ONE TO O...

Bilingual Dictionary

CW00747074

English-Portuguese
Portuguese-English
Dictionary

Compiled by
Dina Teresa

STAR Foreign Language BOOKS

© Publishers

ISBN : 978 1 908357 44 1

This Edition : 2021

Published by
STAR Foreign Language BOOKS
a unit of
Star Books
56, Langland Crescent
Stanmore HA7 1NG, U.K.
info@starbooksuk.com
www.bilingualbooks.co.uk

Printed in India at
Star Print-O-Bind, New Delhi-110 020

About this Dictionary

Developments in science and technology today have narrowed down distances between countries, and have made the world a small place. A person living thousands of miles away can learn and understand the culture and lifestyle of another country with ease and without travelling to that country. Languages play an important role as facilitators of communication in this respect.

To promote such an understanding, **STAR Foreign Language BOOKS** has planned to bring out a series of bilingual dictionaries in which important English words have been translated into other languages, with Roman transliteration in case of languages that have different scripts. This is a humble attempt to bring people of the word closer through the medium of language, thus making communication easy and convenient.

Under this series of *one-to-one dictionaries*, we have published almost 57 languages, the list of which has been given in the opening pages. These have all been compiled and edited by teachers and scholars of the relative languages.

Publishers

Bilingual Dictionaries in this Series

English-Afrikaans / Afrikaans-English	Abraham Venter
English-Albanian / Albanian-English	Theodhora Blushi
English-Amharic / Amharic-English	Girun Asanke
English-Arabic / Arabic-English	Rania-al-Qass
English-Bengali / Bengali-English	Amit Majumdar
English-Bosnian / Bosnian-English	Boris Kazanegra
English-Bulgarian / Bulgarian-English	Vladka Kocheshkova
English-Burmese (Myanmar) / Burmese (Myanmar)-English	Kyaw Swar Aung
English-Cambodian / Cambodian-English	Engly Sok
English-Cantonese / Cantonese-English	Nisa Yang
English-Chinese (Mandarin) / Chinese (Mandarin)-Eng	Y. Shang & R. Yao
English-Croatian / Croatain-English	Vesna Kazanegra
English-Czech / Czech-English	Jindriska Poulova
English-Danish / Danish-English	Rikke Wend Hartung
English-Dari / Dari-English	Amir Khan
English-Dutch / Dutch-English	Lisanne Vogel
English-Estonian / Estonian-English	Lana Haleta
English-Farsi / Farsi-English	Maryam Zaman Khani
English-French / French-English	Aurélie Colin
English-Georgian / Georgina-English	Eka Goderdzishvili
English-Gujarati / Gujarati-English	Sujata Basaria
English-German / German-English	Bicskei Hedwig
English-Greek / Greek-English	Lina Stergiou
English-Hindi / Hindi-English	Sudhakar Chaturvedi
English-Hungarian / Hungarian-English	Lucy Mallows
English-Italian / Italian-English	Eni Lamllari
English-Japanese / Japanese-English	Miruka Arai & Hiroko Nishimura
English-Korean / Korean-English	Mihee Song
English-Latvian / Latvian-English	Julija Baranovska
English-Levantine Arabic / Levantine Arabic-English	Ayman Khalaf
English-Lithuanian / Lithuanian-English	Regina Kazakeviciute
English-Malay / Malay-English	Azimah Husna
English-Nepali / Nepali-English	Anil Mandal
English-Norwegian / Norwegian-English	Samuele Narcisi
English-Pashto / Pashto-English	Amir Khan
English-Polish / Polish-English	Magdalena Herok
English-Portuguese / Portuguese-English	Dina Teresa
English-Punjabi / Punjabi-English	Teja Singh Chatwal
English-Romanian / Romanian-English	Georgeta Laura Dutulescu
English-Russian / Russian-English	Katerina Volobuyeva
English-Serbian / Serbian-English	Vesna Kazanegra
English-Sinhalese / Sinhalese-English	Naseer Salahudeen
English-Slovak / Slovak-English	Zuzana Horvathova
English-Slovenian / Slovenian-English	Tanja Turk
English-Somali / Somali-English	Ali Mohamud Omer
English-Spanish / Spanish-English	Cristina Rodriguez
English-Swahili / Swahili-English	Abdul Rauf Hassan Kinga
English-Swedish / Swedish-English	Madelene Axelsson
English-Tagalog / Tagalog-English	Jefferson Bantayan
English-Tamil / Tamil-English	Sandhya Mahadevan
English-Thai / Thai-English	Suwan Kaewkongpan
English-Tigrigna / Tigrigna-English	Tsegazeab Hailegebriel
English-Turkish / Turkish-English	Nagme Yazgin
English-Ukrainian / Ukrainian-English	Katerina Volobuyeva
English-Urdu / Urdu-English	S. A. Rahman
English-Vietnamese / Vietnamese-English	Hoa Hoang
English-Yoruba / Yoruba-English	O. A. Temitope

STAR Foreign Language BOOKS

ENGLISH-PORTUGUESE

A

a *a.* um

aback *adv.* atrás

abandon *v.t.* abandonar

abase *v.* humilhar

abashed *adj.* embaraçado

abate *v.t.* abater

abbey *n.* abadia

abbot *n.* abade

abbreviate *v.t.* abreviar

abbreviation *n.* abreviatura

abdicate *v.t.* abdicar

abdication *n.* abdicação

abdomen *n.* abdómen

abdominal *a.* abdominal

abduct *v.t.* raptar

abduction *n.* rapto

aberrant *adj.* aberrante

aberration *n.* aberração

abet *v.* estimular

abeyance *n.* suspensão

abhor *v.* abominar

abhorrence *n.* aversão

abhorrent *adj.* repugante

abide *v.i* permanecer

abiding *adj.* permanente

ability *n.* capacidade

abject *adj.* desprezível

abjure *v.* repudiar

ablaze *adv.* entusiasmante

able *adj.* capaz

ablutions *n.* abluções

abnormal *adj.* anormal

aboard *adv.* a bordo

abode *n.* domicílio

abolish *v.t* abolir

abolition *v.* abolição

abominable *adj.* abominável

abominate *v.* abominar

aboriginal *adj.* aborígene

abort *v.i* abortar

abortion *n.* aborto

abortive *adj.* abortado

abound *v.i.* abundar

about *adv.* aproximadamente

about *prep.* sobre

above *adv.* acima

above *prep.* acima

abrasion *n.* abrasão

abrasive *adj.* abrasivo

abreast *adv.* lado a lado

abridge *v.t* abreviar

abroad *adv.* no estrangeiro

abrogate *v.* revogar

abrupt *adj.* abrupto

abscess *n.* abcesso

abscond *v.* fugir

absence *n.* ausente

absent *adj.* ausente

absentee *n.* pessoa ausente

absolute *adj.* absoluto

absolution *n.* absolvição

absolve *v.* absolver

absorb *v.* absorver

abstain *v.* evitar

abstinence *n.* abstinência
abstract *adj.* abstrato
abstruse *adj.* obscuro
absurd *adj.* absurdo
absurdity *n.* absurdo
abundance *n.* abundância
abundant *v.t.* abundante
abuse *v.* abuso
abusive *adj.* abusivo
abut *v.* confinar
abysmal *adj.* abismal
abyss *n.* abismo
academic *adj.* académico
academy *n.* academia
accede *v.* aderir
accelerate *v.* acelerar
accelerator *n.* acerelador
accent *n.* sotaque
accentuate *v.* acentuar
accept *v.* aceitar
acceptable *adj.* aceitável
acceptance *n.* aceitação
access *n.* acessar
accessible *adj.* acessível
accession *n.* adesão
accessory *n.* acessório
accident *n.* acidente
accidental *adj.* acidental
acclaim *v.* aclamar
acclimatise *v.t* aclimatar
accolade *n.* elogio
accommodate *v.* acomodar
accommodation *n.* alojamento

accompaniment *n.* acompanhamento
accompany *v.* acompanhar
accomplice *n.* cúmplice
accomplish *v.* completar
accomplished *adj.* concluído
accomplishment *n.* realização
accord *v.* conceder
accordance *n.* conformidade
according *adv.* conforme
accordingly *adv.* adequadamente
accost *v.* abordar
account *n.* conta
accountable *adj.* responsável
accountancy *n.* contabilidade
accountant *n.* contabilista
accoutrement *n.* farda
accredit *v.* acreditar
accredited *adj.* acreditado
accretion *n.* acreção
accrue *v.t.* advir
accumulate *v.* acumular
accumulation *n.* acumulação
accurate *adj.* exato
accusation *n.* acusação
accuse *v.* acusar
accused *v.t.* acusado
accustom *v.* acostumar
accustomed *adj.* acostumado
ace *n.* ás
acerbic *adj.* amargo
acetate *n.* acetato
acetone *n.* acetona
ache *n.* dor
achieve *v.* alcançar

achievement *n.* conquista
acid *n.* ácido
acidity *n.* acidez
acknowledge *v.* acusar
acknowledgement *n.* reconhecimento
acme *n.* apogeu
acne *n.* acne
acolyte *n.* acólito
acorn *n.* bolota
acoustic *adj.* acústico
acquaint *v.* familiarizar
acquaintance *n.* conhecimento
acquiesce *v.* concordar com
acquiescence *n.* concordância
acquire *v.* adquirir
acquisition *n.* aquisição
acquit *v.* absolver
acquittal *n.* absolvição
acre *n.* acre
acrid *adj.* acre
acrimony *n.* amargor
acrobat *n.* acrobata
acrobatic *adj.* acrobático
across *adv.* transversalmente
acrylic *adj.* acrílico
act *v.* agir
acting *n.* atuação
acting *adj.* em exercício
actinium *n.* actínio
action *n.* ação
actionable *adj.* litigável
activate *v.* ativar
active *adj.* ativo
activist *n.* ativista

activity *n.* atividade
actor *n.* ator
actress *a.* atriz
actual *adj.* real
actually *adv.* efetivamente
actuary *n.* atuário
actuate *v.* acionar
acumen *n.* perspicácia
acupuncture *n.* acupuntura
acute *adj.* perspicaz
adamant *adj.* duro
adapt *v.* adaptar
adaptation *n.* adaptação
add *v.* adicionar
addendum *n.* adenda
addict *n.* viciado
addicted *adj.* viciado
addiction *n.* vício
addition *n.* adição
additional *adj.* adicional
additive *n.* aditivo
addled *adj.* podre
address *n.* morada
addressee *n.* destinatário
adduce *v.* aduzir
adept *adj.* competente
adequacy *n.* adequação
adequate *adj.* adequado
adhere *v.* aderir
adherence *n.* aderência
adhesive *n.* adesivo
adieu *n.* adeus
adjacent *adj.* adjacente
adjective *n.* adjetivo

adjoin v. juntar

adjourn v. adiar

adjournment n. adiamento

adjudge v.t. julgar

adjudicate v. adjudicar

adjunct n. adjunto

adjust v. adaptar

adjustment n. correção

administer v. administrar

administration n. adminsitração

administrative adj. administrativo

administrator adj. administrador

admirable adj. admirável

admiral n. almirante

admiration n. admiração

admire v. admirar

admissible adj. admissível

admission n. admissão

admit v. admitir

admittance n. admissão

admonish v. admoestar

ado n. barulho

adobe n. adobe

adolescence n. adolescente

adolescent adj. adolescência

adopt v. adotar

adoption n. adoção

adoptive adj. adotivo

adorable adj. adorável

adoration n. adoração

adore v.t. adorar

adorn v. adornar

adrift adj. sem rumo

adroit adj. hábil

adsorb v. absorver

adulation n. bajulação

adult n. adulto

adulterate v. adulterar

adulteration n. adulteração

adultery n. adultério

advance v. avançar

advance n. avanço

advancement n. avanço

advantage v.t. beneficiar

advantage n. vantagem

advantageous adj. vantajoso

advent n. advento

adventure n. aventura

adventurous adj. aventureiro

adverb n. advérbio

adversary n. adversário

adverse adj. adverso

adversity n. adversidade

advertise v. anunciar

advertisement n. anúncio

advice n. conselho

advisable adj. aconselhável

advise v. avisar

advocate n. defensor

advocate v. defender

aegis n. égide

aerial n. aéreo

aeon n. eternidade

aerobatics n. acrobacia aérea

aerobics n. aeróbica

aerodrome n. aeródromo

aeronautics n. aeronáutica

aeroplane n. aeroplano

aerosol *n.* aerosol	**African** *adj.* africano
aerospace *n.* aerospaço	**aft** *adv.* atrás
aesthetic *adj.* estético	**after** *adv.* depois
aesthetics *n.* estética	**after** *conj.* depois que
afar *adv.* longe	**after** *prep.* após
affable *adj.* afável	**again** *adv.* novamente
affair *n.* assunto	**against** *prep.* contra
affect *v.* afetar	**agate** *n.* ágata
affectation *n.* afetàção	**age** *n.* idade
affected *adj.* afetado	**aged** *adj.* idoso
affection *n.* afeto	**ageism** *n.* ageismo
affectionate *adj.* afetuoso	**ageless** *adj.* eterno
affidavit *n.* declaração	**agency** *n.* agência
affiliate *v.* afiliar	**agenda** *n.* agenda
affiliation *n.* afiliação	**agent** *n.* agente
affinity *n.* afinidade	**agglomerate** *v.* aglomerar
affirm *v.* afirmar	**aggravate** *v.* agravar
affirmation *n.* afirmação	**aggravation** *n.* agramento
affirmative *adj.* afirmativo	**aggregate** *n.* agregar
affix *v.t.* afixar	**aggression** *n.* agressão
afflict *v.* afligir	**aggressive** *adj.* agressivo
affliction *n.* aflição	**aggressor** *n.* agressor
affluence *n.* afluência	**aggrieve** *v.* afligir
affluent *adj.* afluente	**aghast** *adj.* horrorizado
afford *v.t.* proporcionar	**agile** *adj.* ágil
afforestation *n.* arborização	**agility** *n.* agilidade
affray *n.* tumulto	**agitate** *v.* agitar
affront *n.* afronta	**agitation** *n.* agitação
afield *adv.* longe	**agnostic** *n.* agnóstico
aflame *adj.* em chamas	**ago** *adv.* desde
afloat *adj.* flutuante	**agog** *adj.* curioso
afoot *adv.* andante	**agonize** *v.* agonizar
afraid *adj.* receoso	**agony** *n.* agonia
afresh *adv.* outra vez	**agrarian** *adj.* agrário

agree *v.* concordar
agreeable *adj.* agradável
agreement *n.* acordo
agricultural *adj.* agrícola
agriculture *n.* acricultura
aground *adj.* imobilizadamente
ahead *adv.* na frente
aid *n.* ajuda
aide *n.* assessor
aids *n.* sida
ail *v.* afligir
ailing *adj.* doente
ailment *n.* doença
aim *v.i.* visar
aim *n.* objetivo
aimless *adj.* sem objetivo
air *n.* ar
aircraft *n.* aeronave
airy *adj.* arejado
aisle *n.* corredor
ajar *adv.* em contradição
akin *adj.* consaguíneo
alacritous *n.* ágil
alacrity *n.* espontaneidade
alarm *n* alarme
alarm *v* alarmar
alas *conj.* ai de mim!
albeit *conj.* embora
album *n* album
albumen *n.* albumina
alchemy *n.* alquimia
alcohol *n.* álcool
alcoholic *adj.* alcoólico
alcove *n.* alcova

ale *n.* cerveja
alert *adj.* alerta
algebra *n.* álgebra
alias *adv.* aliás
alias *n.* pseudómino
alibi *n.* alibi
alien *adj.* alienígena
alienate *v.i.* alienar
alight *v.t.* pousar
align *v.* alinhar
alignment *n.* alinhamento
alike *adj.* como
alimony *n.* alimentício
alive *adj.* vivo
alkali *n.* alcalino
all *adj.* todo
allay *v.* acalmar
allegation *n.* alegação
allege *v.* alegar
allegiance *n.* fidelidade
allegory *n.* alegoria
allergen *n.* alérgeno
allergic *adj.* alérgico
allergy *n.* alergia
alleviate *v.* aliviar
alleviation *n.* alívio
alley *n.* beco
alliance *n.* aliança
allied *adj.* aliado
alligator *n.* jacaré
alliterate *v.* aliterar
alliteration *n.* aliteração
allocate *v.* repartir
allocation *n.* atribuição

allot *v.* distribuir
allotment *n.* distribuição
allow *v.* permitir
allowance *n.* permissão
alloy *n.* liga
allude *v.t.* aludir
allure *n.* seduzir
alluring *adj.* sedutor
allusion *n.* alusão
ally *n.* aliado
almanac *n.* almanaque
almighty *adj.* omnipotente
almond *n.* amêndoa
almost *adv.* quase
alms *n.* esmolas
aloft *adv.* em cima
alone *adv.* sozinho
along *prep.* ao longo de
alongside *prep.* ao lado de
aloof *adj.* indiferente
aloud *adv.* alto
alpha *n.* alfa
alphabet *n.* alfabeto
alphabetical *adj.* alfabético
alpine *adj.* alpino
already *adv.* já
also *adv.* também
altar *n.* altar
alter *v.* alterar
alteration *n.* alteração
altercation *n.* altercação
alternate *v.t.* alternar
alternative *adj.* alternativa
although *conj.* apesar de

altitude *n.* altitude
altogether *adv.* completamente
altruism *n.* altruísmo
aluminium *n.* alumínio
alumnus *n.* estudante universitário
always *adv.* sempre
amalgam *n.* amálgama
amalgamate *v.* amalgamar
amalgamation *n.* amalgamação
amass *v.* acumular
amateur *n.* amador
amateurish *adj.* superficial
amatory *adj.* amatório
amaze *v.* surpreender
amazement *n.* assombro
Amazon *n.* Amazonas
ambassador *n.* embaixador
amber *n.* âmbar
ambient *adj.* ambiente
ambiguity *n.* ambiguidade
ambiguous *adj.* ambíguo
ambit *n.* âmbito
ambition *n.* ambição
ambitious *adj.* ambicioso
ambivalent *adj.* ambivalente
amble *v.* andar lentamente
ambrosia *n.* ambrósia
ambulance *n.* ambulância
ambush *n.* emboscada
ameliorate *v.* melhorar
amelioration *n.* melhoria
amend *v.* corrigir
amendment *n.pl.* melhoramento
amenable *adj.* dócil

amiable *adj.* amável	**analogue** *adj.* análogo
amicable *adj.* cordial	**analogy** *n.* analogia
amid *prep.* entre	**analyse** *v.* analisar
amiss *adj.* errado	**analysis** *n.* análise
amity *n.* amizade	**analyst** *n.* analista
ammunition *n.* munição	**analytical** *adj.* analítico
amnesia *n.* amnésia	**anarchism** *n.* anarquismo
amnesty *n.* amnistia	**anarchist** *n.* anarquista
amok *adv.* possesso de fúria	**anarchy** *n.* anarquia
among *prep.* entre	**anatomy** *n.* anatomia
amoral *adj.* amoral	**ancestor** *n.* antepassado
amorous *adj.* amoroso	**ancestral** *adj.* ancestral
amorphous *adj.* amorfo	**ancestry** *n.* descendência
amount *n.* quantia	**anchor** *n.* ancôra
ampere *n.* ampére	**anchorage** *n.* ancoragem
ampersand *n.* e comercial (&)	**ancient** *adj.* idoso
amphibian *n.* anfíbio	**ancillary** *adj.* auxiliar
amphitheatre *n.* anfiteatro	**and** conj. e
ample *adj.* amplo	**android** *n.* andróide
amplification *n.* amplificação	**anecdote** *n.* anedota
amplifier *n.* amplificador	**anew** *adv.* mais uma vez
amplify *v.* amplificar	**angel** *n.* anjo
amplitude *n.* amplitude	**anger** *n.* raiva
amulet *n.* amuleto	**angina** *n.* angina
amuse *v.* divertir	**angle** *n.* ângulo
amusement *n.* divertimento	**angry** *adj.* irritado
an *adj.* um / uma	**anguish** *n.* angústia
anachronism *n.* anacronismo	**angular** *adj.* angular
anaemia *n.* anemia	**animal** *n.* animal
anaesthesia *n.* anestesia	**animate** *v.* animar
anaesthetic *n.* anestético	**animated** *adj.* animado
anal *adj.* anal	**animation** *n.* animação
analgesic *n.* analgésico	**animosity** *n.* animosidade
analogous *adj.* análogo	**aniseed** *n.* anis

ankle *n.* tornozelo	**antelope** *n.* antílope
anklet *n.* peúga	**antenna** *n.* antena
annals *n.* anais	**anthem** *n.* hino
annex *v.* anexo	**anthology** *n.* antologia
annexation *n.* anexação	**anthropology** *n.* antropologia
annihilate *v.* aniquilar	**anthrax** *n.* antrax
annihilation *n.* aniquilação	**anti** *n.* anti
anniversary *n.* aniversário	**antibiotic** *n.* antibiótico
annotate *v.* anotar	**antibody** *n.* anticorpos
announce *v.* anunciar	**antic** *n.* excentricidade
announcement *n.* anúncio	**anticipate** *v.* antecipar
annoy *v.* aborrecer	**anticipation** *n.* antecipação
annoyance *n.* aborrecimento	**anticlimax** *n.* anticlímax
annual *adj.* anual	**antidote** *n.* antídoto
annuity *n.* anuidade	**antioxidant** *n.* antioxidante
annul *v.* anular	**antipathy** *n.* antipatia
anode *n.* anódio	**antiperspirant** *n.* desodorizante
anoint *v.* ungir	**antiquarian** *adj.* antiquário
anomalous *adj.* anómalo	**antiquated** *adj.* antiquado
anomaly *n.* anomalia	**antique** *n.* antigo
anonymity *n.* anonimato	**antiquity** *n.* antiguidade
anonymous *adj.* anónimo	**antiseptic** *adj.* antisséptico
anorexia *n.* anorexia	**antisocial** *adj.* anti-social
another *adj.* outro	**antithesis** *n.* antítese
answer *n.* resposta	**antler** *n.* chifre
answerable *adj.* responsável	**antonym** *n.* antónimo
ant *n.* formiga	**anus** *n.* anus
antacid *adj.* antiácido	**anvil** *n.* bigorna
antagonism *n.* antagonismo	**anxiety** *n.* ansiedade
antagonist *n.* antagonista	**anxious** *adj.* ansioso
antagonize *v.* antagonizar	**any** *adj.* qualquer
Antarctic *adj.* Antártica	**anyhow** *adv.* de qualquer maneira
antecedent *n.* antecedente	**anyone** *pron.* qualquer um
antedate *v.* antecipar	**anything** *pron.* algo

anywhere *adv.* em qualquer lugar
apace *adv.* rapidamente
apart *adv.* à parte
apartheid *n.* apartheid
apartment *n.* apartamento
apathy *n.* apatia
ape *n.* macaco
aperture *n.* abertura
apex n ápice
aphorism *n.* aforismo
apiary *n.* colmeia
aplomb *n.* aprumo
apocalypse *n.* apócalipse
apologize *v.* desculpar
apology *n.* desculpa
apoplectic *adj.* apoplético
apostate *n.* apóstata
apostle *n.* apóstolo
apostrophe *n.* apóstrefe
appal *v.* assustar
apparatus *n.* aparato
apparel *n.* vestuário
apparent *adj.* aparente
appeal *v.t.* apelar
appear *v.* aparecer
appearance *n.* aparência
appease *v.* apaziguar
append *v.* anexar
appendage *n.* apêndice
appendicitis *n.* apendicite
appendix *n.* anexo
appetite *n.* apetite
appetizer *n.* aperitivo
applaud *v.* aplaudir

applause *n.* aplauso
apple *n.* maçã
appliance *n.* aplicação
applicable *adj.* aplicável
applicant *n.* candidato
application *n.* solicitação
apply *v.t.* solicitar
appoint *v.* nomear
appointment *n.* compromisso
apportion *v.t.* repartir
apposite *adj.* apropriado
appraise *v.* avaliar
appreciable *adj.* apreciável
appreciate *v.* apreciar
appreciation *n.* apreciação
apprehend *v.* apreender
apprehension *n.* apreensão
apprehensive *adj.* apreensivo
apprentice *n.* aprendiz
apprise *v.* informar
approach *v.* aproximar
appropriate *adj.* adequado
appropriation *n.* apropriação
approval *n.* aprovação
approve *v.* aprovar
approximate *adj.* aproximado
apricot *n.* pêssego
apron *n.* avental
apt *adj.* apto
aptitude *n.* atitude
aquarium *n.* aquário
aquatic *adj.* aquático
aqueous *adj.* aquoso
Arab *n.* Árabe

Arabian *n.* árabe	**arithmetical** *adj.* aritmético
Arabic *n.* arábico	**ark** *n.* arca
arable *adj.* arável	**arm** *n.* braço
arbiter *n.* árbitro	**armada** *n.* armada
arbitrary *adj.* arbitrário	**Armageddon** *n.* Armagedão
arbitrate *v.* arbitrar	**armament** *n.* armamento
arbitration *n.* arbitragem	**armistice** *n.* armistício
arbitrator *n.* árbitro	**armour** *n.* armadura
arbour *n.* mandril	**armoury** *n.* arsenal
arc *n.* arco	**army** *n.* exército
arcade *n.* arcada	**aroma** *n.* aroma
arch *n.* arco	**aromatherapy** *n.* aromaterapia
archaeology *n.* arqueologia	**around** *adv.* ao redor
archaic *adj.* arcaico	**arouse** *v.* despertar
archangel *n.* arcanjo	**arrange** *v.* organizar
archbishop *n.* arcebispo	**arrangement** *n.* arranjo
archer *n.* arqueiro	**arrant** *adj.* notório
architect *n.* arquiteto	**array** *n.* ordem
architecture *n.* arquitetura	**arrears** *n.* atraso
archives *n.* arquivos	**arrest** *v.* prender
Arctic *adj.* Ártico	**arrival** *n.* chegada
ardent *adj.* ardente	**arrive** *v.* chegar
ardour *n.* ardor	**arrogance** *n.* arrogância
arduous *adj.* árduo	**arrogant** *adj.* arrogante
area *n.* área	**arrogate** *v.* arrogar-se
arena *n.* arena	**arrow** *n.* seta
argue *v.* argumentar	**arsenal** *n.* arsenal
argument *n.* argumento	**arsenic** *n.* arsénico
argumentative *adj.* argumentativo	**arson** *n.* incendiário
anrid *adj.* árido	**art** *n.* arte
arinse *v.* surgir	**artefact** *n.* artefato
aristnocracy *n.* aristocracia	**artery** *n.* artéria
aristocrat *n.* aristócrata	**artful** *adj.* astuto
arithmetic *n.* aritmética	**arthritis** *n.* artrite

artichoke *n.* alcachofra	**asphyxiate** *v.* asfixiar
article *n.* artigo	**aspirant** *n.* aspirante
articulate *adj.* articulado	**aspiration** *n.* aspiração
artifice *n.* artifício	**aspire** *v.* aspirar
artificial *adj.* artificial	**ass** *n.* cú
artillery *n.* artilharia	**assail** *v.* assaltar
artisan *n.* artesão	**assassin** *n.* assassino
artist *n.* artista	**assassinate** *v.* assassinar
artistic *adj.* arstístico	**assassination** *n.* assassinato
artless *adj.* incendiário	**assault** *n.* assalto
as *adv.* como	**assemblage** *n.* montagem
asbestos *n.* amianto	**assemble** *v.* montar
ascend *v.* ascender	**assembly** *n.* assembléia
ascendant *adj.* ascendente	**assent** *n.* consentimento
ascent *n.* ascenção	**assert** *v.* afirmar
ascertain *v.* determinar	**assess** *v.* avaliar
ascetic *adj.* ascético	**assessment** *n.* avaliação
ascribe *v.* atribuir	**asset** *n.* ativo
aseptic *adj.* asséptico	**assiduous** *adj.* assíduo
asexual *adj.* assexuado	**assign** *v.* atribuir
ash *n.* cinza	**assignation** *n.* designação
ashamed *adj.* envergonhado	**assignment** *n.* atribuição
ashore *adv.* em terra firme	**assimilate** *v.* assimilar
Asian *adj.* Asiático	**assimilation** *n.* assimilação
aside *adv.* aparte	**assist** *v.* auxiliar
asinine *adj.* asinino	**assistance** *n.* auxílio
ask *v.* perguntar	**assistant** *n.* ajudante
askance *adv.* desconfiadamente	**associate** *v.* associar
askew *adv.* torto	**association** *n.* associação
asleep *adj.* adormecido	**assonance** *n.* assonância
asparagus *n.* espargos	**assorted** *adj.* variado
aspect *n.* aparência	**assortment** *n.* classificação
asperity *n.* aspereza	**assuage** *v.* amenizar
aspersions *n.* difamações	**assume** *v.* assumir

assumption *n.* suposição
assurance *n.* garantia
assure *v.* assegurar
assured *adj.* seguro
asterisk *n.* asterisco
asteroid *n.* asteróide
asthma *n.* asma
astigmatism *n.* astigmatismo
astonish *v.* surpreender
astonishment *n.* espanto
astound *v.* espantar
astral *adj.* astral
astray *adv.* extraviado
astride *prep.* montado sobre
astrologer *n.* astrólogo
astrology *n.* astrologia
astronaut *n.* astraounata
astronomer *n.* astrónomo
astronomy *n.* astronomia
astute *adj.* astuto
asunder *adv.* separadamente
asylum *n.* asilo
at *prep.* em
atavistic *adj.* atávico
atheism *n.* ateísmo
atheist *n.* ateu
athlete *n.* atleta
athletic *adj.* atlético
atlas *n.* atlas
atmosphere *n.* atmosfera
atoll *n.* atol
atom *n.* átomo
atomic *adj.* atómico
atone *v.* reparar

atonement *n.* reaparação
atrium *n.* átrio
atrocious *adj.* atroz
atrocity *n.* atrocidade
attach *v.* anexar
attache *n.* adido
attachment *n.* anexo
attack *v.* atacar
attain *v.* atingir
attainment *n.* realização
attempt *v.* atentar
attend *v.* atender
attendance *n.* comparecimento
attendant *n.* assistente
attention *n.* atenção
attentive *adj.* atento
attest *v.* atestar
attic *n.* sótão
attire *n.* vestuário
attitude *n.* atitude
attorney *n.* advogado
attract *v.* atrair
attraction *n.* atração
attractive *adj.* atrativo
attribute *v.* atribuir
aubergine *n.* beringela
auction *n.* leilão
audible *adj.* audível
audience *n.* audiência
audio *n.* audio
audit *n.* balanço
audition *n.* audição
auditorium *n.* aufitório
augment *v.* aumentar

August n Agosto
aunt *n.* tia
aura *n.* aura
auspicious *adj.* auspicioso
austere *adj.* austero
Australian *n.* Australiano
authentic *adj.* autêntico
authenticity *n.* autenticidade
author *n.* autor
authoritative *adj.* oficial
authority *n.* autoridade
authorize *v.* autorizar
autism *n.* autismo
autobiography *n.* autobiografia
autocracy *n.* autocracia
autocrat *n.* autocrata
autocratic *adj.* autocrata
autograph *n.* autógrafo
automatic *adj.* automático
automobile *n.* automóvel
autonomous *adj.* autónomo
autopsy *n.* autópsia
autumn *n.* outono
auxiliary *adj.* auxiliar
avail *v.* aproveitar
available *adj.* disponível
avalanche *n.* avalanche
avarice *n.* avareza
avenge *v.* vingança
avenue *n.* avenida
average *n.* média
averse *adj.* adverso
aversion *n.* aversão
avert *v.* evitar

aviary *n.* aviário
aviation *n.* aviação
aviator *n.* aviador
avid *adj.* ávido
avidly *adv.* avidamente
avocado *n.* abacate
avoid *v.* evitar
avoidance *n.* anulação
avow *v.* confessar
avuncular *adj.* avuncular
await *v.* aguardar
awake *v.* acordar
awaken *v.* despertar
award *v.* premiar
aware *adj.* consciente
away *adv.* embora
awe *n.* temor
awesome *adj.* pavoroso
awful *adj.* horrível
awhile *adv.* por algum tempo
awkward *adj.* inábil
awry *adv.* erradamente
axe *n.* machado
axis *n.* eixo
axle *n.* eixo

B

babble *v.* balbuciar
babe *n.* bébé
Babel *n.* Babel
baboon *n.* babuíno
baby *n.* bébé
bachelor *n.* bacharel
back *n.* costas

backbone *n.* espinha dorsal	**bald** *adj.* careca
backdate *v.* pré-datar	**bale** *n.* fardo
backdrop *n.* pano de fundo	**ball** *n.* bola
backfire *v.* tiro pela culatra	**ballad** *n.* balada
background *n.* fundo	**ballet** *n.* balet
backhand *n.* revés	**balloon** *n.* balão
backing *n.* apoio	**ballot** *n.* cédula
backlash *n.* folga	**balm** *n.* bálsamo
backlog *n.* acúmulo	**balsam** *n.* bálsamo
backpack *n.* mochila	**bamboo** *n.* bamboo
backside *n.* traseiro	**ban** *v.* proibir
backstage *adv.* no fundo do palco	**banal** *adj.* vulgar
backtrack *v.* recuar	**banana** *n.* banana
backward *adj.* inverso	**band** *n.* banda
backwater *n.* ressaca	**bandage** *n.* faixa
bacon *n.* bacon	**bandit** *n.* bandido
bacteria *n.* bactéria	**bane** *n.* perdição
bad *adj.* mau	**bang** *n.* estrondo
badge *n.* distintivo	**banger** *n.* sucata
badly *adv.* mal	**bangle** *n.* bracelete
badminton *n.* badminton	**banish** *v.* banir
baffle *v.* confundir	**banishment** *n.* expulsão
bag *n.* saco	**banisters** *n.* corrimão
baggage *n.* bagagem	**banjo** *n.* banjo
baggy *adj.* folgado	**bank** *n.* banco
baguette *n.* baguete	**banker** *n.* banqueiro
bail *n.* fiança	**bankrupt** *adj.* falido
bailiff *n.* meirinho	**bankruptcy** *n.* falência
bait *n.* isco	**banner** *n.* banner
bake *v.* assar	**banquet** *n.* banquete
baker *n.* padeiro	**banter** *n.* brincadeira
bakery *n.* padaria	**baptism** *n.* batismo
balance *n.* equlibrar	**Baptist** *n.* Batista
balcony *n.* varanda	**baptize** *v.* batizar

bar *n.* bar
barb *n.* farpa
barbarian *n.* bárbaro
barbaric *adj.* bárbaro
barbecue *n.* churrasco
barbed *adj.* farpado
barber *n.* barbeiro
bard *n.* bardo
bare *adj.* nu
barely *adv.* apenas
bargain *n.* pechincha
barge *n.* barcaça
bark *n.* casca
barley *n.* cevada
barn *n.* celeiro
barometer *n.* barómetro
baron *n.* barão
barrack *n.* quartel
barracuda *n.* barracuda
barrage *n.* barragem
barrel *n.* barril
barren *adj.* estéril
barricade *n.* barricada
barrier *n.* barreira
barring *prep.* exceto
barrister *n.* advogado
barter *v.* permutar
base *n.* base
baseless *adj.* infundado
basement *n.* cave
bashful *adj.* tímido
basic *n.* básico
basil *n.* manjericão
basilica *n.* basílica

basin *n.* bacia
basis *n.* base
bask *v.* aquecer
basket *n.* cesto
bass *n.* baixo
bastard *n.* bastardo
baste *v.* alinhavar
bastion *n.* bastião
bat *n.* morcego
batch *n.* fornada
bath *n.* banho
bathe *v.* banhar
bathos *n.* anticlímax
batik *n.* batik
baton *n.* bastão
battalion *n.* batalhão
batten *n.* sarrafo
batter *n.* golpear
battery *n.* bateria
battle *n.* batalha
bauble *n.* bugiganga
baulk *v.* relinga
bawl *v.* berrar
bay *n.* baía
bayonet *n.* baioneta
bazaar *n.* bazar
bazooka *n.* bazuca
be *v.* ser/ estar
beach *n.* praia
beacon *n.* farol
bead *n.* pérola
beady *adj.* lustroso
beagle *n.* beagle
beak *n.* bico

beaker *n.* proveta	**befall** *v.* acontecer
beam *n.* viga	**befit** *v.* convir
bean *n.* feijão	**before** *adv.* antes
bear *v.t* suportar	**beforehand** *adv.* antecipadamente
bear *n.* urso	**befriend** *v.* favorecer
beard *n.* barba	**befuddled** *adj.* confuso
bearing *n.* rolamento	**beg** *v.* implorar
beast *n.* besta	**beget** *v.* gerar
beastly *adj.* bestial	**beggar** *n.* mendigo
beat *v.* derrotar	**begi** *v.* começar
beautician *n.* esteticista	**beginning** *n.* início
beautiful *adj.* bonito	**beguile** *v.* seduzir
beautify *v.* embelezar	**behalf** *n.* favor
beatitude *n.* benção	**behave** *v.* comportar-se
beauty *n.* beleza	**behaviour** *n.* comportamento
beaver *n.* castor	**behead** *v.* decapitar
becalmed *adj.* calmaria	**behemoth** *n.* gigante
because *conj.* porque	**behest** *n.* ordem
beck *n.* aceno	**behind** *prep.* atrás de
beckon *v.* acenar	**behold** *v.* observar
become *v.* vir a ser	**beholden** *adj.* reconhecido
bed *n.* cama	**beige** *n.* bege
bedding *n.* cama	**being** *n.* ser
bedlam *n.* confusão	**belabour** *v.* ridicularizar
bedraggled *adj.* sujo	**belated** *adj.* atrasado
bee *n.* abelha	**belay** *v.* apertar
beech *n.* faia	**belch** *v.* arrotar
beef *n.* bife	**beleaguered** *adj.* sitiada
beefy *adj.* carnudo	**belie** *v.* desmentir
beep *n.* bip	**belief** *n.* crença
beer *n.* cerveja	**believe** *v.* acreditar
beet *n.* beterraba	**belittle** *v.* depreciar
beetle *n.* besouro	**bell** *n.* campainha
beetroot *n.* raiz de beterraba	**belle** *n.* bela

bellicose *adj.* belicoso
belligerent *adj.* agressivo
bellow *v.* berrar
bellows *n.* fole
belly *n.* barriga
belong *v.* pertencer
belongings *n.* pertences
beloved *adj.* amado
below *prep.* abaixo
belt *n.* cinto
bemoan *v.* lamentar
bemused *adj.* confuso
bench *n.* banco
bend *v.* dobrar
beneath *adv.* abaixo
benediction *n.* benção
benefactor *n.* benfeitor
benefice *n.* benefício
beneficent *adj.* beneficiente
beneficial *adj.* benéfico
benefit *n.* benefício
benevolence *n.* benevolência
benevolent adj benevolente
benign *adj.* benigno
bent *adj.* dobrado
bequeath *v.* legar
bequest *n.* legado
berate *v.* repreender
bereaved *v.* desolar
bereavement *n.* perda
bereft *adj.* desolado
bergamot *n.* bergamota
berk *n.* idiota
berry *n.* baga

berserk *adj.* furioso
berth *n.* ancoradouro
beseech *v.* implorar
beset *v.* assaltar
beside *prep.* ao lado de
besiege *v.* sitiar
besmirch *v.* manchar
besom *n.* vassoura
besotted *adj.* obcecado
bespoke *adj.* feito sob medida
best *adj.* o melhor
bestial *adj.* bestial
bestow *v.* outorgar
bestride *v.* cavalgar
bet *v.* apostar
betake *v.* recorrer
betray *v.* trair
betrayal *n.* traição
better *adj.* melhor
between *adv.* entre
bevel *n.* bisel
beverage *n.* bebida
bevy *n.* bando
bewail *v.* lamentar
beware *v.* ter cuidado
bewilder *v.t* confundir
bewitch *v.* enfeitiçar
beyond *adv.* além
bi comb. bi
biannual *adj.* semestral
bias *n.* viés
biased *adj.* tendenciosa
bib *n.* babete
Bible *n.* Bíblia

bibliography *n.* bibliografia	**binocular** *adj.* binocular
bibliophile *n.* bibliófilo	**biochemistry** *n.* bioquímica
bicentenary *n.* bicentenário	**biodegradable** *adj.* biodegradável
biceps *n.* bíceps	**biodiversity** *n.* biodeversidade
bicker *v.* brigar	**biography** *n.* biografia
bicycle *n.* bicicleta	**biologist** *n.* biologista
bid *v.* licitar	**biology** *n.* biologia
biddable *adj.* dócil	**biopsy** *n.* biópsia
bidder *n.* licitante	**bipartisan** *adj.* bipartidário
bide *v.* esperar	**birch** *n.* bétula
bidet *n.* bidé	**bird** *n.* pássaro
biennial *adj.* beinal	**bird** flu *n.* gripe aviária
bier *n.* caixão	**birth** *n.* nascimento
bifocal *adj.* bifocal	**biscuit** *n.* biscoito
big *adj.* grande	**bisect** *v.* bifurcar
bigamy *n.* bigamia	**bisexual** *adj.* bissexual
bigot *n.* intolerante	**bishop** *n.* bispo
bigotry *n.* intolerância	**bison** *n.* bisão
bike *n.* bicicleta	**bit** *n.* bocado
bikini *n.* biquini	**bitch** *n.* prostituta
bilateral *adj.* bilateral	**bite** *v.* morder
bile *n.* bílis	**biting** *adj.* cortante
bilingual *adj.* bilingue	**bitter** *adj.* amargo
bill *n.* conta	**bizarre** *adj.* bizarro
billet *n.* boleto	**blab** *v.* tagarelar
billiards *n.* bilhar	**black** *adj.* negro
billion *n.* bilhão	**blackberry** *n.* amora
billionaire *n.* bilionário	**blackboard** *n.* quadro (de lousa)
billow *v.* ondear	**blacken** *v.* denegrir
bin *n.* contentor	**blacklist** *n.* lista negra
binary *adj.* binário	**blackmail** *n.* chantagem
bind *v.* vincular	**blackout** *n.* apagão
binding *n.* ligação	**blacksmith** *n.* ferreiro
binge *n.* farra	**bladder** *n.* bexiga

blade *n.* lâmina	**blithe** *adj.* alegre
blain *n.* pústula	**blitz** *n.* ataque repentino
blame *v.* culpar	**blizzard** *n.* nevão
blanch *v.* branquear	**bloat** *v.* inchar
bland *adj.* suave	**bloater** *n.* arenque defumado
blank *adj.* inexpressivo	**blob** *n.* gota
blanket *n.* cobertor	**bloc** *n.* bloco
blare *v.* retumbar	**block** *n.* bloquear
blarney *n.* lisonja	**blockade** *n.* obstruir
blast *n.* explosão	**blockage** *n.* bloqueio
blatant *adj.* ruidoso	**blog** *n.* blog
blaze *n.* labareda	**bloke** *n.* sujeito
blazer *n.* blazer	**blonde** *adj.* loira
bleach *adj.* descolorante	**blood** *n.* sangue
bleak *adj.* desabrigado	**bloodshed** *n.* derramamento sangue
bleat *v. i* balir	**bloody** *adj.* sangrento
bleed *v.* sangrar	**bloom** *v.* florescer
bleep *n.* bip	**bloomers** *n.* culotes
blemish *n.* defeito	**blossom** *n.* florir
blench *v.* empalidecer	**blot** *n.* borrar
blend *v. t* misturar	**blotch** *n.* manchar
blender *n.* liquidificador	**blouse** *n.* blusa
bless *v.* abençoar	**blow** *v.* soprar
blessed *adj.* abençoado	**blowsy** *adj.* corado
blessing *n.* benção	**blub** *v.* choramingar
blight *n.* ferrugem	**bludgeon** *n.* cacete
blind *adj.* cego	**blue** *adj.* azul
blindfold *v.* vendar os olhos	**bluff** *v.* enganar
blindness *n.* cegueira	**blunder** *n.* tolice
blink *v.* pestanejar	**blunt** *adj.* brusco
blinkers *n.* antolhos	**blur** *v.* ofuscar
blip *n.* som intermitente	**blurb** *n.* nota de publicidade
bliss *n.* felicidade	**blurt** *v.* dizer
blister *n.* bolha	**blush** *v.* corar

blusher *n.* blush	**bonfire** *n.* fogueira
bluster *v.* vociferar	**bonnet** *n.* gorro
boar *n.* javali	**bonus** *n.* bónus
board *n.* conselho	**bony** *adj.* esquelético
boast *v.* alardear	**book** *n.* livro
boat *n.* barco	**booklet** *n.* folheto
bob *v.* sacudir	**bookmark** *n.* marcador de livros
bobble *n.* pompom	**bookseller** *n.* livreiro
bode *v.* agourar	**bookish** *adj.* estudioso
bodice *n.* corpete	**boom** *n.* estrondo
bodily *adv.* completamente	**boon** *n.* benefício
body *n.* corpo	**boor** *n.* traste
bodyguard n guarda-costas	**boost** *v.* impulsionar
bog *n.* atolar	**booster** *n.* intensificador
bogey *n.* espantalho	**boot** *n.* bota
boggle *v.* recuar	**booth** *n.* cabine
bogus *adj.* falso	**bootleg** *adj.* ilícito
boil *v.i.* ferver	**booty** *n.* saque
boiler *n.* caldeira	**border** *n.* fronteira
boisterous *adj.* violento	**bore** *v.* aborrecer
bold *adj.* negrito	**born** *adj.* nascido
boldness *n.* ousadia	**borough** *n.* vila
bole *n.* tronco	**borrow** *v.* emprestar
bollard *n.* abita	**bosom** *n.* seio
bolt *n.* parafuso	**boss** *n.* chefe
bomb *n.* bomba	**bossy** *adj.* mandão
bombard *v.* bombardear	**botany** *n.* botânica
bombardment *n.* bombardeamento	**both** *adj. & pron.* ambos & ambos
bomber *n.* bombista	**bother** *v.* incomodar
bonafide *adj.* genuíno	**bottle** *n.* garrafa
bonanza *n.* prosperidade	**bottom** *n.* fundo
bond *n.* vínculo	**bough** *n.* galho
bondage *n.* servidão	**boulder** *n.* pedregulho
bone *n.* osso	**boulevard** *n.* avenida

bounce v. ressaltar

bouncer n. exagero

bound v. limitar

boundary n. limite

boundless adj. ilimitado

bountiful adj. beneficiente

bounty n. recompensa

bouquet n. ramo (flores)

bout n. ataque

boutique n. boutique

bow n. arco

bow v. curvar

bowel n. intestino

bower n. caramanchão

bowl n. tigela

box n. caixa

boxer n. pugilista

boxing n boxe

boy n. rapaz

boycott v. boicotar

boyhood n infância

bra n. sutiã

brace n. braçadeira

bracelet n. pulseira

bracket n. suporte

brag v. fazer alarde

Braille n. Braille

brain n. cérebro

brake n. travão

branch n. ramo (de negócios)

brand n. marca comercial

brandish v. brandir

brandy n. brandy

brash adj. impertinente

brass n. latão

brave adj. corajoso

bravery n. coragem

brawl n. rixa

bray v. triturar

breach v. violar

bread n. pão

breadth n. largura

break v. quebrar

breakage n. rutura

breakfast n. pequeno-almoço

breast n. peito

breath n. respiração

breathe v. respirar

breech n. culatra

breeches n. bermudas

breed v. reproduzir

breeze n. brisa

brevity n. brevidade

brew v. fermentar

brewery n. cervejaria

bribe v. t. subornar

brick n. tijolo

bridal adj. nupcial

bride n. noiva

bridegroom n. noivo

bridge n. ponte

bridle n. freio

brief adj. breve

briefing n. instruções

brigade n. brigada

brigadier n. brigadeiro

bright adj. brilhante

brighten v. clarear

brilliance *n.* brilho	**bruise** *n.* equimose
brilliant *adj.* brilhante	**brunch** *n.* peq-almoço reforçado
brim *n.* borda	**brunette** *n.* morena
brindle *adj.* mancha	**brunt** *n.* peso
brine *n.* salmoura	**brush** *n.* escovar
bring *v.* trazer	**brusque** *adj.* brusco
brinjal *n.* beringela	**brutal** *adj.* brutal
brink *n.* beira	**brute** *n.* bruto
brisk *adj.* vivo	**bubble** *n.* bolha
bristle *n.* pêlos	**buck** *n.* pinote
British *adj.* Britânico	**bucket** *n.* balde
brittle *adj.* frágil	**buckle** *n.* fivela
broach *adj.* abordar	**bud** *n.* botão
broad *adj.* amplo	**budge** *v.* mover
broadcast *v.* t difundir	**budget** *n.* orçamento
brocade *n.* brocado	**buffalo** *n.* bufalo
broccoli *n.* bróculos	**buffer** *n.* amortecedor
brochure *n.* brochura	**buffet** *n.* bufet
broke *adj.* quebrado	**buffoon** *n.* bobo
broken *adj.* quebrado	**bug** *n.* inseto
broker *n.* corretor	**buggy** *n.* infestado
bronchial *adj.* bronquial	**bugle** *n.* corneta
bronze *n.* bronze	**build** *v.* construir
brood *n.* ninhada	**building** *n.* construção
brook *n.* ribeiro	**bulb** *n.* bulbo
broom *n.* vassoura	**bulge** *n.* proteburância
broth *n.* caldo	**bulimia** *n.* bulimia
brothel *n.* bordel	**bulk** *n.* massa
brother *n.* irmão	**bulky** *adj.* volumoso
brotherhood *n.* irmandade	**bull** *n.* touro
brow *n.* sobrancelha	**bulldog** *n.* buldogue
brown *n.* castanho	**bullet** *n.* bala
browse *v.* procurar	**bulletin** *n.* boletim
browser *n.* navegador	**bullion** *n.* lingote

bullish *adj.* em alta
bullock *n.* boi castrado
bully *n.* valentão
bulwark *n.* baluarte
bum *n.* vagabundo
bumble *v.* fracassar
bump *n.* colisão
bumper *n.* pára-choques
bumpkin *n.* rústico
bumpy *adj.* instável
bun *n.* pão de forma
bunch *n.* punhado
bundle *n.* pacote
bung *n.* tampão
bungalow *n.* bungalow
bungle *v.* estragar
bunk *n.* beliche
bunker *n.* paiol
buoy *n.* bóia
buoyant *adj.* flutuante
buoyancy *n.* flutuabilidade
burble *v.* gaguejar
burden *n.* fardo
bureau *n.* escritório
bureaucracy *n.* burocracia
bureaucrat *n.* burocrata
burgeon *v.* brotar
burger *n.* hambúrguer
burglar *n.* ladrão
burglary *n.* roubo
burial *n.* enterro
burlesque *n.* burlesco
burn *v.* queimar
burner *n.* queimador

burning *adj.* ardente
burrow *n.* toca
bursar *n.* tesoureiro
bursary *n.* bolsa
burst *v.* estourar
bury *v.* enterrar
bus *n.* autocarro
bush *n.* arbusto
bushy *adj.* espesso
business *n.* negócio
businessman *n.* empresário
bust *n.* busto
bustle *v.* apressar
busy *adj.* ocupado
but conj. mas
butcher *n.* açougueiro
butler *n.* mordomo
butter *n.* manteiga
butterfly *n.* borboleta
buttock *n.* nádega
button *n.* botão
buy *v.* comprar
buyer *n.* comprador
buzz *n.* zumbido
buzzard *n.* urubu
buzzer *n.* cigarra
by *prep.* através
by-election *n.* por intermédio
bygone *adj.* passado
by-**line** *n.* linha de assinatura
bypass *n.* ignorar
byre *n.* vacaria
bystander *n.* espetador
byte *n.* byte

C

cab *n.* táxi
cabaret *n.* cabaré
cabbage *n.* repolho
cabin *n.* cabine
cabinet *n.* gabinete
cable *n.* cabo
cacao *n.* cacau
cache *n.* esconderijo
cachet *n.* selo (referente qualidade)
cackle *n.* cacrejo
cactus *n.* cacto
cad *n.* criado
cadaver *n.* cadáver
caddy *n.* caddie
cadet *n.* cadete
cadmium *n.* cádmio
cadre *n.* quadro
caesarean *n.* cesariana
cafe *n.* café
cafeteria *n.* cafeteria
cage *n.* jaula
cahoots *n.* acordo secreto
cajole *v.* persuadir
cake *n.* bolo
calamity *n.* calamidade
calcium *n.* cálcio
calculate *v.* calcular
calculator *n.* calculadora
calculation *n.* cálculo
calendar *n.* calendário
calf *n.* bezerro
calibrate *v.* calibrar

calibre *n.* calibre
call *v.* chamar
calligraphy *n.* caligrafia
calling *n.* chamada
callous *adj.* insensível
callow *adj.* inexperiente
calm *adj.* calmo
calorie *n.* caloria
calumny *n.* calúnia
camaraderie *n.* camaradagem
camber *n.* curvatura
cambric *n.* cambraia
camcorder *n.* vídeo câmara
camel *n.* camelo
cameo *n.* veio
camera *n.* máquina fotográfica
camp *n.* acampamento
campaign *n.* campanha
camphor *n.* cânfora
campus *n.* terrenos universidade
can *n.* lata
can *v.* poder
canal *n.* canal
canard *n.* mentira
cancel *v.* cancelar
cancellation *n.* cancelamento
cancer *n.* cancro
candela *n.* vela
candid *adj.* sincero
candidate *n.* candidato
candle *n.* vela
candour *n.* candura
candy *n.* doce
cane *n.* cana

canine *adj.* canino

canister *n.* vasilha

cannabis *n.* canabis

cannibal *n.* canibal

cannon *n.* canhão

canny *adj.* sagaz

canoe *n.* canoa

canon *n.* canhão

canopy *n.* dossel

cant *n.* hipocrisia

cantankerous *adj.* impertinente

canteen *n.* cantina

canter *n.* trote

canton *n.* cantão

cantonment *n.* acantonamento

canvas *n.* lona

canvass *v.* apurar

canyon *n.* desfiladeiro

cap *n.* boné

capability *n.* aptidão

capable *adj.* capaz

capacious *adj.* espaçoso

capacitor *n.* capacitor

capacity *n.* capacidade

caparison *v.* enfeitar

cape *n.* capa

capital *n.* capital

capitalism *n.* capitalismo

capitalist *n. &adj.* capitalista

capitalize *v.* capitalizar

capitation *n.* capitação

capitulate *v.* capitular

caprice *n.* capricho

capricious *adj.* caprichoso

capsicum *n.* pimento

capsize *v.* emborcar

capstan *n.* cabrestante

capsule *n.* cápsula

captain *n.* capitão

captaincy *n.* capitania

caption *n.* título

captivate *v.* cativar

captive *n.* cativo

captivity *n.* cativeiro

captor *n.* captor

capture *v.* captura

car *n.* carro

caramel *n.* caramelo

carat *n.* quilate

caravan *n.* caravana

carbohydrate *n.* carbohidrato

carbon *n.* carbono

carbonate *adj.* carbonato

carboy *n.* garrafão

carcass *n.* carcaça

card *n.* cartão

cardamom *n.* cardamomo

cardboard *n.* cartão

cardiac *adj.* cardíaco

cardigan *n.* cardigã

cardinal *n.* cardinal

cardiograph *n.* cardiógrafo

cardiology *n.* cardiologia

care *n.* cuidar

career *n.* carreira

carefree *adj.* despreocupado

careful *adj.* cuidadoso

careless *adj.* descuidado

carer *n.* cuidador

caress *v.* carícia

caretaker *n.* zelador

cargo *n.* carga

caricature n caricatura

carmine *n.* carmim

carnage *n.* carnificina

carnal *adj.* carnal

carnival *n.* carnaval

carnivore *n.* carnívoro

carol *n.* cântico

carpal *adj.* carpiano

carpenter *n.* carpinteiro

carpentry *n.* carpintaria

carpet *n.* tapete

carriage *n.* transporte

carrier *n.* portador

carrot *n.* cenoura

carry *v.* transportar

cart *n.* carrinho

cartel *n.* cartel

cartilage *n.* cartilagem

carton *n.* cartão

cartoon *n.* desenho animado

cartridge *n.* cartucho

carve *v.* esculpir

carvery *n.* rodízio

Casanova *n.* Casanova

cascade *n.* cascata

case *n.* caso

casement *n.* armação

cash *n.* numerário

cashew *n.* caju

cashier *n.* caixa

cashmere *n.* casimira

casing *n.* invólucro

casino *n.* casino

cask *n.* barril

casket *n.* caixão

casserole *n.* caçarola

cassock *n.* batina

cast *v.* lançar

castaway *n.* náufrago

caste *n.* casta

castigate *v.* castigar

casting *n.* casting

castle *n.* castelo

castor *n.* castor

castrate *v.* castrar

castor oil *a.* óleo de rícino

casual *adj.* casual

casualty *n.* casualidade

cat *n.* gato

cataclysm *n.* cataclismo

catalogue *n.* catálogo

catalyse *v.* catalisar

catalyst *n.* catalisador

cataract *n.* catarata

catastrophe *n.* catástrofe

catch *v.* apanhar

catching *adj.* atraente

catchy *adj.* cativante

catechism *n.* catecismo

categorical *adj.* categórico

categorize *v.* classificar

category *n.* categoria

cater *v.* fornecer

caterpillar *n.* caterpillar

catharsis *n.* catarse	**celebration** *n.* celebração
cathedral *n.* catedral	**celebrity** *n.* celebridade
catholic *adj.* católico	**celestial** *adj.* divino
cattle *n.* gado	**celibacy** *n.* celibato
catty *n.* calúnia	**celibate** *adj.* celibatário
Caucasian *adj.* Caucasiano	**cell** *n.* célula
cauldron *n.* caldeirão	**cellar** *n.* adega
cauliflower *n.* couve-flor	**cell phone** *n.* telemóvel
causal *adj.* causal	**cellular** *adj.* celular
causality *n.* causualidade	**cellulite** *n.* celulite
cause *n.* causar	**celluloid** *n.* celulóide
causeway *n.* dique	**cellulose** *n.* celulose
caustic *adj.* cáustico	**Celsius** *n.* Celsius
caution *n.* cautela	**Celtic** *adj.* Céltico
cautionary *adj.* cauteloso	**cement** *n.* cimento
cautious *adj.* prudente	**cemetery** *n.* cemitério
cavalcade *n.* cavalgada	**censer** *n.* insensório
cavalier *adj.* improvisado	**censor** *n.* censor
cavalry *n.* cavalaria	**censorship** *n.* censura
cave *n.* gruta	censorious *adj.* severo
caveat *n.* embargo	**censure** *v.* censurar
cavern *n.* caverna	**census** *n.* censo
cavernous *adj.* cavernoso	**cent** *n.* cêntimo
cavity *n.* cavidade	**centenary** *n.* secular
cavort *v.* pinotear	**centennial** *n.* centenário
cease *v.* cessar	**center** *n.* centro
ceasefire *n.* cessar fogo	**centigrade** *adj.* centígrados
ceaseless *adj.* incessante	**centimetre** *n.* centímetro
cedar *n.* cedro	**centipede** *n.* centopéia
cede *v.* ceder	**central** *adj.* fundamental
ceiling *n.* teto	**centralize** *v.* centralizar
celandine *n.* celidónia	**centre** *n.* meio
celebrant *n.* celebrante	**century** *n.* século
celebrate *v.* celebrar	**ceramic** *n.* cerâmica

cereal *n.* cereal	**chaotic** *adj.* caótico
cerebral *adj.* cerebral	**chapel** *n.* capela
ceremonial *adj.* cerimonial	**chaplain** *n.* capelão
ceremonious *adj.* cerimonioso	**chapter** *n.* capítulo
ceremony *n.* cerimónia	**char** *v.* carbonizar
certain *adj.* certo	**character** *n.* caráter
certainly *adv.* certamente	**characteristic** *n.* característica
certifiable *adj.* certificável	**charcoal** *n.* carvão
certificate *n.* certidão	**charge** *v.* cobrar
certify *v.* certificar	**charge** *n.* carga
certitude *n.* certeza	**charger** *n.* carregador
cervical *adj.* cervical	**chariot** *n.* coche
cessation *n.* cessação	**charisma** *n.* carisma
cession *n.* cessão	**charismatic** *adj.* carismático
chain *n.* corrente	**charitable** *adj.* caridoso
chair *n.* cadeira	**charity** *n.* caridade
chairman *n.* presidente	**charlatan** *n.* charlatão
chaise *n.* cabriolé	**charm** *n.* encanto
chalet *n.* chalé	**charming** *adj.* encantador
chalice *n.* cálice	**chart** *n.* gráfico
chalk *n.* giz	**charter** *n.* fretar
challenge *n.* desafio	**chartered** *adj.* fretado
chamber *n.* câmara	**chary** *adj.* cuidadoso
chamberlain *n.* camareiro	**chase** *v.* perseguir
champagne *n.* champanhe	**chassis** *n.* chassis
champion *n.* campeão	**chaste** *adj.* casto
chance *n.* oportunidade	**chasten** *v.* castigar
chancellor *n.* chanceler	**chastise** *v.* punir
Chancery *n.* Chancelaria	**chastity** *n.* castidade
chandelier *n.* lustre	**chat** *v. i.* conversar
change *v.* alterar	**chateau** *n.* castelo
channel *n.* canal	**chattel** *n.* bens imóveis
chant *n.* cântico	**chatter** *v.* tagalerice
chaos *n.* caos	**chauffeur** *n.* motorista

chauvinism *n.* chauvinismo
chauvinist *n.* &*adj.* chauvinista
cheap *adj.* barato
cheapen *v.* t. pechinchar
cheat *v.* enganar
cheat *n.* batota
check *v.* verificar
checkmate n cheque-mate
cheek *n.* bochecha
cheeky *adj.* atrevido
cheep *n.* pio
cheer *v.* t. animar
cheerful *adj.* alegre
cheerless *adj.* triste
cheery *adj.* alegre
cheese *n.* queijo
cheetah *n.* chita
chef *n.* chefe
chemical *adj.* químico
chemist *n.* químico
chemistry *n.* química
chemotherapy *n.* quimioterapia
cheque *n.* cheque
cherish *v.* acalentar
chess *n.* xadrez
chest *n.* peito
chestnut *n.* castanha
chevron *n.* divisa
chew *v.* mastigar
chic *adj.* elegante
chicanery *n.* sofisma
chicken *n.* galinha
chickpea *n.* grão de bico
chide *v.* censurar

chief *n.* chefe
chiefly *adv.* principalmente
chieftain *n.* chefe
child *n.* criança
childhood *n.* infância
childish *adj.* infantil
chill *n.* frio
chilli *n.* pimenta-caiena
chilly *adj.* friorento
chime *n.* carrilhão
chimney *n.* chaminé
chimpanzee *n.* chimpazé
chin *n.* queixo
china *n.* China
chip *n.* lasca
chirp *v.* chilrear
chisel *n.* cinzel
chit *n.* pivete
chivalrous *adj.* cavalheiresco
chivalry *n.* cavalheirismo
chlorine *n.* cloro
chloroform *n.* clorofórmio
chocolate *n.* chocolate
choice *n.* escolha
choir *n.* coro
choke *v.* sufocar
cholera *n.* cólera
choose *v.* t escolher
chop *v.* picar
chopper *n.* cutelo
chopstick *n.* pauzinho
choral *adj.* cantado em coro
chord *n.* acorde
chorus *n.* coro

Christ n. Cristo
Christian adj. Cristão
Christianity n. Cristandade
Christmas n. Natal
chrome n. cromo
chronic adj. crónico
chronicle n. crónica
chronology n. cronologia
chronograph n. cronógrafo
chuckle v. cacarejar
chum n. companheiro
chunk n. naco
church n. igreja
churchyard n. adro
churn v. batedeira
chutney n. molho picante
cider n. cidra
cigar n. charuto
cigarette n. cigarro
cinema n cinema
cinnamon n. canela
circle n. círculo
circuit n. circuito
circular adj. circular
circulate v. circular
circulation n. circulação
circumcise v. circuncidar
circumference n. circunferência
circumscribe v. circunscrever
circumspect adj. circusnpecto
circumstance n. circunstância
circus n. circo
cist n. cista
cistern n. cisterna

citadel n. citadela
cite v. citar
citizen n. cidadão
citizenship n. cidadania
citrus n. cítrico
citric adj. cítrico
city n. cidade
civic adj. cívico
civics n. educação cívica
civil adj. civil
civilian n. civil
civilization n. civilização
civilize v. civilizar
clad adj. revestido
cladding n. revestimento
claim v. reinvidicar
claimant n. reclamante
clammy adj. húmido
clamour n. clamor
clamp n. braçadeira
clan n. clã
clandestine adj. clandestino
clap v. aplaudir
clarify v. esclarecer
clarification n. esclarecimento
clarion adj. clarim
clarity n. clareza
clash v. colidir
clasp v. apertar
class n. aula
classic adj. clássico
classical adj. clássico
classification n. classificação
classify v. classificar

clause *n.* cláusula	**cloister** *n.* claustro
claustrophobia *n.* claustrofobia	**clone** *n.* clone
claw *n.* garra	**close** *adj.* próximo
clay *n.* argila	**closet** *n.* armário
clean *adj.* limpo	**closure** *n.* encerramento
cleanliness *n.* limpeza	**clot** *n.* coágulo
cleanse *v.* limpar	**cloth** *n.* pano
clear *adj.* evidente	**clothe** *v.* vestir
clearance *n.* folga	**clothes** *n.* roupa
clearly *adv.* claramente	**clothing** *n.* vestuário
cleave *v.* fender	**cloud** *n.* nuvem
cleft *n.* fenda	**cloudy** *adj.* nublado
clemency *n.* clemência	**clove** *n.* dente de alho
clement *adj.* clemente	**clown** *n.* palhaço
Clementine *n.* Clementina	**cloying** *adj.* enjoativo
clench *v.* cerrar	**club** *n.* clube
clergy *n.* clero	**clue** *n.* pista
cleric *n.* clérigo	**clumsy** *adj.* trapalhão
clerical *adj.* eclesiástico	**cluster** *n.* grupo
clerk *n.* escriturário	**clutch** *v. t.* apertar
clever *adj.* inteligente	**coach** *n.* treinador
click *n.* clique	**coal** *n.* carvão
client *n.* cliente	**coalition** *n.* aliança
cliff *n.* penhasco	**coarse** *adj.* grosseiro
climate *n.* clima	**coast** *n.* costa
climax *n.* clímax	**coaster** *n.* montanha-russa
climb *v.i* subir	**coat** *n.* casaco
clinch *v.* rebitar	**coating** *n.* revestimento
cling *v.* agarrar	**coax** *v.* persuadir
clinic *n.* clínica	**cobalt** *n.* cobalto
clink *n.* tinido	**cobble** *n.* godo
clip *n.* clip	**cobbler** *n.* tarte de frutas
cloak *n.* manto	**cobra** *n.* cobra
clock *n.* relógio	**cobweb** *n.* teia de aranha

cocaine *n.* cocaína

cock *n.* galo

cockade *n.* laço (insígnia)

cockpit *n.* cabine do piloto

cockroach *n.* barata

cocktail *n.* cocktail

cocky *adj.* convencido

cocoa *n.* cacau

coconut *n.* côco

cocoon *n.* casulo

code *n.* código

co-education *n.* co-educação

coefficient *n.* coeficiente

coerce *v.* coagir

coeval *adj.* coevo

coexist *v.* coexistir

coexistence *n.* coexistência

coffee *n.* café

coffer *n.* cofre

coffin *n.* caixão

cog *n.* roda dentada

cogent *adj.* convicente

cogitate *v.* cogitar

cognate *adj.* cognato

cognizance *n.* conhecimento

cohabit *v.* coabitar

cohere *v.* aderir

coherent *adj.* coerente

cohesion *n.* coesão

cohesive *adj.* coesivo

coil *n.* bobina

coin *n.* moeda

coinage *n.* cunhagem

coincide *v.* coincidir

coincidence *n.* coincidência

coir *n.* fibra de coco

coke *n.* coca-cola

cold *adj.* frio

colic *n.* cólica

collaborate *v.* colaborar

collaboration *n.* colaboração

collage *n.* colagem

collapse *v.* colapso

collar *n.* colarinho

collate *v.* confrontar

collateral *n.* colateral

colleague *n.* colega

collect *v.* coletar

collection *n.* coleção

collective *adj.* coletivo

collector *n.* coletor

college *n.* faculdade

collide *v.* colidir

colliery *n.* mina de carvão

collision *n.* colisão

colloquial *adj.* coloquial

collusion *n.* conspiração

cologne *n.* colónia (perfume)

colon *n.* cólon

colonel *n.* coronel

colonial *adj.* colonial

colony *n.* colónia

colossal *adj.* colossal

colossus *n.* colosso

column *n.* coluna

colour *n.* cor

colouring *n.* coloração

colourless *n.* incolor

coma *n.* coma
comb *n.* pente
combat *n.* combate
combatant n combatente
combination *n.* combinação
combine *v.* combinar
combustible *adj.* combustível
combustion *n.* combustão
come *v.* chegar
comedian *n.* comediante
comedy n comédia
comet *n.* cometa
comfort *n.* conforto
comfort *v.* confortar
comfortable *adj.* confortável
comic *adj.* cómico
comma *n.* vírgula
command *v.* comandar
commandant *n.* comandante
commander *n.* comandante
commando *n.* comando
commemorate *v.* comemorar
commemoration *n.* comemoração
commence *v.* começar
commencement *n.* começo
commend *v.* recomendar
commendable *adj.* louvável
commendation *n.* recomendação
comment *n.* comentário
commentary *n.* comentário
commentator *n.* comentador
commerce *n.* comércio
commercial *adj.* comercial
commiserate *v.* lamentar

commission *n.* comissão
commissioner *n.* comissário
commissure *n.* comissura
commit *v.* cometer
commitment *n.* compromisso
committee *n.* comité
commode *n.* cómoda
commodity *n.* comodidade
common *adj.* vulgar
commoner *n.* plebeu
commonplace *adj.* banal
commonwealth *n.* comunidade
commotion *n.* comoção
communal *adj.* comum
commune *n.* comuna
communicable *adj.* comunicável
communicant *n.* comunicante
communicate *v.* comunicar
communication *n.* comunicação
communion *n.* comunhão
communism *n.* comunismo
community *n.* comunidade
commute *v.* comutar
compact *adj.* compacto
companion *n.* companheiro
company *n.* companhia
comparative *adj.* comparativo
compare *v.* comparar
comparison *n.* comparação
compartment *n.* compartimento
compass *n.* bússola
compassion *n.* compaixão
compatible *adj.* compatível
compatriot *n.* compatriota

compel *v.* obrigar
compendious *adj.* resumido
compendium *n.* compêndio
compensate *v.* compensar
compensation *n.* compensação
compere *n.* patrão
compete *v.* competir
competence *n.* competência
competent *adj.* competente
competition *n.* competição
competitive *adj.* competitivo
competitor *n.* concorrente
compile *v.* compilar
complacent *adj.* complacente
complain *v.* criticar
complaint *n.* queixa
complaisant *adj.* amável
complement *n.* complementar
complementary *adj.* complementar
complete *adj.* completo
completion *n.* realização
complex *adj.* complexo
complexity *n.* complexidade
complexion *n.* compleição
compliance *n.* observância
compliant *adj.* condescendente
complicate *v.* complicar
complication *n.* complicação
complicit *adj.* cúmplice
complicity *n.* cumplicidade
compliment *n.* elogio
compliment *v.* i cumprimentar
comply *v.* obedecer
component *n.* componente

comport *v.* comportar-se
compose *v.* compor
composer *n.* compositor
composite *adj.* composto
composition *n.* composição
compositor *n.* compositor
compost *n.* adubo
composure *n.* compostura
compound *n.* composto
comprehend *v.* compreender
comprehensible *adj.* compreensível
comprehension *n.* compreensão
comprehensive *adj.* compreensivo
compress *v.* comprimir
compression *n.* compressão
comprise *v.* abranger
compromise *n.* compromisso
compulsion *n.* compulsão
compulsive *adj.* compulsivo
compulsory *adj.* obrigatório
compunction *n.* compunção
computation *n.* computação
compute *v.* calcular
computer *n.* computador
computerize *v.* informatizar
comrade *n.* camarada
concatenation *n.* concatenação
concave *adj.* côncavo
conceal *v.* esconder
concede *v.* conceder
conceit *n.* presunção
conceivable *adj.* concebível
conceive *v.* t conceber
concentrate *v.* concentrar

concentration *n.* concentração
concept *n.* conceito
conception *n.* concepção
concern *v.* interessar
concerning *prep.* concernente
concert *n.* concerto
concerted *adj.* combinado
concession *n.* concessão
conch *n.* concha
conciliate *v.* conciliar
concise *adj.* conciso
conclude *n.* concluir
conclusion *n.* conclusão
conclusive *adj.* conclusivo
concoct *v.* inventar
concoction *n.* mistura
concomitant *adj.* simultâneo
concord *n.* concórdia
concordance *n.* acordo
concourse *n.* concurso
concrete *n.* betão
concubine *n.* concubina
concur *v.* concorrer
concurrent *adj.* concorrente
concussion *n.* concussão
condemn *v.* condenar
condemnation *n.* condenação
condense *v.* condensar
condescend *v.* condescender
condiment *n.* condimento
condition *n.* condição
conditional *adj.* condicional
conditioner *n.* condicionador
condole *v.* exprimir condolências

condolence *n.* condolências
condom *n.* preservativo
condominium *n.* condomínio
condone *v.* perdoar
conduct *n.* conduzir
conduct *v.* conduzir
conductor *n.* condutor
cone *n.* cone
confection *n.* confecção
confectioner *n.* confeiteiro
confectionery *n.* confeitaria
confederate *adj.* confederado
confederation *n.* confederação
confer *v.* conferir
conference *n.* conferência
confess *v.* confessar
confession *n.* confissão
confidant *n.* confidente
confide *v.* confiar
confidence *n.* confiança
confident *adj.* confiante
confidential *adj.* confidencial
configuration *n.* configuração
confine *v.* limitar
confinement *n.* reclusão
confirm *v.* confirmada
confirmation *n.* confirmação
confiscate *v.* confiscar
confiscation *n.* confisco
conflate *v.* fundir
conflict *n.* conflito
confluence *n.* afluência
confluent *adj.* afluência
conform *v.* obedecer

conformity *n.* conformidade

confront *v.* enfrentar

confrontation *n.* confronto

confuse *v.* confundir

confusion *n.* confusão

confute *v.* refutar

congenial *adj.* agradável

congenital *adj.* congénito

congested *adj.* congestionado

congestion *n.* congestão

conglomerate *n.* conglomerado

conglomeration *n.* conglomeração

congratulate *v.* felicitar

congratulation *n.* parabéns

congregate *v.* congregar

congress *n.* congresso

congruent *adj.* congruente

conical *adj.* cónico

conjecture *n.* conjetura

conjecture *v.* conjeturar

conjugal *v.t.* & *i.* conjugal

conjugate *v.* conjugar

conjunct *adj.* conjunto

conjunction *n.* conjunção

conjunctivitis *n.* conjutivite

conjuncture *n.* conjuntura

conjure *v.* conjurar

conker *n.* castanha da índia ·

connect *v.* conectar

connection *n.* conexão

connive *v.* conspirar

conquer *v.* conquistar

conquest *n.* conquista

conscience *n.* consciência

conscious *adj.* consciente

consecrate *v.* consagrar

consecutive *adj.* consecutivo

consecutively *adv.* consecutivamente

consensus *n.* consenso

consent *n.* consentimento

consent *v.t.* consentir

consequence *n.* consequência

consequent *adj.* consequente

conservation *n.* conservação

conservative *adj.* conservador

conservatory *n.* conservatório

conserve *v. t* conservar

consider *v.* considerar

considerable *adj.* considerável

considerate *adj.* considerado

consideration *n.* consideração

considering *prep.* pensando bem

consign *v.* consignar

consignment *n.* consignação

consist *v.* consistir em

consistency *n.* consistência

consistent *adj.* consistente

consolation *n.* consolo

console *v. t.* consolar

consolidate *v.* consolidar

consolidation *n.* consolidação

consonant *n.* consoante

consort *n.* consorciar

consortium *n.* consórcio

conspicuous *adj.* conspícuo

conspiracy *n.* conspiração

conspirator *n.* conspirador

conspire *v.* conspirar

constable n. policial
constabulary n. polícia
constant adj. constante
constellation n. constelação
consternation n. consternação
constipation n. obstipação
constituency n. eleitorado
constituent adj. constituinte
constitute v. constituir
constitution n. constituição
constitutional adj. constitucional
constrain v. constranger
constraint n. constragimento
constrict v. contrair
construct v. construir
construction n. construção
constructive adj. construtivo
construe v. interpretar
consul n. cônsul
consular n. consular
consulate n. consulado
consult v. consultar
consultant n. consultor
consultation n. consultar
consume v. consumir
consumer n. consumidor
consummate v. consumar
consumption n. consumo
contact n. contato
contagion n. contágio
contagious adj. contagioso
contain v.t. conter
container n. contentor
containment n. contenção

contaminate v. contaminar
contemplate v. contemplar
contemplation n. contemplação
contemporary adj. contemporâneo
contempt n. desprezo
contemptuous adj. desdenhoso
contend v. lutar
content adj. contente
content n. teor
contention n. contenção
contentment n. contentamento
contentious adj. contentamento
contest n. competição
contestant n. contestante
context n. contexto
contiguous adj. contíguo
continent n. continente
continental adj. continental
contingency n. contigência
continual adj. contínuo
continuation n. extensão
continue v. prosseguir
continuity n. continuidade
continuous adj. contínuo
contort v. contorcer
contour n. contorno
contra prep. contra
contraband n. contrabando
contraception n. contracepção
contraceptive n. contraceptivo
contract n. contrato
contractual adj. contratual
contractor n. contratante
contraction n. contratação

contradict *v.* contradizer	**convivial** *adj.* jovial
contradiction *n.* contradição	**convocation** *n.* convocação
contrary *adj.* oposto	**convoy** *n.* escolta
contrast *n.* contraste	**convulse** *n.* convulsionar
contravene *v.* infringir	**convulsion** *n.* convulsão
contribute *v.* contribuir	**cook** *n.* cozinheiro
contribution *n.* contribuição	**cook** *v.* cozinhar
contrivance *n.* invenção	**cooker** *n.* fogão
contrive *v.* inventar	**cookie** *n.* bolacha
control *n.* controlar	**cool** *adj.* fresco
controller *n.* controlador	**coolant** *n.* refrigerante
controversial *adj.* controverso	**cooler** *n.* refrigerador
controversy *n.* controvérsia	**cooper** *n.* tanoeiro
contusion *n.* contusão	**cooperate** *v.* cooperar
conundrum *n.* enigma	**cooperation** *n.* cooperação
conurbation *n.* aglomeração	**cooperative** *adj.* cooperativo
convene *v.* convocar	**coordinate** *v. t* coordenar
convenience *n.* conveniência	**coordination** *n.* coordenação
convenient *adj.* conveniente	**cope** *v.* competir
convent *n.* convento	**copier** *n.* copiadora
convention *n.* convenção	**copious** *adj.* abundante
converge *v.* convergir	**copper** *n.* cobre
conversant *adj.* familiarizado	**copulate** *v.* copular
conversation *n.* conversa	**copy** *n.* cópia
converse *v.* conversar	**copy** *v.* copiar
conversion *n.* conversão	**coral** *n.* coral
convert *n.* convertido	**cord** *n.* cordel
convert *v.* converter	**cordial** *adj.* cordial
convey *v.* transmitir	**cordon** *n.* cordão
conveyance *n.* transporte	**core** *n.* núcleo
convict *n.* condenado	**coriander** *n.* coentro
convict *v.* condenar	**cork** *n.* cortiça
conviction *n.* condenação	**corn** *n.* milho
convince *v.* convencer	**cornea** *n.* córnea

corner *n.* esquina

cornet *n.* corneta

coronation *n.* coroação

coroner *n.* médico legista

coronet *n.* diadema

corporal *n.* corporal

corporate *adj.* coletivo

corporation *n.* corporação

corps *n.* corpo

corpse *n.* cadáver

corpulent *adj.* corpulento

correct *adj.* correto

correct *v.* corrigir

correction *n.* correção

corrective *adj.* corretivo

correlate *v.* correlacionar

correlation *n.* correlação

correspond *v.* corresponder

correspondence *n.* correspondência

correspondent *n.* correspondente

corridor *n.* corredor

corroborate *v.* corroborar

corrode *v.* corroer

corrosion *n.* corrosão

corrosive *adj.* corrosivo

corrugated *adj.* ondulado

corrupt *adj.* corrupto

corrupt *n.* corrupto

corruption *n.* corrupção

cortisone *n.* cortisona

cosmetic *adj.* cosmético

cosmetic *n.* cosmético

cosmic *adj.* cósmico

cosmology *n.* cosmologia

cosmopolitan *adj.* cosmopólita

cosmos *n.* universo

cost *v.* custar

costly *adj.* dispendioso

costume *n.* traje

cosy *adj.* aconchegante

cot *n.* berço

cottage *n.* chalé

cotton *n.* algodão

couch *n.* sofá

couchette *n.* beliche

cough *v.* tossir

council *n.* conselho

councillor *n.* conselheiro

counsel *n.* conselho

counsel *v.* aconselhar

counsellor *n.* conselheiro

count *v.* contar

countenance *n.* semblante

counter *n.* contador

counter *v.t.* opor

counteract *v.* contrariar

counterfeit *adj.* falsificado

counterfoil *n.* talão de cheques

countermand *v.* revogar

counterpart *n.* contrapartida

countless *adj.* incontável

country *n.* país

county *n.* condado

coup *n.* golpe

coupe *n.* coupe

couple *n.* casal

couplet *n.* par

coupon *n.* cupão

courage *n.* coragem	**cram** *v.* empinar
courageous *adj.* corajoso	**cramp** *n.* cãibra
courier *n.* correio	**crane** *n.* grua
course *n.* curso	**crank** *v.* manivela
court *n.* tribunal	**crash** *v.* colidir
courteous *adj.* cortês	**crass** *adj.* crasso
courtesan *n.* cortesã	**crate** *n.* engraçado
courtesy *n.* cortesia	**cravat** *n.* gravata
courtier *n.* cortesão	**crave** *v.* t desejar
courtly *adj.* polido	**craven** *adj.* covarde
courtship *n.* namoro	**crawl** *v.* rastejar
courtyard *n.* pátio	**crayon** *n.* lápis
cousin *n.* primo	**craze** *n.* mania
cove *n.* enseada	**crazy** *adj.* maluco
covenant *n.* pacto	**creak** *n.* rangido
cover *n.* cobrir	**creak** *v.* ranger
cover *v.* cobrir	**cream** *n.* natas
covert *adj.* encoberto	**crease** *n.* amarrotar
covet *v.* cobiçar	**create** *v.* criar
cow *n.* vaca	**creation** *n.* criação
coward *n.* cobarde	**creative** *adj.* criativo
cowardice *n.* covardia	**creator** *n.* criador
cower *v.* encolher-se	**creature** *n.* criatura
coy *adj.* recatado	**creche** *n.* creche
cosy *adj.* acolhedor	**credentials** *n.* credenciais
crab *n.* caranguejo	**credible** *adj.* credível
crack *n.* rachar	**credit** *n.* crédito
crack *v.* partir	**creditable** *adj.* honroso
cracker *n.* biscoito	**creditor** *n.* credor
crackle *v.* crepitação	**credulity** *adv.* credulidade
cradle *n.* berço	**creed** *n.* credo
craft *n.* artesanato	**creek** *n.* enseada
craftsman *n.* artesão	**creep** *v.* gatinhar
crafty *adj.* astuto	**creeper** *n.* trepadeira

cremate v. cremar	**crow** n. corvo
cremation n. cremação	**crowd** n. multidão
crematorium n. crematório	**crown** n. coroa
crescent n. crescente	**crown** v. coroar
crest n. crista	**crucial** adj. decisivo
crew n. tripulação	**crude** adj. cru
crib n. manjedoura	**cruel** adj. cruel
cricket n. críquete	**cruelty** adv. crueldade
crime n. crime	**cruise** v. cruzeiro
criminal n. criminal	**cruiser** n. cruzador
criminology n. criminologia	**crumb** n. migalha
crimson n. carmesin	**crumble** v. esmigalhar
cringe v. adular	**crumple** v. amarrotar
cripple n. aleijado	**crunch** v. triturar
crisis n. crise	**crusade** n. cruzada
crisp adj. quebradiço	**crush** v. esmagar
criterion n. critério	**crust** n. crosta
critic n. crítico	**crutch** n. muleta
critical adj. crítico	**crux** n. ponto crucial
criticism n. crítica	**cry** n. chorar
criticize v. criticar	**cry** v. chorar
critique n. crítica	**crypt** n. cripta
croak n. coaxar	**crystal** n. cristal
crochet n. crochet	**cub** n. cria
crockery n. louça de barro	**cube** n. cubo
crocodile n. crocodilo	**cubical** adj. cúbico
croissant n. croissant	**cubicle** n. cúbiculo
crook n. panela de barro	**cuckold** n. corno
crooked adj. adoecido	**cuckoo** n. cuco
crop n. colheita	**cucumber** n. pepino
cross n. atravessar	**cuddle** v. abraço
crossing n. travessia	**cuddly** adj. fofinho
crotchet n. capricho	**cudgel** n. clava
crouch v. rastejar	**cue** n. deixa

cuff *n.* algemar

cuisine *n.* cozinha

culinary *adj.* culinária

culminate *v.* culminar

culpable *adj.* culpável

culprit *n.* culpado

cult *n.* culto

cultivate *v.* cultivar

cultural *adj.* cultural

culture *n.* cultura

cumbersome *adj.* pesado

cumin *n.* cominhos

cumulative *adj.* acumulativo

cunning *adj.* astuto

cup *n.* chávena

cupboard *n.* armário

cupidity *n.* avareza

curable *adj.* curável

curative *adj.* curativo

curator *n.* curador

curb *v.* t refrear

curd *n.* coalhada

cure *v.* t. curar

curfew *n.* toque de recolher

curiosity *n.* curiosidade

curious *adj.* curioso

curl *v.* enrolar

currant *n.* groselha

currency *n.* moeda

current *adj.* atual

current *n.* corrente

curriculum *n.* currículo

curry *n.* caril

curse *n.* maldição

cursive *adj.* cursivo

cursor *n.* cursor

cursory *adj.* apressado

curt *adj.* curto

curtail *v.* reduzir

curtain *n.* cortina

curve *n.* curva

cushion *n.* amortecer

custard *n.* creme

custodian *n.* zelador

custody *n.* custódia

custom *n.* personalizado

customary *adj.* habitual

customer *n.* cliente

customize *v.* personalizar

cut *v.* cortar

cute *adj.* bonito

cutlet *n.* costoleta

cutter *n.* cortador

cutting *n.* corte

cyan *n.* ciano

cyanide *n.* cianeto

cyber *comb.* cibernético

cyberspace *n.* ciberespaço

cycle *n.* ciclo

cyclic *adj.* cíclico

cyclist *n.* ciclista

cyclone *n.* ciclone

cylinder *n.* cilindro

cynic *n.* cínico

cynosure *n.* cinosura

cypress *n.* cipreste

cyst *n.* cisto

cystic *adj.* cístico

D

dab v. alisar
dabble v. salpicar
dacoit n. salteador
dad n pai
daffodil n. abrótea
daft adj. maluco
dagger n. adaga
daily adj. diário
dainty adj. delicado
dairy n. laticínio
dais n. estrado
daisy n. margarida
dale n. ladrilho
dally v. flertar
dalliance n. namorico
dam n. barragem
damage n. dano
dame n. dama
damn v. amaldiçoar
damnable adj. condenável
damnation n. condenação
damp adj. húmido
dampen v. amortecer
damper n. amortecedor
dampness n. humidade
damsel n. donzela
dance v. dançar
dancer n. dançarino
dandelion n. dente de leão
dandle v. embalar
dandruff n. caspa
dandy n. estiloso

danger n. perigo
dangerous adj. perigoso
dangle v. i. balançar-se
dank adj. frio e húmido
dapper adj. elegante
dapple v. salpicar
dare v. ousar
daring adj. ousado
dark adj. escuro
darkness n. escuridão
darken v. escurecer
darling n. querida
darn v. cerzir
dart n. dardo
dash v. colidir
dashboard n. painél instrumentos
dashing adj. arrojado
dastardly adj. covarde
data n. dados
database n. base de dados
date n. data
datum n. dado
daub v. emplastrar
daughter n. filha
daughter-in-law n. nora
daunt v. assustar
dauntless adj. destemido
dawdle v. mandriar
dawn n. madrugada
day n. dia
daze v. atordoar
dazzle v. t. deslumbrar
dead adj. morto
deadline n. prazo de entrega

deadlock *n.* impasse
deadly *adj.* mortal
deaf *adj.* surdo
deafening *adj.* ensurdecedor
deal *n.* acordo
deal *v.* i tratar
dealer *n.* negociante
dean *n.* decano
dear *adj.* querido
dearly *adv.* caro
dearth *n.* escassez
death *n.* morte
debacle *n.* desastre
debar *v.* t. excluir
debase *v.* rebaixar
debatable *adj.* discutível
debate *n.* debate
debate *v.* t. debater
debauch *v.* debochar
debauchery *n.* devassidão
debenture *n.* obrigacionista
debilitate *v.* debilitar
debility *n.* debilidade
debit *n.* débito
debonair *adj.* afável
debrief *v.* interrogar
debris *n.* detritos
debt *n.* dívida
debtor *n.* devedor
debunk *v.* desacreditar
debut *n.* estreia
debutante *n.* debutante
decade *n.* década
decadent *adj.* decadente

decaffeinated *adj.* descafeínado
decamp *v.* desacampar
decant *v.* decantar
decanter *n.* decanter
decapitate *v.* decapitar
decay *v.* i decair
decease *n.* falecimento
deceased *adj.* falecido
deceit *n.* engano
deceitful *adj.* traiçoeiro
deceive *v.* enganar
decelerate *v.* desacelerar
December *n.* Dezembro
decency *n.* decência
decent *adj.* decente
decentralize *v.* descentralizar
deception *n.* deceção
deceptive *adj.* enganoso
decibel *n.* decíbel
decide *v.* decidir
decided *adj.* decidido
decimal *adj.* decimal
decimate *v.* dizimar
decipher *v.* decifrar
decision *n.* decisão
decisive *adj.* decisivo
deck *n.* convés
declaim *v.* declamar
declaration *n.* declaração
declare n declarar
declassify *v.* desclassificar
decline *v.* t. diminuir
declivity *n.* declive
decode *v.* descodificar

decompose *n.* decompor

decomposition *v. t* decomposição

decompress *v.* descomprimir

decongestant *n.* descongestionante

deconstruct *v.* desconstruir

decontaminate *v.* descontaminar

decor *n.* decoração

decorate *v.* decorar

decoration *n.* decoração

decorative *adj.* decorativo

decorous *adj.* decoroso

decorum *n.* decoro

decoy *n.* chamariz

decrease *v.* reduzir

decree *n.* decreto

decrement *v. t.* diminuir

decrepit *adj.* decrépito

decriminalize *v.* descriminalizar

decry *v.* desacreditar

dedicate *v.* dedicar

dedication *n.* dedicação

deduce *v.* deduzir

deduct *v.* subtrair

deduction *n.* dedução

deed *n.* ação

deem *v.* julgar

deep *adj.* profundo

deer *n.* veado

deface *v.* desfigurar

defamation *n.* difamação

defame *v.* difamar

default *n.* omissão

defeat *v. t.* derrotar

defeatist *n.* derrotista

defecate *v.* defecar

defect *n.* defeito

defective *adj.* defeituoso

defence *n.* defesa

defend *v.* defender

defendant *n.* réu

defensible *adj.* justificável

defensive *adj.* defensiva

defer *v.* adiar

deference *n.* deferência

defiance *n.* desafio

deficiency *n.* deficiência

deficient *adj.* deficiente

deficit *n.* défice

defile *v. t* macular

define *v.* definir

definite *adj.* definido

definition *n.* definição

deflate *v.* esvaziar

deflation *n.* deflação

deflect *v.* desviar

deforest *v.* desflorestar

deform *v.* desfigurar

deformity *n.* deformação

defraud *v.* defraudar

defray *v.* custear

defrost *v.* descongelar

deft *adj.* hábil

defunct *adj.* defunto

defuse *v.* desarmar

defy *v.* desafiar

degenerate *v.* degenerar

degrade *v.* degradar

degree *n.* grau

dehumanize v. desumanizar
dehydrate v. desidratar
deify v. divinizar
deign v. condescender
deity n. divindade
deja vu n. deja vu
deject v. abater
dejection n. abatimento
delay v. t atrasar
delectable adj. delicioso
delectation n. deleite
delegate n. delegar
delegation n. delegação
delete v. i excluir
deletion n. eliminação
deleterious adj. pernicioso
deliberate adj. deliberado
deliberation n. deliberação
delicacy n. delicadeza
delicate adj. delicado
delicatessen n. guloseimas
delicious adj. delicioso
delight v. t. deliciar
delightful adj. delicioso
delineate v. delinear
delinquent adj. delinquente
delirious adj. delirante
delirium n. delírio
deliver v. entregar
deliverance n. libertação
delivery n. entrega
dell n. dell
delta n. delta
delude v. iludir

deluge n. dilúvio
delusion n. ilusão
deluxe adj. de luxo
delve v. aprofundar
demand n. procura
demanding adj. exigente
demarcation n. demarcação
demean v. rebaixar
demented adj. demente
dementia n. demência
demerit n demérito
demise n. morte
demobilize v. desmobilizar
democracy n. democracia
democratic adj. democrático
demography n. demografia
demolish v. demolir
demon n. demónio
demonize v. endiabrar
demonstrate v. demonstrar
demonstration n. manifestação
demoralize v. desmoralizar
demote v. rebaixar
demur v. escrúpulo
demure adj. acanhado
demystify v. desmistificar
den n. covil
denationalize v. desnacionalizar
denial n. negação
denigrate v. denegrir
denomination n. denominação
denominator n. denominador
denote v. t denotar
denounce v. denunciar

dense *adj.* denso
density *n.* densidade
dent *n.* dente
dental *adj.* dental
dentist *n.* dentista
denture *n.* dentadura
denude *v.* desnudar
denunciation *n.* denúncia
deny *v. i.* negar
deodorant *n.* desodorizante
depart *v.* partir
department *n.* departamento
departure *n.* partida
depend *v.* depender
dependant *n.* dependente
dependency *n.* dependência
dependent *adj.* dependente
depict *v.* descrever
depilatory *adj.* depilatório
deplete *v.* esgotar
deplorable *adj.* deplorável
deploy *v.* implantar
deport *v. t* deportar
depose *v.* depor
deposit *n.* depósito
depository *n.* depositário
depot *n.* depósito
deprave *v.* depravar
deprecate *v.* desaprovar
depreciate *v.* depreciar
depreciation *n.* depreciação
depress *v.* deprimir
depression *n.* depressão
deprive *v.* privar

depth *n.* profundidade
deputation *n.* purificação
depute *v.* delegar
deputy *n.* deputado
derail *v. t.* descarrilhar
deranged *adj.* demente
deregulate *v.* desregulamentar
deride *v.* ridicularizar
derivative *adj.* derivado
derive *v.* derivar
derogatory *adj.* depreciativo
descend *v.* descer
descendant *n.* descendente
descent *n.* descida
describe *v.* descrever
description *n.* descrição
desert *v.* deserto
deserve *v. t.* merecer
design *n.* projeto
designate *v.* designar
desirable *adj.* desejável
desire *n.* desejo
desirous *adj.* desejoso
desist *v.* desistir
desk *n.* secretária
desolate *adj.* desolado
despair *n.* desespero
desperate *adj.* desesperado
despicable *adj.* desprezível
despise *v.* desprezar
despite *prep.* apesar de
despondent *adj.* desanimado
despot *n.* déspota
dessert *n.* sobremesa

destabilize v. desestabilizar	**deviant** adj. depravado
destination n. destino	**deviate** v. desviar
destiny n. destino	**device** n. dispositivo
destitute adj. destituído	**devil** n. diabo
destroy v. destruir	**devious** adj. desonesto
destroyer n. destruidor	**devise** v. inventar
destruction n. destruição	**devoid** adj. desprovido
detach v. separar	**devolution** n. devolução
detachment n. destacamento	**devolve** v. devolver
detail n. pormenor	**devote** v. dedicar
detain v. t deter	**devotee** n. devoto
detainee n. impedidor	**devotion** n. devoção
detect v. descobrir	**devour** v. devorar
detective n. detetive	**devout** adj. devoto
detention n. detenção	**dew** n. orvalho
deter v. deter	**dexterity** n. destreza
detergent n. detergente	**diabetes** n. diabetes
deteriorate v. deteriorar	**diagnose** v. diagnosticar
determinant n. determinante	**diagnosis** n. diagnóstico
determination v. t determinação	**diagram** n. diagrama
determine v. t determinar	**dial** n. discar
deterrent n. impedimento	**dialect** n. dialeto
detest v. detestar	**dialogue** n. diálogo
dethrone v. destronar	**dialysis** n. diálise
detonate v. detonar	**diameter** n. diâmetro
detour n. desvio	**diamond** n. diamante
detoxify v. desentoxicar	**diaper** n. fralda
detract v. diminuir	**diarrhoea** n. diarréia
detriment n. detrimento	**diary** n. diário
detritus n. detrito	**Diaspora** n. Diáspora
devalue v. desvalorizar	**dice** n. dados
devastate v. devastar	**dictate** adj. ditar
develop v. desenvolver	**dictation** n. ditado
development n. desenvolvimento	**dictator** n. ditador

diction *n.* dicção

dictionary *n.* dicionário

dictum *n.* dito

didactic *adj.* didático

die *v.* morrer

diesel *n.* gasóleo

diet *n.* dieta

dietician *n.* nutricionista

differ *v.* diferir

difference *n.* diferença

different *adj.* diferente

difficult *adj.* difícil

difficulty *n.* dificuldade

diffuse *v.* difundir

dig *v.* cavar

digest *v.* digerir

digestion *n.* digestão

digit *n.* dígito

digital *adj.* digital

dignified *adj.* digno

dignify *v.* dignificar

dignitary *n.* dignitário

dignity *n.* dignidade

digress *v.* divagar

dilapidated *adj.* dilapidado

dilate *v.* dilatar

dilemma *n.* dilema

diligent *adj.* diligente

dilute *v.* diluir

dim *adj.* escuro

dimension *n.* dimensão

diminish *v.* diminuir

diminution *n.* diminuição

din *n.* barulho

dine *v.* jantar (ato de jantar)

diner *n.* jantar (pessoa que janta)

dingy *adj.* sombrio

dinner *n.* jantar

dinosaur *n.* dinossauro

dip *v. t* mergulhar

diploma *n.* diploma

diplomacy *n.* diplomacia

diplomat *n.* diplomata

diplomatic *adj.* diplomático

dipsomania *n.* dipsomania

dire *adj.* terrível

direct *adj.* direto

direction *n.* direção

directive *n.* directiva

directly *adv.* diretamente

director *n.* diretor

directory *n.* diretório

dirt *n.* sujo

dirty *adj.* sujo

disability *n.* incapacidade

disable *v.* incapacitar

disabled *adj.* inválido

disadvantage *n.* desvantagem

disaffected *adj.* desafeto

disagree *v.* discordar

disagreeable *adj.* desagradável

disagreement *n.* desacordo

disallow *v.* desaprovar

disappear *v.* desaparecer

disappoint *v.* desiludir

disapproval *n.* desaprovação

disapprove *v.* desaprovar

disarm *v.* desarmar

disarmament *n.* desarmamento	**discreet** *adj.* discreto
disarrange *v.* desordenar	**discrepancy** *n.* discrepância
disarray *n.* desordem	**discrete** *adj.* discreto
disaster *n.* desastre	**discriminate** *v.* discriminar
disastrous *adj.* desastroso	**discursive** *adj.* discursivo
disband *v.* dispersar	**discuss** *v.* discutir
disbelief *n.* descrença	**discussion** *n.* discussão
disburse *v.* desembolsar	**disdain** *n.* desdém
disc *n.* disco	**disease** *n.* doença
discard *v.* descartar	**disembark** *v.* desembarcar
discern *v.* discernir	**disembodied** *adj.* desencarnado
discharge *v.* descarga	**disempower** *v.* desapoderar
disciple *n.* discípulo	**disenchant** *v.* desencantar
discipline *n.* disciplina	**disengage** *v.* desengatar
disclaim *v.* renunciar	**disentangle** *v.* desembaraçar
disclose *v.* divulgar	**disfavour** *n.* desfavor
disco *n.* discoteca	**disgrace** *n.* desgraça
discolour *v.* descolorir	**disgruntled** *adj.* desapontado
discomfit *v.* frustar	**disguise** *v.* disfarçar
discomfort *n.* desconforto	**disgust** *n.* desgosto
disconcert *v.* desconcertar	**dish** *n.* prato
disconnect *v.* desligar	**dishearten** *v.* desanimar
disconsolate *adj.* desconsolado	**dishonest** *adj.* desonesto
discontent *n.* descontentamento	**dishonour** *n.* desonra
discontinue *v.* descontinuar	**disillusion** *v.* desilusão
discord *n.* discórdia	**disincentive** *n.* desincentivo
discordant *adj.* discordante	**disinfect** *v.* desinfetar
discount *n.* desconto	**disingenuous** *adj.* dissimulado
discourage *v.* desencorajar	**disinherit** *v.* deserdar
discourse *n.* discurso	**disintegrate** *v.* desintegrar
discourteous *adj.* descortês	**disjointed** *adj.* deslocado
discover *v.* descobrir	**dislike** *v.* antipatizar
discovery *n.* descoberta	**dislocate** *v.* deslocar
discredit *v.* desacreditar	**dislodge** *v.* desalojar

disloyal *adj.* desleal

dismal *adj.* sombrio

dismantle *v.* desmantelar

dismay *n.* desalento

dismiss *v.* demitir

dismissive *adj.* desconsiderado

disobedient *adj.* desobediente

disobey *v.* desobedecer

disorder *n.* desordem

disorganized *adj.* desorganizado

disorientate *v.* desorientar

disown *v.* renegar

disparity *n.* disparidade

dispassionate *adj.* imparcial

dispatch *v.* expedição

dispel *v.* dissipar

dispensable *adj.* dispensável

dispensary *n.* dispensário

dispense *v.* dispensar

disperse *v.* dispersar

dispirited *adj.* desanimado

displace *v.* t deslocar

display *v.* exibir

displease *v.* contrariar

displeasure *n.* descontentamento

disposable *adj.* descartável

disposal *n.* disposição

dispose *v.* t dispor

dispossess *v.* livrar

disproportionate *adj.* desproporcion.

disprove *v.* refutar

dispute *v.* i disputar

disqualification *n.* desqualificação

disqualify *v.* desqualificar

disquiet *n.* inquietação

disregard *v.* t desconsiderar

disrepair *n.* ruína

disreputable *adj.* vergonhoso

disrepute *n.* descrédito

disrespect *n.* desrespeito

disrobe *v.* despir

disrupt *v.* romper

dissatisfaction *n.* descontentamento

dissect *v.* dissecar

dissent *v.* divergir

dissertation *n.* dissertação

dissident *n.* dissidente

dissimulate *v.* dissimular

dissipate *v.* dissipar

dissolve *v.* t dissolver

dissuade *v.* dissuadir

distance *n.* distância

distant *adj.* distante

distaste *n.* desgosto

distil *v.* destilar

distillery *n.* destilaria

distinct *adj.* distinto

distinction *n.* distinção

distinguish *v.* t distinguir

distort *v.* distorcer

distract *v.* distrair

distraction *n.* distração

distress *n.* aflição

distribute *v.* distribuir

distributor *n.* distribuidor

district *n.* distrito

distrust *n.* desconfiança

disturb *v.* perturbar

ditch *n.* vala	**dollar** *n.* dólar
dither *v.* estremecer	**domain** *n.* domínio
ditto *n.* idem	**dome** *n.* cúpula
dive *v.* mergulho	**domestic** *adj.* doméstico
diverge *v.* divergir	**domicile** *n.* domicílio
diverse *adj.* diverso	**dominant** *adj.* dominante
diversion *n.* desvio	**dominate** *v.* dominar
diversity *n.* diversidade	**dominion** *n.* domínio
divert *v.* t desviar	**donate** *v.* doar
divest *v.* despojar	**donkey** *n.* burro
divide *v.* dividir	**donor** *n.* doador
dividend *n.* dividendo	**doom** *n.* condenação
divine *adj.* divino	**door** *n.* porta
divinity *n.* divindade	**dormitory** *n.* dormitório
division *n.* divisão	**dose** *n.* dose
divorce *n.* divórcio	**dossier** *n.* dossier
divorcee *n.* divorciado	**dot** *n.* ponto
divulge *v.* divulgar	**dote** *v.* caducar
do *v.* fazer	**double** *adj.* duplo
docile *adj.* dócil	**doubt** *n.* duvido
dock *n.* doca	**dough** *n.* massa (dinheiro)
docket *n.* rótulo	**down** *adv.* para baixo
doctor *n.* médico	**downfall** *n.* queda
doctorate *n.* doutorado	**download** *v.* dowload
doctrine *n.* doutrina	**downpour** *n.* aguaceiro
document *n.* documento	**dowry** *n.* dote
documentary *n.* documentário	**doze** *v.* i dormitar
dodge *v.* t esquivar	**dozen** *n.* dúzia
doe *n.* corça	**drab** *adj.* monótono
dog *n.* cão	**draft** *n.* rascunho
dogma *n.* dogma	**drag** *v.* t arrastar
dogmatic *adj.* dogmático	**dragon** *n.* dragão
doldrums *n.* depressão	**drain** *v.* t drenar
doll *n.* boneca	**drama** *n.* drama

dramatic *adj.* dramático	**dual** *adj.* duplo
dramatist *n.* dramaturgo	**dubious** *adj.* duvidoso
drastic *adj.* drástico	**duck** *n.* pato
draught *n.* rascunho	**duct** *n.* canal
draw *v.* desenhar	**dudgeon** *n.* indignação
drawback *n.* desvantagem	**due** *adj.* devido
drawer *n.* gaveta	**duel** *n.* duelo
drawing *n.* desenho	**duet** *n.* dueto
dread *v.t* pavor	**dull** *adj.* aborrecido
dreadful *adj.* terrível	**dullard** *n.* bronco
dream *n.* sonho	**duly** *adv.* devidamente
dreary *adj.* triste	**dumb** *adj.* estúpido
drench *v.* humedecer	**dummy** *n.* manequim
dress *v.* vestir	**dump** *n.* lixeira
dressing *n.* roupa	**dung** *n.* esterco
drift *v.* flutuar	**dungeon** *n.* calabouço
drill *n.* broca	**duo** *n.* duo
drink *v.t* beber	**dupe** *v.* enganar
drip *v.i* gotejar	**duplex** *n.* duplo
drive *v.* conduzir	**duplicate** *adj.* duplicar
driver *n.* motorista	**duplicity** *n.* duplicidade
drizzle *n.* chuvisco	**durable** *adj.* durável
droll *adj.* divertido	**duration** *n.* duração
droop *v.* inclinar	**during** *prep.* durante
drop *v.* cair	**dusk** *n.* crepúsculo
dross *n.* escória	**dust** *n.* pó
drought *n.* seca	**duster** *n.* espanador
drown *v.* afogar	**dutiful** *adj.* obediente
drowse *v.* dormitar	**duty** *n.* dever
drug *n.* droga	**duvet** *n.* edredom
drum *n.* tambor	**dwarf** *n.* anão
drunkard *adj.* bêbado	**dwell** *v.* habitar
dry *adj.* seco	**dwelling** *n.* habitação
dryer *n.* secador	**dwindle** *v.t* diminuir

dye n. tingir	**ebony** n. ébano
dynamic adj. dinâmico	**ebullient** adj. efervescente
dynamics n. dinâmica	**eccentric** adj. excêntrico
dynamite n. dinamite	**echo** n. eco
dynamo n. dínamo	**eclipse** n. eclipse
dynasty n. dinastia	**ecology** n. ecologia
dysentery n. disenteria	**economic** adj. económico
dysfunctional adj. disfuncional	**economical** adj. económico
dyslexia n. dislexia	**economics** n. economia
dyspepsia n. dispepsia	**economy** n. economia
	ecstasy n. êxtase
	edge n. borda

E

	edgy adj. irritável
each adj. cada	**edible** adj. comestível
eager adj. ansioso	**edict** n. édito
eagle n. águia	**edifice** n. edifício
ear n. ouvido	**edit** v. editar
earl n. conde	**edition** n. edição
early adj. cedo	**editor** n. editor
earn v. ganhar	**editorial** adj. editorial
earnest adj. sério	**educate** v. educar
earth n. terra	**education** n. educação
earthen adj. térreo	**efface** v. apagar
earthly adj. terrestre	**effect** n. efeito
earthquake n. terremoto	**effective** adj. eficaz
ease n. facilidade	**effeminate** adj. efeminado
east n. leste	**effete** adj. estéril
Easter n. Páscoa	**efficacy** n. eficácia
eastern adj. oriental	**efficiency** n. eficiência
easy adj. fácil	**efficient** adj. eficiente
eat v. comer	**effigy** n. efígie
eatery n. restaurante	**effort** n. esforço
eatable adj. comestível	**egg** n. ovo
ebb n. vazante	**ego** n. ego

egotism *n.* egoísmo

eight *adj. & n.* oito

eighteen *adj. & n.* dezoito

eighty *adj. & n.* oitenta

either *adv.* também

ejaculate *v.* ejacular

eject *v.* t ejetar

elaborate *adj.* elaborado

elapse *v.* decorrer

elastic *adj.* elástico

elbow *n.* cotovelo

elder *adj.* mais velho

elderly *adj.* idoso

elect *v.* eleger

election *n.* eleição

elective *adj.* eletivo

electorate *n.* eleitorado

electric *adj.* elétrico

electrician *n.* eletricista

electricity *n.* eletricidade

electrify *v.* eletrificar

electrocute *v.* eletrocutar

electronic *adj.* eletrónico

elegance *n.* elegância

elegant *adj.* elegante

element *n.* elemento

elementary *adj.* elementar

elephant *n.* elefante

elevate *v.* elevar

elevator *n.* elevador

eleven *adj. & n.* onze

elf *n.* elfo

elicit *v.* extrair

eligible *adj.* elegível

eliminate *v.* eliminar

elite *n.* elite

ellipse *n.* elipse

elocution *n.* elocução

elongate *v.* alongar

elope *v.* fugir

eloquence *n.* eloquência

else *adv.* outro

elucidate *v.* t elucidar

elude *v.* iludir

elusion *n.* ardil

elusive *adj.* ilusório

emaciated *adj.* descarnado

email *n.* e-mail

emancipate *v.* t emancipar

emasculate *v.* castrar

embalm *v.* embalsamar

embankment *n.* aterro

embargo *n.* embargo

embark *v.* t embarcar

embarrass *v.* embaraçar

embassy *n.* embaixada

embattled *adj.* preparado p/combate

embed *v.* embutir

embellish *v.* embelezar

embitter *v.* amargar

emblem *n.* emblema

embodiment *n.* encarnação

embolden *v.* encorajar

emboss *v.* realçar

embrace *v.* abraçar

embroidery *n.* bordado

embryo *n.* embrião

emend *v.* emendar

emerald *n.* esmeralda
emerge *v.* emergir
emergency *n.* emergência
emigrate *v.* emigrar
eminence *n.* eminência
eminent *adj.* eminente
emissary *n.* emissário
emit *v.* emitir
emollient *adj.* emoliente
emolument *n.* emolumento
emotion *n.* emoção
emotional *adj.* emocional
emotive *adj.* emotivo
empathy *n.* empatia
emperor *n.* imperador
emphasis *n.* ênfase
emphasize *v.* enfatizar
emphatic *adj.* enfático
empire *n.* império
employ *v.* empregar
employee *n.* empregado
employer *n.* empregador
empower *v.* autorizar
empress *n.* imperatriz
empty *adj.* vazio
emulate *v.* t emular
enable *v.* permitir
enact *v.* decretar
enamel *n.* esmalte
enamour *v.* t enamorar
encapsulate *v.* encapsular
encase *v.* encerrar
enchant *v.* encantar
encircle *v.* t cercar

enclave *n.* enclave
enclose *v.* anexar
enclosure *n.* recinto
encode *v.* codificar
encompass *v.* envolver
encore *n.* bis
encounter *v.* encontrar
encourage *v.* encorajar
encroach *v.* invadir
encrypt *v.* criptografar
encumber *v.* sobrecarregar
encyclopaedia *n.* enciclopédia
end *n.* final
endanger *v.* arriscar
endear *v.* cativar
endearment *n.* carinho
endeavour *v.* esforçar
endemic *adj.* endémico
endorse *v.* endossar
endow *v.* dotar
endure *v.* suportar
enemy *n.* inimigo
energetic *adj.* enérgico
energy *n.* energia
enfeeble *v.* debilitar
enfold *v.* envolver
enforce *v.* executar
enfranchise *v.* emanecipar
engage *v.* empenhar
engagement *n.* compromisso
engine *n.* motor
engineer *n.* engenheiro
English *n.* Inglês
engrave *v.* gravar

engross v. ocupar	**entity** n. entidade
engulf v. engolir	**entomology** n. entomologia
enigma n. enigma	**entourage** n. comitiva
enjoy v. desfrutar	**entrails** n. entranhas
enlarge v. ampliar	**entrance** n. entrada
enlighten v. iluminar	**entrap** v. t. capturar
enlist v. alistar	**entreat** v. suplicar
enliven v. animar	**entreaty** v. t súplica
enmity n. inimizade	**entrench** v. entrincheirar
enormous adj. enorme	**entrepreneur** n. empresário
enough adj. suficiente	**entrust** v. confiar
enquire v. inquirir	**entry** n. entrada
enquiry n. inquérito	**enumerate** v. t enumerar
enrage v. enfurecer	**enunciate** v. enunciar
enrapture v. arrebatar	**envelop** v. envolver
enrich v. enriquecer	**envelope** n. envelope
enrol v. matricular	**enviable** adj. invejável
enshrine v. conservar	**envious** adj. invejoso
enslave v. escravizar	**environment** n. ambiente
ensue v. acontecer	**envisage** v. encarar
ensure v. garantir	**envoy** n. enviado
entangle v. t embaraçar	**envy** n. inveja
enter v. entrar	**epic** n. épico
enterprise n. empresa	**epicure** n. gastrónomo
entertain v. entreter	**epidemic** n. epidemia
entertainment n. diversão	**epidermis** n. epiderme
enthral v. encantar	**epigram** n. epigrama
enthrone v. empossar	**epilepsy** n. epilepsia
enthusiasm n. entusiasmo	**epilogue** n. epílogo
enthusiastic n. entusiasta	**episode** n. episódio
entice v. seduzir	**epistle** n. epístola
entire adj. todo	**epitaph** n. epitáfio
entirety n. totalidade	**epitome** n. epítome
entitle v. intitular	**epoch** n. época

equal *adj.* igual

equalize *v.* t igualar

equate *v.* equiparar

equation *n.* equação

equator *n.* equador

equestrian *adj.* equestre

equidistant *adj.* equidistante

equilateral *adj.* equilátero

equilibrium *n.* equilíbrio

equip *v.* equipar

equipment *n.* equipamento

equitable *adj.* equitativo

equity *n.* equidade

equivalent *adj.* equivalente

equivocal *adj.* equívoco

era *n.* era

eradicate *v.* erradicar

erase *v.* apagar

erect *adj.* erguer

erode *v.* corroer

erogenous *adj.* erógeno

erosion *n.* erosão

erotic *adj.* erótico

err *v.* errar

errand *n.* incumbência

errant *adj.* errante

erratic *adj.* errático

erroneous *adj.* erróneo

error *n.* erro

erstwhile *adj.* outrora

erudite *adj.* erudito

erupt *v.* estourar (entrar erupção)

escalate *v.* escalar

escalator *n.* escada rolante

escapade *n.* escapada

escape *v.i* escapar

escort *n.* escolta

esoteric *adj.* esotérico

especial *adj.* especial

especially *adv.* especialmente

espionage *n.* espionagem

espouse *v.* desposar

espresso *n.* café expresso

essay *n.* ensaio

essence *n.* essência

essential *adj.* essencial

establish *v.* estabelecer

establishment *n.* estabelecimento

estate *n.* propriedade

esteem *n.* estima

estimate *v.* t estimar

estranged *adj.* distante

et cetera *adv.* etc.

eternal *adj.* eterno

eternity *n.* eternidade

ethic n ético

ethical *n.* éticamoral

ethnic *adj.* étnico

ethos *n.* ética

etiquette *n.* etiqueta

etymology *n.* etimologia

eunuch *n.* eunuco

euphoria *n.* euforia

euro *n.* euro

European *n.* Europeu

euthanasia *n.* eutanásia

evacuate *v.* evacuar

evade *v.* t evadir

evade v. t evadir

evaluate v. i avaliar

evaporate v. evaporar

evasion n. evasão

evasive adj. evasivo

eve n. véspera

even adj. mesmo

evening n. noite

event n. evento

eventually adv. eventualmente

ever adv. sempre

every adj. cada

evict v. despejar

eviction n. despejo

evidence n. evidência

evident adj. evidente

evil adj. mal

evince v. evidenciar

evoke v. evocar

evolution n. evolução

evolve v. desenvolver

exact adj. exato

exaggerate v. exagerar

exaggeration n. exagero

exalt v. exaltar

exam n. exame

examination n. exame

examine v. examinar

examinee n. examinando

example n. exemplo

exasperate v. exasperar

excavate v. escavar

exceed v. exceder

excel v. sobressair

excellence n. excelência

Excellency n. Excelência

excellent adj. excelente

except prep. exceto

exception n. exceção

excerpt n. excerto

excess n. excesso

excessive adj. excessivo

exchange v. t trocar

exchequer n. erário

excise n. imposto

excite v.i excitar

excitement n. excitação

exclaim v. exclamar

exclamation n. exclamação

exclude v. excluir

exclusive adj. exclusivo

excoriate v. escoriar

excrete v. excretar

excursion n. excursão

excuse v. desculpar

execute v. executar

execution n. execução

executive n. executivo

executor n. executor

exempt adj. isento

exercise n. exercer

exert v. exercer

exhale v. exalar

exhaust v. esgotar

exhaustive adj. exaustivo

exhibit v. apresentar

exhibition n. exposição

exhilarate v. animar

exhort *v.* exortar
exigency *n.* exigência
exile *n.* exílio
exist *v.* existir
existence *n.* existência
exit *n.* sair
exonerate *v.* exonerar
exorbitant *adj.* exorbitante
exotic *adj.* exótico
expand *v.* expandir
expanse *n.* extensão
expatriate *n.* expatriado
expect *v.* esperar
expectant *adj.* expectante
expedient *adj.* expediente
expedite *v.* expedir
expedition *n.* expedição
expel *v.* t expelir
expend *v.* despender
expenditure *n.* despesa
expense *n.* despesa
expensive *adj.* caro
experience *n.* experiência
experiment *n.* experiência
expert *n.* especialista
expertise *n.* perícia
expiate *v.* expiar
expire *v.* expirar
expiry *n.* término
explain *v.* explicar
explicit *adj.* explícito
explode *v.* explodir
exploit *v.* t explorar
exploration *n.* exploração

explore *v.* explorar
explosion *n.* explosão
explosive *adj.* explosivo
exponent *n.* expoente
export *v.* t. exportar
expose *v.* expor
exposure *n.* exposição
express *v.* expresso
expression *n.* expressão
expressive *adj.* expressivo
expropriate *v.* expropriar
expulsion *n.* expulsão
extant *adj.* existente
extend *v.* estender
extension *n.* extensão
extent *n.* extensão
exterior *adj.* exterior
external *adj.* externo
extinct *adj.* extinto
extinguish *v.* extinguir
extirpate *v.* extirpar
extort *v.* extorquir
extra *adj.* extra
extract *v.* t extrair
extraction *n.* extração
extraordinary *adj.* extraordinário
extravagance *n.* extravagância
extravagant *adj.* extravagante
extravaganza *n.* extravagância
extreme *adj.* extremo
extremist *n.* extremista
extricate *v.* desenredar
extrovert *n.* extrovertido
extrude *v.* expulsar

exuberant *adj.* exuberante
exude *v.* transpirar
eye *n.* olho
eyeball *n.* globo ocular
eyesight *n.* visão
eyewash *n.* colírio
eyewitness *n.* testemunha ocular

fable *n.* fábula
fabric *n.* tecido
fabricate *v.* fabricar
fabulous *adj.* fabuloso
facade *n.* fachada
face *n.* face
facet *n.* faceta
facetious *adj.* brincalhão
facial *adj.* facial
facile *adj.* fácil
facilitate *v.* facilitar
facility *n.* facilidade
facing *n.* revestimento
facsimile *n.* fax
fact *n.* fato
faction *n.* facção
factitious *adj.* fictício
factor *n.* fator
factory *n.* fábrica
faculty *n.* faculdade
fad *n.* mania
fade *v.i* desvanecer
Fahrenheit *n.* Fahrenheit
fail *v.* falhar
failing *n.* falta

failure *n.* falha
faint *adj.* fraco
fair *adj.* justo
fairing *n.* capota
fairly *adv.* bastante
fairy *n.* fadas
faith *n.* fé
faithful *adj.* fiel
faithless *adj.* infiel
fake *adj.* falsificação
falcon *n.* falcão
fall *v.* cair
fallacy *n.* ilusão
fallible *adj.* falível
fallow *adj.* inculto
false *adj.* falso
falsehood *n.* falsidade
falter *v.* vacilar
fame *n.* fama
familiar *adj.* familiar
family *n.* família
famine *n.* fome
famished *adj.* faminto
famous *adj.* famoso
fan *n.* ventoinha
fanatic *n.* fanático
fanciful *adj.* caprichoso
fancy *n.* fantasia
fanfare *n.* fanfarra
fang *n.* presa
fantasize *v.* fantasiar
fantastic *adj.* fantástico
fantasy *n.* fantasia
far *adv.* longe

farce *n.* farsa
fare *n.* tarifa
farewell interj. despedida
farm *n.* fazenda
farmer *n.* agricultor
fascia *n.* fascia
fascinate *v.* fascinar
fascism *n.* fascismo
fashion *n.* moda
fashionable *adj.* elegante
fast *adj.* rápido
fasten *v.* prender
fastness *n.* solidez
fat *n.* gordura
fatal *adj.* fatal
fatality *n.* fatalidade
fate *n.* destino
fateful *adj.* fatídico
father *n.* pai
fathom *n.* braça
fatigue *n.* fadiga
fatuous *adj.* fátuo
fault *n.* culpa
faulty *adj.* defeituoso
fauna *n.* fauna
favour *n.* favorecer
favourable *adj.* favorável
favourite *adj.* favorito
fax *n.* fax
fear *n.* medo
fearful *adj.* terrível
fearless *adj.* destemido
feasible *adj.* possível
feast *n.* festa

feat *n.* façanha
feather *n.* pena
feature *n.* característica
febrile *adj.* febril
February *n.* Fevereiro
feckless *adj.* ineficaz
federal *adj.* federal
federate *v.* federado
federation *n.* federação
fee *n.* taxa
feeble *adj.* débil
feed *v.* alimentar
feeder *n.* alimentador
feel *v.* sentir
feeling *n.* sentimento
feign *v.* fingir
feisty *adj.* mal-humorada
felicitate *v.* felicitar
felicitation *n.* felicitação
felicity *n.* felicidade
fell *v.* derrubar
fellow *n.* companheiro
fellowship *n.* amizade
felon *n.* criminoso
female *adj.* fêmea
feminine *adj.* feminino
feminism *n.* feminismo
fence *n.* cerca
fencing *n.* esgrima
fend *v.* cuidar-se
feng shui *n.* feng shui
fennel *n.* funcho
feral *adj.* selvagem
ferment *v.* fermentar

fermentation *n.* fermentação	**fierce** *adj.* feroz
fern *n.* feto	**fiery** *adj.* ardente
ferocious *adj.* feroz	**fifteen** *adj. & n.* quinze
ferry *n.* balsa	**fifty** *adj. & n.* cinquenta
fertile *adj.* fértil	**fig** *n.* figo
fertility *n.* fertilidade	**fight** *v.t* lutar
fertilize *v.* fertilizar	**fighter** *n.* lutador
fertilizer *n.* fertilizante	**figment** *n.* invenção
fervent *adj.* fervente	**figurative** *adj* figurativo
fervid *adj.* ardente	**figure** *n.* figura
fervour *n.* fervor	**figurine** *n.* estatueta
fester *v.* apodrecer	**filament** *n.* filamento
festival *n.* festival	**file** *n.* arquivo
festive *adj.* festivo	**filings** *n.* limalha
festivity *n.* festividade	**fill** *v.* preencher
fetch *v.* buscar	**filler** *n.* enchedor
fete *n.* festejar	**filling** *n.* enchimento
fetish *n.* fetiche	**fillip** *n.* estímulo
fettle *n.* aspeto	**film** *n.* filme
feud *n.* feudo	**filter** *n.* filtro
feudalism *n.* feudalismo	**filth** *n.* imundície
fever *n.* febre	**filtrate** *n.* filtrado
few *adj.* poucos	**fin** *n.* barbatana
fey *adj.* visionário	**final** *adj.* final
fiance *n.* noivo	**finalist** *n.* finalista
fiasco *n.* fiasco	**finance** *n.* finança
fibre *n.* fibra	**financial** *adj.* financeiro
fickle *adj.* inconstante	**financier** *n.* financeiro
fiction *n.* ficção	**find** *v.* encontrar
fictitious *adj.* fictício	**fine** *adj.* fino
fiddle *n.* rabeca	**finesse** *n.* subtileza
fidelity *adj.* fidelidade	**finger** *n.* dedo
field *n.* campo	**finial** *n.* florão
fiend *n.* demónio	**finicky** *adj.* mimado

finish v. terminar	**flagrant** adj. flagrante
finite adj. limitado	**flair** n. faro
fir n. abeto	**flake** n. floco
fire n. fogo	**flamboyant** adj. extravagante
firewall n. firewall	**flame** n. chama
firm adj. firme	**flammable** adj. inflamável
firmament n. firmamento	**flank** n. flanco
first adj. & n. principal & primeiro	**flannel** n. flanela
first aid n. primeiros socorros	**flap** v. bater
fiscal adj. fiscal	**flapjack** n. flapjack
fish n. peixe	**flare** n. labareda
fisherman n. pescador	**flash** v. flash
fishery n. pesca	**flash** light n. lanterna
fishy adj. duvidoso	**flask** n. frasco
fissure n. fissura	**flat** adj. plano
fist n. punho	**flatten** v.t. achatar
fit adj. apto	**flatter** v. lisonjear
fitful adj. irregular	**flatulent** adj. flatulento
fitter n. montador	**flaunt** v. exibir
fitting n. apropriado	**flavour** n. sabor
five adj. & n. cinco	**flaw** n. falha
fix v. fixar	**flea** n. pulga
fixation n. fixação	**flee** v. fugir
fixture n. fixação	**fleece** n. velo
fizz v. assobio	**fleet** n. frota
fizzle v. fracassar	**flesh** n. carne
fizzy adj. efervescente	**flex** v. retesar
fjord n. fiorde	**flexible** adj. flexível
flab n. flacidez	**flexitime** n. flexitime
flabbergasted adj. boquiabertos	**flick** v. agitar
flabby adj. flácido	**flicker** v.t tremer
flaccid adj. flácido	**flight** n. vôo
flag n. bandeira	**flimsy** adj. fraco
flagellate v. flagelar	**flinch** v. recuar

fling *v.* atirar

flint *n.* pedra

flip *v.* sacudir

flippant *adj.* irreverente

flipper *n.* barbatana

flirt *v.i* namorar

flit *v.* voar

float *v.* flutuar

flock *n.* rebanho

floe *n.* campo de gelo

flog *v.* açoitar

flood *n.* inundação

floodlight *n.* holofote

floor *n.* piso

flop *v.* fracassar

floppy *adj.* frouxo

flora *n.* flora

floral *adj.* floral

florist *n.* florista

floss *n.* fio dental

flotation *n.* flutuação

flounce *v.* espernear

flounder *v.* tropeçar

flour *n.* farinha

flourish *v.* florescer

flow *v.i* fluir

flower *n.* flor

flowery *adj.* florido

flu *n.* gripe

fluctuate *v.* flutuar

fluent *adj.* fluente

fluff *n.* buço

fluid *n.* fluído

fluke *n.* casualidade

fluorescent *adj.* fluorescente

fluoride *n.* fluoreto

flurry *n.* aguaceiro

flush *v.* corar

fluster *v.* afobar

flute *n.* flauta

flutter *v.* ágitar

fluvial *adj.* fluvial

flux *n.* fluxo

fly *v.i* voar

foam *n.* espuma

focal *adj.* focal

focus *n.* foco

fodder *n.* forragem

foe *n.* inimigo

fog *n.* nevoeiro

foil *v.* frustrar

fold *v.t* dobrar

foliage *n.* folhagem

folio *n.* fólio

folk *n.* povo

follow *v.* seguir

follower *n.* seguidor

folly *n.* loucura

fond *adj.* afeiçoado

fondle *v.* acariciar

font *n.* fonte

food *n.* comida

fool *n.* idiota

foolish *adj.* tolo

foolproof *adj.* infalível

foot *n.* pé

footage *n.* metragem

football *n.* futebol

footing *n.* posição
footling *adj.* frívolo
for *prep.* para
foray *n.* incursão
forbear *v.* tolerar
forbid *v.* proibir
force *n.* força
forceful *adj.* forte
forceps *n.* fórceps
forcible *adj.* convicente
fore *adj.* anteriormente
forearm *n.* antebraço
forebear *n.* antepassado
forecast *v.t* prever
forefather *n.* antecessor
forefinger *n.* dedo indicador
forehead *n.* testa
foregoing *adj.* acima mencionado
foreign *adj.* estrangeiro
foreigner *n.* forasteiro
foreknowledge *n.* previsão
foreleg *n.* perna dianteira
foreman *n.* capataz
foremost *adj.* principal
forename *n.* prenome
forensic *adj.* forense
foreplay *n.* preliminares
forerunner *n.* precursor
foresee *v.* prever
foresight *n.* previdência
forest *n.* floresta
forestall *v.* prevenir
forestry *n.* silvicultura
foretell *v.* predizer

forever *adv.* para sempre
foreword *n.* prefácio
forfeit *v.* multa
forge *v.t* forjar
forgery *n.* falsificação
forget *v.* esquecer
forgetful *adj.* esquecido
forgive *v.* perdoar
forgo *v.* abdicar
fork *n.* garfo
forlorn *adj.* desamparado
form *n.* forma
formal *adj.* formal
formality *n.* formalidade
format *n.* formato
formation *n.* formação
former *adj.* antigo
formerly *adv.* antigamente
formidable *adj.* formidável
formula *n.* fórmula
formulate *v.* formular
forsake *v.* abandonar
forswear *v.* renegar
fort *n.* forte
forte *n.* forte
forth *adv.* adiante
forthcoming *adj.* próximo
forthwith *adv.* imediatamente
fortify *v.* fortificar
fortitude *n.* força moral
fortnight *n.* quinzena
fortress *n.* fortaleza
fortunate *adj.* afortunado
fortune *n.* fortuna

forty adj.& n. quarenta	**fraud** n. fraude
forum n. fórum	**fraudulent** adj. fraudulento
forward adv. adiante	**fraught** adj. cheio
forward adj. para frente	**fray** v. desgastar
fossil n. fóssil	**freak** n. aberração
foster v. criar	**freckle** n. sardas
foul adj. imundo	**free** adj. livre
found v. fundar	**freebie** n. brinde
foundation n. fundação	**freedom** n. liberdade
founder n. fundador	**freeze** v. congelar
foundry n. fundição	**freezer** n. congelador
fountain n. fonte	**freight** n. frete
four adj.& n. quatro	**freighter** n. fretador
fourteen adj.& n. catorze	**French** adj. Francês
fourth adj.& n. quarto	**frenetic** adj. frenético
fowl n. frango	**frenzy** n. frenesim
fox n. raposa	**frequency** n. frequência
foyer n. vestíbulo	**frequent** adj. frequente
fraction n. fração	**fresh** adj. fresco
fractious adj. rebelde	**fret** v.t. atormentar
fracture v.t fraturar	**fretful** adj. irritável
fragile adj. frágil	**friable** adj. frágil
fragment n. fragmento	**friction** n. fricção
fragrance n. fragrância	**Friday** n. Sexta-feira
fragrant adj. perfumado	**fridge** n. frigorífico
frail adj. frágil	**friend** n. amigo
frame n. quadro	**fright** n. medo
framework n. armação	**frighten** v. assustar
franchise n. franquia	**frigid** adj. frígido
frank adj. franco	**frill** n. babado
frankfurter n. salsichão	**fringe** n. franja
frantic adj. frenético	**frisk** v. saltar
fraternal adj. fraternal	**fritter** v. desperdiçar
fraternity n. fraternidade	**frivolous** adj. frívolo

frock n. sobrecasaca	**fundamental** adj. fundamental
frog n. sapo	**funeral** n. funeral
frolic v.i. brincar	**fungus** n. fungo
from prep. de	**funky** adj. medroso
front n. frente	**funnel** n. funil
frontbencher n. bancada da frente	**funny** adj. engraçado
frontier n. fronteira	**fur** n. pele
frost n. geada	**furious** adj. furioso
frosty adj. gelado	**furl** v. enrolar
froth n. espuma	**furlong** n. medida comprimento
frown v.i franzir	**furnace** n. forno
frowsty adj. bafiento	**furnish** v. fornecer
frugal adj. frugal	**furnishing** n. mobiliário
fruit n. fruta	**furniture** n. mobília
fruitful adj. frutífero	**furore** n. furor
frump n. careta	**furrow** n. sulco
frustrate v. frustrar	**further** adv. mais
fry v. fritar	**furthermore** adv. além disso
fudge n. disparate	**furthest** adj.& adv. extremo
fuel n. combustível	**fury** n. fúria
fugitive n. fugitivo	**fuse** v. fusível
fulcrum n. fulcro	**fusion** n. fusão
fulfil v. cumprir	**fuss** n. espalhafato
fulfilment n. cumprimento	**fussy** adj. espalhafatoso
full adj. completo	**fusty** adj. bolorento
fulsome adj. servil	**futile** adj. fútil
fumble v. tatear	**futility** n. futilidade
fume n. fumo	**future** n. futuro
fumigate v. fumigar	**futuristic** adj. futurista
fun n. diversão	
function n. função	**G**
functional adj. funcional	
functionary n. funcionário	**gab** v. tagarelar
fund n. fundo	**gabble** v.t. palrar
	gadget n. dispositivo

gaffe *n.* gafe	**garage** *n.* garagem
gag *n.* mordaça	**garb** *n.* traje
gaga *adj.* decrépito	**garbage** *n.* lixo
gaiety *n.* alegria	**garble** *v.* adulterar
gaily *adv.* alegremente	**garden** *n.* jardim
gain *v.* ganhar	**gardener** *n.* jardineiro
gainful *adj.* lucrativo	**gargle** *v.* gargarejar
gait *n.* marcha	**garish** *adj.* extravagante
gala *n.* gala	**garland** *n.* grinalda
galaxy *n.* galáxia	**garlic** *n.* alho
gale *n.* ventania	**garment** *n.* vestuário
gall *n.* bílis	**garner** *v.* celeiro
gallant *adj.* valente	**garnet** *n.* granada
gallantry *n.* bravura	**garnish** *v.* enfeitar
gallery *n.* galeria	**garret** *n.* sótão
gallon *n.* galão	**garrulous** *adj.* tagarela
gallop *n.* galope	**garter** *n.* liga
gallows *n.* forca	**gas** *n.* gás
galore *adj.* abundância	**gasket** *n.* gaxeta
galvanize *v.i.* galvanizar	**gasp** *v.i* suspiro
gambit *n.* gambito	**gastric** *adj.* gástrico
gamble *v.* jogar	**gastronomy** *n.* gastronomia
gambler *n.* apostador	**gate** *n.* portão
gambol *v.* brincar	**gateau** *n.* cancela
game *n.* jogo	**gather** *v.* reunir
gamely *adj.* corajosamente	**gaudy** *adj.* exagerado
gammy *adj.* aleijado	**gauge** *n.* aferir
gamut *n.* gama	**gaunt** *adj.* magro
gang *n.* quadrilha	**gauntlet** *n.* manopla
gangling *adj.* desengonçado	**gauze** *n.* gaze
gangster *n.* bandido	**gawky** *adj.* desajeitado
gangway *n.* passadiço	**gay** *adj.* homossexual
gap *n.* lacuna	**gaze** *v.* pasmar
gape *v.* bocejar	**gazebo** *n.* mirante

gazette *n.* gazeta

gear *n.* engrenagem

geek *n.* parvo

gel *n.* gel

geld *v.* capar

gem *n.* jóia

gender *n.* género

general *adj.* geral

generalize *v.* generalizar

generate *v.* gerar

generation *n.* geração

generator *n.* gerador

generosity *n.* generosidade

generous *adj.* generoso

genesis *n.* génese

genetic *adj.* genético

genial *adj.* simpático

genius *n.* génio

genteel *adj.* distinto

gentility *n.* nobreza

gentle *adj.* suave

gentleman *n.* cavalheiro

gentry *n.* antiquado

genuine *adj.* genuíno

geographer *n.* geógrafo

geographical *adj.* geográfico

geography *n.* geografia

geologist *n.* geólogo

geology *n.* geologia

geometric *adj.* geométrico

geometry *n.* geometria

germ *n.* germe

German *n.* Alemão

germane *adj.* germano

germinate *v.* germinar

germination *n.* germinação

gerund *n.* gerúndio

gestation *n.* gestação

gesture *n.* gesto

get *v.* obter

geyser *n.* geyser

ghastly *adj.* terrivelmente

ghost *n.* fantasma

giant *n.* gigante

gibber *v.* produzir

gibe *v.* escarnecer

giddy *adj.* vertiginoso

gift *n.* presente

gifted *adj.* dotado

gigabyte *n.* gigabyte

gigantic *adj.* gigantesco

giggle *v.t.* dar risadinhas

gild *v.* dourar

gilt *adj.* dourado

gimmick *n.* artifício

ginger *n.* gengibre

gingerly *adv.* cautelosamente

giraffe *n.* girafa

girder *n.* viga

girdle *n.* cinturão

girl *n.* menina

girlish *adj.* feminino

giro *n.* vale postal

girth *n.* perímetro

gist *n.* essência

give *v.* dar

given *adj.* dado

glacial *adj.* glacial

glacier n. geleira

glad adj. feliz

gladden v. alegrar

glade n. clareira

glamour n. fascinação

glance v.i. insinuar

gland n. glândula

glare v.i deslumbrar

glass v.t. espelhar

glaze v. esmaltar

glazier n. vidraceiro

gleam v. brilhar

glean v. respigar

glee n. alegria

glide v. deslizar

glider n. planador

glimmer v. vislumbrar

glimpse n. vislumbre

glisten v. brilhar

glitch n. falha

glitter v. brilhar

gloat v. regozijar

global adj. global

globalization n. globalização

globe n. globo

globetrotter n. viajante incansável

gloom n. melancolia

gloomy adj. sombrio

glorification n. glorificação

glorify v. glorificar

glorious adj. glorioso

glory n. glória

gloss n. lustro

glossary n. glossário

glossy adj. acetinado

glove n. luva

glow v. brilhar

glucose n. glicose

glue n. cola

glum adj. mal-humorado

glut n. excesso

glutton n. glutão

gluttony n. gulodice

glycerine n. glicerina

gnarled adj. nodoso

gnat n. mosquito

gnaw v. roer

go v.t ir

goad v. incitar

goal n. objetivo

goalkeeper n. guarda-redes

goat n. cabra

gob n. expetoração

gobble v. devorar

goblet n. taça

god n. Deus

godchild n. afilhado

goddess n. deusa

godfather n. padrinho

godly adj. piedoso

godmother n. madrinha

goggle n. espanto

going n. ida

gold n. ouro

golden adj. dourado

goldsmith n. ourives

golf n. golfe

gondola n. gôndola

gong n. gongo	**graft** n. enxerto
good adj. bom	**grain** n. grão
goodbye excl. adeus	**gram** n. grama
goodness n. bondade	**grammar** n. gramática
goodwill n. boa vontade	**gramophone** n. gramofone
goose n. ganso	**granary** n. celeiro
gooseberry n. groselha	**grand** adj. grande
gore n. sangue derramado	**grandeur** n. grandeza
gorgeous adj. deslumbrante	**grandiose** adj. grandioso
gorilla n. gorila	**grandmother** n. avó
gory adj. sangrento	**grange** n. granja
gospel n. doutrina	**granite** n. granito
gossip n. mexerico	**grant** v. conceder
gouge v. entalhar	**granule** n. grânulo
gourd n. cabaça	**grape** n. uva
gourmand n. guloso	**graph** n. gráfico
gourmet n. gourmet	**graphic** adj. gráfico
gout n. gota	**graphite** n. grafite
govern v. governar	**grapple** v.t. lutar
governance n. governo	**grasp** v. compreender
governess n. governanta	**grass** n. relva
government n. governo	**grasshopper** n. gafanhoto
governor n. governador	**grate** v.t ralar
gown n. toga	**grateful** n. grato
grab v. agarrar	**grater** n. ralador
grace n. graça	**gratification** n. gratificação
graceful adj. gracioso	**gratify** v. gratificar
gracious adj. gracioso	**grating** n. irritante
gradation n. gradação	**gratis** adv. &adj. grátis & grátis
grade n. grau	**gratitude** n. gratidão
gradient n. gradiente	**gratuitous** adj. gratuito
gradual adj. gradual	**gratuity** n. gratificação
graduate n. licenciado	**grave** n. sepultura
graffiti n. grafitti	**gravel** n. cascalho

graveyard *n.* cemitério

gravitas *n.* sereidade

gravitate *v.* gravitar

gravitation *n.* gravitação

gravity *n.* gravidade

gravy *n.* molho

graze *v.* arranhar

grease *n.* graxa

great *adj.* excelente

greatly *adv.* muito

greed *n.* ganância

greedy *adj.* ganancioso

green *adj. & n.* verde

greengrocer *n.* merceeiro

greenery *v.t.* verdura

greet *n.* cumprimentar

greeting *n.* saudação

grenade a. granada

grey *n.* cinza

greyhound *n.* galgo

grid *n.* grade

griddle *n.* chapa de ferro (culinária)

grief *n.* dor

grievance *n.* queixa

grieve *v.* afligir

grievous *adj.* grave

grill *v.* grelha

grim *adj.* cruel

grime *n.* guligem

grin *v.* arreganhar

grind *v.* moer

grinder *n.* afiador

grip *v.* apertar

gripe *v.* agarrar

grit *n.* areia

groan *v.* gemer

grocer *n.* merceeiro

grocery *n.* mercearia

groggy *adj.* embriagado

groin *n.* virilha

groom *v.* cuidar de cavalo

groove *n.* sulco

grope *v.* tatear

gross *adj.* bruto

grotesque *adj.* grotesco

grotto *n.* gruta

ground *n.* chão

groundless *adj.* infundado

group *n.* grupo

grouping *n.* agrupamento

grout *n.* argamassa

grovel *v.* rastejar

grow *v.i.* crescer

growl *v.* rosnar

growth *n.* crescimento

grudge n rancor

grudging *adj.* invejoso

gruel *n.* papa de aveia

gruesome *adj.* macabro

grumble *v.* resmungar

grumpy *adj.* amuado

grunt *v.i.* roncar

guarantee *v.t* garantir

guarantor *n.* fiador

guard *v.* guardar

guarded *adj.* guardado

guardian *n.* guardião

guava *n.* goiaba

gudgeon n. cavilha

guerrilla n. guerrilha

guess v.i adivinhar

guest n. convidado

guffaw n. gargalhada

guidance n. orientação

guide n. guia

guidebook n. roteiro

guild n. corporação

guile n. malícia

guillotine n. guilhotina

guilt n. culpa

guilty adj. culpado

guise n. aparência

guitar n. guitarra

gulf n. golfo

gull n. lorpa

gullet n. esófago

gullible adj. crédulo

gully n. ravina

gulp v. tragar

gum n. pastilha

gun n. arma

gurdwara n. gurdwara

gurgle v. gorgolejar

gust n. rajada

gut n. intestino

gutsy adj. audaz

gutter n. callha

guy n. gajo

guzzle v. regabofe

gymnasium n. ginásio

gymnast n. ginasta

gymnastic n. ginástico

gynaecology n. ginecologia

gypsy n. cigano

gyrate v. girar

H

habit n. hábito

habitable adj. habitável

habitat n. habitat

habitation n. habitação

habituate v.t. habituar

habitue n. habitué

hack v. piratear

hackneyed adj. banal

haemoglobin n. hemoglobina

haemorrhage n. hemorragia

haft n. punho

hag n. bruxa

haggard adj. desfigurado

haggle v. pechinchar

hail n. granizo

hair n. cabelo

haircut n. corte de cabelo

hairstyle n. penteado

hairy adj. peludo

hajj n. hadj

halal adj. halal

hale adj. são

halitosis n. mau hálito

hall n. hall de entrada

hallmark n. carimbo

hallow v. venerar

hallucinate v. alucinar

halogen n. halogénio

halt v. deter

halter *n.* cabresto
halting *adj.* hesitante
halve *v.* dividir
halyard *n.* adriça
ham *n.* presunto
hamburger *n.* hamburguer
hamlet *n.* lugarejo
hammer *n.* martelo
hammock *n.* rede
hamper *n.* cesto
hamster *n.* hamster
hamstring *n.* tendão
hand *n.* mão
handbag *n.* bolsa
handbill *n.* anúncio
handbook *n.* manual
handcuff *n.* algema
handful *n.* punhado
handicap *n.* desvantagem
handicapped *n.* deficientes
handicraft *n.* artesanato
handiwork *n.* obra
handkerchief *n.* lenço
handle *v.t* manusear
handout *n.* folheto
handshake *n.* aperto de mão
handsome *adj.* bonito
handy *adj.* conveniente
hang *v.i.* pendurar
hangar *n.* hangar
hanger *n.* cabide
hanging *n.* enforcamento
hangover *n.* ressaca
hank *n.* meada

hanker *v.* ansiar
haphazard *adj.* acidental
hapless *adj.* infeliz
happen *v.* acontecer
happening *n.* acontecimento
happiness *n.* felicidade
happy *adj.* feliz
harass *v.* molestar
harassment *n.* provocação
harbour *n.* porto
hard *adj.* difícil
hard drive *n.* disco rígido
hardback *n.* livro de capa dura
harden *v.* endurecer
hardly *adv.* dificilmente
hardship *n.* dificuldade
hardy *adj.* destemido
hare *n.* lebre
harelip *n.* fenda palatina
harem *n.* harém
hark *v.* escutar
harlequin *n.* arlequim
harm *n.* mal
harmful *adj.* prejudicial
harmless *adj.* inofensivo
harmonious *adj.* harmonioso
harmonium *n.* harmónio
harmonize *v.* harmonizar
harmony *n.* harmonia
harness *n.* arreio
harp *n.* harpa
harpy *n.* predador
harrow *n.* ancinho
harrowing *adj.* cruciante

harsh *adj.* áspero	**headlight** *n.* farol
harvest *n.* colheita	**headline** *n.* manchete
harvester *n.* quem colhe	**headmaster** *n.* diretor
hassle *n.* aborrecimento	**headphone** *n.* auscultadores
hassock *n.* puff	**headquarters** *n.* sede
haste *n.* haste	**headstrong** *adj.* obstinado
hasten *v.* apressar	**heady** *adj.* inebriante
hasty *adj.* apressado	**heal** *v.* curar
hat *n.* chapéu	**health** *n.* saúde
hatch *n.* escotilha	**healthy** *adj.* saudável
hatchet *n.* machadinha	**heap** *n.* pilha
hate *v.t.* odiar	**hear** *v.* ouvir
hateful *adj.* odioso	**hearing** *n.* audição
haughty *adj.* altivo	**hearse** *n.* carro fúnebre
haulage *n.* transporte	**heart** *n.* coração
haulier *n.* transportador	**heartache** *n.* mágoa
haunch *n.* pernil	**heartbreak** *n.* desgosto
haunt *v.* assombrar	**heartburn** *n.* azia
haunted *adj.* assombrada	**hearten** *v.* animar
have *v.* ter	**heartening** *adj.* animador
haven *n.* refúgio	**heartfelt** *adj.* sincero
havoc *n.* devastação	**hearth** *n.* lareira
hawk *n.* falcão	**heartless** *adj.* impiedoso
hawker *n.* vendedor ambulante	**hearty** *adj.* caloroso
hawthorn *n.* espinheiro-alvar	**heat** *n.* calor
hay *n.* feno	**heater** *n.* aquecedor
hazard *n.* perigo	**heath** *n.* charneca
hazardous *adj.* perigoso	**heathen** *n.* ateu
haze *n.* neblina	**heather** *n.* urze
hazy *adj.* nebuloso	**heating** *n.* aquecimento
he *pron.* ele	**heave** *v.* levantar
head *n.* cabeça	**heaven** *n.* céu
headache *n.* dor de cabeça	**heavenly** *adj.* celestial
heading *n.* título	**heavy** *adj.* pesado

heckle *v.* importunar	**herald** *n.* liço
hectare *n.* hectare	**herb** *n.* erva
hectic *adj.* agitado	**herculean** *adj.* hercúleo
hector *v.* intimidar	**herd** *n.* rebanho
hedge *n.* sebe	**here** *adv.* aqui
hedonism *n.* hedonismo	**hereabouts** *adv.* perto daqui
heed *v.* prestar atenção	**hereafter** *adv.* a seguir
heel *n.* calcanhar	**hereby** *adv.* por este meio
hefty *adj.* robusto	**hereditary** *adj.* hereditário
hegemony *n.* hegemonia	**heredity** *n.* hereditariedade
height *n.* altura	**heritage** *n.* herança
heighten *v.* intensificar	**hermetic** *adj.* hermético
heinous *adj.* hediondo	**hermit** *n.* eremita
heir *n.* herdeiro	**hermitage** *n.* eremitério
helicopter *n.* helicóptero	**hernia** *n.* hérnia
heliport *n.* heliporto	**hero** *n.* herói
hell *n.* inferno	**heroic** *adj.* heróico
helm *n.* leme	**heroine** *n.* heroína
helmet *n.* capacete	**herpes** *n.* herpes
help *v.* ajudar	**herring** *n.* arenque
helpful *adj.* útil	**hers** *pron.* dela
helping *n.* ajuda	**herself** *pron.* ela mesma
helpless *adj.* desamparado	**hesitant** *adj.* hesitante
hem *n.* bainha	**hesitate** *v.* hesitar
hemisphere *n.* hemisfério	**heterogeneous** *adj.* heterogéneo
hen *n.* galinha	**heterosexual** *adj.* heterossexual
hence *adv.* por isso	**hew** *v.* talhar
henceforth *adv.* doravante	**hexogen** *n.* hexogeno
henchman *n.* escudeiro	**heyday** *n.* apogeu
henna *n.* hena	**hibernate** *v.* hibernar
henpecked *adj.* dominar o conjuge	**hiccup** *n.* soluço
hepatitis *adj.* hepatite	**hide** *v.t* esconder
heptagon *n.* heptágono	**hideous** *adj.* hediondo
her *pron.* seu	**hierarchy** *n.* hierarquia

high *adj.* alto

highlight *v.* realçar

highly *adv.* altamente

Highness *n.* Alteza

highway *n.* autoestrada

hijack *v.* assaltar

hike *n.* caminhada

hilarious *adj.* divertido

hilarity *n.* hilaridade

hill *n.* colina

hillock *n.* outeiro

hilt *n.* cabo

him *pron.* ele

himself *pron.* ele próprio

hinder *v.* atrapalhar

hindrance *n.* impedimento

hindsight *n.* retrospetiva

hinge *n.* dobradiça

hint *n.* dica

hip *n.* anca

hire *v.t* contratar

hirsute *adj.* hirsuto

his *adj.* seu (s)/ sua (s)

hiss *v.i* assobiar

histogram *n.* histograma

historian *n.* historiador

historic *adj.* histórico

historical *adj.* histórico

history *n.* história

hit *v.* acertar

hitch *v.* amarrar

hither *adv.* cá

hitherto *adv.* até agora

hive *n.* colmeia

hoard *n.* tesouro escondido

hoarding *n.* acumulação

hoarse *adj.* rouco

hoax *n.* brincadeira

hob *n.* fogão

hobble *v.* mancar

hobby *n.* hobby

hobgoblin *n.* duende

hockey *n.* hóquei

hoist *v.* içar

hold *v.t* manter

holdall *n.* saco de viagem

hole *n.* buraco

holiday *n.* férias

holistic *adj.* holística

hollow *adj.* oco

holly *n.* azevinho

holmium *n.* hólmio

holocaust *n.* holocausto

hologram *n.* holograma

holster *n.* coldre

holy *adj.* santo

homage *n.* homenagem

home *n.* lar

homely *adj.* simples

homicide *n.* homicídio

homogeneous *adj.* homogéneo

homoeopath *n.* homeopata

homeopathy *n.* homeopatia

homogeneous *a.* homogéneo

homophobia *n.* homofobia

homosexual *n.* homossexual

honest *adj.* honesto

honesty *n.* honestidade

honey *n.* mel		**horror** *n.* horror
honeycomb *n.* favo de mel		**horse** *n.* cavalo
honeymoon *n.* lua de mel		**horsepower** *n.* cavalo-vapor
honk *n.* grasnido do ganso		**horticulture** *n.* horticultura
honorary *adj.* honorário		**hose** *n.* mangueira
honour *n.* honra		**hosiery** *n.* meias
honourable *adj.* honroso		**hospice** *n.* hospício
hood *n.* capuz		**hospitable** *adj.* hospitaleiro
hoodwink *v.* enganar		**hospital** *n.* hospital
hoof *n.* casco		**hospitality** *n.* hospitalidade
hook *n.* gancho		**host** *n.* hospedeiro
hooked *adj.* curvo		**hostage** *n.* refém
hooligan *n.* rufião		**hostel** *n.* albergue
hoop *n.* aro		**hostess** *n.* anfitriã
hoopla *n.* informal		**hostile** *adj.* hostil
hoot *n.* pio		**hostility** *n.* hostilidade
Hoover *n.* Hoover		**hot** *adj.* quente
hop *v.* salto		**hotchpotch** *n.* confusão
hop *v.t.* saltar		**hotel** *n.* hotel
hope *n.* esperança		**hound** *n.* cão de caça
hopefully *adv.* esperançosamente		**hour** *n.* hora
hopeless *adj.* sem esperança		**house** *n.* casa
horde *n.* horda		**housewife** *n.* dona de casa
horizon *n.* horizonte		**housing** *n.* habitação
horizontal *adj.* horizontal		**hovel** *n.* alpendre
hormone *n.* hormona		**hover** *v.* pairar
horn *n.* chifre		**how** *adv.* como
hornet *n.* vespão		**however** *adv.* porém
horoscope *n.* horóscopo		**howl** *n.* gemido
horrendous *adj.* horrendo		**howler** *n.* gafe
horrible *adj.* horrível		**hub** *n.* cubo
horrid *adj.* horrível		**hubbub** *n.* tumulto
horrific *adj.* horroroso		**huddle** *v.* amontoar
horrify *v.* horrorizar		**hue** *n.* matiz

huff *n.* jactância
hug *v.* abraçar
huge *adj.* enorme
hulk *n.* carcaça (navio velho)
hull *n.* casco
hum *v.* zumbir
human *adj.* humano
humane *adj.* humanitário
humanism *n.* humanismo
humanitarian *adj.* humanitário
humanity *n.* humanidade
humanize *v.* humanizar
humble *adj.* humilde
humid *adj.* húmido
humidity *n.* humidade
humiliate *v.* humilhar
humility *n.* humildade
hummock *n.* montículo de terra
humorist *n.* humorista
humorous *adj.* engraçado
humour *n.* humor
hump *n.* corcunda
hunch *v.* curvar
hundred *adj.& n.* cem
hunger *n.* fome
hungry *adj.* faminto
hunk *n.* naco
hunt *v.* caçar
hunter *n.* caçador
hurdle *n.* barreira
hurl *v.* arremessar
hurricane *n.* furacão
hurry *v.* apressar
hurt *v.* doer

hurtle *v.* chocar
husband *n.* marido
husbandry *n* gestão
hush *v.i* acalmar
husk *n.* casca
husky *adj.* rouco
hustle *v.* apressar
hut *n.* cabana
hutch *n.* coelheira
hybrid *n.* híbrido
hydrant *n.* hidrante
hydrate *v.* hidrato
hydraulic *adj.* hidráulico
hydrofoil *n.* hidrodinâmica
hydrogen *n.* hidrogénio
hyena *n.* hiena
hygiene *n.* higiene
hymn *n.* hino
hype *n.* exagero
hyper *pref.* hiper
hyperactive *adj.* hiperativo
hyperbole *n.* hipérbole
hypertension *n.* hipertensão
hyphen *n.* hífen
hypnosis *n.* hipnose
hypnotism *n.* hipnotismo
hypnotize *v.* hipnotizar
hypocrisy *n.* hipocrisia
hypocrite *n.* hipócrita
hypotension *n.* hipotensão
hypothesis *n.* hipótese
hypothetical *adj.* hipotético
hysteria *n.* histeria
hysterical *adj.* histérico

I

I *pron.* Eu
ice *n.* gelo
iceberg *n.* icebergue
ice-cream *n.* gelados
icicle *n.* sincelo
icing *n.* glacê
icon *n.* ícone
icy *n.* gelado
idea *n.* idéia
ideal *n.* ideal
ideally *adv.* idealmente
idealism *n.* idealismo
idealist *n.* idealista
idealistic *adj.* idealista
idealize *v.* idealizar
identical *adj.* idêntico
identification *n.* identificação
identity *n.* identidade
identity *v.* identificar
ideology *n.* ideologia
idiocy *n.* idiota
idiom *n.* idioma
idiomatic *adj.* idiomático
idiosyncrasy *n.* idiossincrasia
idiot *n.* idiota
idiotic *adj.* idiota
idle *adj.* inativo
idleness *n.* ociosidade
idler *n.* ocioso
idol *n.* ídolo
idolatry *n.* idolatria
idolize *v.* idolatrar

idyll *n.* idílio
if *conj.* se
igloo *n.* iglu
igneous *adj.* ígneo
ignite *v.* incendiar
ignition *n.* ignição
ignoble *adj.* ignóbil
ignominy *n.* infâmia
ignominious *adj.* infame
ignoramus *n.* ignorante
ignorance *n.* ignorância
ignorant *adj.* ignorante
ignore *v.* ignorar
ill *adj.* doente
illegal *adj.* ilegal
illegible *adj.* ilegível
illegibility *n.* ilegibilidade
illegitimate *adj.* ilegítimo
illicit *adj.* ilícito
illiteracy *n.* analfabetismo
illiterate *n.* analfabeto
illness *n.* doença
illogical *adj.* ilógico
illuminate *v.* iluminar
illumination *n.* iluminação
illusion *n.* ilusão
illusory *adj.* ilusório
illustrate *n.* ilustrar
illustration *n.* ilustração
illustrious *adj.* ilustre
image *n.* imagem
imagery *n.* imagens
imaginary *adj.* imaginário
imagination *n.* imaginação

imaginative adj. imaginativo
imagine v.t. imaginar
imbalance n. desequilíbrio
imbibe v. absorver
imbroglio n. confusão
imbue v. incutir
imitate v. imitar
imitation n. imitação
imitator n. imitador
immaculate adj. imaculado
immanent adj. imanente
immaterial adj. imaterial
immature adj. imaturo
immaturity n. imaturidade
immeasurable adj. imensurável
immediate adj. imediato
immemorial adj. imemorial
immense adj. imenso
immensity n. imensidão
immerse v. imergir
immersion n. imersão
immigrant n. imigrante
immigrate v. imigrar
immigration n. imigração
imminent adj. iminente
immoderate adj. imoderado
immodest n. imodesto
immodesty a. imodéstia
immolate v. imolar
immoral adj. imoral
immorality n. imoralidade
immortal adj. imortal
immortality n. imortalidade
immortalize v. imortalizar

immovable adv. imóvel
immune adj. imune
immunity n. imunidade
immunize v. imunizar
immunology n. imunologia
immure v. emparedar
immutable adj. imutável
impact n. impacto
impair v. prejudicar
impalpable adj. impalpável
impart v. transmitir
impartial adj. imparcial
impartiality n. imparcialidade
impassable adj. intransitável
impasse n. impasse
impassioned adj. apaixonado
impassive adj. impassível
impatient adj. impaciente
impeach v. acusar
impeachment n. impugnação
impeccable adj. impecável
impede v. impedir
impediment n. impedimento
impel v. impelir
impending adj. iminente
impenetrable adj. impenetrável
imperative adj. imperativo
imperfect adj. imperfeito
imperfection n. imperfeição
imperial adj. imperial
imperialism n. imperialismo
imperil v. perigar
impersonal adj. impessoal
impersonate v. personificar

impersonation n. representação
impertinence n impertinência
impertinent adj. impertinente
impervious adj. impenetrável
impetuous adj. impetuoso
impetus n. ímpeto
impious adj. ímpio
implacable adj. implacável
implant v. implantar
implausible adj. inverossímil
implement n. implementar
implicate v. implicar
implication n. implicação
implicit adj. implícito
implode v. implodir
implore v.t. implorar
imply v. implicar
impolite adj. indelicado
import v. importar
importer n. importador
importance n. importância
important adj. importante
impose v. impor
imposing adj. imponente
imposition n. imposição
impossibility n. impossibilidade
impossible adj. impossível
imposter n. impostor
impotence n. impotência
impotent adj. impotente
impound v. encurralar
impoverish v. empobrecer
impracticable adj. impraticável
impractical adj. impraticável

impress v. impressionar
impression n. impressão
impressive adj. impressionante
imprint v. impressionar
imprison v. aprisionar
improbable adj. improvável
improper adj. impróprio
impropriety n. inconveniência
improve v. melhorar
improvement n. melhoria
improvident adj. incauto
improvise v. improvisar
imprudent adj. imprudente
impudent adj. insolente
impulse n. impulso
impulsive adj. impulsivo
impunity n. impunidade
impure adj. impuro
impurity n. impureza
impute v. imputar
in prep. em
inability n. incapacidade
inaccurate adj. inexato
inaction n. inatividade
inactive adj. inativo
inadequate adj. inadequado
inadmissible adj. inadmissível
inadvertent adj. inadvertido
inane adj. fútil
inanimate adj. inanimado
inapplicable adj. inaplicável
inappropriate adj. impróprio
inarticulate adj. inarticulado
inattentive adj. desatento

inaudible adj. inaudível

inaugural adj. inaugural

inaugurate v. inaugurar

inauspicious adj. pouco auspicioso

inborn adj. inato

inbred adj. natural

incalculable adj. incalculável

incapable adj. incapaz

incapacity n. incapacidade

incarcerate v. encarcerar

incarnate adj. encarnado

incarnation n. encarnação

incense n. incenso

incentive n. incentivo

inception n. início

incest n. incesto

inch n. polegada

incidence n. incidência

incident n. incidente

incidental adj. acidental

incisive adj. incisivo

incite v. incitar

inclination n. inclinação

incline v. inclinar

include v. incluir

inclusion n. inclusão

inclusive adj. inclusivo

incoherent adj. incoerente

income n. renda

incomparable adj. incomparável

incompatible adj. incompatível

incompetent adj. incompetente

incomplete adj. incompleto

inconclusive adj. inconclusivo

inconsiderate adj. imprudente

inconsistent adj. inconsistente

inconsolable adj. inconsolável

inconspicuous adj. imperceptível

inconvenience n. inconveniente

incorporate v. incorporar

incorporation n. incorporação

incorrect adj. incorreto

incorrigible adj. incorrigível

incorruptible adj. íntegro

increase v. aumentar

incredible adj. incrível

increment n. incrementar

incriminate v.i. incriminar

incubate v. incubar

inculcate v. inculcar

incumbent adj. incumbente

incur v. incorrer

incurable adj. incurável

incursion n. incursão

indebted adj. endividado

indecency n. indecência

indecent adj. indecente

indecision n. indecisão

indeed adv. de fato

indefensible adj. insustentável

indefinite adj. indefinido

indemnity n. indemnização

indent v. recortar

indenture n. recorte

independence n. independência

independent adj. independente

indescribable adj. indescritível

index n. índice

Indian *n.* Indiano

indicate *v.* indicar

indication *n.* indicação

indicative *adj.* indicativo

indicator *n.* indicador

indict *v.* acusar

indictment *n.* acusação

indifference *n.* indiferença

indifferent *adj.* indiferente

indigenous *adj.* indígena

indigestible *adj.* indigesto

indigestion *n.* indigestão

indignant *adj.* indignado

indignation *n.* indignação

indignity *n.* indignidade

indigo *n.* índigo

indirect *adj.* indireto

indiscipline *n.* indisciplina

indiscreet *adj.* indiscreto

indiscretion *n.* indiscrição

indiscriminate *adj.* indiscriminado

indispensable *adj.* indispensável

indisposed *adj.* indisposto

indisputable *adj.* indisputável

indistinct *adj.* indistinto

individual *adj.* individual

individualism *n.* individualismo

individuality *n.* individualidade

indivisible *adj.* indivisível

indolent *adj.* indolente

indomitable *adj.* indomado

indoor *adj.* interior

induce *v.* induzir

inducement *n.* incitamento

induct *v.* introduzir

induction *n.* indução

indulge *v.* poupar

indulgence *n.* indulgência

indulgent *adj.* indulgente

industrial *adj.* industrial

industrious *adj.* trabalhador

industry *n.* indústria

ineffective *adj.* ineficaz

inefficient *adj.* ineficiente

ineligible *adj.* inelegível

inequality *n.* desigualdade

inert *adj.* inerte

inertia *n.* inércia

inescapable *adj.* inevitável

inevitable *adj.* inevitável

inexact *adj.* inexato

inexcusable *adj.* indesculpável

inexhaustible *adj.* inesgotável

inexorable *adj.* inexorável

inexpensive *adj.* barato

inexperience *n.* inexperiência

inexplicable *adj.* inexplicável

inextricable *adj.* inextricável

infallible *adj.* infalível

infamous *adj.* infame

infamy *n.* infâmia

infancy *n.* infância

infant *n.* infantil

infanticide *n.* infanticídio

infantile *adj.* infantil

infantry *n.* infantaria

infatuate *v.* enfatuar

infatuation *n.* paixão

infect v. infectar

infection n. infecção

infectious adj. infeccioso

infer v. supor

inference n. dedução

inferior adj. inferior

inferiority n. inferioridade

infernal adj. infernal

infertile adj. infértil

infest v. infestar

infidelity n. infidelidade

infighting n. boxe

infiltrate v. infiltrar

infinite adj. infinito

infinity n. infinidade

infirm adj. enfermo

infirmity n. enfermidade

inflame v. inflamar

inflammable adj. inflamável

inflammation n. inflamação

inflammatory adj. inflamatório

inflate v. inflar

inflation n. inflação

inflect v. modular

inflexible adj. inflexível

inflict v. infligir

influence n. influenciar

influential adj. influente

influenza n. gripe

influx n. afluxo

inform v. informar

informal adj. informal

information n. informação

informative adj. informativo

informer n. informante

infrastructure n. infra-estrutura

infrequent adj. raro

infringe v. infringir

infringement n. violação

infuriate v. enfurecer

infuse v. infundir

infusion n. infusão

ingrained adj. impregnado

ingratitude n. ingratidão

ingredient n. ingrediente

inhabit v. habitar

inhabitable adj. habitável

inhabitant n. habitante

inhale v. inalar

inhaler n. inalador

inherent adj. inerente

inherit v. herdar

inheritance n. herança

inhibit v. inibir

inhibition n. inibição

inhospitable adj. inóspito

inhuman adj. desumano

inimical adj. hostil

inimitable adj. inimitável

initial adj. inicial

initiate v. iniciar

initiative n. iniciativa

inject v. injetar

injection n. injeção

injudicious adj. imprudente

injunction n. injunção

injure v. ferir

injurious adj. prejudicial

injury *n.* ferimento

injustice *n.* injustiça

ink *n.* tinta

inkling *n.* pressentimento

inland *adj.* interior

inmate *n.* pensionista

inmost *adj.* íntimo

inn *n.* pousada

innate *adj.* inato

inner *adj.* interior

innermost *adj.* íntimo

innings *n.* turno

innocence *n.* inocência

innocent *adj.* inocente

innovate *v.* inovar

innovation *n.* inovação

innovator *n.* inovador

innumerable *adj.* inumerável

inoculate *v.* inocular

inoculation *n.* inoculação

inoperative *adj.* inoperante

inopportune *adj.* inoportuno

inpatient *n.* internado

input *n.* entrada

inquest *n.* inquérito

inquire *v.* inquirir

inquiry *n.* inquérito

inquisition *n.* inquisição

inquisitive *adj.* curioso

insane *adj.* insano

insanity *n.* insanidade

insatiable *adj.* insaciável

inscribe *v.* inscrever

inscription *n.* inscrição

insect *n.* inseto

insecticide *n.* inseticida

insecure *adj.* inseguro

insecurity *n.* insegurança

insensible *adj.* insensível

inseparable *adj.* inseparável

insert *v.* inserir

insertion *n.* inserção

inside *n.* dentro

insight *n.* introspeção

insignificance *n.* insignificância

insignificant *adj.* insignificante

insincere *adj.* falso

insincerity *adv.* falsidade

insinuate *v.* insinuar

insinuation *n.* insinuação

insipid *adj.* insípido

insist *v.* insistir

insistence *n.* insistência

insistent *adj.* insistente

insolence *n.* insolência

insolent *adj.* insolente

insoluble *adj.* insolúvel

insolvency *n.* insolvência

insolvent *adj.* insolvente

inspect *v.* inspecionar

inspection *n.* inspeção

inspector *n.* inspetor

inspiration *n.* inspiração

inspire *v.* inspirar

instability *n.* instabilidade

install *v.* instalar

installation *n.* instalação

instalment *n.* prestação

instance *n.* instância
instant *adj.* imediato
instantaneous *adj.* instantâneo
instead *adv.* em vez
instigate *v.* instigar
instil *v.* instilar
instinct *n.* instinto
instinctive *adj.* instintivo
institute *n.* instituto
institution *n.* instituição
instruct *v.* instruir
instruction *n.* instrução
instructor *n.* instrutor
instrument *n.* instrumento
instrumental *adj.* instrumental
instrumentalist *n.* instrumentalista
insubordinate *adj.* insubordinado
insubordination *n.* insubordinação
insufficient *adj.* insuficiente
insular *adj.* insular
insulate *v.* isolar
insulation *n.* isolamento
insulator *n.* isolador
insulin *n.* insulina
insult *v.t.* insultar
insupportable *adj.* insuportável
insurance *n.* seguro
insure *v.* garantir
insurgent *n.* insurgente
insurmountable *adj.* intransponível
insurrection *n.* insurreição
intact *adj.* intacto
intake *n.* admissão
intangible *adj.* intangível

integral *adj.* integral
integrity *n.* integridade
intellect *n.* intelecto
intellectual *adj.* intelectual
intelligence *n.* inteligência
intelligent *adj.* inteligente
intelligible *adj.* inteligível
intend *v.* pretender
intense *adj.* intenso
intensify *v.* intensificar
intensity *n.* intensidade
intensive *adj.* intensivo
intent *n.* intenção
intention *n.* intenção
intentional *adj.* intencional
interact *v.* interagir
intercede *v.* interceder
intercept *v.* intercetar
interception *n.* interceptação
interchange *v.* permutar
intercom *n.* intercomunicador
interconnect *v.* interconectar
intercourse *n.* relações
interdependent *adj.* interdependente
interest *n.* interesse
interesting *adj.* interessante
interface *n.* interface
interfere *v.* interferir
interference *n.* interferência
interim *n.* interino
interior *adj.* interior
interject *v.* interpor
interlink *v.* encadear
interlock *v.* entreligar

interlocutor *n.* interlocutor
interloper *n.* intruso
interlude *n.* interlúdio
intermediary *n.* intermediário
intermediate *adj.* intermédio
interminable *adj.* interminável
intermission *n.* intervalo
intermittent *adj.* intermitente
intern *v.* internar
internal *adj.* interno
international *adj.* internacional
internet *n.* Internet
interplay *n.* interação
interpret *v.* interpretar
interpreter *n.* intérprete
interracial *adj.* misto
interrelate *v.* inter-relacionar
interrogate *v.* interrogar
interrogative *adj.* interrogativo
interrupt *v.* interromper
interruption *n.* interrupção
intersect *v.* intercetar
interstate *n.* interestadual
interval *n.* intervalo
intervene *v.* intervir
intervention *n.* intervenção
interview *n.* entrevista
intestine *n.* intestino
intimacy *n.* intimidade
intimate *adj.* íntimo
intimidate *v.* intimidar
intimidation *n.* intimidação
into *prep.* em
intolerable *adj.* intolerável

intolerant *adj.* intolerante
intone *v.* entoar
intoxicate *v.* intoxicar
intoxication *n.* intoxicação
intractable *adj.* intratável
intranet *n.* intranet
intransitive *adj.* intransitivo
intrepid *adj.* intrépido
intricate *adj.* intricado
intrigue *v.* intriga
intrinsic *adj.* intrínseco
introduce *v.* introduzir
introduction *n.* introdução
introductory *adj.* introdutório
introspect *v.* fazer uma introspeção
introspection *n.* introspeção
introvert *n.* introvertido
intrude *v.* introduzir
intrusion *n.* intrusão
intrusive *adj.* intrusivo
intuition *n.* intuição
intuitive *n.* intuitivo
inundate *v.* inundar
invade *v.* invadir
invalid *n.* inválido
invalidate *v.* invalidar
invaluable *adj.* inestimável
invariable *adj.* invariável
invasion *n.* invasão
invective *n.* invetiva
invent *v.* inventar
invention *n.* invenção
inventor *n.* inventor
inventory *n.* inventário

inverse *adj.* inverso	**irregularity** *n.* irregularidade
invert *v.* inverter	**irrelevant** *adj.* irrelevante
invest *v.t.* investir	**irreplaceable** *adj.* insubstituível
investigate *v.* investigar	**irresistible** *adj.* irresistível
investigation *n.* investigação	**irresolute** *adj.* irresoluto
investment *n.* investimento	**irrespective** *adj.* independente
invigilate *adj.* fiscalizar	**irresponsible** *adj.* irresponsável
invigilator *n.* vigilante	**irreversible** *adj.* irreversível
invincible *adj.* invencível	**irrevocable** *adj.* irrevogável
inviolable *adj.* inviolável	**irrigate** *v.* irrigar
invisible *adj.* invisível	**irrigation** *n.* irrigação
invitation *n.* convite	**irritable** *adj.* irritável
invite *v.* convidar	**irritant** *n.* irritante
inviting *adj.* convidativo	**irritate** *v.* irritar
invocation *n.* invocação	**irruption** *n.* irrupção
invoice *n.* fatura	**Islam** *n.* Islão
invoke *v.* invocar	**island** *n.* ilha
involuntary *adj.* involuntário	**isle** *n.* ilha
involve *v.* envolver	**islet** *n.* ilhota
invulnerable *adj.* invulnerável	**isobar** *n.* isóbaro
inward *adj.* interior	**isolate** *v.* isolar
irate *adj.* enfurecido	**isolation** *n.* isolamento
ire *n.* ira	**issue** *n.* questão
iris *n.* íris	**it** *pron.* ele
irksome *adj.* maçador	**italic** *adj.* itálico
iron *n.* ferro	**itch** *v.i.* coçar
ironical *adj.* irónico	**itchy** *adj.* sarnento
irony *n.* ironia	**item** *n.* item
irradiate *v.* irradiar	**iterate** *v.* repetir
irrational *adj.* irracional	**itinerary** *n* itinerário
irreconcilable *adj.* irreconciliável	**itself** *pron.* se
irredeemable *adj.* irremediável	**ivory** *n.* marfim
irrefutable *adj.* irrefutável	**ivy** *n.* hera
irregular *adj.* irregular	

J

jab *v.* picar

jabber *v.* tagarelar

jack *n.* tomada

jackal *n.* chacal

jackass *n.* burro

jacket *n.* jaqueta

jackpot *n.* prémio

Jacuzzi *n.* jacuzzi

jade *n.* jade

jaded *adj.* cansado

jagged *adj.* denteado

jail *n.* prisão

jailer *n.* carcereiro

jam *v.t.* espremer

jam *n.* congestionamento

jamboree *n.* comemoração

janitor *n.* zelador

January *n.* Janeiro

jar *n.* jarra

jargon *n.* jargão

jasmine *n.* jasmim

jaundice *n.* icterícia

jaunt *n.* passeata

jaunty *adj.* desenvolto

javelin *n.* dardo

jaw *n.* mandíbula

jay *n.* gaio

jazz *n.* jazz

jazzy *adj.* jazzístico

jealous *adj.* ciumento

jealousy *n.* ciúme

jeans *n.* jeans

jeep *n.* jipe

jeer *v.* zombar

jelly *n.* geléia

jellyfish *n.* medusa

jeopardize *v.* expor

jeopardy *n.* perigo

jerk *n.* idiota

jerkin *n.* justilho

jerry can *n.* bidão

jersey *n.* camisola

jest *n.* brincadeira

jester *n.* bobo

jet *n.* jato

jet lag *n.* jet lag

jewel *n.* jóia

jeweller *n.* joalheiro

jewellery *n.* jóias

jibe *n.* brincadeira

jig *n.* rapaziada

jiggle *v.* sacudir

jigsaw *n.* puzzle

jingle *n.* tilintar

jinx *n.* enguiço

jitters *n.* nervosismo

job *n.* trabalho

jockey *n.* jóquei

jocose *adj.* jocoso

jocular *adj.* jovial

jog *v.* empurrar

joggle *v.* embutir

join *v.* juntar

joiner *n.* marceneiro

joint *n.* articulação

joist *n.* viga

joke *n.* piada
joker *n.* joker
jolly *adj.* alegre
jolt *v.t.* abalar
jostle *v.t.* empurar
jot *v.t.* apontar
journal *n.* revista
journalism *n.* jornalismo
journalist *n.* jornalista
journey *n.* jornada
jovial *adj.* jovial
joviality *adv.* jovialidade
joy *n.* alegria
joyful *adj.* alegre
joyous *adj.* alegre
jubilant *adj.* jubiloso
jubilation *n.* júbilo
jubilee *n.* jubileu
judge *n.* juiz
judgement *n.* julgamento
judicial *adj.* judicial
judiciary *n.* judiciário
judicious *adj.* judicioso
judo *n.* judo
jug *n.* jarro
juggle *v.* mistificar
juggler *n.* malabarista
juice *n.* sumo
juicy *adj.* suculento
July *n.* Julho
jumble *n.* confusão
jumbo *adj.* colosso
jump *v.i* saltar
jumper *n.* saltador

jumper *n.* saltador
junction *n.* junção
juncture *n.* conjuntura
June *n.* Junho
jungle *n.* selva
junior *adj.* júnior
junior *n.* júnior
junk *n.* tralha
Jupiter *n.* Júpiter
jurisdiction *n.* jurisdição
jurisprudence *n.* jurisprudência
jurist *n.* jurista
juror *n.* jurado
jury *n.* júri
just *adj.* justo
justice *n.* justiça
justifiable *adj.* justificável
justification *n.* justificação
justify *v.* justificar
jute *n.* juta
juvenile *adj.* juvenil

K

kaftans *n.* Cafetãs
kaleidoscope *n.* caleidoscópio
kangaroo *n.* canguru
karaoke *n.* karaoke
karate *n.* karaté
karma *n.* carma
kebab *n.* kebab
keel *n.* quilha
keen *adj.* afiado
keenness *n.* perspicácia
keep *v.* manter

keeper *n.* guarda
keeping *n.* manutenção
keepsake *n.* lembrança
keg *n.* barril
kennel *n.* canil
kerb *n.* berma
kerchief *n.* lenço
kernel *n.* núcleo
kerosene *n.* querosene
ketchup *n.* ketchup
kettle *n.* chaleira
key *n.* chave
keyboard *n.* teclado
keyhole *n.* buraco de fechadura
kick *v.* chutar
kid *n.* criança
kidnap *v.* raptar
kidney *n.* rim
kill *v.* matar
killing *n.* matança
kiln *n.* forno
kilo *n.* quilo
kilobyte *n.* kilobyte
kilometre *n.* quilómetro
kilt *n.* kilt
kimono *n.* quimono
kin *n.* parentes
kind *n.* tipo
kindergarten *n.* jardim de infância
kindle *v.* acender
kindly *adv.* amavelmente
kinetic *adj.* cinético

king *n.* rei
kingdom *n.* reino
kink *n.* torção
kinship *n.* parentesco
kiss *v.t.* beijar
kit *n.* conjunto
kitchen *n.* cozinha
kite *n.* pipa
kith *n.* amigos
kitten *n.* gatinho
kitty *n.* gatinho
knack *n.* habilidade
knacker *v.* abater
knave *n.* valete
knead *v.* amassar
knee *n.* joelho
kneel *v.* ajoelhar
knickers *n.* cuecas
knife *n.* faca
knight *n.* cavaleiro
knighthood *n.* fidalguia
knit *v.* tricotar
knob *n.* botão
knock *v.* bater
knot *n.* nó
knotty *adj.* nodoso
know *v.* saber
knowing *adj.* conhecedor
knowledge *n.* conhecimento
knuckle *n.* junta
kosher *adj.* kosher (alimento limpo)
kudos *n.* renome
kung fu *n.* kung fu

L

label n. etiqueta
labial adj. labial
laboratory n. laboratório
laborious adj. penoso
labour n. trabalho
labourer n. trabalhador
labyrinth n. labirinto
lace n. renda
lacerate v. dilacerar
lachrymose adj. lacrimoso
lack n. falta
lackey n. lacaio
lacklustre adj. desbotado
laconic adj. lacónico
lacquer n. laca
lacrosse n. lacrosse
lactate v. amamentar
lactose n. lactose
lacuna n. lacuna
lacy adj. rendado
lad n. puto
ladder n. escadote
laden n. carregado
ladle n. concha
lady n. senhora
ladybird n. joaninha
lag v. atrasar
lager n. lager (tipo de cerveja)
laggard n. lento
lagging n. atraso
lagoon n. lagoa
lair n. covil

lake n. lago
lamb n. cordeiro
lambast v. desaprovar
lame adj. coxo
lament n. lamento
lamentable adj. lamentável
laminate v. laminar
lamp n. lâmpada
lampoon v. satirizar
lance n. lança
lancer n. lanceiro
lancet n. lanceta
land n. terra
landing n. aterragem
landlady n. senhoria
landlord n. senhorio
landscape n. paisagem
lane n. pista
language n. linguagem
languid adj. lânguido
languish v. desfalecer
lank adj. magro
lanky adj. esguio
lantern n. lanterna
lap n. colo
lapse n. lapso
lard n. banha de porco
larder n. despensa
large adj. grande
largesse n. generosidade
lark n. cotovia
larva n. larva
larynx n. laringe
lasagne n. lasanha

lascivious *adj.* lascivo
laser *n.* laser
lash *v.* chicotear
lashings *n.* abundância
lass *n.* moça
last *adj.* último
lasting *adj.* duradouro
latch *n.* trinco
late *adj.* tarde
lately *adv.* recentemente
latent *adj.* latente
lath *n.* ripa
lathe *n.* torno mecânico
lather *n.* espuma
latitude *n.* latitude
latrine *n.* latrina
latte *n.* café com leite
latter *adj.* último
lattice *n.* gelosia
laud *v.* elogiar
laudable *adj.* louvável
laugh *v.* rir
laughable *adj.* ridículo
laughter *n.* riso
launch *v.* lançar
launder *v.* lavar
launderette *n.* lavandaria
laundry *n.* lavandaria
laurel *n.* loureiro
laureate *n.* laureado
lava *n.* lava
lavatory *n.* lavatório
lavender *n.* lavanda
lavish *adj.* pródigo

law *n.* lei
lawful *adj.* legal
lawless *adj.* sem lei
lawn *n.* relvado
lawyer *n.* advogado
lax *adj.* frouxo
laxative *n.* laxante
laxity *n.* frouxidão
lay *v.* colocar
layer *n.* camada
layman *n.* leigo
laze *v.* preguiçar
lazy *adj.* preguiçoso
leach *v.* coar
lead *n.* liderança
lead *v.* conduzir
leaden *adj.* plúmbeo
leader *n.* líder
leadership *n.* chefia
leaf *n.* folha
leaflet *n.* folheto
league *n.* liga
leak *v.* vazar
leakage *n.* fuga
lean *v.* inclinar
leap *v.* saltar
learn *v.* aprender
learned *adj.* aprendido
learner *n.* aprendiz
learning *n.* aprendizagem
lease *n.* arrendamento
leash *n.* coleira
least *adj.* mínimo
leather *n.* couro

leave v.t. deixar

lecture n. palestra

lecturer n. conferencista

ledge n. saliência

ledger n. registro

leech n. sanguessuga

leek n. alho-porro

left n. esquerdo

leftist n. esquerdista

leg n. perna

legacy n. legado

legal adj. legal

legality n. legalidade

legalize v. legalizar

legend n. lenda

legendary adj. lendário

leggings n. perneiras

legible adj. legível

legion n. legião

legislate v. legislar

legislation n. legislação

legislative adj. legislativo

legislator n. legislador

legislature n. legislatura

legitimacy n. legitimidade

legitimate adj. legítimo

leisure n. lazer

leisurely adj. vagaroso

lemon n. limão

lemonade n. limonada

lend v. emprestar

length n. comprimento

lengthy adj. longo

leniency n. suavidade

lenient adj. brando

lens n. lente

lentil n. lentilha

Leo n. Leo

leopard n. leopardo

leper n. leproso

leprosy n. lepra

lesbian n. lésbica

less adj. menos

lessee n. arrendatário

lessen v. diminuir

lesser adj. menor

lesson n. lição

lessor n. senhorio

lest conj. para que não

let v. deixar

lethal adj. letal

lethargic adj. letárgico

lethargy n. letargia

letter n. carta

level n. nível

lever n. alavanca

leverage n. alavancagem

levity n. leviandade

levy v. arrecadar

lewd adj. lascivo

lexical adj. lexical

lexicon n. léxico

liability n. responsabilidade

liable adj. passível

liaise v. colaborar

liaison n. ligação

liar n. mentiroso

libel n. difamação

liberal *adj.* liberal	**likely** *adj.* provável
liberate *v.* libertar	**liken** *v.* assemelhar
liberation *n.* libertação	**likeness** *n.* semelhança
liberator *n.* libertador	**likewise** *adv.* também
liberty *n.* liberdade	**liking** *n.* gosto
libido *n.* libido	**lilac** *n.* lilás
Libra *n.* Libra	**lily** *n.* lírio
librarian *n.* bibliotecário	**limb** *n.* membro
library *n.* biblioteca	**limber** *v.* engatar
licence *n.* licença	**limbo** *n.* limbo
licensee *n.* licenciado	**lime** *n.* lima
licentious *adj.* desregado	**limelight** *n.* ribalta
lick *v.* lamber	**limerick** *n.* quintilha humorística
lid *n.* tampa	**limit** *n.* limitar
lie *v.* mentir	**limitation** *n.* limitação
liege *n.* suserano	**limited** *adj.* limitado
lien *n.* penhor	**limousine** *n.* limusine
lieu *n.* lugar	**limp** *v.* mancar
lieutenant *n.* tenente	**line** *n.* linha
life *n.* vida	**lineage** *n.* linhagem
lifeless *adj.* inanimado	**linen** *n.* linho
lifelong *adj.* vitalício	**linger** *v.* demorar
lift *v.t.* levantar	**lingerie** *n.* lingerie
ligament *n.* ligamento	**lingo** *n.* dialeto
light *n.* luz	**lingua** *n.* língua
lighten *v.* iluminar	**lingual** *n.* lingual
lighter *n.* isqueiro	**linguist** *adj.* linguista
lighting *n.* iluminação	**linguistic** *adj.* linguístico
lightly *adv.* levemente	**lining** *n.* revestimento
lightening *n.* relâmpago	**link** *n.* ligação
lignite *n.* linhita	**linkage** *n.* acoplamento
like *prep.* como	**linseed** *n.* linhaça
likeable *adj.* simpático	**lintel** *n.* lintel
likelihood *n.* probabilidade	**lion** *n.* leão

lip n. lábio
liposuction n. lipoaspiração
liquefy v. liquidificar
liquid n. líquido
liquidate v. liquidar
liquidation n. liquidação
liquor n. licor
lisp n. ceceio
lissom adj. ágil
list n. lista
listen v. ouvir
listener n. ouvinte
listless adj. apático
literal adj. literal
literary adj. literário
literate adj. alfabetizado
literature n. literatura
lithe adj. flexível
litigant n. litigante
litigate v. litigar
litigation n. litígio
litre n. litro
litter n. liteira
little adj. pouco
live v. viver
livelihood n. sustento
lively adj. animado
liven v. animar
liver n. fígado
livery n. libré
living n. vivo
lizard n. lagarto
load n. carregar
loaf n. pão

loan n. empréstimo
loath adj. relutante
loathe v. detestar
loathsome adj. repugnante
lobby n. entrada
lobe n. lóbulo
lobster n. lagosta
local adj. local
locale n. localidade
locality n. vizinhança
localize v. localizar
locate v. instalar
location n. localização
lock n. fechadura
locker n. cacifo
locket n. medalhão
locomotion n. locomoção
locomotive n. locomotiva
locum n. coloquial
locus n. local
locust n. gafanhoto
locution n. locução
lodge n. alojamento
lodger n. inquilino
lodging n. alojamento
loft n. sótão
lofty adj. elevado
log n. toro
logarithm n. logaritmo
logic n. lógica
logical adj. lógico
logistics n. logística
logo n. logotipo
loin n. lombo

loiter v. tardar
loll v. relaxar-se
lollipop n. chupa-chupa
lolly n. sorvete
lone adj. solitário
loneliness n. solidão
lonely adj. sozinho
loner n. solitário
lonesome adj. só
long adj. longo
longevity n. longevidade
longing n. ancioso
longitude n. longitude
loo n. sanita
look v. olhar
look n olhadela
lookalike n. sósia
loom n. tear
loop n. laço
loose adj. solto
loosen v. livrar
loot n. pilhagem
lop v. podar
lope v. galopar
lopsided adj. assimétrico
lord n. senhor
lordly adj. altivamente
lore n. sabedoria
lorry n. camião
lose v. perder
loss n. perda
lot pron. tudo
lotion n. loção
lottery n. lotaria

lotus n. lótus
loud adj. alto
lounge v. deitar
lounge n. salão
louse n. piolho
lousy adj. piolhento
lout n. labrego
Louvre n. Louvre
lovable adj. adorável
love n. amor
lovely adj. encantador
lover n. amante
low adj. baixo
lower adj. o mais baixo
lowly adj. humilde
loyal adj. leal
loyalist n. lealista
lozenge n. losango
lubricant n. lubrificante
lubricate v. lubrificar
lubrication n. lubrificação
lucent adj. brilhante
lucid adj. lúcido
lucidity adv. lucidez
luck n. sorte
luckless adj. infeliz
lucky adj. sortudo
lucrative adj. lucrativo
lucre n. lucro
ludicrous adj. ridículo
luggage n. bagagem
lukewarm adj. indiferente
lull v. acalmar
lullaby n. canção

luminary *n.* celebridade
luminous *adj.* luminoso
lump *n.* pedaço
lunacy *n.* loucura
lunar *adj.* lunar
lunatic *n.* lunático
lunch *n.* almoço
luncheon *n.* almoço
lung *n.* pulmão
lunge *n.* picadeiro
lurch *n.* deserção
lure *v.* atrair
lurid *adj.* lúgubre
lurk *v.* espreitar
luscious *adj.* delicioso
lush *adj.* exuberante
lust *n.* luxúria
lustful *adj.* libidinoso
lustre *n.* brilho
lustrous *adj.* brilhante
lusty *adj.* vigoroso
lute *n.* alaúde
luxuriant *adj.* luxuriante
luxurious *adj.* luxuoso
luxury *n.* luxo
lychee *n.* lichia
lymph *n.* linfa
lynch *n.* linchamento
lyre *n.* lira
lyric *n.* lírica
lyrical *adj.* sentimental
lyricist *n.* lírico

M

macabre *adj.* macabro
machine *n.* máquina
machinery *n.* maquinaria
macho *adj.* macho
mackintosh *n.* impermeável
mad *adj.* louco
madam *n.* madame
madcap *adj.* estouvado
Mafia *n.* máfia
magazine *n.* revista
magenta *n.* magenta
magic *n.* magia
magician *n.* mágico
magisterial *adj.* magistral
magistrate *n.* magistrado
magnanimous *adj.* magnânimo
magnate *n.* magnata
magnet *n.* íman
magnetic *adj.* magnético
magnetism *n.* magnetismo
magnificent *adj.* magnífico
magnify *v.* ampliar
magnitude *n.* magnitude
magpie *n.* pega
mahogany *n.* mogno
mahout *n.* cornaca
maid *n.* empregada
maiden *n.* donzela
mail *n.* correio
mail order *n.* ordem de correio
maim *v.* mutilar
main *adj.* principal

mainstay *n.* esteio
maintain *v.* manter
maintenance *n.* manutenção
maisonette *n.* Casinha
majestic *adj.* majestoso
majesty *n.* majestade
major *adj.* maior
majority *n.* maioria
make *v.* fazer
make-up *n.* maquilhagem
making *n.* realização
maladjusted *adj.* desajustado
maladministration *n.* desgoverno
malady *n.* doença
malaise *n.* mal-estar
malaria *n.* malária
malcontent *n.* descontente
male *n.* masculino
malediction *n.* maldição
malefactor *n.* malfeitor
malformation *n.* deformidade
malfunction *v.* avariar
malice *n.* malícia
malicious *adj.* malicioso
malign *adj.* maléfico
malignant *adj.* maligno
mall *n.* centro comercial
malleable *adj.* maleável
mallet *n.* macete
malnutrition *n.* subnutrição
malpractice *n.* culpa
malt *n.* malte
maltreat *v.* maltratar
mammal *n.* mamífero

mammary *adj.* mamário
mammon *n.* mamona
mammoth *n.* mamute
man *n.* homem
manage *v.* gerir
manageable *adj.* manejável
management *n.* gestão
manager *n.* gerente
managerial *adj.* administrativo
mandate *n.* mandato
mandatory *adj.* obrigatório
mane *n.* crina
manful *adj.* viril
manganese *n.* manganésio
manger *n.* manjedoura
mangle *v.* mutilar
mango *n.* manga
manhandle *n.* maltratar
manhole *n.* vala
manhood *n.* masculinidade
mania *n.* mania
maniac *n.* maníaco
manicure *n.* manicure
manifest *adj.* manifesto
manifestation *n.* manifestação
manifesto *n.* manifesto
manifold *adj.* múltiplo
manipulate *v.* manipular
manipulation *n.* manipulação
mankind *n.* humanidade
manly *adj.* viril
manna *n.* maná
mannequin *n.* manequim
manner *n.* maneira

mannerism *n.* maneirismo	**marionette** *n.* marioneta
manoeuvre *n.* manobra	**marital** *adj.* marital
manor *n.* solar	**maritime** *adj.* marítimo
manpower *n.* mão de obra	**mark** *n.* marca
mansion *n.* mansão	**marker** *n.* marcador
mantel *n.* prateleira do fogão	**market** *n.* mercado
mantle *n.* manto	**marketing** *n.* marketing
mantra *n.* mantra	**marking** *n.* marcas
manual *adj.* manual	**marksman** *n.* bom atirador
manufacture *v.* fabricar	**marl** *n.* marga
manufacturer *n.* fabricante	**marmalade** *n.* marmelada
manumission *n.* alforria	**maroon** *n.* marrom
manure *n.* estrume	**marquee** *n.* marquesinha
manuscript *n.* manuscrito	**marriage** *n.* casamento
many *adj.* muitos	**marriageable** *adj.* núbil
map *n.* mapa	**marry** *v.* casar
maple *n.* ácer	**Mars** *n.* Marte
mar *v.* estragar	**marsh** n pântano
marathon *n.* maratona	**marshal** *n.* marechal
maraud *v.* saquear	**marshmallow** *n.* marshmallow
marauder *n.* saqueador	**marsupial** *n.* marsupial
marble *n.* mármore	**mart** *n.* mercado
march *n.* marcha	**martial** *adj.* marcial
march *v.* marchar	**martinet** *n.* meticuloso
mare *n.* égua	**martyr** *n.* mártir
margarine *n.* margarina	**martyrdom** *n.* martírio
margin *n.* margem	**marvel** *v.i* maravilhar-se
marginal *adj.* marginal	**marvellous** *adj.* maravilhoso
marigold *n.* malmequer	**Marxism** *n.* Marxismo
marina *n.* marina	**marzipan** *n.* maçapão
marinade *n.* escabeche	**mascara** *n.* rímel
marinate *v.* marinar	**mascot** *n.* mascote
marine *adj.* marinha	**masculine** *adj.* masculino
mariner *n.* marinheiro	**mash** *v.t* triturar

mask *n.* máscara
masochism *n.* masoquismo
mason *n.* pedreiro
masonry *n.* alvenaria
masquerade *n.* mascarada
mass *n.* massa
massacre *n.* massacre
massage *n.* massagem
masseur *n.* massagista
massive *adj.* maciço
mast *n.* mastro
master *n.* mestre
mastermind *n.* mentor
masterpiece *n.* obra-prima
mastery *n.* mestria
masticate *v.* mastigar
masturbate *v.* masturbar
mat *n.* tapete
matador *n.* matador
match *n.* fósforo
matchmaker *n.* casamenteiro
mate *n.* companheiro
material *n.* material
materialism *n.* materialismo
materialize *v.* materializar
maternal *adj.* maternal
maternity *n.* maternidade
mathematical *adj.* matemático
mathematician *n.* matemático
mathematics *n.* matemática
matinee *n.* matiné
matriarch *n.* matriarca
matricide *n.* matricídio
matriculate *v.* matricular

matriculation *n.* matrícula
matrimonial *adj.* matrimonial
matrimony *n.* matrimónio
matrix *n.* matriz
matron *n.* matrona
matter *n.* assunto
mattress *n.* colchão
mature *adj.* maduro
maturity *n.* maturidade
maudlin *adj.* sentimental
maul *v.* agredir
maunder *v.* vaguear
mausoleum *n.* mausoléu
maverick *n.* dissidente
maxim *n.* máxima
maximize *v.* maximizar
maximum *n.* máximo
May *n.* Maio
may *v.* poder
maybe *adv.* talvez
mayhem *n.* barafunda
mayonnaise *n.* maionese
mayor *n.* Presidente da Câmara
maze *n.* labirinto
me *pron.* mim
mead *n.* hidromel
meadow *n.* prado
meagre *adj.* magro
meal *n.* refeição
mealy *adj.* farinhento
mean *v.* significar
meander *v.* sepentear
meaning *n.* significado
means *n.* meios

meantime *adv.* entretanto
meanwhile *adv.* entretanto
measles *n.* sarampo
measly *adj.* com sarampo
measure *v.* medir
measure a. medida
measured *adj.* medido
measurement *n.* medição
meat *n.* carne
mechanic *n.* mecânico
mechanical *adj.* mecânico
mechanics *n.* mecânica
mechanism *n.* mecanismo
medal *n.* medalha
medallion *n.* medalhão
medallist *n.* medalhista
meddle *v.* intrometer-se
media *n.* media
median *adj.* mediana
mediate *v.* mediar
mediation *n.* mediação
medic *n.* médico
medical *adj.* médico
medication *n.* medicação
medicinal *adj.* medicinal
medicine *n.* medicina
medieval *adj.* medieval
mediocre *adj.* medíocre
mediocrity *n.* mediocridade
meditate *v.* meditar
mediation *n.* mediação
meditative *adj.* reflexivo
Mediterranean *adj.* Mediterrâneo
medium *n.* medium

medley *n.* mistura
meek *adj.* manso
meet *v.* reunir
meeting *n.* reunião
mega *adj.* fantástico
megabyte *n.* megabyte
megahertz *n.* megahertz
megalith *n.* megálito
megalithic *adj.* megalítico
megaphone *n.* megafone
megapixel *n.* megapixel
melamine *n.* melamina
melancholia *n.* melancolia
melancholy *n.* melancolia
melange *n.* mistura
meld *n.* fundir
melee *n.* tumulto
meliorate *v.* aperfeiçoar
mellow *adj.* jovial
melodic *adj.* melódico
melodious *adj.* melodioso
melodrama *n.* melodrama
melodramatic *adj.* melodramático
melody *n.* melodia
melon *n.* melão
melt *v.* derreter
member *n.* membro
membership *n.* adesão
membrane *n.* membrana
memento *n.* lembrança
memo *n.* memorando
memoir *n.* autobiografia
memorable *adj.* memorável
memorandum *n.* memorando

memorial n. memorial
memory n. memória
menace n. ameaça
mend v. consertar
mendacious adj. mentiroso
mendicant adj. mendicante
menial adj. servil
meningitis n. meningite
menopause n. menopausa
menstrual adj. menstrual
menstruation n. menstruação
mental adj. mental
mentality n. mentalidade
mention v. mencionar
mentor n. mentor
menu n. menu
mercantile adj. mercantil
mercenary adj. mercenário
merchandise n. mercadoria
merchant n. comerciante
merciful adj. misericordioso
mercurial adj. mercurial
mercury n. mercúrio
mercy n. misericórdia
mere adj. mero
meretricious adj. meretriz
merge v. fundir
merger n. fusão
meridian n. meridiano
merit n. merecer
meritorious adj. meritório
mermaid n. sereia
merry adj. alegre
mesh n. engrenar

mesmeric adj. mesmérico
mesmerize v. hipnotizar
mess n. confusão
message n. mensagem
messenger n. mensageiro
messiah n. messias
messy adj. confuso
metabolism n. metabolismo
metal n. metal
metallic adj. metálico
metallurgy n. metalurgia
metamorphosis n. metamorfose
metaphor n. metáfora
metaphysical adj. metafísico
metaphysics n. metafísica
mete v. medir
meteor n. meteoro
meteoric adj. meteórico
meteorology n. meteorologia
meter n. metro
method n. método
methodical adj. metódico
methodology n. metodologia
meticulous adj. meticuloso
metre n. metro
metric adj. métrico
metrical adj. métrico
metropolis n. metrópole
metropolitan adj. metro
mettle n. impetuosidade
mettlesome n. impetuoso
mew v. confinar
mews n. estábulos
mezzanine n. mezanino

miasma *n.* miasma

mica *n.* mica

microbiology *n.* microbiologia

microchip *n.* microchip

microfilm *n.* microfilme

micrometer *n.* micrómetro

microphone *n.* microfone

microprocessor *n.* microprocessador

microscope *n.* microscópio

microscopic *adj.* microscópico

microsurgery *n.* microcirurgia

microwave *n.* microondas

mid *adj.* médio

midday *n.* meio-dia

middle *adj.* médio

middleman *n.* intermediário

middling *adj.* mediano

midget *n.* anão

midnight *n.* meia-noite

midriff *n.* diafragma

midst *adj.* meio

midsummer *adj.* solistício do verão

midway *adv.* a meio caminho

midwife *n.* parteira

might *v.* poder

mighty *adj.* poderoso

migraine *n.* enxaqueca

migrant *n.* migrante

migrate *v.* migrar

migration *n.* migração

mild *adj.* suave

mile *n.* milha

mileage *n.* quilometragem

milestone *n.* marco miliário

milieu *n.* meio social

militant *adj.* militante

militant *n.* militante

military *adj.* militar

militate *v.* militar

militia *n.* milícia

milk *n.* leite

milkshake *n.* batido

milky *adj.* leitoso

mill *n.* moinho

millennium *n.* milénio

millet *n.* painço

milligram *n.* miligrama

millimetre *n.* milímetro

milliner *n.* modista

million *n.* milhão

millionaire *n.* milionário

millipede *n.* centopeia

mime *n.* mimo

mime *n.* mimo

mimic *n.* mímico

mimicry *n.* imitação

minaret *n.* minarete

mince *v.* picar

mind *n.* mente

mindful *adj.* atento

mindless *adj.* estúpido

mine *pron.* meu

mine *n.* mina

miner *n.* mineiro

mineral *n.* mineral

mineralogy *n.* mineralogia

minestrone *n.* minestrone

mingle *v.* misturar

mini *adj.* Mini	**misapprehend** *v.* compreender mal
miniature *adj.* miniatura	**misapprehension** *n.* equívoco
minibus *n.* miniautocarro	**misappropriate** *v.* apropriar-se mal
minicab *n.* minicarro	**misappropriation** *v.* malversação
minim *n.* mínima	**misbehave** *v.* portar-se mal
minimal *adj.* mínimo	**misbehaviour** *n.* mau comportamento
minimize *v.* minimizar	**misbelief** *n.* heresia
minimum *n.* mínimo	**miscalculate** *v.* calcular mal
minion *n.* lacaio	**miscalculation** *n.* erro de cálculo
miniskirt *n.* minissaia	**miscarriage** *n.* insucesso
minister *n.* ministro	**miscarry** *v.* abortar
ministerial *adj.* governamental	**miscellaneous** *adj.* diverso
ministry *n.* ministério	**mischance** *n.* infortúnio
mink *n.* vison	**mischief** *n.* travessura
minor *adj.* menor	**mischievous** *adj.* malicioso
minority *n.* minoria	**misconceive** *v.* compreender mal
minster *n.* catedral	**misconception** *n.* equívoco
mint *n.* hortelã	**misconduct** *n.* mau comportamento
minus *prep.* menos	**misconstrue** *v.* interpretar mal
minuscule *adj.* minúscula	**miscreant** *n.* canalha
minute *n.* minuto	**misdeed** *n.* delito
minute *adj.* minucioso	**misdemeanour** *n.* contravenção
minutely *adv.* minuciosamente	**misdirect** *v.* equivocar
minx *n.* sirigaita	**miser** *n.* avarento
miracle *n.* milagre	**miserable** *adj.* miserável
miraculous *adj.* milagroso	**miserly** *adj.* avarento
mirage *n.* miragem	**misery** *n.* miséria
mire *n.* lamaçal	**misfire** *v.* falhar alvo
mirror *n.* espelho	**misfit** *n.* inadaptado
mirth *n.* alegria	**misfortune** *n.* infortúnio
mirthful *adj.* alegre	**misgive** *v.* causar apreensões
misadventure *n.* contratempo	**misgiving** *n.* apreensão
misalliance *n.* ligação desigual	**misguide** *v.* desencaminhar
misapply *v.* aplicar mal	**mishandle** *v.* maltratar

mishap n. revés
misinform v. informar mal
misinterpret v. interpretar mal
misjudge v. menosprezar
mislay v. extraviar
mislead v. enganar
mismanagement n. desgoverno
mismatch n. incompatibilidade
misnomer n. nome impróprio
misplace v. deslocar
misprint n. erro de impressão
misquote v. citar mal
misread v. interpretar mal
misrepresent v. deturpar
misrule n. desgoverno
miss v. perder
miss n. menina solteira
missile n. míssil
missing adj. desaparecido
mission n. missão
missionary n. missionário
missive n. missiva
misspell v. soletrar mal
mist n. névoa
mistake n. erro
mistaken adj. equivocado
mistletoe n. visco-branco
mistreat v. maltratar
mistress n. amante
mistrust v. desconfiar
misty adj. nebuloso
misunderstand v. compreender mal
misunderstanding n. mal-entendido
misuse v. fazer mau uso

mite n. ácaro
mitigate v. mitigar
mitigation n. mitigação
mitre n. mitra
mitten n. luva de lã
mix v. misturar
mixer n. batedeira
mixture n. mistura
moan n. gemido
moat n. fosso
mob n. mulridão
mobile adj. móvel
mobility n. mobilidade
mobilize v. mobilizar
mocha n. moca
mock v. zombar
mockery n. zombaria
modality n. modalidade
mode n. modo
model n. modelo
modem n. modem
moderate adj. moderada
moderation n. moderação
moderator n. moderador
modern adj. moderno
modernity n. modernidade
modernize v. modernizar
modernism n. modernismo
modest adj. modesto
modesty n. modéstia
modicum n. bocadinho
modification n. modificação
modify v.t. modificar
modish adj. à moda

modulate v. modular
module n. módulo
moil v. trabalhar duro
moist adj. húmido
moisten v. humedecer
moisture n. humidade
moisturize v. hidratar
molar n. molar
molasses n. melaço
mole n. toupeira
molecular adj. molecular
molecule n. molécula
molest v. molestar
molestation n. molestação
mollify v. tranquilizar
molten adj. fundido
moment n. momento
momentary adj. momentâneo
momentous adj. importante
momentum n. ímpeto
monarch n. monarca
monarchy n. monarquia
monastery n. mosteiro
monastic adj. monástico
monasticism n. monaquismo
Monday n. Segunda-feira
monetarism n. monetarismo
monetary adj. monetário
money n. dinheiro
monger n. vendedor
mongoose n. mangusto
mongrel n. mestiço
monitor n. monitor
monitory adj. monitorial

monk n. monge
monkey n. macaco
mono n. mono
monochrome n. monocromático
monocle n. monóculo
monocular adj. monocular
monody n. monólogo
monogamy n. monogamia
monogram n. monograma
monograph n. monografia
monolatry n. monolatria
monolith n. monolito
monologue n. monólogo
monophonic adj. monofónico
monopolist n. monopolista
monopolize v. monopolizar
monopoly n. monopólio
monorail n. monocarril
monosyllable n. monossílabo
monotheism n. monoteísmo
monotheist n. monoteísta
monotonous adj. monótono
monotony n. monotonia
monsoon n. monção
monster n. monstro
monstrous n. monstruoso
monstrous adj. monstruoso
montage n. montagem
month n. mês
monthly adj. mensal
monument n. monumento
monumental adj. monumental
moo v. mugir
mood n. humor

moody adj. mal-humorado	**mortgagee** n. credor hipotecário
moon n. lua	**mortgagor** n. hipotecário
moonlight n. luar	**mortify** v. mortificar
moor n. charco	**mortuary** n. mortuário
moorings n. amarras	**mosaic** n. mosaico
moot adj. discutível	**mosque** n. mesquita
mop n. esfregona	**mosquito** n. mosquito
mope v. entristecer	**moss** n. musgo
moped n. ciclomotor	**most** n. a maioria
moraine n. morena	**mote** n. partícula
moral adj. moral	**motel** n. motel
morale n. moral	**moth** n. mariposa
moralist n. moralista	**mother** n. mãe
morality n. moralidade	**motherboard** n. motherboard
moralize v. moralizar	**motherhood** n. maternidade
morass n. pântano	**mother-in-law** n. sogra
morbid adj. mórbido	**motherly** adj. maternal
morbidity adv. morbidez	**motif** n. motivo
more n. mais	**motion** n. movimento
moreover adv. além disso	**motionless** adj. imóvel
morganatic adj. morganático	**motivate** v. motivar
morgue n. morgue	**motivation** n. motivação
moribund adj. moribundo	**motive** n. motivo
morning n. manhã	**motley** adj. multicolor
moron n. idiota	**motor** n. motor
morose adj. rabugento	**motorcycle** n. motocicleta
morphine n. morfina	**motorist** n. motorista
morphology n. morfologia	**motorway** n. autoestrada
morrow n. dia seguinte	**mottle** n. mosqueado
morsel n. bocado	**motto** n. moto
mortal adj. mortal	**mould** n. bolor
mortality n. mortalidade	**moulder** v. apoderecer
mortar n. argamassa.	**moulding** n. modelagem
mortgage n. hipoteca	**moult** v. mudar as penas

mound n. montículo	**mug** n. caneca
mount v. montar	**muggy** adj. mormacento
mountain n. montanha	**mulatto** n. mulato
mountaineer n. montanhista	**mulberry** n. amoreira
mountaineering n. montanhismo	**mule** n. mula
mountainous adj. montanhoso	**mulish** adj. obstinado
mourn v. lamentar	**mull** v. ponderar
mourner n. enlutado	**mullah** n. mullah
mournful adj. lúgubre	**mullion** n. batente
mourning n. luto	**multicultural** adj. multicultural
mouse n. rato	**multifarious** adj. múltiplo
mousse n. mousse	**multiform** adj. multiforme
moustache n. bigode	**multilateral** adj. multilateral
mouth n. boca	**multimedia** n. multimédia
mouthful n. bocado	**multiparous** adj. multíparo
movable adj. móvel	**multiple** adj. múltiplo
move v. mover	**multiplex** n. multiplex
movement n. movimento	**multiplication** n. multiplicação
mover n. movedor	**multiplicity** n. multiplicidade
movies n. filmes	**multiply** v. multiplicar
moving adj. em movimento	**multitude** n. multidão
mow v. cortar	**mum** n. mãe
mozzarella n. mozzarella	**mumble** v. resmungar
much pron. muito	**mummer** n. ator de pantominas
mucilage n. mucilagem	**mummify** v. mumificar
muck n. esterco	**mummy** n. múmia
mucous adj. mucoso	**mumps** n. papeira
mucus n. muco	**munch** v. mastigar
mud n. lama	**mundane** adj. mundano
muddle v. atrapalhar	**municipal** adj. municipal
muesli n. muesli	**municipality** n. municipalidade
muffin n. queque	**munificent** adj. magnânimo
muffle v. abafar	**muniment** n. proteção militar
muffler n. amortecedor	**munitions** n. munições

mural *n.* mural	**mutinous** *adj.* amotinado
murder *n.* assassinato	**mutiny** *n.* revolta
murderer *n.* assassino	**mutter** *v.* murmurar
murk *n.* escuridão	**mutton** *n.* carneiro
murky *adj.* sombrio	**mutual** *adj.* mútuo
murmur *v.* murmurar	**muzzle** *n.* focinho
muscle *n.* músculo	**muzzy** *adj.* enfadonho
muscovite *n.* moscovita	**my** *adj.* meu
muscular *adj.* muscular	**myalgia** *n.* mialgia
muse *n.* musa	**myopia** *n.* miopia
museum *n.* museu	**myopic** *adj.* míope
mush *n.* papas	**myosis** *n.* miose
mushroom *n.* cogumelo	**myriad** *n.* miríade
music *n.* música	**myrrh** *n.* mirra
musical *adj.* musical	**myrtle** *n.* murta
musician *n.* músico	**myself** *pron.* eu mesmo
musk *n.* almíscar	**mysterious** *adj.* misterioso
musket *n.* mosquete	**mystery** *n.* mistério
musketeer *n.* mosqueteiro	**mystic** *n.* místico
Muslim *n.* Muçulmano	**mystical** *adj.* mágico
muslin *n.* musselina	**mysticism** *n.* misticismo
mussel *n.* mexilhão	**mystify** *v.* mistificar
must *v.* dever	**mystique** *n.* mística
mustang *n.* mustang (cavalo selvagem)	**myth** *n.* mito
mustard *n.* mostarda	**mythical** *adj.* mítico
muster *v.* reunir	**mythological** *adj.* lendário
musty *adj.* bolorento	**mythology** *n.* mitologia
mutable *adj.* mutável	
mutate *v.* mutar	
mutation *n.* mutação	
mutative *adj.* mutação	**nab** *v.* agarrar
mute *adj.* mudo	**nabob** *n.* nababo
mutilate *v.* mutilar	**nacho** *n.* nacho
mutilation *n.* mutilação	**nadir** *n.* nadir
	nag *v.t.* importunar

nail *n.* unha	**natty** *adj.* elegante
naivety *n.* ingenuidade	**natural** *adj.* natural
naked *adj.* nu	**naturalist** *n.* naturalista
name *n.* nome	**naturalize** *v.* naturalizar
namely *n.* nomeadamente	**naturalization** *n.* naturalização
namesake *n.* homónimo	**naturally** *adv.* naturalmente
nanny *n.* ama	**nature** *n.* natureza
nap *n.* soneca	**naturism** *n.* naturismo
nape *n.* nuca	**naughty** *adj.* desobediente
naphthalene *n.* naftalina	**nausea** *n.* náusea
napkin *n.* guardanapo	**nauseate** *v.* enjoar
nappy *n.* fralda	**nauseous** *adj.* nauseabundo
narcissism *n.* narcisismo	**nautical** *adj.* náutico
narcissus *n.* narciso	**naval** *adj.* naval
narcotic *n.* narcótico	**nave** *n.* nave
narrate *v.* narrar	**navigable** *adj.* navegável
narration *n.* narração	**navigate** *v.* navegar
narrative *n.* narrativa	**navigation** *n.* navegação
narrator *n.* narrador	**navigator** *n.* navegador
narrow *adj.* estreito	**navy** *n.* marinha
nasal *adj.* nasal	**nay** *adv.* ou melhor
nascent *adj.* nascente	**near** *adv.* perto
nasty *adj.* desagradável	**nearby** *adv.* próximo
natal *adj.* natal	**near** *v.i.* aproximar
natant *adj.* nadante	**nearest** *adj.* o mais próximo
nation *n.* nação	**nearly** *adv.* quase
national *adj.* nacional	**neat** *adj.* puro
nationalism *n.* nacionalismo	**nebula** *n.* nébula
nationalist *n.* nacionalista	**nebulous** *adj.* nebuloso
nationality *n.* nacionalidade	**necessarily** *adv.* necessariamente
nationalization *n.* nacionalização	**necessary** *adj.* necessário
nationalize *v.* nacionalizar	**necessitate** *v.* necessitar
native *n.* nativo	**necessity** *n.* necessidade
nativity *n.* nascimento	**neck** *n.* pescoço

necklace *n.* colar
necklet *n.* gola
necromancy *n.* necromancia
necropolis *n.* necrópole
nectar *n.* néctar
nectarine *n.* nectarina
need *v.* necessidade
needful *adj.* necessário
needle *n.* agulha
needless *adj.* desnecessário
needy *adj.* necessitado
nefarious *adj.* nefasto
negate *v.* negar
negation *n.* negação
negative *adj.* negativo
negativity *n.* negatividade
neglect *v.* negligenciar
negligence *n.* negligência
negligent *adj.* negligente
negligible *adj.* desprezível
negotiable *adj.* negociável
negotiate *v.* negociar
negotiation *n.* negociação
negotiator *n.* negociador
negress *n.* preta
negro *n.* negro
neigh *n.* relincho
neighbour *n.* vizinho
neighbourhood *n.* vizinhança
neighbourly *adj.* sociável
neither *adj.* nem
nemesis *n.* vingança
neoclassical *adj.* neoclássico
Neolithic *adj.* Neolítico

neon *n.* néon
neophyte *n.* neófito
nephew *n.* sobrinho
nepotism *n.* nepotismo
Neptune *n.* Neptuno
nerd *n.* totó
Nerve *n.* nervo
nerveless *adj.* sem nervos
nervous *adj.* nervoso
nervy *adj.* nervoso
nest *n.* ninho
nestle *v.* aninhar
nestling *n.* aninhada
net *n.* rede
nether *adj.* inferior
netting *n.* pesca à rede
nettle *n.* urtiga
network *n.* rede
neural *adj.* neural
neurologist *n.* neurologista
neurology *n.* neurologia
neurosis *n.* neurose
neurotic *adj.* neurótico
neuter *adj.* neutro
neutral *adj.* neutral
neutralize *v.* neutralizar
neutron *n.* neutrão
never *adv.* nunca
nevertheless *adv.* não obstante
new *adj.* novo
newly *adv.* recentemente
news *n.* notícia
next *adj.* próximo
nexus *n.* nexo

nib n. bico

nibble v. mordidela

nice adj. bom

nicety n. escrúpulo

niche n. nicho

nick n. entalhe

nickel n. níquel

nickname n. apelido

nicotine n. nicotina

niece n. sobrinha

niggard n. mesquinho

niggardly adj. mesquinho

nigger n. preto

niggle v. mesquinhar

nigh adv. quase

night n. noite

nightingale n. rouxinol

nightmare n. pesadelo

nightie n. camisa de noite

nihilism n. niilismo

nil n. nada

nimble adj. ágil

nimbus n. nimbo

nine adj. & n. nove

nineteen adj. & n. dezanove

nineteenth adj. & n. décimo nono

ninetieth adj. & n. nonagésimo

ninth adj. & n. nono

ninety adj. & n. noventa

nip v. beliscar

nipple n. mamilo

nippy adj. picante

nirvana n. nirvana

nitrogen n. nitrogénio

no adj. não

nobility n. nobreza

noble adj. nobre

nobleman n. nobre

nobody pron. ninguém

nocturnal adj. noturno

nod v. acenar

node n. nó

noise n. ruído

noisy adj. barulhento

nomad n. nómado

nomadic adj. nómado

nomenclature n. nomenclatura

nominal adj. nominal

nominate v. nomear

nomination n. nomeação

nominee n. nomeado

non-alignment n. não-alinhamento

nonchalance n. indiferença

nonchalant adj. indiferente

nonconformist n. inconformista

none pron. nenhum

nonentity n. nulidade

nonplussed adj. perplexo

nonetheless a. no entanto,

nonpareil adj. incomparável

nonplussed adj. embaraçado

nonsense n. absurdo

nonstop adj. direto

noodles n. macarronete

nook n. recanto

noon n. meio-dia

noose n. armadilha

nor conj. nem

Nordic adj. Nórdico

norm n. norma

normal adj. normal

normalcy n. normalidade

normalize v. normalizar

normative adj. normativo

north n. norte

northerly adj. norte

northern adj. do norte

nose n. nariz

nostalgia n. nostalgia

nostril n. narina

nostrum n. droga

nosy adj. intrometido

not adv. nem

notable adj. notável

notary n. notário

notation n. notação

notch n. entalhe

note n. nota

notebook n. caderno

noted adj. notável

noteworthy adj. notável

nothing pron. nada

notice n. notar

noticeable adj. perceptível

noticeboard n. quadro de notícias

notfiable adj. participação obrigatória

notification n. notificação

notify v. notificar

notion n. noção

notional adj. ideal

notoriety n. notoriedade

notorious prep. notório

notwithstanding prep. não obstante

nougat n. nogado

nought n. nada

noun n. substantivo

nourish v. nutrir

nourishment n. nutrição

novel n. novela

novelette n. novela

novelist n. romancista

novelty n. novidade

November n. Novembro

novice n. novato

now adv. agora

nowhere adv. em nenhuma parte

noxious adj. nocivo

nozzle n. bocal

nuance n. nuance

nubile a. núbil

nuclear adj. nuclear

nucleus n. núcleo

nude adj. nu

nudist n. nudista

nudity n. nudez

nudge v. acotevelar

nugatory adj. ineficaz

nugget n. pepita

nuisance n. estorvo

null adj. nulo

nullification n. anulação

nullify v. anular

numb adj. entorpecido

number n. número

numberless adj. inumerável

numeral n. numeral

numerator *n.* numerador
numerical *adj.* numérico
numerous *adj.* numeroso
nun *n.* freira
nunnery *n.* convento de freiras
nuptial *adj.* nupcial
nurse *n.* enfermeira
nursery *n.* berçário
nurture *v.* educar
nut *n.* noz
nutrient *n.* nutriente
nutrition *n.* nutrição
nutritious *adj.* nutritivo
nutritive *adj.* nutritivo
nutty *adj.* amalucado
nuzzle *v.* fossar
nylon *n.* nylon
nymph ninfa

oaf *n.* imbecil
oak *n.* carvalho
oar *n.* remo
oasis *n.* oásis
oat *n.* aveia
oath *n.* juramento
oatmeal *n.* aveia
obduracy *n.* obstinação
obdurate *adj.* obstinado
obedience *n.* obediência
obedient *adj.* obediente
obeisance *n.* obediência
obesity *n.* obesidade
obese *adj.* obeso

obey *v.* obedecer
obfuscate *v.* ofuscar
obituary *n.* obituário
object *n.* objeto
objection *n.* objeção
objectionable *adj.* censurável
objective *adj.* objetivo
objectively *adv.* objetivamente
oblation *n.* oblação
obligated *adj.* obrigado
obligation *n.* obrigação
obligatory *adj.* obrigatório
oblige *v.* obrigar
obliging *adj.* delicado
oblique *adj.* oblíquo
obliterate *v.* obliterar
obliteration *n.* obliteração
oblivion *n.* esquecimento
oblivious *adj.* esquecido
oblong *adj.* oblongo
obloquy *n.* descrédito
obnoxious *adj.* desagradável
obscene *adj.* obsceno
obscenity *n.* obscenidade
obscure *adj.* obscuro
obscurity *n.* obscuridade
observance *n.* observância
observant *adj.* observador
observation *n.* observação
observatory *n.* observatório
observe *v.* observar
obsess *v.* obcecar
obsession *n.* obsessão
obsolescent *adj.* obsolescente

obsolete *adj.* obsoleto
obstacle *n.* obstáculo
obstinacy *n* obstinação
obstinate *adj.* obstinado
obstruct *v.* obstruir
obstruction *n.* obstrução
obstructive *adj.* obstrutivo
obtain *v.* obter
obtainable *adj.* alcançável
obtrude *v.* intrometer
obtuse *adj.* obtuso
obverse *n.* anverso
obviate *v.* prevenir
obvious *adj.* óbvio
occasion *n.* ocasião
occasional *adj.* ocasional
occasionally *adv.* ocasionalmente
occident *n.* Ocidente
occidental *adj.* ocidental
occlude *v.* tapar
occult *n.* oculto
occupancy *n.* ocupação
occupant *n.* ocupante
occupation *n.* ocupação
occupational *adj.* profissional
occupy *v.* ocupar
occur *v.* ocorrer
occurrence *n.* ocorrência
ocean *n.* oceano
oceanic *adj.* oceânico
octagon *n.* octógono
octave *n.* oitava
octavo *n.* octavo
October *n.* Outubro

octogenarian *n.* octogenário
octopus *n.* polvo
octroi *n.* octroi
ocular *adj.* ocular
odd *adj.* estranho
oddity *n.* excentricidade
odds *n.* probabilidade
ode *n.* ode
odious *adj.* odioso
odium *n.* ódio
odorous *adj.* perfumado
odour *n.* odor
odyssey *n.* Odisseia
of *prep.* de
off *adv.* fora
offence *n.* ofensa
offend *v.* ofender
offender *n.* ofensor
offensive *adj.* ofensiva
offer *v.* oferecer
offering *n.* oferta
office *n.* escritório
officer *n.* oficial (militar)
official *adj.* oficial
officially *adv.* oficialmente
officiate *v.* desempenhar
officious *adj.* oficioso
offset *v.* compensar
offshoot *n.* ramificação
offshore *adj.* a pouca distância de
offside *adj.* impedido
offspring *n.* prole
oft *adv.* frequentemente
often *adv.* frequentemente

ogle v. comer (com os olhos)	**ontology** n. ontologia
oil n. óleo	**onus** n. ónus
oil a. óleo	**onward** adv. avante
oily adj. oleoso	**onyx** n. ónix
ointment n. pomada	**ooze** v.i. gotejar
okay adj. Ok	**opacity** n. opacidade
old adj. velho	**opal** n. opala
oligarchy n. oligarquia	**opaque** adj. opaco
olive n. azeitona	**open** adj. aberto
Olympic adj. olímpico	**opening** n. abertura
omelette n. omelete	**openly** adv. abertamente
omen n. presságio	**opera** n. ópera
ominous adj. ameaçador	**operate** v. operar
omission n. omissão	**operation** n. operação
omit v. omitir	**operational** adj. operacional
omnibus n. compêndio	**operative** adj. operativo
omnipotence n. omnipotência	**operator** n. operador
omnipotent adj. omnipotente	**opine** v. opinar
omnipresence n. omnipresença	**opinion** n. opinião
omnipresent adj. omnipresente	**opium** n. ópio
omniscience n. omnisciência	**opponent** n. oponente
omniscient adj. omnisciente	**opportune** adj. oportuno
on prep. em	**opportunism** n. oportunismo
once adv. uma vez	**opportunity** n. oportunidade
one n. & adj. um & um	**oppose** v. opor
oneness n. unicidade	**opposite** adj. oposto
onerous adj. oneroso	**opposition** n. oposição
oneself pron. se	**oppress** v. oprimir
onion n. cebola	**oppression** n. opressão
onlooker n. espectador	**oppressive** adj. opressivo
only adv. apenas	**oppressor** n. opressor
onomatopoeia n. omnomatopeia	**opt** v. optar
onset n. início	**optic** adj. ótico
onslaught n. investida	**optician** n. oculista

optimism *n.* otimismo

optimist *n.* otimista

optimistic *adj.* otimista

optimize *v.* otimizar

optimum *adj.* ótimo

option *n.* opção

optional *adj.* opcional

opulence *n.* opulência

opulent *adj.* opulento

or *conj.* ou

oracle *n.* oráculo

oracular *adj.* oracular

oral *adj.* oral

orally *adv.* oralmente

orange *n.* laranja

oration *n.* oração

orator *n.* orador

oratory *n.* oratória

orb *n.* orbe

orbit *n.* órbita

orbital *adj.* orbital

orchard *n.* pomar

orchestra *n.* orquestra

orchestral *adj.* orquestral

orchid *n.* orquídea

ordeal *n.* prova

order *n.* ordem

orderly *adj.* metódico

ordinance *n.* portaria

ordinarily *adv.* normalmente

ordinary *adj.* comum

ordnance *n.* artilharia

ore *n.* minério

organ *n.* órgão

organic *adj.* orgânico

organism *n.* organismo

organization *n.* organização

organize *v.* organizar

orgasm *n.* orgasmo

orgy *n.* orgia

orient *n.* oriente

oriental *adj.* oriental

orientate *v.* orientar

origami *n.* origami

origin *n.* origem

original *adj.* original

originality *n.* originalidade

originate *v.* originar

originator *n.* originador

ornament *n.* ornamento

ornamental *adj.* ornamental

ornamentation *n.* ornamentação

ornate *adj.* ornamentado

orphan *n.* órfão

orphanage *n.* orfanato

orthodox *adj.* ortodoxo

orthodoxy *n.* ortodoxia

orthopaedics *n.* ortopedia

oscillate *v.* oscilar

oscillation *n.* oscilação

ossify *v.* ossificar

ostensible *adj.* ostensivo

ostentation *n.* ostentação

osteopathy *n.* osteopatia

ostracize *v.* ostracizar

ostrich *n.* avestruz

other *adj. & pron.* outro & outro

otherwise *adv.* senão

otiose *adj.* ocioso	**outmoded** *adj.* fora de moda
otter *n.* lontra	**outnumber** *v.* exceder
ottoman *n.* divã	**outpatient** *n.* ambulatorial (doente)
ounce *n.* onça	**outpost** *n.* posto avançado (militar)
our *adj.* nosso	**output** *n.* rendimento
ourselves *pron.* nós mesmos	**outrage** *n.* ultraje
oust *v.* expulsar	**outrageous** *adj.* ultrajante
out *adv.* fora	**outrider** *n.* criado
outbid *v.* ultrapassar	**outright** *adv.* total
outboard *adj.* para o exterior	**outrun** *v.* ultrapassar
outbreak *n.* surto	**outset** *n.* início
outburst *n.* explosão	**outshine** *v.* ofuscar
outcast *n.* pária	**outside** *n.* fora
outclass *v.* ultrapassar	**outsider** *n.* forasteiro
outcome *n.* resultado	**outsize** *adj.* desmedido
outcry *n.* algazarra	**outskirts** *n.* periferia
outdated *adj.* desatualizado	**outsource** *v.* terceirizar
outdo *v.* exceder	**outspoken** *adj.* franco
outdoor *adj.* exterior	**outstanding** *adj.* marcante
outer *adj.* externo	**outstrip** *v.* ultrapassar
outfit *n.* equipamento	**outward** *adj.* exterior
outgoing *adj.* extrovertido	**outwardly** *adv.* exteriormente
outgrow *v.* superar	**outweigh** *v.* ultrapassar (em peso)
outhouse *n.* telheiro	**outwit** *v.* despistar
outing *n.* passeio	**oval** *adj.* oval
outlandish *adj.* estranho	**ovary** *n.* ovário
outlast *v.* sobreviver	**ovate** *adj.* ovadas
outlaw *n.* bandido	**ovation** *n.* ovação
outlay *n.* despesas	**oven** *n.* forno
outlet *n.* saída	**over** *prep.* sobre
outline *n.* contorno	**overact** *v.* exagerar
outlive *v.* sobreviver	**overall** *adj.* global
outlook *n.* perspectiva	**overawe** *v.* intimidar
outlying *adj.* afastado	**overbalance** *v.* desequilibrar

overbearing *adj.* arrogante
overblown *adj.* empolado
overboard *adv.* pela borda fora
overburden *v.* sobrecarregar
overcast *adj.* entristecido
overcharge *v.* sobrecarregar
overcoat *n.* sobretudo
overcome *v.* superar
overdo *v.* exagerar
overdose *n.* overdose
overdraft *n.* débito a descoberto
overdraw *v.* exagerar
overdrive *n.* overdrive
overdue *adj.* atrasado
overestimate *v.* exagerar
overflow *v.* transbordar
overgrown *adj.* coberto
overhaul *v.* inspecionar
overhead *adv.* em cima
overhear *v.* ouvir por
overjoyed *adj.* radiante
overlap *v.* sobrepor
overleaf *adv.* no verso
overload *v.* sobrecarregar
overlook *v.* negligenciar
overly *adv.* excessivamente
overnight *adv.* de noite
overpass *n.* passagem elevada
overpower *v.* dominar
overrate *v.* sobrestimar
overreach *v.* exceder
overreact *v.* dramatize
override *v.* ultrapassar

overrule *v.* anular
overrun *v.* invadir
overseas *adv.* no exterior
oversee *v.* vigiar
overseer *n.* supervisor
overshadow *v.* ofuscar
overshoot *v.* ultrapassar
oversight *n.* fiscalização
overspill *n.* derramamento
overstep *v.* exceder
overt *adj.* evidente
overtake *v.* ultrapassar
overthrow *v.* derrubar
overtime n horas extras
overtone *n.* conotação
overture *n.* abertura
overturn *v.* derrubar
overview *n.* visão global
overweening *adj.* presunçoso
overwhelm *v.* oprimir
overwrought *adj.* extenuado
ovulate *v.* ovular
owe *n.* dever
owing *adj.* devido
owl *n.* coruja
own *adj.* próprio
owner *n.* proprietário
ownership *n.* propriedade
ox *n.* boi
oxide *n.* óxido
oxygen *n.* oxigénio
oyster *n.* ostra
ozone n ozónio

P

pace *n.* passo
pacemaker *n.* pacemaker
pacific *n.* pacífico
pacifist *n.* pacifista
pacify *v.* pacificar
pack *n.* pacote
package *n.* embalagem
packet *n.* pacote
packing *n.* embalagem
pact *n.* pacto
pad *n.* almofada
padding *n.* acolchoamento
paddle *n.* pagaia
paddock *n.* cercado para cavalos
padlock *n.* cadeado
paddy *n.* arroz com casca
paediatrician *n.* pediatra
paediatrics *n.* pediatria
paedophile *n.* pedófilo
pagan *n.* pagão
page *n.* página
pageant *n.* espetáculo
pageantry *n.* pompa
pagoda *n.* pagode
pail *n.* balde
pain *n.* dor
painful *adj.* doloroso
painkiller *n.* analgésico
painstaking *adj.* meticuloso
paint *n.* pintar
painter *n.* pintor
painting *n.* pintura

pair *n.* par
paisley *n.* desenho (padrão tecido)
pal *n.* amigo
palace *n.* palácio
palatable *adj.* saboroso
palatal *adj.* palatal
palate *n.* paladar
palatial *adj.* grandioso
pale *adj.* pálido
palette *n.* paleta
paling *n.* paliçada
pall *n.* mortalha
pallet *n.* palete
palm *n.* palma
palmist *n.* quiromante
palmistry *n.* quiromantia
palpable *adj.* palpável
palpitate *v.* palpitar
palpitation *n.* palpitação
palsy *n.* paralisia
paltry *adj.* insignificante
pamper *v.* deleitar
pamphlet *n.* panfleto
pamphleteer *n.* panfletista
pan *n.* panela
panacea *n.* panaceia
panache *n.* penacho
pancake *n.* panqueca
pancreas *n.* pâncreas
panda *n.* panda
pandemonium *n.* pandemónio
pane *n.* vidraça
panegyric *n.* panegírico
panel *n.* painel

pang *n.* angústia

panic *n.* pânico

panorama *n.* panorama

pant *v.* arfar

pantaloon *n.* calças

pantheism *n.* panteísmo

pantheist *adj.* panteísta

panther *n.* pantera

panties *n.* calcinhas

pantomime *n.* pantomima

pantry *n.* despensa

pants *n.* calças

papacy *n.* papado

papal *adj.* papal

paper *n.* papel

paperback *n.* brochura

par *n.* paridade

parable *n.* parábola

parachute *n.* paraquedas

parachutist *n.* paraquedista

parade *n.* desfile

paradise *n.* paraíso

paradox *n.* paradoxo

paradoxical *adj.* paradoxal

paraffin *n.* parafina

paragon *n.* protótipo

paragraph *n.* parágrafo

parallel *n.* paralelo

parallelogram *n.* paralelograma

paralyse *v.* paralisar

paralysis *n.* paralisia

paralytic *adj.* paralítico

paramedic *n.* paramédico

parameter *n.* parâmetro

paramount *adj.* supremo

paramour *n.* amante

paraphernalia *n.* parafernália

paraphrase *v.* parafrasear

parasite *n.* parasita

parasol *n.* guarda-sol

parcel *n.* parcela

parched *adj.* ressequido

pardon *n.* perdão

pardonable *adj.* perdoável

pare *v.* aparar

parent *n.* parente

parentage *n.* parentesco

parental *adj.* parental

parenthesis *n.* parênteses

pariah *n.* pária

parish *n.* paróquia

parity *n.* paridade

park *n.* parque

parky *adj.* cortante

parlance *n.* linguagem

parley *n.* parlamentar

parliament *n.* parlamento

parliamentarian *n.* parlamentar

parliamentary *adj.* parlamentar

parlour *n.* salão

parochial *adj.* paroquial

parody *n.* paródia

parole *n.* palavra de honra (militar)

parricide *n.* parricídio

parrot *n.* papagaio

parry *v.* desviar

parse *v.* analisar

parsimony *n.* parcimónia

parson n. pastor	**pastry** n. pastelaria
part n. parte	**pasture** n. pasto
partake v. participar	**pasty** n. pastoso
partial adj. parcial	**pat** v. acariciar
partiality n. parcialidade	**patch** n. remendo
participate v. participar	**patchy** adj. desigual
participant n. participante	**patent** n. patente
participation n. participação	**paternal** adj. paternal
particle n. partícula	**paternity** n. paternidade
particular adj. especial	**path** n. caminho
parting n. despedida	**pathetic** adj. patético
partisan n. partidário	**pathology** n. patologia
partition n. divisória	**pathos** n. patético
partly adv. parcialmente	**patience** n. paciência
partner n. parceiro	**patient** adj. paciente
partnership n. parceria	**patient** n. paciente
party n. festa	**patio** n. pátio
pass v. passar	**patisserie** n. pastelaria
passable adj. passável	**patriarch** n. patriarca
passage n. passagem	**patricide** n. paticídio
passenger n. passageiro	**patrimony** n. património
passing adj. passante	**patriot** n. patriota
passion n. paixão	**patriotic** adj. patriótico
passionate adj. apaixonado	**patriotism** n. patriotismo
passive adj. passiva	**patrol** v. patrulha
passport n. passaporte	**patron** n. protetor
past adj. passado	**patronage** n. patrocínio
pasta n. massa	**patronize** v. apadrinhar
paste n. pasta	**pattern** n. padrão
pastel n. pastel	**patty** n. empada
pasteurized adj. pasteurizado	**paucity** n. escassez
pastime n. passatempo	**paunch** n. pança
pastor n. pastor	**pauper** n. indigente
pastoral adj. pastoral	**pause** n. pausa

pave *v.* pavimentar
pavement *n.* calçada
pavilion *n.* pavilhão
paw *n.* pata
pawn *n.* peão
pawnbroker *n.* penhorista
pay *v.* pagar
payable *n.* pagável
payee *n.* beneficiário
payment *n.* pagamento
pea *n.* ervilha
peace *n.* paz
peaceable *adj.* pacífico
peaceful *adj.* pacífico
peach *n.* pêssego
peacock *n.* pavão
peahen *n.* pavoa
peak *n.* pico
peaky *adj.* pálido
peal *n.* repique
peanut *n.* amendoim
pear *n.* pera
pearl *n.* pérola
peasant *n.* camponês
peasantry *n.* camponeses
pebble *n.* seixo
pecan *n.* noz-pecã
peck *v.i.* bicar
peculiar *adj.* peculiar
pedagogue *n.* pedagogo
pedagogy *n.* pedagogia
pedal *n.* pedal
pedant *n.* pedante
pedantic *adj.* pedante

peddle *v.* traficar
pedestal *n.* pedestal
pedestrian *n.* pedestre
pedicure *n.* pedicure
pedigree *n.* linhagem
pedlar *n.* vendedor ambulante
pedometer *n.* pedómetro
peek *v.* espreitar
peel *n.* casca
peep *v.* piar
peer *n.* par
peer *v.* perscrutar
peerage *n.* nobreza
peerless *adj.* inigualável
peg *n.* cavilha
pejorative *adj.* pejorativo
pelican *n.* pelicano
pellet *n.* bolinha
pelmet *n.* sanefa
pelt *v.* couro
pelvis *n.* pélvis
pen *n.* caneta
penal *adj.* penal
penalize *v.* penalizar
penalty *n.* pena
penance *n.* penitência
penchant *n.* inclinação
pencil *n.* lápis
pendant *n.* pingente
pendent *adj.* pendente
pending *adj.* pendente
pendulum *n.* pêndulo
penetrate *v.* penetrar
penetration *n.* penetração

penguin *n.* pinguim	**perforce** *adv.* necessariamente
peninsula *n.* península	**perform** *v.* realizar
penis *n.* pénis	**performance** *n.* atuação
penitent *adj.* penitente	**performer** *n.* executante
penniless *adj.* pobre	**perfume** *n.* perfume
penny *n.* centavo	**perfume** *adv.* perfume
pension *n.* pensão	**perfunctory** *adj.* superficial
pensioner *n.* pensionista	**perhaps** *adv.* talvez
pensive *adj.* pensativo	**peril** *n.* perigo
pentagon *n.* pentágono	**perilous** *adj.* perigoso
penthouse *n.* penthouse	**period** *n.* período
penultimate *adj.* penúltimo	**periodic** *adj.* periódico
people *n.* pessoas	**periodical** *adj.* periódico
pepper *n.* pimenta	**periphery** *n.* periferia
peppermint *n.* hortelã-pimenta	**perish** *v.* perecer
peptic *adj.* péptico	**perishable** *adj.* perecível
per *prep.* por	**perjure** *v.* mentir
perambulate *v.t.* perambular	**perjury** *n.* perjúrio
perceive *v.* perceber	**perk** *v.* revigorar
perceptible *adj.* perceptível	**perky** *adj.* empertigado
percentage *n.* percentagem	**permanence** *n.* permanência
perceptible *adj.* perceptível	**permanent** *adj.* permanente
perception *n.* percepção	**permeable** *adj.* permeável
perceptive *adj.* perceptivo	**permissible** *adj.* permissível
perch *n.* poleiro	**permission** *n.* permissão
percipient *adj.* perceptivo	**permissive** *adj.* permissivo
percolate *v.* coar	**permit** *v.* permitir
percolator *n.* coador	**permutation** *n.* permutação
perdition *n.* perdição	**pernicious** *adj.* pernicioso
perennial *adj.* perene	**perpendicular** *adj.* perpendicular
perfect *adj.* perfeito	**perpetrate** *v.* perpetrar
perfection *n.* perfeição	**perpetual** *adj.* perpétuo
perfidious *adj.* pérfida	**perpetuate** *v.t.* perpetuar
perforate *v.* perfurar	**perplex** *v.* complicar

perplexity n. perplexidade
perquisite n. regalia
Perry n. Perry (bebida alcoólica)
persecute v. perseguir
persecution n. perseguição
perseverance n. perseverança
persevere v.i. perseverar
persist v. persistir
persistence n. persistência
persistent adj. persistente
person n. pessoa
persona n. personalidade
personage n. personagem
personal adj. pessoal
personality n. personalidade
personification n. personificação
personify v. personificar
personnel n. pessoal
perspective n. perspectiva
perspicuous adj. límpido
perspiration n. transpiração
perspire v.t. transpirar
persuade v. persuadir
persuasion n. persuasão
pertain v. pertencer
pertinent adj. pertinente
perturb v. perturbar
perusal n. leitura (cuidadosa)
peruse v. considerar
pervade v. impregnar
perverse adj. perverso
perversion n. perversão
perversity n. perversidade
pervert v. perverter

pessimism n. pessimismo
pessimist n. pessimista
pessimistic adj. pessimista
pest n. praga
pester v. atazanar
pesticide n. pesticida
pestilence n. peste
pet n. animal de estimação
petal n. pétala
petite adj. diminuto
petition n. petição
petitioner n. peticionário
petrify v. petrificar
petrol n. gasolina
petroleum n. petróleo
petticoat n. saiote
pettish adj. rabugento
petty adj. pequeno
petulance n. petulância
petulant adj. petulante
phantom n. fantasma
pharmaceutical adj. farmacêutico
pharmacist n. farmacêutico
pharmacy n. farmácia
phase n. fase
phenomenal adj. fenomenal
phenomenon n. fenómeno
phial n. frasco
philanthropic adj. filantrópico
philanthropist n. filantropo
philanthropy n. filantropia
philately n. filatelia
philological adj. filológico
philologist n. filólogo

philology *n.* filologia

philosopher *n.* filósofo

philosophical *adj.* filosófico

philosophy *n.* filosofia

phlegmatic *adj.* fleumático

phobia *n.* fobia

phoenix *n.* fénix

phone *n.* telefone

phonetic *adj.* fonético

phosphate *n.* fosfato

phosphorus *n.* fósforo

photo *n.* foto

photocopy *n.* fotocópia

photograph *n.* fotografia

photographer *n.* fotógrafo

photographic *adj.* fotográfico

photography *n.* fotografia

photostat *n.* fotocopiadora

phrase *n.* frase

phraseology *n.* fraseologia

physical *adj.* físico

physician *n.* médico

physics *n.* física

physiognomy *n.* fisionomia

physiotherapy *n.* fisioterapia

physique *n.* físico

pianist *n.* pianista

piano *n.* piano

piazza *n.* praça

pick *v.* escolher

picket *n.* piquete

pickings *n.* sobras

pickle *n.* conserva

picnic *n.* piquenique

pictograph *n.* pictograma

pictorial *adj.* pictórico

picture *n.* quadro

picturesque *adj.* pitoresco

pie *n.* tarte

piece *n.* peça

piecemeal *adv.* fragmentário

pier *n.* paredão

pierce *v.* penetrar

piety *n.* piedade

pig *n.* porco

pigeon *n.* pombo

pigeonhole *n.* ninho de pombo

piggery *n.* pocilga

pigment *n.* pigmento

pigmy *n.* pigmeu

pike *n.* pique

pile *n.* monte

pilfer *v.* furtar

pilgrim *n.* peregrino

pilgrimage *n.* peregrinação

pill *n.* pílula

pillar *n.* pilar

pillow *n.* travesseiro

pilot *n.* piloto

pimple *n.* borbulha

pin *n.* alfinete

pincer *n.* pinça

pinch *v.* beliscar

pine *v.* pinho

pineapple *n.* ananás

pink *adj.* rosa

pinnacle *n.* pináculo

pinpoint *v.* apontar

pint *n.* quartilho
pioneer *n.* pioneiro
pious *adj.* piedoso
pipe *n.* tubo
pipette *n.* pipeta
piquant *adj.* picante
pique *n.* ressentimento
piracy *n.* pirataria
pirate *n.* pirata
pistol *n.* pistola
piston *n.* pistão
pit *n.* cova
pitch *n.* passo
pitcher *n.* jarro
piteous *adj.* lamentável
pitfall *n.* armadilha
pitiful *adj.* lamentável
pitiless *adj.* impiedoso
pity *n.* pena
pivot *n.* eixo
pivotal *adj.* giratório
pixel *n.* pixel
pizza *n.* pizza
placard *n.* letreiro
placate *v.* aplacar
place *n.* lugar
placement *n.* localização
placid *adj.* plácido
plague *n.* praga
plain *adj.* liso
plaintiff *n.* queixoso
plaintive *adj.* lamurioso
plait *n.* trança
plan *n.* plano

plane *n.* avião
planet *n.* planeta
planetary *adj.* planetário
plank *n.* prancha
plant *n.* planta
plantain *n.* tanchagem
plantation *n.* plantação
plaque *n.* placa
plaster *n.* gesso
plastic *n.* plástico
plate *n.* prato
plateau *n.* planalto
platelet *n.* plaqueta
platform *n.* plataforma
platinum *n.* platina
platonic *adj.* platónico
platoon *n.* pelotão
platter *n.* travessa
plaudits *n.* aplausos
plausible *adj.* plausível
play *v.i.* jogar
playground *n.* recreio
playwright *n.* dramaturgo
player *n.* jogador
plaza *n.* praça
plea *n.* apelo
plead *v.* alegar
pleasant *adj.* agradável
pleasantry *n.* jovialidade
please *v.* por favor
pleasure *n.* prazer
pleat *n.* prega
plebeian *adj.* plebeu
plebiscite *n.* plebiscito

pledge *n.* penhor	**pod** *n.* vagem
plenty *pron.* abundância	**podcast** *n.* podcast
plethora *n.* pletora	**podium** *n.* pódio
pliable *adj.* maleável	**poem** *n.* poema
pliant *adj.* flexível	**poet** *n.* poeta
pliers *n.* alicate	**poetry** *n.* poesia
plight *n.* apuro	**poignancy** *n.* mordacidade
plinth *n.* plinto	**poignant** *adj.* mordaz
plod *v.* meditar	**point** *n.* ponto
plot *n.* enredo	**pointing** *n.* indicação
plough *n.* arado	**pointless** *adj.* supérfluo
ploughman *n.* lavrador	**poise** *n.* equilíbrio
ploy *n.* estratagema	**poison** *n.* veneno
pluck *v.* arrancar	**poisonous** *adj.* venenoso
plug *n.* ficha (elétrica)	**poke** *v.* impelir
plum *n.* ameixa	**poker** *n.* poker
plumage *n.* plumagem	**poky** *adj.* pequeno
plumb *v.* sondar	**polar** *adj.* polar
plumber *n.* canalizador	**pole** *n.* pólo
plume *n.* pluma	**polemic** *n.* polémica
plummet *v.* mergulhar (verticalmente)	**police** *n.* polícia
plump *adj.* roliço	**policeman** *n.* polícia
plunder *v.* pilhar	**policy** *n.* política
plunge *v.* mergulhar	**polish** *n.* polimento
plural *adj.* plural	**polite** *adj.* educado
plurality *n.* pluralidade	**politeness** *n.* polidez
plus *prep.* mais	**politic** *adj.* político
plush *n.* pelúcia	**political** *adj.* político
ply *n.* camada	**politician** *n.* político
pneumatic *adj.* pneumático	**politics** *n.* política
pneumonia *n.* pneumonia	**polity** *n.* governo
poach *v.* escaldar	**poll** *n.* sondagem
pocket *n.* bolso	**pollen** *n.* pólen
	pollster *n.* entrevistador

pollute v. poluir
pollution n. poluição
polo n. pólo
polyandry n. poliandria
polygamous adj. polígamo
polygamy n. poligamia
polyglot adj. poliglota
polygraph n. polígrafo
polytechnic n. politécnico
polytheism n. politeísmo
polytheistic adj. politeísta
pomegranate n. romã
pomp n. pompa
pomposity n. pomposidade
pompous adj. pomposo
pond n. lagoa
ponder v. ponderar
pontiff n. pontífice
pony n. pónei
pool n. piscina
poor adj. pobre
poorly adv. pobremente
pop v. pop
pope n. papa
poplar n. álamo
poplin n. popelina
populace n. população
popular adj. popular
popularity n. popularidade
popularize v. popularizar
populate v. povoar
population n. população
populous adj. populoso
porcelain n. porcelana

porch n. átrio
porcupine n. porco-espinho
pore n. poro
pork n. carne de porco
pornography n. pornografia
porridge n. papas
port n. porto
portable adj. portátil
portage n. transporte
portal n. portal
portend v. prognosticar
portent n. mau agouro
porter n. porteiro
portfolio n. pasta
portico n. pórtico
portion n. parcela
portrait n. retrato
portraiture n. retrato
portray v. retratar
portrayal n. retrato
pose v. pose
posh adj. elegante
posit v. propor
position n. posição
positive adj. positivo
possess v. possuir
possession n. posse
possessive adj. possessivo
possibility n. possibilidade
possible adj. possível
post n. correios
postage n. franquia
postal adj. postal
postcard n. postal

postcode n. código postal
poster n. poster
posterior adj. posterior
posterity n. posteridade
postgraduate n. pós-graduado
posthumous adj. póstumo
postman n. carteiro
postmaster n. chefe dos correios
post-mortem n. autópsia
post office n. correios
postpone v. adiar
postponement n. adiamento
postscript n. posfácio
posture n. postura
pot n. pote
potato n. batata
potency n. potência
potent adj. potente
potential adj. potencial
potentiality n. potencialidade
potter v. malbaratar
pottery n. cerâmica
pouch n. bolsa
poultry n. aves domésticas
pounce v. decalcar
pound n. libra
pour v. derramar
poverty n. pobreza
powder n. pó
power n. poder
powerful adj. poderoso
practicability n. praticabilidade
practicable adj. praticável
practical adj. prático

practice n. prática
practise v. praticar
practitioner n. profissional
pragmatic adj. pragmático
pragmatism n. pragmatismo
praise v.t. elogiar
praline n. pralina
pram n. carrinho de bébé
prank n. partida
prattle v. tagarelar (de modo infantil)
pray v. rezar
prayer n. oração
preach v. rezar
preacher n. padre
preamble n. preâmbulo
precarious adj. precário
precaution n. precaução
precautionary adj. precaucionário
precede v. preceder
precedence n. precedência
precedent n. precedente
precept n. preceito
precinct n. recinto
precious adj. precioso
precipitate v. precipitar
precis n. resumo
precise adj. preciso
precision n. precisão
precognition n. predição
precondition n. pré-requisito
precursor n. precursor
predator n. predador
predecessor n. antecessor

predestination *n.* predestinação	**premiere** *n.* estreia
predetermine *v.* predeterminar	**premise** *n.* premissa
predicament *n.* predicamento	**premises** *n.* premissa
predicate *n.* predicado	**premium** *n.* prémio
predict *v.* predizer	**premonition** *n.* pressentimento
prediction *n.* predição	**preoccupation** *n.* preocupação
predominance *n.* predomínio	**preoccupy** *v.* preocupar
predominant *adj.* predominante	**preparation** *n.* preparação
predominate *v.* predominar	**preparatory** *adj.* preparatória
pre-eminence *n.* preeminência	**prepare** *v.* preparar
pre-eminent *adj.* preeminente	**preponderance** *n.* preponderância
pre-empt *v.* antecipar-se	**preponderate** *v.* preponderar
prefabricated *adj.* pré-fabricadas	**preposition** *n.* preposição
preface *n.* prefácio	**prepossessing** *adj.* atraente
prefect *n.* prefeito	**preposterous** *adj.* absurdo
prefer *v.* preferir	**prerequisite** *n.* pré-requisito
preference *n.* preferência	**prerogative** *n.* prerrogativa
preferential *adj.* preferencial	**presage** *v.* presságio
preferment *n.* nomeação	**prescience** *n.* presciência
prefix *n.* prefixo	**prescribe** *v.* prescrever
pregnancy *n.* gravidez	**prescription** *n.* prescrição
pregnant *adj.* grávida	**presence** *n.* presença
prehistoric *adj.* pré-histórico	**present** *adj.* presente
prejudge *v.* pré-julgar	**present** *n.* presente
prejudice *n.* prejuízo	**present** *v.* apresentar
prejudicial *adj.* prejudicial	**presentation** *n.* apresentação
prelate *n.* prelado	**presently** *adv.* atualmente
preliminary *adj.* preliminar	**preservation** *n.* preservação
prelude *n.* prelúdio	**preservative** *n.* preservativo
premarital *adj.* pré-nupcial	**preserve** *v.* preservar
premature *adj.* prematuro	**preside** *v.* presidir
premeditate *v.* premeditar	**president** *n.* presidente
premeditation *n.* premeditação	**presidential** *adj.* presidencial
premier *adj.* principal	**press** *v.* apertar

pressure *n.* pressão

pressurize *v.* pressurizar

prestige *n.* prestígio

prestigious *adj.* prestigioso

presume *v.* presumir

presumption *n.* presunção

presuppose *v.* pressupor

presupposition *n.* pressuposto

pretence *n.* pretensão

pretend *v.* fingir

pretension *n.* pretensão

pretentious *adj.* pretensioso

pretext *n.* pretexto

prettiness *n.* beleza

pretty *adj.* bastante

pretzel *n.* rosquilha

prevail *v.* prevalecer

prevalence *n.* predomínio

prevalent *adj.* predominante

prevent *v.* evitar

prevention *n.* prevenção

preventive *adj.* preventivo

preview *n.* visualização

previous *adj.* anterior

prey *n.* presa

price *n.* preço

priceless *adj.* inestimável

prick *v.* picar

prickle *n.* espinho

pride *n.* orgulho

priest *n.* padre

priesthood *n.* sacerdócio

prim *adj.* empertigado

primacy *n.* primazia

primal *adj.* primitivo

primarily *adv.* principalmente

primary *adj.* primário

primate *n.* primata

prime *adj.* primeiro

primer *n.* cartilha

primeval *adj.* primitivo

primitive *adj.* primitivo

prince *n.* príncipe

princely *adj.* princípesco

princess *n.* princesa

principal *adj.* principal

principal *n.* principal

principle *n.* princípio

print *v.* imprimir

printout *n.* cópia impressa

printer *n.* impressora

prior *adj.* prévio

priority *n.* prioridade

priory *n.* priorado

prism *n.* prisma

prison *n.* prisão

prisoner *n.* prisioneiro

pristine *adj.* primitivo

privacy *n.* privacidade

private *adj.* privado

privation *n.* privação

privatize *v.* privatizar

privilege *n.* privilégio

privy *adj.* privado

prize *n.* prémio

pro *n.* pró

proactive *adj.* proativa

probability *n.* probabilidade

probable *adj.* provável
probably *adv.* provavelmente
probate *n.* homologação
probation *n.* provação
probationer *n.* estagiário
probe *n.* sonda
probity *n.* honradez
problem *n.* problema
problematic *adj.* problemático
procedure *n.* procedimento
proceed *v.* prosseguir
proceedings *n.* procedimento
proceeds *n.* receitas (dinheiro)
process *n.* processo
procession *n.* procissão
proclaim *v.* proclamar
proclamation *n.* proclamação
proclivity *n.* propensão
procrastinate *v.* adiar
procrastination *n.* adiamento
procreate *v.* procriar
procure *v.* obter
procurement *n.* obtenção
prod *v.* acotovelar
prodigal *adj.* pródigo
prodigious *adj.* prodigioso
prodigy *n.* prodígio
produce *v.* produzir
producer *n.* produtor
product *n.* produto
production *n.* produção
productive *adj.* produtivo
productivity *n.* produtividade
profane *adj.* profano

profess *v.* professar
profession *n.* profissão
professional *adj.* profissional
professor *n.* professor
proficiency *n.* proficiência
proficient *adj.* proficiente
profile *n.* perfil
profit *n.* lucro
profitable *adj.* rentável
profiteering *n.* exploração
profligacy *n.* desregramento
profligate *adj.* libertino
profound *adj.* profundo
profundity *n.* profundidade
profuse *adj.* profuso
profusion *n.* profusão
progeny *n.* descendência
prognosis *n.* prognóstico
prognosticate *v.* prognosticar
programme *n.* programa
progress *n.* progresso
progressive *adj.* progressivo
prohibit *v.* proibir
prohibition *n.* proibição
prohibitive *adj.* proibitivo
project *n.* projeto
projectile *n.* projétil
projection *n.* projeção
projector *n.* projetor
prolapse *n.* prolapso
proliferate *v.* proliferar
proliferation *n.* proliferação
prolific *adj.* prolífico
prologue *n.* prólogo

prolong v. prolongar
prolongation n. prolongamento
promenade n. passeio público
prominence n. proeminência
prominent adj. proeminente
promiscuous adj. promíscuo
promise n. promessa
promising adj. promissor
promote v. promover
promotion n. promoção
prompt v. incitar
prompter n. incitador
promulgate v. promulgar
prone adj. inclinado
pronoun n. pronome
pronounce v. pronunciar
pronunciation n. pronúncia
proof n. prova
prop n. escora
propaganda n. propaganda
propagate v. propagar
propagation n. propagação
propel v. impulsionar
propeller n. hélice
proper adj. adequado
property n. propriedade
prophecy n. profecia
prophesy v. profetizar
prophet n. profeta
prophetic adj. profético
propitiate v. propiciar
proportion n. proporção
proportional adj. proporcional
proportionate adj. proporcionado

proposal n. proposta
propose v. propor
proposition n. proposição
propound v. propor
proprietary adj. proprietário
proprietor n. proprietário
propriety n. propriedade
prorogue v. prorrogar
prosaic adj. prosaico
prose n. prosa
prosecute v. processar
prosecution n. acusação
prosecutor n. promotor
prospect n. prospecto
prospective adj. em perspectiva
prospectus n. prospecto
prosper v. prosperar
prosperity n. prosperidade
prosperous adj. próspero
prostate n. próstata
prostitute n. prostituta
prostitution n. prostituição
prostrate adj. prostrado
prostration n. prostração
protagonist n. protagonista
protect v. proteger
protection n. proteção
protective adj. protetor
protectorate n. protetorado
protein n. proteína
protest n. protesto
protestation n. protesto
protocol n. protocolo
prototype n. protótipo

protracted *adj.* prolongado
protractor *n.* transferidor
protrude *v.* sobressair
proud *adj.* orgulhoso
prove *v.* provar
provenance *n.* proveniência
proverb *n.* provérbio
proverbial *adj.* proverbial
provide *v.* fornecer
providence *n.* providência
provident *adj.* providente
providential *adj.* providencial
province *n.* província
provincial *adj.* provincial
provision *n.* provisão
provisional *adj.* provisório
proviso *n.* condição
provocation *n.* provocação
provocative *adj.* provocante
provoke *v.* provocar
prowess *n.* proeza
proximate *adj.* próximo
proximity *n.* proximidade
proxy *n.* procuração
prude *n.* puritana
prudence *n.* prudência
prudent *adj.* prudente
prudential *adj.* prudencial
prune *n.* ameixa
pry *v.* bisbilhotar
psalm *n.* salmo
pseudo *adj.* pseudo
pseudonym *n.* pseudónimo
psyche *n.* psique

psychiatrist *n.* psiquiatra
psychiatry *n.* psiquiatria
psychic *adj.* psíquico
psychological *adj.* psicológico
psychologist *n.* psicólogo
psychology *n.* psicologia
psychopath *n.* psicopata
psychosis *n.* psicose
psychotherapy *n.* psicoterapia
pub *n.* pub
puberty *n.* puberdade
pubic *adj.* púbico
public *adj.* público
publication *n.* publicação
publicity *n.* publicidade
publicize *v.* divulgar
publish *v.* publicar
publisher *n.* editor
pudding *n.* pudim
puddle *n.* charco
puerile *adj.* pueril
puff *n.* sopro
puffy *adj.* ofegante
pull *v.* puxar
pulley *n.* polia
pullover *n.* pulôver
pulp *n.* polpa
pulpit *n.* púlpito
pulsar *n.* pulsar
pulsate *v.* pulsar
pulsation *n.* pulsação
pulse *n.* pulso
pummel *v.* golpear
pump *n.* bomba

pumpkin *n.* abóbora
pun *n.* trocadilho
punch *v.* soco
punctual *adj.* pontual
punctuality *n.* pontualidade
punctuate *v.* pontuar
punctuation *n.* pontuação
puncture *n.* punção
pungency *n.* pungência
pungent *adj.* pungente
punish *v.* punir
punishment *n.* punição
punitive *adj.* punitivo
punter *n.* apostador
puny *adj.* insignificante
pup *n.* cachorro
pupil *n.* aluno
puppet *n.* fantoche
puppy *n.* cachorro
purblind *adj.* obtuso
purchase *v.* comprar
pure *adj.* puro
purgation *n.* purgação
purgative *adj.* purgante
purgatory *n.* purgatório
purge *v.* purga
purification *n.* purificação
purify *v.* purificar
purist *n.* purista
puritan *n.* puritano
puritanical *adj.* puritana
purity *n.* pureza
purple *n.* roxo
purport *v.* significar

purpose *n.* propósito
purposely *adv.* intencionalmente
purr *v.* ronronar
purse *n.* bolsa
purser *n.* comissário de bordo
pursuance *n.* execução
pursue *v.* perseguir
pursuit *n.* busca
purvey *v.* aprovisionar
purview *n.* alcance
pus *n.* pus
push *v.* empurrar
pushy *adj.* agressivo
puss *n.* bichano
put *v.* colocar
putative *adj.* putativo
putrid *adj.* pútrido
puzzle *v.t.* decifrar
pygmy *n.* pigmeu
pyjamas *n.* pijama
pyorrhoea *n.* piorreia
pyramid *n.* pirâmide
pyre *n.* pira funerária
pyromania *n.* piromania
python píton

quack n charlatão
quackery *n.* charlatanismo
quad *n.* quadrângulo
quadrangle a. quadrilátero
quadrangular *n.* quadrangular
quadrant *n.* quadrante
quadrilateral *n.* quadrilátero

quadruped n. quadrúpede
quadruple adj. quádruplo
quadruplet n. quádrupla
quaff v. absorver
quail n. codorniz
quaint adj. singular
quaintly adv. curiosamente
quake v. tremer
Quaker n. quacre
qualification n. qualificação
qualify v. qualificar
qualitative adj. qualitativo
quality n. qualidade
qualm n. escrúpulo
quandary n. dilema
quango n. quango
quantify v. quantificar
quantitative adj. quantitativo
quantity n. quantidade
quantum n. quantidade
quarantine n. quarentena
quark n. quark
quarrel n. disputa
quarrelsome adj. conflituoso
quarry n. pedreira
quart n. quarto
quarter n. trimestre
quarterly adj. trimestral
quartet n. quarteto
quartz n. quartzo
quash v. revogar
quaver v. trinar
quay n. cais
queasy adj. enjoado

queen n. rainha
queer adj. esquisito
quell v. reprimir
quench v. extinguir
querulous adj. impertinente
query n. pergunta
quest n. busca
question n. pergunta
questionable adj. questionável
questionnaire n. questionário
queue n. fila
quibble n. trocadilho
quick adj. rápido
quicken v. acelerar
quickly adv. rapidamente
quid n. libra estrelina
quiescent adj. quiescente
quiet adj. silencioso
quieten v. aquietar
quietetude n. quietetude
quiff n. madeixa
quilt n. colcha
quilted adj. acolchoado
Quinn n. Quinn
quince n. marmelo
quinine n. quinina
quintessence n. quinta-essência
quip n. sofisma
quirk n. equívoco
quit v. desistir
quite adv. bastante
quits adj. quite
quiver v. tiritar
quixotic adj. quixotesco

quiz *n.* enigma
quizzical *adj.* irónico
quondam *adj.* antigo
quorum *n.* quorum
quota *n.* quota
quotation *n.* citação
quote *v.* citar
quotient *n.* quociente

R

rabbit *n.* coelho
rabble *n.* multidão
rabid *adj.* fanático
rabies *n.* raiva
race *n.* corrida
race *v.* correr
racial *adj.* racial
racialism *n.* racismo
rack *n.* prateleira
racket *n.* raquete
racketeer *n.* escroque
racy *adj.* picante
radar *n.* radar
radial *adj.* radial
radiance *n.* esplendor
radiant *adj.* radiante
radiate *v.* irradiar
radiation *n.* radiação
radical *adj.* radical
radio *n.* rádio
radioactive *adj.* radioativo
radiography *n.* radiografia
radiology *n.* radiologia
radish *n.* rabanete

radium *n.* rádio
radius *n.* raio
raffle *n.* tômbola
raft *n.* jangada
rag *n.* trapo
rage *n.* raiva
ragged *adj.* irregular
raid *n.* incursão
rail *n.* trilho
railing *n.* corrimão
raillery *n.* troça
railway *n.* caminho de ferro
rain n chuva
rainbow *n.* arco-íris
raincoat *n.* capa de chuva
rainfall *n.* aguaceiro
rainforest *n.* floresta
rainy *adj.* chuvoso
raise *v.* levantar
raisin *n.* passa de uva
rake *n.* ancinho
rally *n.* desânimo
ram *n.* carneiro
ramble *v.* divagar
ramification *n.* ramificação
ramify *v.* ramificar
ramp *n.* rampa
rampage *v.* enlouquecer
rampant *adj.* excessivo
rampart *n.* baluarte
ramshackle *adj.* decrépito
ranch *n.* rancho
rancid *adj.* rançoso
rancour *n.* rancor

random *adj.* acaso	**rational** *adj.* racional
range *n.* alcance	**rationale** *n.* fundamentação lógica
ranger *n.* guarda-florestal	**rationalism** *n.* racionalismo
rank *n.* graduação	**rationalize** *v.* racionalizar
rank *v.* classificar	**rattle** *v.* chocalhar
rankle *v.* magoar	**raucous** *adj.* rouco
ransack *v.* pilhar	**ravage** *v.t.* devastar
ransom *n.* resgate	**rave** *v.* delirar
rant *v.* endoidecer	**raven** *n.* corvo
rap *v.* censurar	**ravenous** *adj.* voraz
rapacious *adj.* voraz	**ravine** *n.* ravina
rape *v.* violar	**raw** *adj.* cru
rapid *adj.* rápido	**ray** *n.* raio
rapidity *n.* rapidez	**raze** *v.* arrasar
rapier *n.* florete	**razor** *n.* navalha
rapist *n.* violador	**reach** *v.* alcançar
rapport *n.* harmonia	**react** *v.* reagir
rapprochement *n.* aproximação	**reaction** *n.* reação
rapt *adj.* arrebatado	**reactionary** *adj.* reacionário
rapture *n.* arrebatamento	**reactor** *n.* reator
rare *adj.* muito	**read** *v.* ler
raring *adj.* desejoso	**reader** *n.* leitor
rascal *n.* patife	**readily** *adv.* prontamente
rash *adj.* precipitado	**reading** *n.* leitura
rasp *n.* grosa	**readjust** *v.* reajustar
raspberry *n.* framboesa	**ready** *adj.* pronto
rat *n.* rato	**reaffirm** *v.* reafirmar
ratchet *n.* roquete	**real** *adj.* real
rate *n.* taxa	**realism** *n.* realismo
rather *adv.* bastante	**realistic** *adj.* realista
ratify *v.* ratificar	**reality** *n.* realidade
rating *n.* classificação	**realization** *n.* realização
ratio *n.* relação	**realize** *v.* perceber
ration *n.* ração	**really** *adv.* realmente

realm *n.* reino
ream *n.* resma
reap *v.* colher
reaper *n.* ceifeiro
reappear *v.* reaparecer
reappraisal *n.* reavaliação
rear *n.* cauda
rearrange *v.* rearranjar
reason *n.* razão
reasonable *adj.* razoável
reassess *v.* reavaliar
reassure *v.* reassegurar
rebate *n.* desconto
rebel *v.* rebelar
rebellion *n.* rebelião
rebellious *adj.* rebelde
rebirth *n.* renascimento
rebound *v.* ressaltar
rebuff *v.* recusar
rebuild *v.* reconstruir
rebuke *v.* repreender
rebuke *v.t.* repreender
recall *v.* recordar
recap *v.* recapitular
recapitulate *v.* resumir
recapture *v.* recapturar
recede *v.* recuar
receipt *n.* recebimento
receive *v.* receber
receiver *n.* recebedor
recent *adj.* recente
recently *adv.* recentemente
receptacle *n.* recetáculo
reception *n.* receção

receptionist *n.* rececionista
receptive *adj.* recetivo
recess *n.* intervalo
recession *n.* recessão
recessive *adj.* regressivo
recharge *v.* recarregar
recipe *n.* receita
recipient *n.* destinatário
reciprocal *adj.* recíproco
reciprocate *v.* retribuir
recital *n.* recital
recite *v.* recitar
reckless *adj.* imprudente
reckon *v.t.* contar
reclaim *v.* exigir
reclamation *n.* correção
recline *v.* reclinar
recluse *n.* recluso
recognition *n.* reconhecimento
recognize *v.i.* reconhecer
recoil *v.* recuar
recollect *v.* recordar
recollection *n.* recordação
recommend *v.* recomendar
recommendation *n.* recomendação
recompense *v.* recompensar
reconcile *v.* reconciliar
reconciliation *n.* reconciliação
recondition *v.* recondicionar
reconsider *v.* reconsiderar
reconstitute *v.* reconstituir
reconstruct *v.* reconstruir
record *n.* registo
recorder *n.* gravador

recount *v.* narrar

recoup *v.* recuperar

recourse *n.* recurso

recover *v.* reaver

recovery *n.* recuperação

recreate *v.* recrear

recreation *n.* recreação

recrimination *n.* recriminação

recruit *v.* recrutar

rectangle *n.* retângulo

rectangular *adj.* retangular

rectification *n.* retificação

rectify *v.* retificar

rectitude *n.* retidão

rectum *n.* reto

recumbent *adj.* reclinado

recuperate *v.* recuperar

recur *v.* retornar

recurrence *n.* retorno

recurrent *adj.* recorrente

recycle *v.* reciclar

red *adj.* vermelho

reddish *adj.* avermelhado

redeem *v.* redimir

redemption *n.* redenção

redeploy *v.* transferir

redolent *adj.* fragrante

redouble *v.* redobrar

redoubtable *adj.* temível

redress *v.* reparar

reduce *v.* reduzir

reduction *n.* redução

reductive *adj.* simplista

redundancy *n.* redundância

redundant *adj.* redundante

reef *n.* recife

reek *v.* emanar

reel *n.* carretel

refer *v.* referir

referee *n.* árbitro

reference *n.* referência

referendum *n.* referendo

refill *v.* reabastecer

refine *v.* refinar

refinement *n.* refinação

refinery *n.* refinaria

refit *v.* reparar

reflect *v.* refletir

reflection *n.* reflexão

reflective *adj.* reflexo

reflex *n.* reflexo

reflexive *adj.* reflexivo

reflexology *n.* reflexologia

reform *v.* reformar

reformation *n.* reforma

reformer *n.* reformador

refraction *n.* refração

refrain *v.t.* privar-se

refresh *v.* refrescar

refreshment *n.* refresco

refrigerate *v.* refrigerar

refrigeration *n.* refrigeração

refrigerator *n.* frigorífico

refuge *n.* refúgio

refugee *n.* refugiado

refulgence *adj.* resplendor

refulgent *adj.* refulgente

refund *v.* reembolsar

refurbish v. renovar
refusal n. recusa
refuse v. recusar
refuse n. resíduos
refutation n. refutação
refute v. refutar
regain v. recuperar
regal adj. real
regard v. respeitar
regarding prep. em relação a
regardless adv. indiferente
regenerate v. regenerar
regeneration n. regeneração
regent n. regente
reggae n. reggae
regicide n. regicídio
regime n. regime
regiment n. regimento
region n. região
regional adj. regional
register n. registo
registrar n. escrivão
registration n. registo
registry n. registo
regress v. retroceder
regret n. tristeza
regrettable adj. lamentável
regular adj. normal
regularity n. regularidade
regularize v. regularizar
regulate v. regular
regulation n. regulação
regulator n. regulador
rehabilitate v. reabilitar

rehabilitation n. reabilitação
rehearsal n. ensaio
rehearse v. ensaiar
reign v. reinar
reimburse v. reembolsar
rein n. rédea
reincarnate v. reencarnar
reinforce v. reforçar
reinforcement n. reforço
reinstate v. restabelecer
reinstatement n. reintegração
reiterate v. reiterar
reiteration n. reiteração
reject v. rejeitar
rejection n. rejeição
rejoice v. regozijar
rejoin v. reunir
rejoinder n. réplica
rejuvenate v. rejuvenescer
rejuvenation n. rejuvenescimento
relapse v. reincidir
relate v. relacionar (-se)
relation n. relação
relationship n. relacionamento
relative adj. parente
relativity n. relatividade
relax v. relaxar
relaxation n. relaxamento
relay n. relé
release v. libertar
relegate v. relegar
relent v. abrandar
relentless adj. implacável
relevance n. relevância

relevant *adj.* relevante
reliable *adj.* confiável
reliance *n.* confiança
relic *n.* relíquia
relief *n.* alívio
relieve *v.* aliviar
religion *n.* religião
religious *adj.* religioso
relinquish *v.* abandonar
relish *v.* saborear
relocate *v.* mudar
reluctance *n.* relutância
reluctant *adj.* relutante
rely *v.* depender
remain *v.* permanecer
remainder *n.* restante
remains *n.* restos
remand *v.* aprisionar
remark *v.* observar
remarkable *adj.* notável
remedial *adj.* curativo
remedy *n.* remédio
remember *v.* relembrar
remembrance *n.* lembrança
remind *v.* lembrar
reminder *n.* lembrete
reminiscence *n.* reminiscência
reminiscent *adj.* recordativo
remiss *adj.* remisso
remission *n.* remissão
remit *n.* perdão
remittance *n.* remessa
remnant *n.* resto
remonstrate *v.* protestar

remorse *n.* remorso
remote *adj.* remoto
removable *adj.* removível
removal *n.* remoção
remove *v.* remover
remunerate *v.* remunerar
remuneration *n.* remuneração
remunerative *adj.* remunerativo
renaissance *n.* renascimento
render *v.* retribuir
rendezvous *n.* encontro
renegade *n.* renegado
renew *v.* renovar
renewal *adj.* renovação
renounce *v.t.* renunciar a
renovate *n.* renovar
renovation *n.* renovação
renown *n.* renome
renowned *adj.* famoso
rent *n.* renda
rental *n.* aluguel
renunciation *n.* renúncia
reoccur *v.* acontecer
reorganize *v.* reorganizar
repair *v.* reparar
repartee *n.* réplica
repatriate *v.* repatriar
repatriation *n.* repatriação
repay *v.* reembolsar
repayment *n.* reembolso
repeal *v.* revogar
repeat *v.* repetir
repel *v.* repelir
repellent *adj.* repelente

repent v. arrepender-se

repentance n. arrependimento

repentant adj. arrependido

repercussion n. repercussão

repetition n. repetição

replace v. substituir

replacement n. substituição

replay v. repetir

replenish v. reabastecer

replete adj. repleto

replica n. réplica

replicate v. repetir

reply v. responder

report v. denunciar

reportage n. reportagem

reporter n. repórter

repose n. repouso

repository n. repositório

repossess v. reaver

reprehensible adj. repreensível

represent v. representar

representation n. representação

representative adj. representativo

repress v. reprimir

repression n. repressão

reprieve v. adiar

reprimand v. reprimenda

reprint v. reimprimir

reprisal n. represália

reproach v. repreender

reprobate n. réprobo

reproduce v. reproduzir

reproduction n. reprodução

reproductive adj. reprodutivo

reproof n. censura

reprove v. reprovar

reptile n. réptil

republic n. república

republican adj. republicano

repudiate v. repudiar

repudiation n. repúdio

repugnance n. repugnância

repugnant adj. repugnante

repulse v. repelir

repulsion n. repulsão

repulsive adj. repugnante

reputation n. reputação

repute n. reputação

request n. pedido

requiem n. réquiem

require v. exigir

requirement n. exigência

requisite adj. necessário

requisite n. requisito

requisition n. requisição

requite v.t. pagar

rescind v. rescindir

rescue v. resgatar

research n. pesquisa

resemblance n. semelhança

resemble v. assemelhar

resent v. ressentir

resentment n. ressentimento

reservation n. reserva

reserve v. reservar

reservoir n. reservatório

reshuffle v. remodelar

reside v. residir

residence *n.* residência

resident *n.* residente

residential *adj.* residencial

residual *adj.* residual

residue *n.* resíduo

resign *v.* renunciar a

resignation *n.* renúncia

resilient *adj.* elástico

resist *v.* resistir

resistance *n.* resistência

resistant *adj.* resistente

resolute *adj.* resoluto

resolution *n.* resolução

resolve *v.* resolver

resonance *n.* ressonância

resonant *adj.* ressonante

resonate *v.* ressoar

resort *n.* recurso

resound *v.* ressoar

resource *n.* recurso

resourceful *adj.* engenhoso

respect *n.* respeito

respectable *adj.* respeitável

respectful *adj.* respeitoso

respective *adj.* respetivo

respiration *n.* respiração

respirator *n.* respirador

respire *v.* respirar

respite *n.* pausa

resplendent *adj.* resplandecente

respond *v.* responder

respondent *n.* inquirido

response *n.* resposta

responsibility *n.* responsabilidade

responsible *adj.* responsável

responsive *adj.* responsivo

rest *v.* descansar

restaurant *n.* restaurante

restaurateur *n.* dono de restaurante

restful *adj.* repousante

restitution *n.* restituição

restive *adj.* inquieto

restoration *adj.* restauração

restore *v.* restaurar

restrain *v.* conter

restraint *n.* limitação

restrict *n.* restringir

restriction *n.* restrição

restrictive *adj.* restritivo

result *n.* resultado

resultant *adj.* resultante

resume *v.* retomar

resumption *n.* recomeço

resurgence *a.* ressurgimento

resurgent *adj.* que ressurge

resurrect *v.* ressuscitar

retail *n.* retalho

retailer *n.* retalhista

retain *v.i.* reter

retainer *n.* retentor

retaliate *v.* retaliar

retaliation *n.* retaliação

retard *v.* retardar

retardation *n.* retardo

retarded *adj.* retardado

retch *v.* esforçar (para vomitar)

retention *n.* retenção

retentive *adj.* retentivo

rethink *v.* repensar
reticent *adj.* reticente
retina *n.* retina
retinue *n.* séquito
retire *v.* aposentar
retirement *n.* aposentadoria
retiring *adj.* retraído
retort *v.* replicar
retouch *v.* retocar
retrace *v.t.* remontar
retract *v.* retrair
retread *v.* recauchutar
retreat *v.t.* recuar
retrench *v.* restringir
retrenchment *n.* redução
retrial *n.* novo julgamento
retribution *n.* retribuição
retrieve *v.* recuperar
retriever *n.* retriever (raça de cão)
retro *adj.* rétro
retroactive *adj.* retroativo
retrograde *adj.* retrógrado
retrospect *n.* retrospecto
retrospective *adj.* retrospetivo
return *v.* voltar
return *n.* retorno
reunion *n.* reunião
reunite *v.* reunir
reuse *v.* reutilizar
revamp *v.* renovar
reveal *v.* revelar
revel *v.* desvairar
revelation *n.* revelação
revenge *n.* vingança

revenue *n.* receita
reverberate *v.* ecoar
revere *v.* venerar
revered *adj.* respeitado
reverence *n.* reverência
reverend *adj.* venerável
reverent *adj.* respeitoso
reverential *adj.* reverencial
reverie *n.* devaneio
reversal *n.* reversão
reverse *v.* reverter
reversible *adj.* reversível
revert *v.* reverter
review *n.* crítica
revile *v.* insultar
revise *v.* rever
revision *n.* revisão
revival *n.* renascimento
revivalism *n.* revivalismo
revive *v.* reviver
revocable *adj.* revogável
revocation *n.* revogação
revoke *v.* revogar
revolt *v.* revoltar
revolution *n.* revolução
revolutionary *adj.* revolucionário
revolutionize *v.* revolucionar
revolve *v.* revolver
revolver *n.* revólver
revulsion *n.* asco
reward *n.* recompensa
rewind *v.* rebobinar
rhapsody *n.* rapsódia
rhetoric *n.* retórica

rhetorical *adj.* retórico	**right** *adj.* correto
rheumatic *adj.* reumático	**right** *n* direito
rheumatism *n.* reumatismo	**righteous** *adj.* justo
rhinoceros *n.* rinoceronte	**rightful** *adj.* legítimo
rhodium *n.* ródio	**rigid** *adj.* rígido
rhombus *n.* rombo	**rigmarole** *n.* ladainha
rhyme *n.* rima	**rigorous** *adj.* rigoroso
rhythm *n.* ritmo	**rigour** *n.* rigor
rhythmic *adj.* rítmico	**rim** *n.* aro
rib *n.* costela	**ring** *n.* anel
ribbon *n.* fita	**ring** *v.* tocar (sino)
rice *n.* arroz	**ringlet** *n.* anelzinho
rich *adj.* rico	**ringworm** *n.* micose
richly *adv.* ricamente	**rink** *n.* pista de gelo
richness *n.* riqueza	**rinse** *v.* enxaguar
rick *n.* meda	**riot** *n.* tumulto
rickets *n.* raquitismo	**rip** *v.* rasgar
rickety *adj.* frágil	**ripe** *adj.* maduro
rickshaw *n.* riquexó	**ripen** *v.* amadurecer
rid *v.* livrar	**riposte** *n.* contragolpe
riddance *n.* alívio	**ripple** *n.* ondulação
riddle *n.* enigma	**rise** *v.* subir
riddled *adj.* crivado	**risible** *adj.* rídiculo
ride *v.* montar	**rising** *n.* subida
rider *n.* cavaleiro	**risk** *n.* risco
ridge *n.* cume	**risky** *adj.* arriscado
ridicule *n.* troça	**rite** *n.* rito
ridiculous *adj.* ridículo	**ritual** *n.* ritual
rife *adj.* frequente	**rival** *n.* rival
rifle *n.* arma	**rivalry** *n.* rivalidade
rifle *v.* assaltar	**rive** *v.* despedaçar
rift *n.* fenda	**river** *n.* rio
rig *v.* burlar	**rivet** *n.* rebite
rigging *n.* cordame	**rivulet** *n.* regato

road *n.* estrada	**roof** *n.* telhado
roadwork *n.* obras na estrada	**roofing** *n.* cobertura
roadworthy *adj.* veículo bom estado	**rook** *n.* gralha (pássaro)
roadster *n.* descapotável antigo	**rookery** *n.* espelunca
roam *v.* vaguear	**room** *n.* quarto
roar *n.* rugido	**roomy** *adj.* espaçoso
roar *v.* rugir	**roost** *n.* poleiro
roast *v.* assar	**rooster** *n.* galo
rob *v.* roubar	**root** *n.* raiz
robber *n.* ladrão	**rooted** *adj.* enraizado
robbery *n.* roubo	**rope** *n.* corda
robe *n.* robe	**rosary** *n.* rosário
robot *n.* robô	**rose** *n.* rosa
robust *adj.* robusto	**rosette** *n.* roseta
rock *n.* rocha	**roster** *n.* lista
rocket *n.* foguete	**rostrum** *n.* tribuna
rocky *adj.* rochoso	**rosy** *adj.* rosado
rod *n.* haste	**rot** *v.* apodrecer
rodent *n.* roedor	**rota** *n.* rota
rodeo *n.* rodeio	**rotary** *adj.* rotativo
roe *n.* cabrito-montês	**rotate** *v.* rodar
rogue *n.* trapaceiro	**rotation** *n.* rotação
roguery *n.* velhacaria	**rote** *n.* hábito
roguish *adj.* malandro	**rotor** *n.* rotor
roister *v.* bradar	**rotten** *adj.* podre
role *n.* papel	**rouge** *n.* vermelhão
roll *v.i.* girar	**rough** *adj.* áspero
roll *n.* rolo	**roulette** *n.* roleta
roll-call *n.* lista de chamada	**round** *adj.* redondo
roller *n.* rolete	**roundabout** *n.* carrossel
rollercoaster *n.* montanha-russa	**rounded** *adj.* arredondado
romance *n.* romance	**roundly** *adv.* redondamente
romantic *adj.* romântico	**rouse** *v.* despertar
romp *v.* traquinar	**rout** *n.* confusão

route *n.* rota
routine *n.* rotina
rove *v.* deambular
rover *n.* vagabundo
roving *adj.* errante
row *n.* linha
rowdy *adj.* turbulento
royal *n.* real
royalist *n.* realista
royalty *n.* realeza
rub *n.* atrito
rub *v.* esfregar
rubber *n.* borracha
rubbish *n.* lixo
rubble *n.* cascalho
rubric *n.* rubrica
ruby *n.* rubi
rucksack *n.* mochila
ruckus *n.* zaragata
rudder *n.* leme
rude *adj.* rude
rudiment *n.* rudimento
rudimentary *adj.* rudimentar
rue *v.* lamentar
rueful *adj.* pesaroso
ruffian *n.* rufião
ruffle *v.* irritar
rug *n.* tapete
rugby *n.* rugby
rugged *adj.* acidentado
ruin *n.* ruína
ruinous *adj.* ruinoso
rule *n.* regra
rule *v.* governar

ruler *n.* governante
ruling *n.* dirigente
rum *n.* rum
rumble *v.* retumbar
rumbustious *adj.* barulhento
ruminant *n.* ruminante
ruminate *v.* ruminar
rumination *n.* ruminação
rummage *v.* esquadrinhar
rummy *n.* borrachão
rumour *n.* rumor
rumple *v.* amarrotar
rumpus *n.* zaragata
run *n.* corrida
run *v.* correr
runaway *adj.* fugitivo
rundown *adj.* resumo
runway *n.* caminho
rung *n.* degrau
runnel *n.* regato
runner *n.* corredor
runny *adj.* corredio
rupture *v.t.* quebrar
rural *adj.* rural
ruse *n.* estratagema
rush *v.* apressar
Rusk *n.* Rusk
rust *n.* ferrugem
rustic *adj.* rústico
rusticate *v.* viver no campo
rustication *n.* vida rural
rusticity *n.* rusticidade
rustle *v.* sussurro
rusty *adj.* enferrujado

rut *n.* cio
ruthless *adj.* implacável
rye *n.* centeio

S

Sabbath *n.* Sabbat
sabotage *v.* sabotar
sabre *n.* sabre
saccharin *n.* sacarina
saccharine *adj.* sacarina
sachet *n.* saché
sack *n.* saco
sack *v.* demitir
sacrament *n.* sacramento
sacred *adj.* sagrado
sacrifice *n.* sacrifício
sacrifice *v.* sacrificar
sacrificial *adj.* sacrificial
sacrilege *n.* sacrilégio
sacrilegious *adj.* sacrílego
sacrosanct *adj.* sacrossanto
sad *adj.* triste
sadden *v.* entristecer
saddle *n.* sela
saddier *n.* seleiro
sadism *n.* sadismo
sadist *n.* sádico
safari *n.* safari
safe *adj.* seguro
safe *n.* cofre
safeguard *n.* salvaguarda
safety *n.* segurança
saffron *n.* açafrão
sag *v.* afundar

saga *n.* saga
sagacious *adj.* sagaz
sagacity *n.* sagacidade
sage *n.* salva
sage *adj.* sábio
sail *n.* vela
sail *v.* velejar
sailor *n.* marinheiro
saint *n.* santo
saintly *adj.* santo
sake *n.* causa
saleable *adj.* próprio para venda
salad *n.* salada
salary *n.* salário
sale *n.* venda
salesman *n.* vendedor
salient *adj.* saliente
saline *adj.* salino
salinity *n.* salinidade
saliva *n.* saliva
sallow *adj.* pálido
sally *n.* saída
salmon *n.* salmão
salon *n.* salão
saloon *n.* salão
salsa *n.* salsa
salt *n.* sal
salty *adj.* salgado
salutary *adj.* salutar
salutation *n.* saudação
salute *n.* saudação
salvage *v.* salvar
salvation *n.* salvação
salver *n.* salva

salvo *n.* artilharia

Samaritan *n.* Samaritano

same *adj.* mesmo

sample *n.* amostra

sampler *n.* espécime

sanatorium *n.* sanatório

sanctification *n.* santificação

sanctify *v.* santificar

sanctimonious *adj.* hipócrita

sanction *v.* sancionar

sanctity *n.* santidade

sanctuary *n.* santuário

sanctum *n.* sacrário

sand *n.* areia

sandal *n.* sandália

sandalwood *n.* sândalo

sander *n.* lixadeira

sandpaper *n.* lixa

sandwich *n.* sanduíche

sandy *adj.* arenoso

sane *adj.* são

sangfroid *n.* sangue-frio

sanguinary *adj.* sanguinário

sanguine *adj.* sanguíneo

sanatorium *n.* sanatório

sanitary *adj.* sanitário

sanitation *n.* saneamento

sanitize *v.* higienizar

sanity *n.* sanidade

sap *n.* seiva

sapling *n.* adolescente

sapphire *n.* safira

sarcasm *n.* sarcasmo

sarcastic *adj.* sarcástico

sarcophagus *n.* sarcófago

sardonic *adj.* sardónico

sari *n.* sari

sartorial *adj.* relativo a alfaiate

sash *n.* faixa

Satan *n.* Satanás

satanic *adj.* satânico

Satanism *n.* Satanismo

satchel *n.* sacola

sated *adj.* saciado

satellite *n.* satélite

satiable *adj.* saciável

satiate *v.* saciar

satiety *n.* saciedade

satin *n.* cetim

satire *n.* sátira

satirical *adj.* satírico

satirist *n.* satirista

satirize *v.* satirizar

satisfaction *n.* satisfação

satisfactory *adj.* satisfatório

satisfy *v.* satisfazer

saturate *v.* saturar

saturation *n.* saturação

Saturday *n.* Sábado

saturnine *adj.* saturnino

sauce *n.* molho

saucer *n.* pires

saucy *adj.* atrevido

sauna *n.* sauna

saunter *v.* passear

sausage *n.* salsicha

savage *adj.* selvagem

savagery *n.* selvageria

save v. salvar

savings n. poupança

saviour n. salvador

savour v.t. saborear

savoury adj. saboroso

saw n. serra

saw v. serrar

sawdust n. serradura

saxophone n. saxofone

say n. opinião

saying n. provérbio

scab n. sarnenta

scabbard n. bainha

scabies n. sarna

scabrous adj. obsceno

scaffold n. andaime

scaffolding n. andaime

scald v. escaldar

scale n. escala

scallop n. castanhola

scalp n. couro cabeludo

scam n. esquema (desonesto)

scamp n. maroto

scamper v.t. fugir

scan v. digitalizar

scanner n. digitalizador

scandal n. escândalo

scandalize v. escandalizar

scant adj. escasso

scanty adj. escasso

scapegoat n. bode expiatório

scar n. cicatriz

scarce adj. raro

scarcely adv. dificilmente

scare v. assustar

scarecrow n. espantalho

scarf n. cachecol

scarlet n. escarlate

scarp n. escarpa

scary adj. assustador

scathing adj. mordaz

scatter v. espalhar

scavenge v. limpar

scenario n. cenário

scene n. cena

scenery n. cenário

scenic adj. cénico

scent n. perfume

sceptic n. cético

sceptical adj. incrédulo

sceptre n. cetro

schedule n. horário

schematic adj. esquemático

scheme n. esquema

schism n. cisma

schizophrenia n. esquizofrenia

scholar n. estudioso

scholarly adj. erudito

scholarship n. bolsa de estudo

scholastic adj. académico

school n. escola

sciatica n. ciática

science n. ciência

scientific adj. científico

scientist n. cientista

scintillating adj. cintilante

scissors n. tesoura

scoff v.i. ridicularizar

scold v. repreender

scoop n. concha

scooter n. scooter

scope n. âmbito

scorch v. queimar

score n. resultado

score v. pontuar

scorer n. marcador

scorn n. desprezo

scornful adj. desdenhoso

scorpion n. escorpião

Scot n. Escocês

scot-free adv. impune

scoundrel n. canalha

scour v. limpar

scourge n. açoite

scout n. escoteiro

scowl n. carrancudo

scrabble v. rabiscar

scraggy adj. magricela

scramble v. misturar

scrap n. sucata

scrape v. raspar

scrappy adj. desconexo

scratch v.t. arranhar

scrawl v. gatafunhar

scrawny adj. magricela

scream v. gritar

screech n. guincho

screed n. discurso

screen n. ecrã

screw n. parafuso

screwdriver n. chave de fenda

scribble v. rabiscar

scribe n. escriba

scrimmage n. escaramuça

scrimp v. estreitar

script n. escrita

scripture n. escritura

scroll n. rolo de pergaminho

scrooge n. avarento

scrub v. esfregar

scruffy adj. mal vestido

scrunch v. mastigar

scruple n. escrúpulos

scrupulous adj. escrupuloso

scrutinize v. escrutinar

scrutiny n. escrutínio

scud v. deslizar

scuff v. arrastar

scuffle n. rixa

sculpt v. esculpir

sculptor n. escultor

sculptural adj. escultural

sculpture n. escultura

scum n. escumalha

scurrilous adj. indecente

scythe n. gadanha

sea n. mar

seagull n. gaivota

seal n. sela

sealant n. selante

seam n. costura

seamless adj. sem costura

seamy adj. desagradável

sear v. tostar

search v. procurar

seaside n. beira-mar

season *n.* temporada
seasonable *adj.* oportuno
seasonal *adj.* sazonal
seasoning *n.* tempero
seat *n.* assento
seating *n.* lugares sentados
secede *v.* abandonar
secession *n.* secessão
seclude *v.* isolar
secluded *adj.* isolado
seclusion *n.* isolamento
second *adj.* segundo
secondary *adj.* secundário
secrecy *n.* sigilo
secret *adj.* secreto
secretariat *n.* secretariado
secretary *n.* secretário
secrete *v.* ocultar
secretion *n.* secreção
secretive *adj.* secreto
sect *n.* fação
sectarian *adj.* sectário
section *n.* seção
sector *n.* setor
secular *adj.* secular
secure *adj.* protegido
security *n.* segurança
sedan *n.* sedan
sedate *adj.* calmo
sedation *n.* sedação
sedative *n.* sedativo
sedentary *adj.* sedentário
sediment *n.* sedimento
sedition *n.* sedição

seditious *adj.* sedicioso
seduce *v.* seduzir
seduction *n.* sedução
seductive *adj.* sedutor
sedulous *adj.* assíduo
see *v.* ver
seed *n.* semente
seedy *adj.* puído
seek *v.i.* procurar
seem *v.* parecer
seemly *adj.* decoroso
seep *v.* infiltrar
seer *n.* vidente
see-saw *n.* balancé
segment *n.* segmento
segregate *v.* separar
segregation *n.* separação
seismic *adj.* sísmico
seize *v.* apreender
seizure *n.* apreensão
seldom *adv.* raramente
select *v.* selecionar
selection *n.* seleção
selective *adj.* seletivo
self *n.* eu
selfish *adj.* egoísta
selfless *adj.* altruísta
self-made *adj.* por si mesmo
sell *v.* vender
seller *n.* vendedor
selvedge *n.* ourela
semantic *adj.* semântico
semblance *n.* aparência
semen *n.* sémen

semester *n.* semestre

semicircle *n.* semicírculo

semicolon *n.* ponto e vírgula

seminal *adj.* seminal

seminar *n.* seminário

Semitic *adj.* Semítico

senate *n.* senado

senator *n.* senador

senatorial *adj.* senatorial

send *v.* enviar

senile *adj.* senil

senility *n.* senilidade

senior *adj.* sénior

seniority *n.* antiguidade

sensation *n.* sensação

sensational *adj.* sensacional

sensationalize *v.* exagerar

sense *n.* sentido

senseless *adj.* disparatado

sensibility *n.* sensibilidade

sensible *adj.* sensato

sensitive *adj.* sensível

sensitize *v.* sensibilizar

sensor *n.* sensor

sensory *adj.* sensorial

sensual *adj.* sensual

sensualist *n.* sensualista

sensuality *n.* sensualidade

sensuous *adj.* sensual

sentence *n.* sentença

sententious *adj.* sentencioso

sentient *adj.* senciente

sentiment *n.* sentimento

sentimental *adj.* sentimental

sentinel *n.* sentinela

sentry *n.* vigia

separable *adj.* separável

separate *v.* separar

separation *n.* separação

separatist *n.* separatista

sepsis *n.* sepsia

September *n.* Setembro

septic *adj.* sético

sepulchral *adj.* sepulcral

sepulchre *n.* sepulcro

sequel *n.* continuação

sequence *n.* sequência

sequential *adj.* sequente

sequester *v.* sequestrar

serene *adj.* sereno

serenity *n.* serenidade

serf *n.* servo

serge *n.* sarja

sergeant *n.* sargento

serial *adj.* serial

serialize *v.* seriar

series *n.* série

serious *adj.* sério

sermon *n.* sermão

sermonize *v.* pregar

serpent *n.* serpente

serpentine *adj.* sinuoso

serrated *adj.* dentado

servant *n.* criado

serve *v.* servir

server *n.* servidor

service *n.* serviço

serviceable *adj.* aproveitável

serviette *n.* guardanapo
servile *adj.* servil
servility *n.* servilismo
serving *n.* servidor
sesame *n.* sésamo
session *n.* sessão
set *v.* pôr
set n conjunto
settee *n.* sofá
setter *n.* montador
setting *n.* montagem
settle *v.* resolver
settlement *n.* liquidação
settler *n.* colono
seven *adj. & n.* sete
seventeen *adj. & n.* dezessete
seventeenth *adj. & n.* décimo sétimo
seventh *adj. & n.* sétimo
seventieth *adj. & n.* septuagésimo
seventy *adj. & n.* setenta
sever *v.* cortar
several *adj. & pron.* vários & muitos
severance *n.* separação
severe *adj.* grave
severity *n.* gravidade
sew *v.* costurar
sewage *n.* águas residuais
sewer *n.* esgoto
sewerage *n.* rede de esgotos
sex *n.* sexo
sexism *n.* sexismo
sexton *n.* sacristão
sextuplet *n.* sêxtuplo
sexual *adj.* sexual

sexuality *n.* sexualidade
sexy *adj.* sensual
shabby *adj.* gasto
shack *n.* cabana
shackle *n.* manilha
shade *n.* sombra
shade *v.* escurecer
shadow *n.* sombra
shadow *a.* sombra
shadowy *adj.* sombrio
shady *adj.* suspeito
shaft *n.* eixo
shag *n.* guedelha
shake *v.* tremer
shaky *adj.* trémulo
shall *v.* dever
shallow *adj.* raso
sham *n.* fraude
shamble *v.* bambolear
shambles *n.* ruínas
shame *n.* vergonha
shameful *adj.* vergonhoso
shameless *adj.* desavergonhado
shampoo *n.* champô
shank *n.* canela (perna)
shanty *n.* choupana
shape *n.* forma
shapeless *adj.* disforme
shapely *adj.* simétrico
shard *n.* caco
share *n.* parte
shark *n.* tubarão
sharp *adj.* afiado
sharpen *v.* afiar

sharpener *n.* afiador

shatter *v.t.* estilhaçar

shattering *adj.* terrível

shave *v.* barbear

shaven *adj.* barbeado

shaving *n.* barbear

shawl *n.* xaile

she *pron.* ela

sheaf *n.* molho (de palha)

shear *v.* tosquiar

sheath *n.* bainha

shed *n.* barracão

sheen *n.* brilho

sheep *n.* ovelha

sheepish *adj.* envergonhado

sheer *adj.* puro

sheet *n.* folha

shelf *n.* prateleira

shell *n.* concha

shelter *n.* abrigo

shelve *v.* colocar em prateleira

shepherd *n.* pastor

shield *n.* escudo

shift *v.* transferir

shiftless *adj.* indolente

shifty *adj.* matreiro

shimmer *v.* cintilar

shin *n.* canela (perna)

shine *v.* brilhar

shingle *n.* telha

shiny *adj.* brilhante

ship *n.* navio

shipment *n.* remessa

shipping *n.* expedição

shipwreck *n.* naufrágio

shipyard *n.* estaleiro

shire *n.* condado

shirk *v.* esquivar

shirker *n.* mandrião

shirt *n.* camisa

shiver *v.* tiritar

shoal *n.* cardume

shock *n.* choque

shock *v.* chocar

shocking *adj.* chocante

shoddy *adj.* falso

shoe *n.* sapato

shoestring *n.* atacador

shoot *v.* atirar

shooting *n.* tiroteio

shop *n.* compras

shopkeeper *n.* comerciante

shoplifting *n.* roubo em lojas

shopping *n.* compras

shore *n.* costa

short *adj.* curto

shortage *n.* escassez

shortcoming *n.* deficiência

shortcut *n.* atalho

shorten *v.* encurtar

shortfall *n.* défice

shortly *adv.* bruscamente

should *v.* dever (obrigatoriedade)

shoulder *n.* ombro

shout *v.i.* gritar

shove *v.* empurrar

shovel *n.* pá

show *v.* mostrar

showcase *n.* expositor

showdown *n.* confronto

shower *n.* chuveiro

showy *adj.* vistoso

shrapnel *n.* estilhaços

shred *n.* farrapo

shrew *n.* megera

shrewd *adj.* sagaz

shriek *v.* guinchar

shrill *adj.* estridente

shrine *n.* santuário

shrink *v.* encolher

shrinkage *n.* encolhimento

shrivel *v.* murchar

shroud *n.* mortalha

shrub *n.* arbusto

shrug *v.* encolher os ombros

shudder *v.* estremecer

shuffle *v.t.* iludir

shun *v.t.* evitar

shunt *v.* desviar

shut *v.* fechar

shutter *n.* persiana

shuttle *n.* máquina de costurar

shuttlecock *n.* volante (badminton)

shy *adj.* tímido

sibilant *adj.* sibilante

sibling *n.* irmão

sick *adj.* doente

sickle *n.* foice

sickly *adj.* doentio

sickness *n.* doença

side *n.* lado

sideline *n.* linha lateral

siege *n.* cerco

siesta *n.* sesta

sieve *n.* peneira

sift *v.* peneirar

sigh *v.i.* suspirar

sight *n.* vista

sighting *n.* avistamento

sightseeing *n.* turismo

sign *n.* signo

signal *n.* sinal

signatory *n.* signatário

signature *n.* assinatura

significance *n.* significado

significant *n.* significativo

signification *n.* sentido

signify *v.* significar

silence *n.* silêncio

silencer *n.* silenciador

silent *adj.* silencioso

silhouette *n.* silhueta

silicon *n.* silício

silk *n.* seda

silken *adj.* sedoso

silkworm *n.* bicho-da-seda

silky *adj.* sedoso

sill *n.* parapeito

silly *adj.* bobo

silt *n.* lodo

silver *n.* prata

similar *adj.* similar

similarity *n.* similaridade

simile *n.* símile

simmer *v.* ferver

simper *v.* sorrir afetadamente

simple *adj.* simples	**sisterhood** *n.* irmandade
simpleton *n.* simplório	**sisterly** *adj.* de irmã
simplicity *n.* simplicidade	**sit** *v.* sentar
simplification *n.* simplificação	**site** *n.* local
simplify *v.* simplificar	**sitting** *n.* sessão
simulate *v.* simular	**situate** *v.* situar
simultaneous *adj.* simultâneo	**situation** *n.*, a situação
sin *n.* pecado	**six** *adj.& n.* seis
since *prep.* desde	**sixteen** *adj. & n.* dezasseis
sincere *adj.* sincero	**sixteenth** *adj. & n.* décimo sexto
sincerity *n.* sinceridade	**sixth** *adj. & n.* sexto
sinecure *n.* sinecura	**sixtieth** *adj. & n.* sexagésimo
sinful *adj.* pecador	**sixty** *adj. & n.* sessenta
sing *v.* cantar	**size** *n.* tamanho
singe *v.* chamuscar	**sizeable** *adj.* considerável
singer *a.* cantor	**sizzle** *v.* chiar
single *adj.* único	**skate** *n.* patim
singlet *n.* camisola interior s/ mangas	**skateboard** *n.* skate
singleton *n.* carta singular	**skein** *n.* meada
singular *adj.* peculiar	**skeleton** *n.* esqueleto
singularity *n.* singularidade	**sketch** *n.* esboço
singularly *adv.* singularmente	**sketchy** *adj.* superficial
sinister *adj.* sinistro	**skew** *v.* enviesar
sink *v.* afundar	**skewer** *n.* espada
sink *n.* lavatório	**ski** *n.* ski
sinner *n.* pecador	**skid** *v.* derrapar
sinuous *adj.* sinuoso	**skilful** *adj.* hábil
sinus *n.* seio	**skill** *n.* habilidade
sip *v.* sorver	**skilled** *adj.* hábil
siphon *n.* sifão	**skim** *v.* roçar
sir *n.* senhor	**skimp** *adj.* parco
siren *n.* sereia	**skin** *n.* pele
sissy *n.* maricas	**skinny** *adj.* magro
sister *n.* irmã	**skip** *v.* pular

skipper *n.* capitão

skirmish *n.* escaramuça

skirt *n.* saia

skirting *n.* rodapé

skit *n.* sátira

skittish *adj.* assustadiço

skittle *n.* disparate

skull *n.* crânio

sky *n.* céu

skylight *n.* clarabóia

skyscraper *n.* arranha-céu

slab *n.* laje

slack *adj.* negligente

slacken *v.* afrouxar

slag *n.* escória

slake *v.t.* caldear

slam *v.* bater

slander *n.* calúnia

slanderous *adj.* difamatório

slang *n.* calão

slant *v.* inclinar

slap *v.t.* esbofetear

slash *v.* retalhar

slat *n.* ripa

slate *n.* ardósia

slattern *n.* mulher desmazelada

slatternly *adj.* desleixado

slaughter *n.* matança

slave *n.* escravo

slavery *n.* escravidão

slavish *adj.* servil

slay *v.* matar

sleaze *n.* corrupção

sleazy *adj.* frágil

sledge *n.* trenó

sledgehammer *n.* marreta

sleek *adj.* lustroso

sleep *n.* sono

sleeper *n.* dorminhoco

sleepy *adj.* sonolento

sleet *n.* fiapos de neve

sleeve *n.* manga

sleigh *n.* trenó

sleight *n.* prestidigitação

slender *adj.* delgado

sleuth *n.* sabujo

slice *n.* fatia

slick *adj.* liso

slide *v.* deslizar

slight *adj.* leve

slightly *adv.* levemente

slim *adj.* esbelto

slime *n.* lodo

slimy *adj.* viscoso

sling *n.* eslinga

slink *v.* escapulir

slip *v.* escorregar

slipper *n.* chinelo

slippery *adj.* escorregadio

slit *v.t.* fender

slither *v.* deslizar

slob *n.* pateta

slobber *v.* babar

slogan *n.* slogan

slope *v.* inclinar-se

sloppy *adj.* desleixado

slot *n.* ranhura

sloth *n.* preguiça

slothful *adj.* preguiçoso
slouch *v.* desleixar
slough *n.* lamaçal
slovenly *adj.* desleixado
slow *adj.* lento
slowly *adv.* lentamente
slowness *n.* lentidão
sludge *n.* lodo
slug *n.* lesma
sluggard *n.* preguiçoso
sluggish *adj.* lento
sluice *n.* comporta
slum *n.* favela
slumber *v.* repousar
slump *v.* desmoronar
slur *v.* difamar
slurp *v.* sorver (ruidosamente)
slush *n.* lodo
slushy *adj.* lamacento
slut *n.* vadia
sly *adj.* astuto
smack *n.* beijoca
small *adj.* pequeno
smallpox *n.* varíola
smart *adj.* inteligente
smarten *v.* avivar
smash *v.* quebrar
smashing *adj.* esmagador
smattering *n.* conhecimento limitado
smear *v.* untar
smell *n.* cheiro
smelly *adj.* malcheiroso
smidgen *n.* pitada
smile *v.* sorrir

smirk *v.* sorrir afetadamente
smith *n.* ferreiro
smock *n.* bata
smog *n.* poluição
smoke *n.* fumar
smoky *adj.* enfumaçado
smooch *v.* estar na marmelada
smooth *adj.* liso
smoothie *n.* bajulador
smother *v.* sufocar
smoulder *v.* lavrar (fogo)
smudge *v.* sujar
smug *adj.* presunçoso
smuggle *v.* contrabandear
smuggler *n.* contrabandista
snack *n.* lanche
snag *n.* dificuldade
snail *n.* caracol
snake *n.* serpente
snap *v.* estalar
snapper *n.* pargo (peixe)
snappy *adj.* irritado
snare *n.* cilada
snarl *v.* rosnar
snarl *v.t.* rosnar
snatch *v.* arrebatar
snazzy *adj.* apelativo
sneak *v.* esquivar-se
sneaker *n.* ténis
sneer *n.* escárnio
sneeze *v.i.* espirrar
snide *adj.* falso
sniff *v.* farejar
sniffle *v.* fungar

snigger *n.* rir à socapa
snip *v.* retalhar
snipe *v.* caçar
snippet *n.* fragmento
snob *n.* snobe
snobbery *n.* snobismo
snobbish *adj.* snobe
snooker *n.* snooker
snooze *n.* dormitar
snore *n.* ronco
snort *n.* resfôlego
snout *n.* focinho
snow *n.* neve
snowball *n.* bola de neve
snowy *adj.* nevoso
snub *v.* desprezar
snuff *v.* fungar
snuffle *v.* falar fanhoso
snug *adj.* confortável
snuggle *v.* aconchegar
so *adv.* assim
soak *v.* embeber
soap *n.* sabão
soapy *adj.* ensaboado
soar *v.i.* planar
sob *v.* soluçar
sober *adj.* sóbrio
sobriety *n.* sobriedade
soccer *n.* futebol
sociability *n.* sociabilidade
sociable *adj.* sociável
social *adj.* social
socialism *n.* socialismo
socialist *n. & adj.* socialista

socialize *v.* socializar
society *n.* sociedade
sociology *n.* sociologia
sock *n.* meia
socket *n.* casquilho
sod *n.* relvado
soda *n.* soda
sodden *adj.* encharcado
sodomy *n.* sodomia
sofa *n.* sofá
soft *adj.* suave
soften *v.* amolecer
soggy *adj.* encharcado
soil *n.* solo
sojourn *n.* estadia
solace *n.* consolo
solar *adj.* solar
solder *n.* solda
soldier *n.* soldado
sole *n.* único
solely *adv.* unicamente
solemn *adj.* solene
solemnity *n.* solenidade
solemnize *v.* solenizar
solicit *v.* solicitar
solicitation *n.* solicitação
solicitor *n.* solicitador
solicitous *adj.* solícito
solicitude *n.* solicitude
solid *adj.* sólido
solidarity *n.* solidariedade
soliloquy *n.* solilóquio
solitaire *n.* solitário
solitary *adj.* solitário

solitude *n.* solidão

solo *n.* solo

soloist *n.* solista

solubility *n.* solubilidade

soluble *adj.* solúvel

solution *n.* solução

solve *v.* resolver

solvency *n.* solvência

solvent *n.* solvente

sombre *adj.* sombrio

some *adj.* alguns

somebody *pron.* alguém

somehow *adv.* de alguma maneira

someone *pron.* alguém

somersault *n.* cambalhota

somnolent *adj.* sonolento

something *pron.* algo

somewhat *adv.* um pouco

somewhere *adv.* algures

somnambulism *n.* sonambulismo

somnambulist *n.* sonâmbulo

somnolence *n.* sonolência

somnolent *adj.* sonolento

son *n.* filho

song *n.* canção

songster *n.* cantor

sonic *adj.* sónico

sonnet *n.* soneto

sonority *n.* sonoridade

soon *adv.* rapidamente

soot *n.* fuligem

soothe *v.* abrandar

sophism *n.* sofisma

sophist *n.* sofista

sophisticate *n.* sofismar

sophisticated *adj.* sofisticado

sophistication *n.* sofisticação

soporific *adj.* soporífero

sopping *adj.* encharcado

soppy *adj.* alagado

sorbet *n.* sorvete

sorcerer *n.* feiticeiro

sorcery *n.* feitiçaria

sordid *adj.* sórdido

sore *adj.* dolorido

sorely *adv.* extremamente

sorrow *n.* tristeza

sorry *adj.* pesaroso

sort *n.* tipo

sortie *n.* surtida

sough *v.* sussurrar

soul *n.* alma

soulful *adj.* emotivo

soulless *adj.* desumano

soul mate *n.* alma gémea

sound *n.* som

soundproof *adj.* à prova de som

soup *n.* sopa

sour *adj.* azedo

source *n.* fonte

souse *v.* humedecer

south *n.* sul

southerly *adj.* meridional

southern *adj.* sulista

souvenir *n.* lembrança

sovereign *n.* soberano

sovereignty *n.* soberania

sow *n.* porca

spa *n.* spa
space *n.* espaço
spacious *adj.* espaçoso
spade *n.* pá
spam *n.* spam
span *n.* palmo
Spaniard *n.* Espanhol
spaniel *n.* spaniel
Spanish *n.* Espanhol
spank *v.* espancar
spanking *adj.* formidável
spanner *n.* chave de fendas
spare *adj.* sobressalente
sparing *adj.* poupado
spark *n.* faísca
sparkle *v.* brilhar
sparkling *n.* brilhante
sparrow *n.* pardal
sparse *adj.* escasso
spasm *n.* espasmo
spasmodic *adj.* espasmódico
spastic *adj.* espamódico
spat *n.* palmada
spate *n.* enchente
spatial *adj.* espacial
spatter *v.* salpicar
spawn *v.* desovar
spay *v.* esterelizar
speak *v.* falar
speaker *n.* falante
spear *n.* lança
spearhead *n.* ponta de lança
spearmint *n.* hortelã
special *adj.* especial

specialist *n.* especialista
speciality *n.* especialidade
specialization *n.* especialização
specialize *v.* especializar
species *n.* espécies
specific *adj.* específico
specification *n.* especificação
specify *v.* especificar
specimen *n.* espécime
specious *adj.* enganador
speck *n.* mancha pequena
speckle *n.* mancha pequena
spectacle *n.* espetáculo
spectacular *adj.* espetacular
spectator *n.* espetador
spectral *adj.* espetral
spectre *n.* espetro
spectrum *n.* espetro
speculate *v.* especular
speculation *n.* especulação
speech *n.* discurso
speechless *adj.* mudo
speed *n.* velocidade
speedway *n.* circuito
speedy *adj.* célere
spell *v.t.* soletrar
spellbound *adj.* tonto
spelling *n.* soletração
spend *v.* gastar
spendthrift *n.* perdulário
sperm *n.* esperma
sphere *n.* esfera
spherical *n.* esférico
spice *n.* tempero

spicy *adj.* picante	**splenetic** *adj.* esplenético
spider *n.* aranha	**splice** *v.* unir
spike *n.* prego	**splint** *n.* tala
spiky *adj.* pontiagudo	**splinter** *n.* lasca
spill *v.* derramar	**split** *v.* dividir
spillage *n.* derrame	**splutter** *v.* crepitar
spin *v.* girar	**spoil** *v.* estragar
spinach *n.* espinafre	**spoiler** *n.* desmancha-prazeres
spinal *adj.* espinhal	**spoke** *n.* raio
spindle *n.* fuso	**spokesman** *n.* porta-voz
spindly *adj.* espigado	**sponge** *n.* esponja
spine *n.* coluna	**sponsor** *n.* patrocinador
spineless *adj.* fraco	**sponsorship** *n.* patrocínio
spinner *n.* fiandeira	**spontaneity** *n.* espontaneidade
spinster *n.* solteirona	**spontaneous** *adj.* espontâneo
spiral *adj.* espiral	**spool** *n.* carretel
spire *n.* pináculo	**spoon** *n.* colher
spirit *n.* espírito	**spoonful** *n.* colherada
spirited *adj.* animado	**spoor** *n.* rasto
spiritual *adj.* espiritual	**sporadic** *adj.* esporádico
spiritualism *n.* espiritualismo	**spore** *n.* esporo
spiritualist *n.* espiritualista	**sport** *n.* desporto
spirituality *n.* espiritualidade	**sporting** *adj.* desportivo
spit *n.* cuspo	**sportive** *adj.* brincalhão
spite *n.* despeito	**sportsman** *n.* desportista
spiteful *adj.* rancoroso	**spot** *n.* local
spittle *n.* saliva	**spotless** *adj.* impecável
spittoon *n.* escarrador	**spousal** *n.* conjugal
splash *v.* salpicar	**spouse** *n.* cônjuge
splatter *v.* ondular	**spout** *n.* bica
splay *v.* alargar	**sprain** *v.t.* torcer
spleen *n.* baço	**sprat** *n.* espadilha (peixe)
splendid *adj.* esplêndido	**sprawl** *v.* estatelar
splendour *n.* esplendor	**spray** *n.* spray

spread v. espalhar	**squid** n. lula
spreadsheet n. folha de cálculo	**squint** v. entortar (os olhos)
spree n. farra	**squire** n. escudeiro
sprig n. raminho	**squirm** v. torcer
sprightly adj. alegre	**squirrel** n. esquilo
spring v. pular	**squirt** v. respingar
sprinkle v.i. borrifar	**squish** v. expelir jato
sprinkler n. borrifador	**stab** v. esfaquear
sprinkling n. aspersão	**stability** n. estabilidade
sprint v. correr velozmente	**stabilization** n. estabilização
sprinter n. sprinter	**stabilize** v. estabilizar
sprout v. brotar	**stable** adj. estável
spry adj. ágil	**stable** n. estábulo
spume n. espuma	**stack** n. pilha
spur n. espora	**stadium** n. estádio
spurious adj. espúrio	**staff** n. pessoal
spurn v. menosprezar	**stag** n. veado
spurt v. esguichar	**stage** n. etapa
sputum n. expetoração	**stagecoach** n. diligência
spy n. espião	**stagger** v. cambalear
squabble n. disputa	**staggering** adj. cambaleante
squad n. esquadra	**stagnant** adj. estagnado
squadron n. esquadrão	**stagnate** v. estagnar
squalid adj. esquálido	**stagnation** n. estagnação
squall n. borrasca	**staid** adj. sério
squander v. esbanjar	**stain** v.t. manchar
square n. quadrado	**stair** n. escada
squash v. achatar	**staircase** n. escadaria
squat v.i. agachar	**stake** n. estaca
squawk v. grasnir	**stale** adj. velho
squeak n. ranger	**stalemate** n. impasse
squeal n. guincho	**staleness** n. bafiento
squeeze v. espremer	**stalk** n. haste
squib n. bicha-de-rabear	**stalker** n. perseguidor

stall *n.* estrebaria	**starve** *v.* morrer de fome
stallion *n.* garanhão	**stash** *v.* acumular
stalwart *adj.* robusto	**state** *n.* estado
stamen *n.* estame	**stateless** *adj.* apátrida
stamina *n.* vigor	**stately** *adj.* imponente
stammer *v.* gaguejar	**statement** *n.* afirmação
stamp *n.* carimbo	**statesman** *n.* estadista
stamp *v.* carimbar	**static** *adj.* estático
stampede *n.* debandada	**statically** *adv.* estaticamente
stance *n.* atitude	**station** *n.* estação
stanchion *n.* pilar	**stationary** *adj.* estacionário
stand *v.* suportar	**stationer** *n.* proprietário papelaria
standard *n.* padrão	**stationery** *n.* artigos de papelaria
standardization *n.* uniformização	**statistical** *adj.* estatístico
standardize *v.* uniformizar	**statistician** *n.* estatístico
standing *n.* em pé	**statistics** *n.* estatística
standpoint *n.* ponto de vista	**statuary** *n.* estatuária
standstill *n.* imobilização	**statue** *n.* estátua
stanza *n.* estrofe	**statuesque** *adj.* escultural
staple *n.* agrafo	**statuette** *n.* estatueta
staple *v.* agrafar	**stature** *n.* estatura
stapler *n.* agrafador	**status** *n.* estado (posição social)
star *n.* estrela	**statute** *n.* estatuto
starch *n.* amido	**statutory** *adj.* estatutário
starchy *adj.* empertigado	**staunch** *adj.* leal
stare *v.* encarar	**stave** *n.* aduela
stark *adj.* forte	**stay** *v.* ficar
starlet *n.* estrelinha	**stead** *n.* lugar
startling *n.* surpreendente	**steadfast** *adj.* firme
starry *adj.* estrelado	**steadiness** *n.* estabilidade
start *v.* começar	**steady** *adj.* estável
starter *n.* arranque	**steak** *n.* bife
startle *v.* assustar	**steal** *v.* roubar
starvation *n.* fome	**stealth** *n.* discrição

stealthily *adv.* furtivamente
stealthy *adj.* furtivo
steam *n.* vapor
steamer *n.* navio a vapor
steed *n.* corcel
steel *n.* aço
steep *adj.* íngreme
steeple *n.* campanário
steeplechase *n.* corrida obstáculos
steer *v.* dirigir
stellar *adj.* estelar
stem *n.* caule
stench *n.* fedor
stencil *n.* estêncil
stenographer *n.* estenógrafo
stenography *n.* estenografia
stentorian *adj.* possante
step *n.* passo
steppe *n.* estepe
stereo *n.* estéreo
stereophonic *adj.* estereofónico
stereoscopic *adj.* estereoscópico
stereotype *n.* estereótipo
sterile *adj.* estéril
sterility *n.* esterilidade
sterilization *n.* esterilização
sterilize *v.* esterilizar
sterling *n.* libra estrelina
stern *adj.* severo
sternum *n.* esterno
steroid *n.* esteróide
stertorous *adj.* estertorante
stethoscope *n.* estetoscópio
stew *n.* ensopado

steward *n.* mordomo
stick *n.* pau
sticker *n.* adesivo
stickleback *n.* espinhela
stickler *n.* picuinhas
sticky *adj.* pegajoso
stiff *adj.* duro
stiffen *v.* enrijecer
stifle *v.* sufocar
stigma *n.* estigma
stigmata *n.* estigmas
stigmatize *v.* estigmatizar
stile *n.* couceira
stiletto *n.* punhal
still *adj.* imóvel
stillborn *n.* nado-morto
stillness *n.* tranquilidade
stilt *n.* pernilongo
stilted *adj.* empolado
stimulant *n.* estimulante
stimulate *v.* estimular
stimulus *n.* estímulo
sting *n.* picada
stingy *adj.* mesquinho
stink *v.* feder
stint *n.* restrição
stipend *n.* estipêndio
stipple *v.* encher de pontos
stipulate *v.* estipular
stipulation *n.* estipulação
stir *v.* movimentar
stirrup *n.* estribo
stitch *n.* ponto
stitch *v.* alinhavar

stock *n.* stock	**straight** *adj.* reto
stockbroker *n.* corretor de Bolsa	**straighten** *v.* endireitar
stockade *n.* paliçada	**straightforward** *adj.* franco
stocking *n.* aprovisionamento	**straightway** *adv.* imediatamente
stockist *n.* armazenista	**strain** *v.* esticar
stocky *adj.* atarracado	**strain** *n.* tensão
stoic *n.* estóico	**strained** *adj.* tenso
stoke *v.* carregar	**strait** *n.* estreito
stoker *n.* fogueiro	**straiten** *v.i.* estreitar
stole *n.* estola	**strand** *v.* encalhar
stolid *adj.* impassível	**strange** *adj.* estranho
stomach *n.* estômago	**stranger** *n.* desconhecido
stomp *n.* sapateado	**strangle** *v.* estrangular
stone *n.* pedra	**strangulation** *n.* estrangulamento
stony *adj.* pedregoso	**strap** *n.* correia
stooge *n.* estarola	**strapping** *adj.* robusto
stool *n.* banquinho	**stratagem** *n.* estratagema
stoop *v.* dobrar	**strategic** *adj.* estratégico
stop *v.* parar	**strategist** *n.* estrategista
stoppage *n.* interrupção	**strategy** *n.* estratégia
stopper *n.* tampão	**stratify** *v.* estratificar
storage *n.* armazenamento	**stratum** *n.* estrato
store *n.* loja	**straw** *n.* palha
storey *n.* pavimento	**strawberry** *n.* morango
stork *n.* cegonha	**stray** *v.* vaguear
storm *n.* tempestade	**streak** *n.* listra
stormy *adj.* tempestuoso	**streaky** *adj.* raiado
story *n.* história	**stream** *n.* corrente
stout *adj.* robusto	**streamer** *n.* flâmula
stove *n.* fogão	**streamlet** *n.* riacho
stow *v.* armazenar	**street** *n.* rua
straddle *v.* andar escarranchado	**strength** *n.* força
straggle *v.* vaguear	**strengthen** *v.* fortalecer
straggler *n.* vagabundo	**strenuous** *adj.* vigoroso

stress *n.* stress	**structure** *n.* estrutura
stress *v.t.* pressionar	**strudel** *n.* strudel
stretch *v.* esticar	**struggle** *v.* lutar
stretch *n.* extensão	**strum** *v.* arranhar
stretcher *n.* esticador	**strumpet** *n.* prostituta
strew *v.* espalhar	**strut** *n.* andar empertigado
striation *n.* estrias	**Stuart** *n.* Stuart
stricken *adj.* ferido	**stub** *n.* cepo
strict *adj.* estrito	**stubble** *n.* restolho
strictly *adv.* estritamente	**stubborn** *adj.* teimoso
stricture *n.* aperto	**stucco** *n.* estuque
stride *v.* cavalgar	**stud** *n.* viga
strident *adj.* estridente	**student** *n.* estudante
strife *n.* conflito	**studio** *n.* estúdio
strike *v.* golpear	**studious** *adj.* estudioso
striker *n.* grevista	**study** *n.* estudo
striking *adj.* impressionante	**study** *v.* estudar
string *n.* corda	**stuff** *n.* coisas
stringency *n.* rigor	**stuffing** *n.* estofamento
stringent *adj.* rigoroso	**stuffy** *adj.* abafado
stringy *adj.* pegajoso	**stultify** *v.* invalidar
strip *v.t.* descascar	**stumble** *v.* tropeçar
stripe *n.* barra	**stump** *n.* toco
stripling *n.* adolescente	**stun** *v.* atordoar
stripper *n.* Stripper	**stunner** *n.* cativante
strive *v.* lutar	**stunning** *adj.* assombroso
strobe *n.* estroboscópio	**stunt** *v.* atrasar
stroke *n.* golpe	**stupefy** *v.* atordoar
stroll *v.* passear	**stupendous** *adj.* estupendo
strong *adj.* forte	**stupid** *adj.* estúpido
stronghold *n.* fortaleza	**stupidity** *n.* estupidez
strop *n.* tira de couro	**stupor** *n.* estupor
stroppy *adj.* esquisito	**sturdy** *adj.* robusto
structural *adj.* estrutural	**stutter** *v.* gaguejar

sty *n.* estábulo

stygian *adj.* infernal

style *n.* estilo

stylish *adj.* elegante

stylist *n.* estilista

stylistic *adj.* estilístico

stylized *adj.* estilizado

stylus *n.* estilete

stymie *v.* boicotar

styptic *adj.* hemostático

suave *adj.* suave

subaltern *n.* subalterno

subconscious *adj.* subconsciente

subcontract *v.* subcontratar

subdue *v.* subjugar

subedit *v.* supervisionar a redação

subject *n.* assunto

subjection *n.* sujeição

subjective *adj.* subjetivo

subjudice *adj.* em segredo

subjugate *v.* subjugar

subjugation *n.* subjugação

subjunctive *adj.* subjuntivo

sublet *v.t.* subalugar

sublimate *v.* sublimar

sublime *adj.* sublime

subliminal *adj.* subliminar

submarine *n.* submarino

submerge *v.* submergir

submerse *v.* submergir

submersible *adj.* submersível

submission *n.* submissão

submissive *adj.* submisso

submit *v.* submeter

subordinate *adj.* subordinado

subordination *n.* subordinação

suborn *v.* subornar

subscribe *v.* subscrever

subscript *adj.* subscrito

subscription *n.* assinatura

subsequent *adj.* subsequente

subservience *n.* subserviência

subservient *adj.* subserviente

subside *v.* baixar

subsidiary *adj.* subsidiário

subsidize *v.* subsidiar

subsidy *n.* subsídio

subsist *v.* subsistir

subsistence *n.* subsistência

subsonic *adj.* subsónico

substance *n.* substância

substantial *adj.* substancial

substantially *adv.* substancialmente

substantiate *v.* fundamentar

substantiation *n.* comprovação

substantive *adj.* substantivo

substitute *n.* substituto

substitution *n.* substituição

subsume *v.* subsumir

subterfuge *n.* subterfúgio

subterranean *adj.* subterrâneo

subtitle *n.* subtítulo

subtle *adj.* subtil

subtlety *n.* subtileza

subtotal *n.* subtotal

subtract *v.* subtrair

subtraction *n.* subtração

subtropical *adj.* subtropical

suburb *n.* subúrbio
suburban *adj.* suburbano
suburbia *n.* subúrbios
subversion *n.* subversão
subversive *adj.* subversivo
subvert *v.i.* subverter
subway *n.* metro
succeed *v.* suceder
success *n.* sucesso
successful *adj.* bem sucedido
succession *n.* sucessão
successive *adj.* sucessivo
successor *n.* sucessor
succinct *adj.* sucinto
succour *n.* socorro
succulent *adj.* suculento
succumb *v.* sucumbir
such *adj.* tal
suck *v.* chupar
sucker *n.* idiota
suckle *v.* mamar
suckling *n.* aleitamento
suction *n.* sucção
sudden *adj.* repentino
suddenly *adv.* subitamente
Sudoku *n.* Sudoku
sue *v.t.* processar
suede *n.* camurça
suffer *v.i.* sofrer
sufferance *n.* sofrimento
suffice *v.* bastar
sufficiency *n.* suficiência
sufficient *adj.* suficiente
suffix *n.* sufixo

suffocate *v.* sufocar
suffocation *n.* sufoco
suffrage *n.* sufrágio
suffuse *v.* inundar
sugar *n.* açúcar
suggest *v.* sugerir
suggestible *adj.* sugestionável
suggestion *n.* sugestão
suggestive *adj.* sugestivo
suicidal *adj.* suicida
suicide *n.* suicídio
suit *n.* fato
suitability *n.* conveniência
suitable *adj.* adequado
suite *n.* suite
suitor *n.* litigante
sulk *v.* amuar
sullen *adj.* taciturno
sully *v.* sujar
sulphur *n.* enxofre
sultana *n.* sultana
sultry *adj.* abafado
sum *n.* soma
summarily *adv.* sumariamente
summarize *v.* resumir
summary *n.* resumo
summer *n.* verão
summit *n.* cume
summon *v.* convocar
summons *n.* convocação
sumptuous *adj.* sumptuoso
sun *n.* sol
sun *v.* insolar
sundae *n.* sundae

Sunday *n.* Domingo

sunder *v.* separar

sundry *adj.* diversos

sunken *adj.* submerso

sunny *adj.* ensolarado

super *adj.* formidável

superabundance *adj.* superabundância

superabundant *adj.* superabundante

superannuation *n.* aposentadoria

superb *adj.* soberbo

supercharger *n.* compressor

supercilious *adj.* arrogante

superficial *adj.* superficial

superficiality *n.* superficialidade

superfine *adj.* superfino

superfluity *n.* superfluidade

superfluous *adj.* supérfluo

superhuman *adj.* sobre-humano

superimpose *v.* sobrepor

superintend *v.* superintender

superintendence *n.* superintendência

superintendent *n.* superintendente

superior *adj.* superior

superiority *n.* superioridade

superlative *adj.* superlativo

supermarket *n.* supermercado

supernatural *adj.* sobrenatural

superpower *n.* superpotência

superscript *adj.* sobrescrito

supersede *v.* suplantar

supersonic *adj.* supersónico

superstition *n.* superstição

superstitious *adj.* supersticioso

superstore *n.* hipermercado

supervene *v.* sobrevir

supervise *v.* supervisionar

supervision *n.* supervisão

supervisor *n.* supervisor

supper *n.* ceia

supplant *v.* suplantar

supple *adj.* flexível

supplement *n.* suplemento

supplementary *adj.* suplementar

suppliant *n.* suplicante

supplicate *v.* suplicar

supplier *n.* fornecedor

supply *v.* fornecer

support *v.* apoiar

support *n.* apoio (moral)

suppose *v.* supor

supposition *n.* suposição

suppository *n.* supositório

suppress *v.* suprimir

suppression *n.* supressão

suppurate *v.* supurar

supremacy *n.* supremacia

supreme *adj.* supremo

surcharge *n.* sobretaxa

sure *adj.* certo

surely *adv.* certamente

surety *n.* fiança

surf *n.* surf

surface *n.* superfície

surfeit *n.* superabundância

surge *n.* onda

surgeon *n.* cirurgião

surgery *n.* cirurgia

surly *adj.* ranzinza

surmise *v.t.* supor
surmount *v.* superar
surname *n.* sobrenome
surpass *v.* superar
surplus *n.* excedente
surprise *n.* surpresa
surreal *adj.* surreal
surrealism *n.* surrealismo
surrender *v.* render-se
surrender *n.* rendição
surreptitious *adj.* sub-reptício
surrogate *n.* substituto
surround *v.* cercar
surroundings *n.* ambiente
surtax *n.* sobretaxa
surveillance *n.* vigilância
survey *v.t.* inspecionar
surveyor *n.* agrimensor
survival *n.* sobrevivência
survive *v.* sobreviver
susceptible *adj.* suscetível
suspect *v.* suspeitar
suspect n suspeito
suspend *v.* suspender
suspense *n.* expectativa
suspension *n.* suspensão
suspicion *n.* suspeita
suspicious *adj.* suspeito
sustain *v.* sustentar
sustainable *adj.* sustentável
sustenance *n.* sustento
suture *n.* sutura
svelte *adj.* esbelto
swab *n.* cotonete

swaddle *v.* enfaixar
swag *n.* saque
swagger *v.* fanfarronar
swallow *v.* engolir
swamp *n.* pântano
swan *n.* cisne
swank *v.* ostentar
swanky *adj.* pretencioso
swap *v.* trocar
swarm *n.* enxame
swarthy *adj.* moreno
swashbuckling *adj.* fanfarrão
swat *v.* golpear
swathe *n.* faixa
sway *v.* oscilar
swear *v.* jurar
sweat *n.* suor
sweater *n.* suéter
sweep *v.* varrer
sweeper *n.* varredor
sweet *adj.* doce
sweet *n.* querido
sweeten *v.* adoçar
sweetheart *n.* amor
sweetmeat *n.* guloseima
sweetener *n.* adoçante
sweetness *n.* doçura
swell *v.* inchar
swell *n.* inchação
swelling *n.* inchaço
swelter *v.* abafar
swerve *v.* desviar
swift *adj.* rápido
swill *v.* enxaguar

swim *v.* nadar

swimmer *n.* nadador

swindle *v.* burlar

swindler *n.* vigarista

swine *n.* suíno

swing *n.* balanço

swing *v.* balançar

swingeing *adj.* enorme

swipe *v.* espancar

swirl *v.* serpentear

swish *adj.* enfeitado

switch *n.* interruptor

swivel *v.* rotar

swoon *v.* desmaiar

swoop *v.* descer

sword *n.* espada

sybarite *n.* sibarita

sycamore *n.* sicómoro

sycophancy *n.* sicofantismo

sycophant *n.* sicofanta

syllabic *adj.* silábico

syllable *n.* sílaba

syllabus *n.* programa de estudos

syllogism *n.* silogismo

sylph *n.* silfo

sylvan *adj.* silvestre

symbiosis *n.* simbiose

symbol *n.* símbolo

symbolic *adj.* simbólico

symbolism *n.* simbolismo

symbolize *v.* simbolizar

symmetrical *adj.* simétrico

symmetry *n.* simetria

sympathetic *adj.* compreensivo

sympathize *v.* simpatizar

sympathy *n.* simpatia

symphony *n.* sinfonia

symposium *n.* simpósio

symptom *n.* sintoma

symptomatic *adj.* sintomático

synchronize *v.* sincronizar

synchronous *adj.* síncrono

syndicate *n.* sindicato

syndrome *n.* síndrome

synergy *n.* sinergia

synonym *n.* sinónimo

synonymous *adj.* sinónimo

synopsis *n.* sinopse

syntax *n.* sintaxe

synthesis *n.* síntese

synthesize *v.* sintetizar

synthetic *adj.* sintético

syringe *n.* seringa

syrup *n.* xarope

system *n.* sistema

systematic *adj.* sistemático

systematize *v.* sistematizar

systemic *adj.* sistémico

T

tab *n.* aba

table *n.* mesa

tableau *n.* quadro

tablet *n.* comprimido

tabloid *n.* tablóide

taboo *n.* tabu

tabular *adj.* tabular

tabulate *v.* classificar

tabulation n. classificação	**tame** adj. manso
tabulator v. tabulador	**tamely** adv. mansamente
tachometer n. tacómetro	**tamp** v. calcar
tacit adj. tácito	**tamper** v. adulterar
taciturn adj. taciturno	**tampon** n. tampão
tack n. tacha	**tan** n. bronzeado
tackle v.t. obstruir	**tandem** n. tandem
tacky adj. pegajoso	**tang** n. travo
tact n. tato	**tangent** n. tangente
tactful adj. delicado	**tangerine** n. tangerina
tactic n. tática	**tangible** adj. tangível
tactician n. tático	**tangle** v.t. enredar
tactical adj. tático	**tank** n. tanque
tactile adj. tátil	**tanker** n. petroleiro
tag n. etiqueta	**tanner** n. curtidor
tail n. cauda	**tannery** n. curtume
tailor n. alfaiate	**tantalize** v. atormentar
taint v. macular	**tantamount** adj. equivalente
take v. tomar	**tantrum** n. birra
takeaway n. takeaway	**tap** n. torneira
takings n. conquista	**tapas** n. tapas
talc n. talco	**tape** n. fita
tale n. conto	**tape** v.i. amarrar
talent n. talento	**taper** v. estreitar
talented adj. talentoso	**tapestry** n. tapeçaria
talisman n. talismã	**tappet** n. ressalto
talk v. falar	**tar** n. alcatrão
talkative adj. falador	**tardy** adj. tardio
tall adj. alto	**target** n. alvo
tallow n. sebo	**tariff** n. tarifa
tally n. registo	**tarn** n. gaivina
talon n. garra	**tarnish** v. empanar
tamarind n. tamarindo	**tarot** n. tarot
tambourine n. pandeireta	**tarpaulin** n. lona

tart *n.* tarte	**technicality** *n.* tecnicismo
tartar *n.* tástaro	**technician** *n.* técnico
task *n.* tarefa	**technique** *n.* técnica
tassel *n.* borla	**technological** *adj.* tecnológica
taste *n.* gosto	**technologist** *n.* tecnólogo
taste *v.* experimentar	**technology** *n.* tecnologia
tasteful *adj.* saboroso	**tedious** *adj.* tedioso
tasteless *adj.* insípido	**tedium** *n.* tédio
tasty *adj.* gostoso	**teem** *v.* abundar
tatter *n.* farrapo	**teenager** *n.* adolescente
tattle *n.* tagarelice	**teens** *n.* adolescentes
tattoo *n.* tatuagem	**teeter** *v.* cambalear
tatty *adj.* pobre	**teethe** *v.* cair os dentes
taunt *n.* sarcasmo	**teetotal** *adj.* abstémio
taut *adj.* tenso	**teetotaller** *n.* abstémio
tavern *n.* taverna	**telecast** *v.t.* televisionar
tawdry *adj.* espalhafatoso	**telecommunications** *n.* telecomunicações
tax *n.* imposto	**telegram** *n.* telegrama
taxable *adj.* tributável	**telegraph** *n.* telégrafo
taxation *n.* tributação	**telegraphic** *adj.* telegráfico
taxi *n.* táxi	**telegraphy** *n.* telegrafia
taxi *v.* movimentar avião na pista	**telepathic** *adj.* telepática
taxonomy *n.* taxonomia	**telepathist** *n.* telepata
tea *n.* chá	**telepathy** *n.* telepatia
teach *v.* ensinar	**telephone** *n.* telefone
teacher *n.* professor	**teleprinter** *n.* teleimpressor
teak *n.* teca	**telescope** *n.* telescópio
team *n.* equipe	**teletext** *n.* teletexto
tear *v.* chorar	**televise** *v.* televisionar
tear *n.* lágrima	**television** *n.* televisão
tearful *adj.* choroso	**tell** *v.* dizer
tease *v.* arreliar	**teller** *n.* contador
teat *n.* mamilo	**telling** *adj.* notável
technical *adj.* técnico	**telltale** *adj.* queixinhas

temerity *n.* temeridade
temper *n.* temperamento
temperament *n.* temperamento
temperamental *adj.* temperamental
temperance *n.* temperança
temperate *adj.* temperado
temperature *n.* temperatura
tempest *n.* tempestade
tempestuous *adj.* tempestuoso
template *n.* modelo
temple *n.* templo
tempo *n.* tempo (música)
temporal *adj.* temporal
temporary *adj.* temporário
temporize *v.* temporizar
tempt *v.* seduzir
temptation *n.* tentação
tempter *n.* tentador
ten *adj. & adv.* dez
tenable *adj.* sustentável
tenacious *adj.* tenaz
tenacity *n.* tenacidade
tenancy *n.* arrendamento
tenant *n.* inquilino
tend *v.* supervisionar
tendency *n.* tendência
tendentious *adj.* tendencioso
tender *adj.* tenro
tender *n.* afetuoso
tendon *n.* tendão
tenement *n.* habitação
tenet *n.* princípio
tennis *n.* ténis
tenor *n.* tenor

tense *adj.* tenso
tensile *adj.* tênsil
tension *n.* tensão
tent *n.* tenda
tentacle *n.* tentáculo
tentative *adj.* experimental
tenterhook *n.* gancho (susp. tecidos)
tenth *adj. & n.* décimo
tenuous *adj.* ténue
tenure *n.* mandato
tepid *adj.* tépido
term *n.* prazo
termagant *n.* megera
terminal *adj.* terminal
terminate *v.* terminar
termination *n.* terminação
terminological *adj.* terminológico
terminology *n.* terminologia
terminus *n.* término
termite *n.* térmite (formiga)
terrace *n.* terraço
terracotta *n.* terracota
terrain *n.* terreno
terrestrial *adj.* terrestre
terrible *adj.* terrível
terrier *n.* terrier
terrific *adj.* formidável
terrify *v.* aterrorizar
territorial *adj.* territorial
territory *n.* território
terror *n.* terror
terrorism *n.* terrorismo
terrorist *n.* terrorista
terrorize *v.* aterrorizar

terry *n.* frisado

terse *adj.* conciso

tertiary *adj.* terciário

test *n.* teste

testament *n.* testamento

testate *adj.* que deixou

testicle *n.* testículo

testify *v.* testemunhar

testimonial *n.* certificado

testimony *n.* testemunho

testis *n.* testículo

testosterone *n.* testosterona

testy *adj.* irritável

tetchy *adj.* irritado

tether *v.t.* acorrentar

text *n.* texto

textbook *n.* manual escolar

textile n têxtil

textual *adj.* textual

texture *n.* textura

thank *v.* agradecer

thankful *adj.* grato

thankless *adj.* ingrato

that *pron.* & *adj.* que & esse

thatch *n.* palha

thaw *v.* derreter

the *adv.* quanto

theatre *n.* teatro

theatrical *adj.* teatral

theft *n.* roubo

their *adj.* seu

theism *n.* teísmo

them *pron.* os, as,

thematic *adj.* temático

theme *n.* tema

themselves *pron.* se

then *adv.* então

thence *adv.* daí

theocracy *n.* teocracia

theodolite *n.* teodolito

theologian *n.* teólogo

theology *n.* teologia

theorem *n.* teorema

theoretical *adj.* teórico

theorist *n.* teórico

theorize *v.* teorizar

theory *n.* teoria

theosophy *n.* teosofia

therapeutic *adj.* terapêutico

therapist *n.* terapeuta

therapy *n.* terapia

there *adv.* lá

thermal *adj.* térmico

thermodynamics *n.* termodinâmica

thermometer *n.* termómetro

thermos *n.* termo

thermosetting *adj.* termoendurecíveis

thermostat *n.* termóstato

thesis *n.* tese

they *pron.* eles

thick *adj.* grosso

thicken *v.* engrossar

thicket *n.* matagal

thief *n.* ladrão

thigh *n.* coxa

thimble *n.* dedal

thin *adj.* fino

thing *n.* coisa

think *v.* pensar
thinker *n.* pensador
third *adj.* terceiro
thirst *n.* sede
thirsty *adj.* sedento
thirteen *adj. & n.* treze & terço
thirteenth *adj. & n.* décimo terceiro
thirtieth *adj. & n.* trigésimo
thirty *adj. & n.* trinta
this *pron.& adj.* isso & este
thistle *n.* cardo
thither *adv.* para lá
thong *n.* correia
thorn *n.* espinho
thorny *adj.* espinhoso
thorough *adj.* completo
thoroughfare *n.* via pública
though *conj.* conquanto
thoughtful *adj.* pensativo
thoughtless *adj.* irrefletido
thousand *adj. & n.* mil
thrall *n.* escravo
thrash *v.* sovar
thread *n.* fio
threat *n.* ameaça
threaten *v.* ameaçar
three *adj. & n.* três
thresh *v.* debulhar
threshold *n.* limiar
thrice *adv.* triplamente
thrift *n.* frugalidade
thrifty *adj.* frugal
thrill *n.* emoção
thriller *n.* tríler

thrive *v.* prosperar
throat *n.* garganta
throaty *adj.* gutural
throb *v.* pulsar
throes *n.* espasmos
throne *n.* trono
throng *n.* multidão
throttle *n.* garganta
through *prep. &adv.* por & através
throughout *prep.* por todo
throw *v.* lançar
thrush *n.* tordo
thrust *v.* empurrar
thud *n.* baque
thug *n.* bandido
thumb *n.* polegar
thunder *n.* trovão
thunderous *adj.* trovejante
Thursday *n.* Quinta-feira
thus *adv.* assim
thwart *v.* impedir
thyroid *n.* tiróide
tiara *n.* tiara
tick *n.* instante
ticket *n.* bilhete
ticking *n.* tiquetaque
tickle *v.* fazer cócegas
ticklish *adj.* delicado
tidal *adj.* das marés
tidally *n.* tidally
tide *n.* dependente
tidings *n.* notícias
tidiness *n.* asseio
tidy *adj.* arrumado

tie v. amarrar

tie n. gravata

tied adj. amarrado

tier n. fila

tiger n. tigre

tight adj. apertado

tighten v. apertar

tile n. azulejo

till prep. até

tiller n. agricultor

tilt v. inclinar

timber n. madeira

time n. tempo

timely adj. oportuno

timid adj. tímido

timidity n. timidez

timorous adj. timorato

tin n. estanho

tincture n. tintura

tinder n. mecha

tinge n. coloração

tingle n. prurido

tinker v. consertar utensílios

tinkle v. tilintar

tinsel n. ouropel

tint n. matiz

tiny adj. minúsculo

tip n. ponta

tipple v. beber

tipster n. informante

tipsy n. embriagado

tiptoe v. andar em bicos de pés

tirade n. tirada

tire v. cansar

tired adj. cansado

tireless adj. incansável

tiresome adj. cansativo

tissue n. tecido

titanic adj. titânico

titbit n. guloseima

tithe n. dízimo

titillate v. deleitar

titivate v. enfeitar

title n. título

titled adj. titular

titular adj. nominal

to prep. para

toad n. sapo

toast n. brinde

toaster n. torradeira

tobacco n. tabaco

today adv. hoje

toddle v. cambalear

toddler n. criança

toe n. dedo do pé

toffee n. caramelo

tog n. trapo

toga n. toga

together adv. juntos

toggle n. cavilha

toil v.i. laborar

toilet n. casa de banho

toiletries n. artigos higiene pessoal

toils n. armadilha

token n. sinal

tolerable adj. tolerável

tolerance n. tolerância

tolerant adj. tolerante

tolerate *v.* tolerar
toleration *n.* tolerância
toll *n.* portagem
tomato *n.* tomate
tomb *n.* túmulo
tomboy *n.* maria-rapaz
tome *n.* tomo
tomfoolery *n.* tolice
tomorrow *adv.* amanhã
ton *n.* tonelada
tone *n.* tom
toner *n.* toner
tongs *n.* tenaz
tongue *n.* língua
tonic *n.* tónico
tonight *adv.* hoje à noite
tonnage *n.* tonelagem
tonne *n.* tonelada
tonsil *n.* amígdala
tonsure *n.* tonsura
too *adv.* também
tool *n.* ferramenta
tooth *n.* dente
toothache *n.* dor de dente
toothless *adj.* desdentado
toothpaste *n.* dentífrico
toothpick *n.* palito
top *n.* topo
topaz *n.* topázio
topiary *n.* topiária
topic *n.* tópico
topical *adj.* tópico
topless *adj.* sem topo
topographer *n.* topógrafo

topographical *adj.* topográfico
topography *n.* topografia
topping *n.* cobertura
topple *v.* tombar
tor *n.* pico rochoso
torch *n.* tocha
toreador *n.* toureiro
torment *n.* tormento
tormentor *n.* atormentador
tornado *n.* tornado
torpedo *n.* torpedo
torpid *adj.* entorpecido
torrent *n.* torrente
torrential *adj.* torrencial
torrid *adj.* tórrido
torsion *n.* torção
torso *n.* torso
tort *n.* dano
tortoise *n.* tartaruga
tortuous *adj.* tortuoso
torture *n.* tortura
toss *v.* lançar
tot *n.* copinho
total *adj.* total
total *n.* total
totalitarian *adj.* totalitário
totality *n.* totalidade
tote *v.* carregar
totter *v.* cambalear
touch *v.* tocar
touching *adj.* tocante
touchy *adj.* suscetível
tough *adj.* difícil
toughen *v.* endurecer

toughness *n.* dureza	**traduce** *v.* difamar
tour *n.* excursão	**traffic** *n.* tráfego
tourism *n.* turismo	**trafficker** *n.* traficante
tourist *n.* turista	**trafficking** *n.* tráfico
tournament *n.* torneio	**tragedian** *n.* trageódico
tousle *v.* despentear	**tragedy** *n.* tragédia
tout *v.* angariar	**tragic** *adj.* trágico
tow *v.* rebocar	**trail** *n.* trilha
towards *prep.* para	**trailer** *n.* caravana
towel *n.* toalha	**train** *n.* comboio
towelling *n.* atoalhado	**train** *v.* instruir
tower *n.* torre	**trainee** *n.* estagiário
town *n.* cidade	**trainer** *n.* treinador
township *n.* distrito	**training** *n.* treino
toxic *adj.* tóxico	**traipse** *v.* caminhar
toxicology *n.* toxicologia	**trait** *n.* traço
toxin *n.* toxina	**traitor** *n.* traidor
toy *n.* brinquedo	**trajectory** *n.* trajetória
trace *v.t.* traçar	**tram** *n.* eléctrico
traceable *adj.* rastreável	**trammel** *v.* confinar
tracing *n.* traçado	**tramp** *v.* vagabundear
track *n.* rasto	**trample** *v.* pisar
tracksuit *n.* fato de treino	**trampoline** *n.* trampolim
tract *n.* trato	**trance** *n.* transe
tractable *adj.* tratável	**tranquil** *adj.* tranquilo
traction *n.* tração	**tranquillity** *n.* tranquilidade
tractor *n.* trator	**tranquillize** *v.* tranquilizar
trade *n.* comércio	**transact** *v.* transacionar
trademark *n.* marca registrada	**transaction** *n.* transação
trader *n.* comerciante	**transatlantic** *adj.* transatlântico
tradesman *n.* comerciante	**transceiver** *n.* transceptor
tradition *n.* tradição	**transcend** *v.* transcender
traditional *adj.* tradicional	**transcendent** *adj.* transcendente
traditionalist *n.* tradicionalista	**transcendental** *adj.* transcendental

transcontinental adj. transcontinental
transcribe v. transcrever
transcript n. cópia
transcription n. transcrição
transfer v. transferir
transferable adj. transferível
transfiguration n. transfiguração
transfigure v. transfigurar
transform v. transformar
transformation n. transformação
transformer n. transformador
transfuse v. transferir
transfusion n. transfusão
transgress v. transgredir
transgression n. transgressão
transient adj. transitório
transistor n. transístor
transit n. trânsito
transition n. transição
transitive adj. transitivo
transitory adj. transitório
translate v. traduzir
translation n. tradução
transliterate v. transliterar
translucent adj. translúcido
transmigration n. transmigração
transmission n. transmissão
transmit v. transmitir
transmitter n. transmissor
transmute v. transmutar
transparency n. transparência
transparent adj. transparente
transpire v. transpirar
transplant v. transplantar

transport v. transportar
transportation n. transporte
transporter n. transportador
transpose v. transpor
transsexual n. transsexual
transverse adj. transverso
transvestite n. travesti
trap n. armadilha
trapeze n. trapézio
trash n. lixo
trauma n. trauma
travel v. viajar
traveller n. viajante
travelogue n. documentário viagem
traverse v. atravessar
travesty n. paródia
trawler n. traineira
tray n. bandeja
treacherous adj. traiçoeiro
treachery n. traição
treacle n. melaço
tread v. pisar
treadle n. pedal
treadmill n. passadeira
treason n. traição
treasure n. tesouro
treasurer n. tesoureiro
treasury n. tesouraria
treat v. tratar
treatise n. tratado
treatment n. tratamento
treaty n. tratado
treble adj. triplo
tree n. árvore

trek *n.* caminhada	**Trier** *n.* Trier
trellis *n.* latada	**trifle** *n.* ninharia
tremble *v.* tremer	**trigger** *n.* gatilho
tremendous *adj.* tremendo	**trigonometry** *n.* trigonometria
tremor *n.* tremor	**trill** *n.* trinado
tremulous *adj.* trémulo	**trillion** *adj.* & *n.* trilião
trench *n.* trincheira	**trilogy** *n.* trilogia
trenchant *adj.* mordaz	**trim** *v.* enfeitar
trend *n.* tendência	**trimmer** *n.* embelezador
trendy *adj.* atual	**trimming** *n.* ornamentação
trepidation *n.* trepidação	**trinity** *n.* trindade
trespass *v.* transgredir	**trinket** *n.* bugiganga
tress *n.* trança	**trio** *n.* trio
trestle *n.* cavalete	**trip** *v.* viajar
trial *n.* julgamento	**tripartite** *adj.* tripartido
triangle *n.* triângulo	**triple** *n.* triplo
triangular *adj.* triangular	**triplet** *n.* trio
triathlon *n.* triatlo	**triplicate** *adj.* triplicado
tribal *adj.* tribal	**tripod** *n.* tripé
tribe *n.* tribo	**triptych** *n.* tríptico
tribulation *n.* tribulação	**trite** *adj.* banal
tribunal *n.* tribunal	**triumph** *n.* triunfo
tributary *n.* tributário	**triumphal** *adj.* triunfal
tribute *n.* tributo	**triumphant** *adj.* triunfante
trice *n.* instante	**trivet** *n.* tripé
triceps *n.* tricípite	**trivia** *n.* trivialidades
trick *n.* truque	**trivial** *adj.* trivial
trickery *n.* embuste	**troll** *n.* troll
trickle *v.* gotejar	**trolley** *n.* carrinho
trickster *n.* trapaceiro	**troop** *n.* tropa
tricky *adj.* complicado	**trooper** *n.* soldado de cavalaria
tricolour *n.* tricolor	**trophy** *n.* troféu
tricycle *n.* triciclo	**tropic** *n.* trópico
trident *n.* tridente	**tropical** *adj.* tropical

trot *v.* trotar	**trusty** *adj.* fiel
trotter *n.* cavalo de trote	**truth** *n.* verdade
trouble *n.* dificuldade	**truthful** *adj.* verdadeiro
trouble-shooter *n.* mediador	**try** *v.* tentar
troublesome *adj.* perturbador	**trying** *adj.* penoso
trough *n.* gamela	**tryst** *n.* encontro
trounce *v.* censurar	**tsunami** *n.* tsunami
troupe *n.* grupo	**tub** *n.* tina
trousers *n.* calças	**tube** *n.* tubo
trousseau *n.* enxoval de noiva	**tubercle** *n.* tubérculo
trout *n.* truta	**tuberculosis** *n.* tuberculose
trowel *n.* espátula	**tubular** *adj.* tubular
troy *n.* peso troy	**tuck** *v.* dobrar
truant *n.* ocioso	**Tuesday** *n.* Terça-feira
truce *n.* trégua	**tug** *v.* rebocar
truck *n.* camião	**tuition** *n.* ensino
trucker *n.* camionista	**tulip** *n.* tulipa
truculent *adj.* cruel	**tumble** *v.* derrubar
trudge *v.* arrastar-se	**tumbler** *n.* copo
true *adj.* verdadeiro	**tumescent** *adj.* tumescente
truffle *n.* trufa	**tumour** *n.* tumor
trug *n.* cesto feito de tiras	**tumult** *n.* tumulto
truism *n.* truísmo	**tumultuous** *adj.* tumultuoso
trump *n.* trunfo	**tun** *n.* tonel
trumpet *n.* trombeta	**tune** *n.* sintonia
truncate *v.* truncar	**tuner** *n.* sintonizador
truncheon *n.* cassetete	**tunic** *n.* túnica
trundle *v.* rolar	**tunnel** *n.* túnel
trunk *n.* tronco	**turban** *n.* turbante
truss *n.* asna	**turbid** *adj.* turvo
trust *n.* confiança	**turbine** *n.* turbina
trustee *n.* provedor	**turbocharger** *n.* turbocompressor
truncheon *n.* cassetete	**turbulence** *n.* turbulência
trustworthy *adj.* fidedigno	**turbulent** *adj.* turbulento

turf *n.* relva
turgid *adj.* túrgido
turkey *n.* peru
turmeric *n.* curcuma
turmoil *n.* tumulto
turn *v.* girar
turner *n.* torneiro
turning *n.* volta
turnip *n.* nabo
turnout *n.* afluência
turnover *n.* volume de negócios
turpentine *n.* terebintina
turquoise *n.* turquesa
turtle *n.* tartaruga
tusk *n.* presa (dente)
tussle *n.* luta
tutelage *n.* tutela
tutor *n.* tutor
tutorial *n.* tutorial
tuxedo *n.* smoking
tweak *v.* beliscar
twee *adj.* efeminado
tweed *n.* tweed
tweet *v.* chilrear
tweeter *n.* alto-falante
tweezers *n.* pinça
twelfth *adj.&n.* décimo segundo
twelve *adj.&n.* doze
twentieth *adj.&n.* vigésimo
twenty *adj.&n.* vinte
twice *adv.* duas vezes
twiddle *v.* girar
twig *n.* galho
twilight *n.* crepúsculo

twin *n.* gémeo
twine *n.* retrós
twinge *n.* pontada
twinkle *v.* piscar
twirl *v.* rodopiar
twist *v.* girar
twitch *v.* contorcer
twitter *v.* chilrear
two *adj.&n.* dois
twofold *adj.* duplo
tycoon *n.* magnata
type *n.* tipo
typesetter *n.* compositor
typhoid *n.* tifóide
typhoon *n.* tufão
typhus *n.* tifo
typical *adj.* típico
typify *v.* tipificar
typist *n.* datilógrafo
tyrannize *v.* tiranizar
tyranny *n.* tirania
tyrant *n.* tirano
tyre *n.* pneu

U

ubiquitous *adj.* ubíquo
udder *n.* úbere
ugliness *n.* fealdade
ugly *adj.* feio
ulcer *n.* úlcera
ulterior *adj.* ulterior
ultimate *adj.* final
ultimately *adv.* finalmente
ultimatum *n.* ultimato

ultra pref. além
ultramarine n. ultramarino
ultrasonic adj. ultrassónico
ultrasound n. ecografia
umber n. ocre
umbilical adj. umbilical
umbrella n. guarda-chuva
umpire n. árbitro
unable adj. incapaz
unanimity a. unanimidade
unaccountable adj. inexplicável
unadulterated adj. autêntico
unalloyed adj. puro
unanimous adj. unânime
unarmed adj. desarmado
unassailable adj. inatacável
unassuming adj. modesto
unattended adj. desacompanhado
unavoidable adj. inevitável
unaware adj. inconsciente
unbalanced adj. desequilibrado
unbelievable adj. inacreditável
unbend v. afrouxar
unborn adj. vindouro
unbridled adj. desenfreado
unburden v. aliviar
uncalled adj. não chamado
uncanny adj. estranho
unceremonious adj. descortês
uncertain adj. incerto
uncharitable adj. injusto
uncle n. tio
unclean adj. imundo
uncomfortable adj. desconfortável

uncommon adj. incomum
uncompromising adj. intransigente
unconditional adj. incondicional
unconscious adj. inconsciente
uncouth adj. rude
uncover v. destapar
unctuous adj. untuoso
undeceive v. desenganar
undecided adj. indeciso
undeniable adj. inegável
under prep. em
underarm adj. axilas
undercover adj. secreto
undercurrent n. corrente
undercut v. escavar
underdog n. desfavorecido
underestimate v. subestimar
undergo v. exprimentar
undergraduate n. estudante universit.
underground adj. subterrâneo
underhand adj. clandestinamente
underlay n. calço
underline v.t. relaçar
underling n. realce
undermine v. minar
underneath prep. embaixo
underpants n. cuecas
underpass n. passagem inferior
underprivileged adj. desprivilegiado
underrate v. subestimar
underscore v. sublinhar
undersigned n. abaixo assinado
understand v.t. entender
understanding n. compreensão

understate v. minimizar

undertake v. empreender

undertaker n. cangalheiro

underwear n. roupa interior

underworld n. submundo

underwrite v. subscrever

undesirable adj. indesejável

undo v. desfazer

undoing n. ruína

undone adj. desfeito

undress v. despir

undue adj. indevido

undulate v. ondular

undying adj. imortal

unearth v. desenterrar

uneasy adj. inquieto

unemployable adj. imprestável

unemployed adj. desempregado

unending adj. interminável

unequalled adj. inigualável

uneven adj. desigual

unexceptionable adj. irrepreensível

unexceptional adj. corriqueiro

unexpected adj. inesperado

unfailing adj. infalível

unfair adj. injusto

unfaithful adj. infiel

unfit adj. impróprio

unfold v. desdobrar

unforeseen adj. imprevisto

unforgettable adj. inesquecível

unfortunate adj. infeliz

unfounded adj. infundado

unfurl v. desfraldar

ungainly adj. desajeitado

ungovernable adj. incontrolável

ungrateful adj. ingrato

unguarded adj. sem proteção

unhappy adj. infeliz

unhealthy adj. insalubre

unheard adj. desconhecido

unholy adj. profano

unification n. unificação

uniform adj. uniforme

unify v. unificar

unilateral adj. unilateral

unimpeachable adj. irrepreensível

uninhabited adj. inabitado

union n. união

unionist n. sindicalista

unique adj. único

unisex adj. unissexo

unison n. unissonância

unit n. unidade

unite v. unir

unity n. união

universal adj. universal

universality adv. universalidade

universe n. universo

university n. universidade

unjust adj. injusto

unkempt adj. despenteado

unkind adj. cruel

unknown adj. desconhecido

unleash v. soltar

unless conj. senão

unlike prep. ao contrário

unlikely adj. improvável

unlimited *adj.* ilimitado

unload *v.* descarregar

unmanned *adj.* não tripulado

unmask *v.* desmascarar

unmentionable *adj.* intocável

unmistakable *adj.* inequívoco

unmitigated *adj.* absoluto

unmoved *adj.* impassível

unnatural *adj.* antinatural

unnecessary *adj.* desnecessário

unnerve *v.* enervar

unorthodox *adj.* heterodoxo

unpack *v.* desempacotar

unpleasant *adj.* desagradável

unpopular *adj.* impopular

unprecedented *adj.* inaudito

unprepared *adj.* desprevenido

unprincipled *adj.* sem princípios

unprofessional *adj.* amador

unqualified *adj.* incompetente

unreasonable *adj.* irracional

unreliable *n.* inseguro

unreserved *adj.* imoderado

unrest *n.* agitação

unrivalled *adj.* incomparável

unruly *adj.* indisciplinado

unscathed *adj.* ileso

unscrupulous *adj.* sem escrúpulos

unseat *v.* destituir

unselfish *adj.* altruísta

unsettle *v.* abalar

unshakeable *adj.* inabalável

unskilled *adj.* inexpriente

unsocial *adj.* insociável

unsolicited *adj.* espontâneo

unstable *adj.* instável

unsung *adj.* não celebrado

unthinkable *adj.* impensável

untidy *adj.* desordenado

until *prep.* até

untimely *adj.* prematuro

untold *adj.* incontável

untouchable *adj.* intocável

untoward *adj.* desagradável

unusual *adj.* incomum

unutterable *adj.* inexprímivel

unveil *v.* desvelar

unwarranted *adj.* injustificável

unwell *adj.* indisposto

unwilling *adj.* relutante

unwind *v.* desenrolar

unwise *adj.* imprudente

unwittingly *adv.* involuntariamente

unworldly *adj.* extraterrestre

unworthy *adj.* indigno

up *adv.* levantado

upbeat *adj.* otimista

upbraid *v.* censurar

upcoming *adj.* iminente

update *v.* atualizar

upgrade *v.* melhorar

upheaval *n.* perturbação

uphold *v.* suportar

upholster *v.* estofar

upholstery *n.* estofamento

uplift *v.* elevar

upload *v.* upload

upper *adj.* superior

upright *adj.* vertical

uprising *n.* insurreição

uproar *n.* tumulto

uproarious *adj.* barulhento

uproot *v.* extirpar

upset *v.* chatear

upshot *n.* conclusão

upstart *n.* arrivista

upsurge *n.* subida

upturn *n.* recuperação

upward *adv.* para cima

urban *adj.* urbano

urbane *adj.* urbano

urbanity *n.* urbanidade

urchin *n.* diabrete

urge *v.* instar

urgent *adj.* urgente

urinal *n.* mictório

urinary *adj.* urinário

urinate *v.* urinar

urine *n.* urina

urn *n.* urna

usable *adj.* utilizável

usage *n.* uso

use *v.t.* usar

useful *adj.* útil

useless *adj.* inútil

user *n.* usuário

usher *n.* porteiro

usual *adj.* usual

usually *adv.* geralmente

usurp *v.* usurpar

usurpation *n.* usurpação

usury *n.* usura

utensil *n.* utensílio

uterus *n.* útero

utilitarian *adj.* utilitário

utility *n.* utilidade

utilization *n.* utilização

utilize *v.* utilizar

utmost *adj.* máximo

utopia *n.* utopia

utopian *adj.* utópico

utter *adj.* total

utterance *n.* enunciação

uttermost *adj.* extremo

uttermost *n.* máximo

vacancy *n.* vaga

vacant *adj.* vago

vacate *v.* desocupar

vacation *n.* férias

vaccinate *v.* vacinar

vaccination *n.* vacinação

vaccine *n.* vacina

vacillate *v.* vacilar

vacillation *n.* vacilação

vacuous *adj.* vazio

vacuum *n.* vácuo

vagabond *n.* vagabundo

vagary *n.* capricho

vagina *n.* vagina

vagrant *n.* vagabundo

vague *adj.* vago

vagueness *n.* imprecisão

vain *adj.* vaidoso

vainglorious *adj.* vanglorioso

vainly *adv.* inutilmente

valance *n.* sanefa

vale *n.* vale

valediction *n.* despedida

valency *n.* valência

valentine *n.* dia dos namorados

valet *n.* criado

valetudinarian *n.* valétudinário

valiant *adj.* valente

valid *adj.* válido

validate *v.* validar

validity *n.* validade

valise *n.* pequena mala de viagem

valley *n.* vale

valour *n.* bravura

valuable *adj.* valioso

valuation *n.* avaliação

value *n.* valor

valve *n.* válvula

vamp *n.* gáspea (de sapato)

vampire *n.* vampiro

van *n.* carrinha

vandal *n.* vândalo

vandalize *v.* vandalizar

vane *n.* cata-vento

vanguard *n.* vanguarda

vanish *v.* desaparecer

vanity *n.* vaidade

vanquish *v.* vencer

vantage *n.* vantagem

vapid *adj.* insípido

vaporize *v.* vaporizar

vapour *n.* vapor

variable *adj.* variável

variance *n.* variação

variant *n.* variante

variation *n.* variação

varicose *adj.* varicoso

varied *adj.* variado

variegated *adj.* diverso

variety *n.* variedade

various *adj.* vário

varlet *n.* escudeiro

varnish *n.* verniz

vary *v.* variar

vascular *adj.* vascular

vase *n.* vaso

vasectomy *n.* vasectomia

vassal *n.* vassalo

vast *adj.* grande

vaudeville *n.* comédia leve

vault *n.* abóbada

vaunted *adj.* ostentado

veal *n.* vitela

vector *n.* vetor

veer *n.* desviar-se

vegan *n.* vegan

vegetable *n.* vegetal

vegetarian *n.* vegetariano

vegetate *v.* vegetar

vegetation *n.* vegetação

vegetative *adj.* vegetativo

vehement *adj.* veemente

vehicle *n.* veículo

vehicular *adj.* veicular

veil *n.* véu

vein *n.* veia

velocity *n.* velocidade
velour *n.* veludo
velvet *n.* veludo
velvety *adj.* aveludado
venal *adj.* venal
venality *n.* venalidade
vend *v.* vender
vendetta *n.* vendeta
vendor *n.* vendedor
veneer *n.* folheado
venerable *adj.* venerável
venerate *v.* venerar
veneration *n.* veneração
venetian *adj.* veneziano
vengeance *n.* vingança
vengeful *adj.* vingativo
venial *adj.* venial
venom *n.* veneno
venomous *adj.* venenoso
venous *adj.* venoso
vent *n.* respiradouro
ventilate *v.* ventilar
ventilation *n.* ventilação
ventilator *n.* ventilador
venture *n.* risco
venturesome *adj.* aventureiro
venue *n.* local
veracious *adj.* verídico
veracity *n.* veracidade
veranda *n.* alpendre
verb *n.* verbo
verbal *adj.* verbal
verbally *adv.* verbalmente
verbalize *v.* verbalizar

verbatim *adv.* literal
verbiage *n.* palavreado
verbose *adj.* verboso
verbosity *n.* verbosidade
verdant *adj.* verdejante
verdict *n.* veredito
verge *n.* beira
verification *n.* verificação
verify *v.* verificar
verily *adv.* verdadeiramente
verisimilitude *n.* verossimilhança
veritable *adj.* autêntico
verity *n.* verdade
vermillion *n.* vermelhão
vermin *n.* bicharada
vernacular *n.* vernáculo
vernal *adj.* vernal
versatile *adj.* versátil
versatility *n.* versatilidade
verse *n.* verso
versed *adj.* versado
versification *n.* versificação
versify *v.* versificar
version *n.* versão
verso *n.* verso
versus *prep.* contra
vertebra *n.* vértebra
vertebrate *n.* vertebrado
vertex *n.* vértice
vertical *adj.* vertical
vertiginous *adj.* vertiginoso
vertigo *n.* vertigem
verve *n.* verve
very *adv.* muito

vesicle *n.* vesícula
vessel *n.* navio
vest *n.* colete
vestibule *n.* vestíbulo
vestige *n.* vestígio
vestment *n.* vestuário
vestry *n.* sacristia
veteran *n.* veterano
veterinary *adj.* veterinário
veto *n.* veto
vex *v.* irritar
vexation *n.* aborrecimento
via *prep.* via
viable *adj.* viável
viaduct *n.* viaduto
vial *n.* frasquinho
viands *n.* mantimentos
vibe *n.* vibração
vibrant *adj.* vibrante
vibraphone *n.* vibrafone
vibrate *v.* vibrar
vibration *n.* vibração
vibrator *n.* vibrador
vicar *n.* vigário
vicarious *adj.* vicário
vice *n.* vício
viceroy *n.* vice-rei
vice-versa *adv.* vice-versa
vicinity *n.* vizinhança
vicious *adj.* vicioso
vicissitude *n.* vicissitude
victim *n.* vítima
victimize *n.* vitimar
victor *n.* vencedor

victorious *adj.* vitorioso
victory *n.* vitória
victualler *n.* abastecedor
victuals *n.* mantimentos
video *n.* vídeo
vie *v.* competir
view *n.* vista
vigil *n.* vigília
vigilance *n.* vigilância
vigilant *adj.* vigilante
vignette *n.* vinheta
vigorous *adj.* vigoroso
vigour *n.* vigor
Viking *n.* Viking
vile *adj.* vil
vilify *v.* vilipendiar
villa *n.* vila
village *n.* aldeia
villager *n.* aldeão
villain *n.* vilão
vindicate *v.* justificar
vindication *n.* justificação
vine *n.* videira
vinegar *n.* vinagre
vintage *n.* vintage
vintner *n.* negociante de vinhos
vinyl *n.* vinil
violate *v.* violar
violation *n.* violação
violence *n.* violência
violent *adj.* violento
violet *n.* violeta
violin *n.* violino
violinist *n.* violinista

virago *n.* virago
viral *adj.* viral
virgin *n.* virgem
virginity *n.* virgindade
virile *adj.* viril
virility *n.* virilidade
virtual *adj.* virtual
virtue *n.* virtude
virtuous *adj.* virtuoso
virulence *n.* virulência
virulent *adj.* virulento
virus *n.* vírus
visa *n.* visto
visage *n.* rosto
viscid *adj.* viscoso
viscose *n.* viscose
viscount *n.* visconde
viscountess *n.* viscondessa
viscous *adj.* viscoso
visibility *n.* visibilidade
visible *adj.* visível
vision *n.* visão
visionary *adj.* visionário
visit *v.* visitar
visitation *n.* visita oficial
visitor *n.* visitante
visor *n.* viseira
vista *n.* vista
visual *adj.* visual
visualize *v.* visualizar
vital *adj.* vital
vitality *n.* vitalidade
vitalize *v.* vitalizar
vitamin *n.* vitamina

vitiate *v.* viciar
viticulture *n.* viticultura
vitreous *adj.* vítreo
vitrify *v.* vitrificar
vitriol *n.* vitríolo
vituperation *n.* vitupério
vivacious *adj.* vivaz
vivacity *n.* vivacidade
vivarium *n.* viveiro
vivid *adj.* vívido
vivify *v.* vivificar
vixen *n.* megera
vocabulary *n.* vocabulário
vocal *adj.* vocal
vocalist *n.* vocalista
vocalize *v.* vocalizar
vocation *n.* vocação
vociferous *adj.* vociferador
vogue *n.* voga
voice *n.* voz
voicemail *n.* voicemail
void *adj.* vazio
voile *n.* voile
volatile *adj.* volátil
volcanic *adj.* vulcânico
volcano *n.* vulcão
volition *n.* volição
volley *n.* vólei
volt *n.* volt
voltage *n.* tensão
voluble *adj.* fluente
volume *n.* volume
voluminous *adj.* volumoso
voluntarily *adv.* voluntariamente

voluntary *adj.* voluntário	**wafer** *n.* bolacha
volunteer *n.* voluntário	**waffle** *v.* waffle
voluptuary *n.* voluptuário	**waft** *v.* soprar
voluptuous *adj.* voluptuoso	**wag** *v.* abanar
vomit *v.* vomitar	**wage** *n.* salário
voodoo *n.* vodu	**wager** *n. & v.* aposta & apostar
voracious *adj.* voraz	**waggle** *v.* abanar
vortex *n.* vórtice	**wagon** *n.* vagão
votary *n.* devoto	**wagtail** *n.* alvéola
vote *n.* voto	**waif** *n.* vira-lata
voter *n.* eleitor	**wail** *n.* pranto
votive *adj.* votivo	**wain** *n.* carroça
vouch *v.* garantir	**wainscot** *n.* lambril
voucher *n.* vale	**waist** *n.* cintura
vouchsafe *v.* condescender	**waistband** *n.* cós
vow *n.* voto	**waistcoat** *n.* colete
vowel *n.* vogal	**wait** *v.* esperar
voyage *n.* viagem	**waiter** *n.* empregado de mesa
voyager *n.* viajante	**waitress** *n.* empregada de mesa
vulcanize *v.* vulcanizar	**waive** *v.* prescindir
vulgar *adj.* vulgar	**wake** *v.* acordar
vulgarian *n.* vulgar	**wakeful** *adj.* desperto
vulgarity *n.* vulgaridade	**waken** *v.* acordar
vulnerable *adj.* vulnerável	**walk** *v.* andar
vulpine *adj.* vulpino	**wall** *n.* parede
vulture *n.* abutre	**wallaby** *n.* canguru

W

	wallet *n.* carteira
	wallop *v.* espancar
wacky *adj.* excêntrico	**wallow** *v.* chafurdar
wad *n.* chumaço	**Wally** *n.* Wally
waddle *v.* andar gingando	**walnut** *n.* nogueira
wade *v.* patinhar	**walrus** *n.* morsa
wader *n.* ave limícola	**waltz** *n.* valsa
wadi *n.* uádi	**wan** *adj.* pálido

207

wand *n.* varinha	**wasp** *n.* vespa
wander *v.* vaguear	**waspish** *adj.* irascível
wane *v.* diminuir	**wassail** *n.* banquete
wangle *v.* falsificar	**wastage** *n.* desperdício
want *v.* querer	**waste** *v.* desperdiçar
wanting *adj.* deficiente	**wasteful** *adj.* imoral
wanton *adj.* arbitrário	**watch** *v.* observar
war *n.* guerra	**watchful** *adj.* vigilante
warble *v.* chilrear	**watchword** *n.* lema
warbler *n.* rouxinol	**water** *n.* água
ward *n.* vigilância	**waterfall** *n.* cascata
warden *n.* governador	**watermark** *n.* marca d'água
warder *n.* carcereiro	**watermelon** *n.* melancia
wardrobe *n.* guarda-roupa	**waterproof** *adj.* impermeável
ware *n.* mercadoria	**watertight** *adj.* inequívoco
warehouse *n.* armazém	**watery** *adj.* aquoso
warfare *n.* guerra	**watt** *n.* watt
warlike *adj.* bélico	**wattage** *n.* potência
warm *adj.* quente	**wattle** *n.* sebe
warmth *n.* calor	**wave** *v.* ondular
warn *v.* advertir	**waver** *v.* hesitar
warning *n.* aviso	**wavy** *adj.* ondulado
warp *v.* deformar	**wax** *n.* cera
warrant *n.* garantia	**way** *n.* maneira
warrantor *n.* fiador	**waylay** *v.* assaltar
warranty *n.* garantia	**wayward** *adj.* desobediente
warren *n.* coelheira	**we** *pron.* nós
warrior *n.* guerreiro	**weak** *adj.* fraco
wart *n.* verruga	**weaken** *v.* enfraquecer
wary *adj.* cauteloso	**weakling** *n.* pessoa fraca
wash *v.* lavar	**weakness** *n.* fraqueza
washable *adj.* lavável	**weal** *n.* bem-estar
washer *n.* máquina de lavar	**wealth** *n.* riqueza
washing *n.* lavagem	**wealthy** *adj.* rico

wean v. desmamar	**welfare** n. bem-estar
weapon n. arma	**well** adv. bem
wear v. vestir	**well** n. poço
wearisome adj. enfadonho	**wellington** n. galochas
weary adj. cansado	**welt** n. vira (de calçado)
weasel n. doninha	**welter** n. amálgama
weather n. tempo	**wen** n. quisto sebáceo
weave v. tecer	**wench** n. prostituta
weaver n. tecelão	**wend** v. andar
web n. teia	**west** n. oeste
webby adj. reticulado	**westerly** adv. para oeste
webpage n. webpage	**western** adj. ocidental
website n. site	**westerner** n. ocidental
wed v. casar	**westernize** v. ocidentalizar
wedding n. casamento	**wet** adj. molhado
wedge n. cunha	**wetness** n. humidade
wedlock n. casamento	**whack** v. bater
Wednesday n. Quarta-feira	**whale** n. baleia
weed n. erva daninha	**whaler** n. baleeiro
week n. semana	**whaling** n. pesca à baleia
weekday n. dia da semana	**wharf** n. cais
weekly adj. semanal	**wharfage** n. depósito no cais
weep v. chorar	**what** pron. & adj. o que & qual
weepy adj. choroso	**whatever** pron. tudo o que
weevil n. gorgulho	**wheat** n. trigo
weigh v. pesar	**wheaten** adj. de trigo
weight n. peso	**wheedle** v. lisonjear
weighting n. lastração	**wheel** n. roda
weightlifting n. halterofilia	**wheeze** v. ofegar
weighty adj. pesado	**whelk** n. búzio
weir n. açude	**whelm** v. soterrar
weird adj. estranho	**whelp** n. cachorrinho
welcome n. boas-vindas	**when** adv. quando
weld v. soldar	**whence** adv. de onde

whenever conj. sempre que

where adv. onde

whereabouts adv. por onde

whereas n. visto que

whet v. afiar

whether conj. se

whey n. coalho

which pron. & adj. que & qual

whichever pron. seja qual for

whiff n. lufada

while n. enquanto

whilst conj. enquanto

whim n. capricho

whimper v. choramingar

whimsical adj. caprichoso

whimsy n. capricho

whine n. choradeira

whinge v. queixar

whinny n. relincho

whip n. chicote

whir n. zunido

whirl v. rodopiar

whirligig n. carrossel

whirlpool n. turbilhão

whirlwind n. furacão

whirr v. zumbir

whisk v. espanar

whisker n. suíças

whisky n. uísque

whisper v. sussurrar

whist n. whisky

whistle n. assobio

whit n. partícula

white adj. branco

whitewash n. cal

whither adv. para onde

whiting n. verdinho (peixe)

whittle v. aguçar

whiz v. zumbir

who pron. que

whoever pron. quem quer que

whole adj. inteiro

whole-hearted adj. sincero

wholesale n. venda por grosso

wholesaler n. grossista

wholesome adj. saudável

wholly adv. totalmente

whom pron. quem

whoop n. excitação

whopper n. colosso

whore n. prostituta

whose adj. do qual

whose pron. de quem

why adv. por que

wick n. pavio

wicked adj. malévolo

wicker n. vime

wicket n. postigo

wide adj. amplo

widen v. ampliar

widespread adj. comum

widow n. viúva

widower n. viúvo

width n. largura

wield v. empunhar

wife n. esposa

wig n. peruca

wiggle v. mexer

Wight *n.* Wight (ilha)

wigwam *n.* cabana

wild *adj.* selvagem

wilderness *n.* deserto

wile *n.* artimanha

wilful *adj.* teimoso

will *v.* auxiliar de futuro

willing *adj.* disposto

willingness *n.* boa vontade

willow *n.* salgueiro

wily *adj.* astuto

wimble *n.* pua

wimple *n.* véu

win *v.* ganhar

wince *v.* estremecer

winch *n.* guincho

wind *n.* vento

windbag *n.* fala-barato

winder *n.* bobinador

windlass *n.* molinete

windmill *n.* moinho de vento

window *n.* janela

windy *adj.* ventoso

wine *n.* vinho

winery *n.* vinícola

wing *n.* asa

wink *v.* piscar os olhos

winkle *n.* molusco gastrópode

winner *n.* vencedor

winning *adj.* vencedor

winnow *v.* joeirar

winsome *adj.* cativante

winter *n.* inverno

wintry *adj.* gelado

wipe *v.* limpar

wire *n.* arame

wireless *adj.* sem fio

wiring *n.* cablagem

wisdom *n.* sabedoria

wise *adj.* sábio

wish *v.* desejar

wishful *adj.* desejoso

wisp *n.* punhado

wisteria *n.* glicínia

wistful *adj.* saudoso

wit *n.* inteligência

witch *n.* bruxa

witchcraft *n.* bruxaria

witchery *n.* feitiçaria

with *prep.* com

withal *adv.* além disso

withdraw *v.* retirar

withdrawal *n.* retirada

withe *n.* verga

wither *v.* murchar

withhold *v.* sonegar

within *prep.* dentro

without *prep.* sem

withstand *v.* resistir

witless *adj.* desmiolado

witness *n.* testemunha

witter *v.* palrar

witticism *n.* graça

witty *adj.* espirituoso

wizard *n.* feiticeiro

wizened *adj.* encarquilhado

woad *n.* pastel-dos-tintureiros (flor)

wobble *v.* oscilar

woe *n.* aflição
woeful *adj.* mísero
wok *n.* wok
wold *n.* descampado
wolf *n.* lobo
woman *n.* mulher
womanhood *n.* feminilidade
womanize *v.* efeminar
womb *n.* útero
wonder *v.* desejar saber
wonderful *adj.* maravilhoso
wondrous *adj.* assombroso
wonky *adj.* vacilante
wont *n.* acostumado
wonted *adj.* costumeiro
woo *v.* cortejar
wood *n.* madeira
wooded *adj.* arborizado
wooden *adj.* de madeira
woodland *n.* bosque
woof *n.* latido
woofer *n.* woofer
wool *n.* lã
woollen *adj.* de lã
woolly *adj.* lanoso
woozy *adj.* confuso
word *n.* palavra
wording *n.* redação
wordy *adj.* palavroso
work *n.* trabalho
workable *adj.* exequível
workaday *adj.* diário
worker *n.* trabalhador
working *n.* trabalho

workman *n.* trabalhador
workmanship *n.* artesanato
workshop *n.* workshop
world *n.* mundo
worldly *adj.* mundano
worm *n.* verme
wormwood *n.* absinto
worried *adj.* preocupado
worrisome *adj.* incómodo
worry *v.* preocupar
worse *adj.* pior
worsen *v.* piorar
worship *n.* veneração
worshipper *n.* adorador
worst *adj.* o pior
worsted *n.* estambre
worth *adj.* digno
worthless *adj.* inútil
worthwhile *adj.* que vale a pena
worthy *adj.* mercedor
would *v.* seria
would-be *adj.* provável
wound *n.* ferida
wrack *n.* sargaço
wraith *n.* espetro
wrangle *n.* disputa
wrap *v.* embalar
wrapper *n.* invólucro
wrath *n.* ira
wreak *v.* desafogar
wreath *n.* coroa
wreathe *v.* entrelaçar
wreck *n.* ruína
wreckage *n.* naufrágio

wrecker *n.* provocador naufrágios
wren *n.* carriça
wrench *v.* arrebatar
wrest *v.* forçar
wrestle *v.* lutar
wrestler *n.* lutador
wretch *n.* desgraçado
wretched *adj.* miserável
wrick *v.* torcer
wriggle *v.* ziguezaguear
wring *v.* torcer
wrinkle *n.* ruga
wrist *n.* pulso
writ *n.* decreto
write *v.* escrever
writer *n.* escritor
writhe *v.* contorcer
writing *n.* escrita
wrong *adj.* errado
wrongful *adj.* ilegal
wry *adj.* torto

X

xenon *n.* xenon
xenophobia *n.* xenofobia
Xerox *n.* Xerox
Xmas *n.* Natal
x-ray *n.* radiografia
xylophages *adj.* xilófagos
xylophilous *adj.* xilófilo
xylophone *n.* xilofone

Y

yacht *n.* iate
yachting *n.* vela
yachtsman *n.* velejador
yak *n.* iaque
yam *n.* inhame
yap *v.* latir
yard *n.* quintal
yarn *n.* fio
yashmak *n.* yashmak (véu)
yaw *v.* guinar
yawn *v.* bocejar
year *n.* ano
yearly *adv.* anual
yearn *v.* ansiar
yearning *n.* ansioso
yeast *n.* levedura
yell *n.* grito
yellow *adj.* amarelo
yelp *n.* ganido
Yen *n.* Yen
yeoman *n.* pequeno proprietário
yes *excl.* sim
yesterday *adv.* ontem
yet *adv.* ainda
yeti *n.* yeti
yew *n.* teixo
yield *v.* produzir
yob *n.* vândalo
yodel *v.* cantar tirolês
yoga *n.* ioga

yogurt *n.* iogurte

yoke *n.* jugo

yokel *n.* campónio

yolk *n.* gema

yonder *adj.* além

yonks *n.* muito tempo

yore *n.* outrora

you *pron.* você

young *adj.* jovem

youngster *n.* jovem

your *adj.* seu

yourself *pron.* você mesmo

youth *n.* juventude

youthful *adj.* jovem

yowl *n.* uivo

yummy *adj.* gostoso

zip *n.* zunido

zircon *n.* zircão

zither *n.* cítara

zodiac *n.* zodíaco

zombie *n.* zombie

zonal *adj.* zonal

zone *n.* zona

zoo *n.* jardim zoológico

zoological *adj.* zoológico

zoologist *n.* zoólogo

zoology *n.* zoologia

zoom *v.* zunir

Z

zany *adj.* Bobo

zap *v.* Matar

zeal *n.* zelo

zealot *n.* fanático

zealous *adj.* Zeloso

zebra *n.* zebra

zebra crossing *n.* passadeira

zenith *n.* zénite

zephyr *n.* zéfiro

zero *adj.* zero

zest *n.* entusiasmo

zigzag *n.* ziguezague

zilch *n.* peva

zinc *n.* zinco

zing *n.* silvo

PORTUGUESE - ENGLISH

A

a bordo *adv.* aboard
a maioria *n.* most
a meio caminho *adv.* midway
à moda *adj.* modish
à parte *adv.* apart
a pouca distância de *adj.* offshore
à prova de som *adj.* soundproof
a seguir *adv.* hereafter
aba *n.* tab
abacate *n.* avocado
abade *n.* abbot
abadia *n.* abbey
abafado *adj.* stuffy
abafar *v.* muffle
abaixo *prep.* & *adv.* below & beneath
abaixo *adv.* beneath
abaixo assinado *n.* undersigned
abalar *v.* unsettle
abanar *v.* waggle
abandonar *v.t.* abandon
abastecedor *n.* victualler
abater *v.t.* abate
abatimento *n.* dejection
abcesso *n.* abscess
abdicação *n.* abdication
abdicar *v.t,* abdicate
abdómen *n.* abdomen
abdominal *a.* abdominal
abelha *n.* bee
abençoado *adj.* blessed
abençoar *v.* bless
aberração *n.* freak

aberrante *adj.* aberrant
abertamente *adv.* openly
aberto *adj.* open
abertura *n.* overture
abeto *n.* fir
abismal *adj.* abysmal
abismo *n.* abyss
abita *n.* bollard
abluções *n.* ablutions
abóbada *n.* vault
abóbora *n.* pumpkin
abolição *v.* abolition
abolir *v.t* abolish
abominar *v.* abhor
abominável *adj.* abominable
abordar *v.* accost
aborígene *adj.* aboriginal
aborrecer *v.* annoy
aborrecido *adj.* dull
aborrecimento *n.* annoyance
abortado *adj.* abortive
abortar *v.i* abort
aborto *n.* abortion
abraçar *v.* embrace
abraço *v.* cuddle
abrandar *v.* relent
abranger *v.* comprise
abrasão *n.* abrasion
abrasivo *adj.* abrasive
abreviar *v.t.* abbreviate
abreviatura *n.* abbreviation
abrigo *n.* shelter
abrótea *n.* daffodil
abrupto *adj.* abrupt

absinto *n.* wormwood
absoluto *adj.* absolute
absolver *v.* absolve
absolvição *n.* absolution
absorver *v.* adsorb
abstémio *n.* teetotaller
abstinência *n.* abstinence
abstrato *adj.* abstract
absurdo *adj.* absurd
absurdo *n.* absurdity
abundância *n.* abundance
abundância *adj.* galore
Abundância *pron.* plenty
abundante *adj.* abundant
abundar *v.i.* & *v.* abound & teem
abusivo *adj.* abusive
abuso *v.* abuse
abutre *n.* vulture
academia *n.* academy
académico *adj.* academic
açafrão *n.* saffron
acalentar *v.* cherish
acalmar *v.* & *v.i.* allay & hush
acampamento *n.* camp
acanhado *adj.* demure
acantonamento *n.* cantonment
ação *n.* action
acariciar *v.* fondle
ácaro *n.* mite
acaso *adj.* random
aceitação *n.* acceptance
aceitar *v.* accept
aceitável *adj.* acceptable
acelerar *v.* accelerate

acenar *v.* beckon
acender *v.* kindle
aceno *n.* beck
acentuar *v.* accentuate
ácer *n.* maple
acerelador *n.* accelerator
acertar *v.* hit
acessar *n.* access
acessível *adj.* accessible
acessório *n.* accessory
acetato *n.* acetate
acetinado *adj.* glossy
acetona *n.* acetone
achatar *v.t.* & *v.* flatten & squash
acidentado *adj.* rugged
acidental *adj.* accidental
acidente *n.* accident
acidez *n.* acidity
ácido *n.* acid
acima *adv.* & *prep.* above
acima mencionado *adj.* foregoing
acionar *v.* actuate
aclamar *v.* acclaim
aclimatar *v.t* acclimatise
acne *n.* acne
aço *n.* steel
açoitar *v.* flog
açoite *n.* scourge
acolchoado *adj.* quilted
acolchoamento *n.* padding
acolhedor *adj.* cosy
acólito *n.* acolyte
acomodar *v.* accommodate
acompanhamento *n.* accompaniment

acompanhar v. accompany
aconchegante adj. cosy
aconchegar v. snuggle
aconselhar v. counsel
aconselhável adj. advisable
acontecer v. befall
acontecer v. happen
acontecimento n. happening
acoplamento n. linkage
acordar v. awake
acorde n. chord
acordo n. agreement
acordo secreto n. cahoots
acorrentar v.t. tether
acostumado adj. accustomed
acostumado n. wont
acostumar v. accustom
acotevelar v. nudge
açougueiro n. butcher
acre n. & adj. acre & acrid
acreção n. accretion
acreditado adj. accredited
acreditar v. believe
acricultura n. agriculture
acrílico adj. acrylic
acrobacia aérea n. aerobatics
acrobata n. acrobat
acrobático adj. acrobatic
actínio n. actinium
açúcar n. sugar
açude n. weir
acumulação n. accumulation
acumular v. accumulate
acumulativo adj. cumulative

acúmulo n. backlog
acupuntura n. acupuncture
acusação n. accusation
acusado v.t. accused
acusar v. accuse
acústico adj. acoustic
adaga n. dagger
adaptação n. adaptation
adaptar v. adapt
adega n. cellar
adenda n. addendum
adequação n. adequacy
adequadamente adv. accordingly
adequado adj. adequate
aderência n. adherence
aderir v. adhere
adesão n. accession
adesivo n. adhesive
adeus n. & excl. adieu & goodbye
adiamento n. postponement
adiante adv. forth
adiante adj. forward
adiar v. postpone
adição n. addition
adicional adj. additional
adicionar v. add
adido n. attache
aditivo n. additive
adivinhar v.i guess
adjacente adj. adjacent
adjetivo n. adjective
adjudicar v. adjudicate
adjunto n. adjunct
administrador adj. administrator

administrar v. administer

administrativo adj. administrative

adminsitração n. administration

admiração n. admiration

admirar v. admire

admirável adj. admirable

admissão n. admission

admissível adj. admissible

admitir v. admit

admoestar v. admonish

adobe n. adobe

adoçante n. sweetener

adoção n. adoption

adoçar v. sweeten

adoecido adj. crooked

adolescência adj. adolescent

adolescente n. adolescence

adolescentes n. teens

adoração n. adoration

adorador n. worshipper

adorar v.t. adore

adorável adj. adorable

adormecido adj. asleep

adornar v. adorn

adotar v. adopt

adotivo adj. adoptive

adquirir v. acquire

adriça n. halyard

adro n. churchyard

adubo n. compost

aduela n. stave

adular v. cringe

adulteração n. adulteration

adulterar v. adulterate

adultério n. adultery

adulto n. adult

aduzir v. adduce

advento n. advent

advérbio n. adverb

adversário n. adversary

adversidade n. adversity

adverso adj. adverse

advertir v. warn

advir v.t. accrue

advogado n. attorney

aéreo n. aerial

aeróbica n. aerobics

aeródromo n. aerodrome

aeronáutica n. aeronautics

aeronave n. aircraft

aeroplano n. aeroplane

aerosol n. aerosol

aerospaço n. aerospace

afastado adj. outlying

afável adj. affable

afeiçoado adj. fond

aferir n. gauge

afetação n. affectation

afetado adj. affected

afetar v. affect

afeto n. affection

afetuoso adj.& n. affectionate & tender

afiado adj. keen

afiador n. grinder

afiar v. sharpen

afilhado n. godchild

afiliação n. affiliation

afiliar v. affiliate

afinidade *n.* affinity

afirmação *n.* affirmation

afirmar *v.* affirm

afirmativo *adj.* affirmative

afixar *v.t.* affix

aflição *n.* affliction

afligir *v.* afflict

afligir *v.* aggrieve

afluência *n.* affluence

afluente *adj.* affluent

afluxo *n.* influx

afobar *v.* fluster

afogar *v.* drown

aforismo *n.* aphorism

afortunado *adj.* fortunate

africano *adj.* African

afronta *n.* affront

afrouxar *v.* slacken

afundar *v.* sink

agachar *v.i.* squat

agarrar *v.* grab

ágata *n.* agate

ageismo *n.* ageism

agência *n.* agency

agenda *n.* agenda

agente *n.* agent

ágil *adj.* & *n.* agile & alacritous

agilidade *n.* agility

agir *v.* act

agitação *n.* unrest

agitado *adj.* hectic

agitar *v.* agitate

aglomeração *n.* conurbation

aglomerar *v.* agglomerate

agnóstico *n.* agnostic

agonia *n.* agony

agonizar *v.* agonize

agora *adv.* now

Agosto *n* August

agourar *v.* bode

agradável *adj.* agreeable

agradecer *v.* thank

agrafador *n.* stapler

agrafar *v.* staple

agrafo *n.* staple

agramento *n.* aggravation

agrário *adj.* agrarian

agravar *v.* aggravate

agredir *v.* maul

agregar *n.* aggregate

agressão *n.* aggression

agressivo *adj.* aggressive

agressor *n.* aggressor

agrícola *adj.* agricultural

agricultor *n.* farmer

agrimensor *n.* surveyor

agrupamento *n.* grouping

água *n.* water

aguaceiro *n.* rainfall

aguardar *v.* await

águas residuais *n.* sewage

aguçar *v.* whittle

águia *n.* eagle

agulha *n.* needle

ai de mim! *conj.* alas

ainda *adv.* yet

ajoelhar *v.* kneel

ajuda *n.* helping

ajudante *n.* assistant

ajudar *v.* help

alagado *adj.* soppy

álamo *n.* poplar

alardear *v.* boast

alargar *v.* splay

alarmar v alarm

alarme n alarm

alaúde *n.* lute

alavanca *n.* lever

alavancagem *n.* leverage

albergue *n.* hostel

album n album

albumina *n.* albumen

alcachofra *n.* artichoke

alcalino *n.* alkali

alcançar *v.* achieve

alcançável *adj.* obtainable

alcance *n.* purview

alcatrão *n.* tar

álcool *n.* alcohol

alcoólico *adj.* alcoholic

alcova *n.* alcove

aldeão *n.* villager

aldeia *n.* village

alegação *n.* allegation

alegar *v.* allege

alegoria *n.* allegory

alegrar *v.* gladden

alegre *adj.* blithe

alegremente *adv.* gaily

alegria *n.* gaiety

aleijado *adj.* gammy

aleitamento *n.* suckling

além *adv.* beyond

além disso *adv.* furthermore

Alemão *n.* German

alérgeno *n.* allergen

alergia *n.* allergy

alérgico *adj.* allergic

alerta *adj.* alert

alfa *n.* alpha

alfabético *adj.* alphabetical

alfabetizado *adj.* literate

alfabeto *n.* alphabet

alfaiate *n.* tailor

alfinete *n.* pin

alforria *n.* manumission

algazarra *n.* outcry

álgebra *n.* algebra

algema *n.* handcuff

algemar *n.* cuff

algo *pron.* anything

algodão *n.* cotton

alguém *pron.* somebody

alguns *adj.* some

algures *adv.* somewhere

alho *n.* garlic

alho-porro *n.* leek

aliado *adj.* allied

aliado *n.* ally

aliança *n.* alliance

aliás *adv.* alias

alibi *n.* alibi

alicate *n.* pliers

alienar *v.i.* alienate

alienígena *adj.* alien

alimentador *n.* feeder

alimentar v. feed	altivo adj. haughty
alimentício n. alimony	alto adj. high
alinhamento n. alignment	alto-falante n. tweeter
alinhar v. align	altruísmo n. altruism
alinhavar v. baste	altruísta adj. selfless
alisar v. dab	altura n. height
alistar v. enlist	alucinar v. hallucinate
aliteração n. alliteration	aludir v.t. allude
aliterar v. alliterate	aluguel n. rental
aliviar v. alleviate	alumínio n. aluminium
alívio n. alleviation	aluno n. pupil
alma n. soul	alusão n. allusion
alma gémea n. soul mate	alvenaria n. masonry
almanaque n. almanac	alvéola n. wagtail
almirante n. admiral	alvo n. target
almíscar n. musk	ama n. nanny
almoço n. lunch	amado adj. beloved
almofada n. pad	amador n. amateur
alojamento n. accommodation	amadurecer v. ripen
alojamento n. lodging	amaldiçoar v. damn
alongar v. elongate	amálgama n. amalgam
alpendre n. hovel	amalgamação n. amalgamation
alpino adj. alpine	amalgamar v. amalgamate
alquimia n. alchemy	amalucado adj. nutty
altamente adv. highly	amamentar v. lactate
altar n. altar	amanhã adv. tomorrow
alteração n. alteration	amante n. lover
alterar v. change	amarelo adj. yellow
altercação n. altercation	amargar v. embitter
alternar v.t. alternate	amargo adj. bitter
alternativa adj. alternative	amargor n. acrimony
Alteza n. Highness	amarrado adj. tied
altitude n. altitude	amarrar v. tie
altivamente adj. lordly	amarras n. moorings

amarrotar n. crease
amassar v. knead
amatório adj. amatory
amável adj. complaisant
amavelmente adv. kindly
Amazonas n. Amazon
âmbar n. amber
ambição n. ambition
ambicioso adj. ambitious
ambiente n. environment
ambiguidade n. ambiguity
ambíguo adj. ambiguous
âmbito n. ambit
ambivalente adj. ambivalent
ambos & ambos adj. & pron. both
ambrósia n. ambrosia
ambulância n. ambulance
ambulatorial (doente) n. outpatient
ameaça n. threat
ameaçador adj. ominous
ameaçar v. threaten
ameixa n. prune
amêndoa n. almond
amendoim n. peanut
amenizar v. assuage
amianto n. asbestos
amido n. starch
amígdala n. tonsil
amigo n. friend
amigos n. kith
amizade n. fellowship
amnésia n. amnesia
amnistia n. amnesty
amolecer v. soften

amontoar v. huddle
amor n. love
amora n. blackberry
amoral adj. amoral
amoreira n. mulberry
amorfo adj. amorphous
amoroso adj. amorous
amortecedor n. buffer
amortecer n. cushion
amostra n. sample
amotinado adj. mutinous
ampére n. ampere
ampliar v. enlarge
amplificação n. amplification
amplificador n. amplifier
amplificar v. amplify
amplitude n. amplitude
amplo adj. ample
amuado adj. grumpy
amuar v. sulk
amuleto n. amulet
anacronismo n. anachronism
anais n. annals
anal adj. anal
analfabetismo n. illiteracy
analfabeto n. illiterate
analgésico n. analgesic
analisar v. analyse
análise n. analysis
analista n. analyst
analítico adj. analytical
analogia n. analogy
análogo adj. analogue
ananás n. pineapple

anão *n.* dwarf

anão *n.* midget

anarquia *n.* anarchy

anarquismo *n.* anarchism

anarquista *n.* anarchist

anatomia *n.* anatomy

anca *n.* hip

ancestral *adj.* ancestral

ancinho *n.* rake

ancioso *n.* longing

ancôra *n.* anchor

ancoradouro *n.* berth

ancoragem *n.* anchorage

andaime *n.* scaffold

andante *adv.* afoot

andar *v.* walk

andar escanrrachado *v.* straddle

andar em bicos de pés *v.* tiptoe

andar empertigado *n.* strut

andar gingando *v.* waddle

andar lentamente *v.* amble

andróide *n.* android

anedota *n.* anecdote

anel *n.* ring

anelzinho *n.* ringlet

anemia *n.* anaemia

anestesia *n.* anaesthesia

anestético *n.* anaesthetic

anexação *n.* annexation

anexar *v.* attach

anexo *v.* annex

anfíbio *n.* amphibian

anfiteatro *n.* amphitheatre

anfitriã *n.* hostess

angariar *v.* tout

angina *n.* angina

angular *adj.* angular

ângulo *n.* angle

angústia *n.* anguish

animação *n.* animation

animado *adj.* animated

animador *adj.* heartening

animal *n.* animal

animal de estimação *n.* pet

animar *v.* animate

animosidade *n.* animosity

aninhada *n.* nestling

aninhar *v.* nestle

aniquilação *n.* annihilation

aniquilar *v.* annihilate

anis *n.* aniseed

aniversário *n.* anniversary

anjo *n.* angel

ano *n.* year

anódio *n.* anode

anomalia *n.* anomaly

anómalo *adj.* anomalous

anonimato *n.* anonymity

anónimo *adj.* anonymous

anorexia *n.* anorexia

anormal *adj.* abnormal

anotar *v.* annotate

ansiar *v.* hanker

ansiedade *n.* anxiety

ansioso *adj.* anxious

ansioso *n.* yearning

antagonismo *n.* antagonism

antagonista *n.* antagonist

antagonizar *v.* antagonize	**antolhos** *n.* blinkers
Antártica *adj.* Antarctic	**antologia** *n.* anthology
antebraço *n.* forearm	**antónimo** *n.* antonym
antecedente *n.* antecedent	**antrax** *n.* anthrax
antecessor *n.* forefather	**antropologia** *n.* anthropology
antecipação *n.* anticipation	**anual** *adj.* & *adv.* annual & yearlly
antecipadamente *adv.* beforehand	**anuidade** *n.* annuity
antecipar *v.* antedate	**anulação** *n.* avoidance
antecipar-se *v.* pre-empt	**anular** *v.* annul
antena *n.* antenna	**anunciar** *v.* advertise
antepassado *n.* ancestor	**anúncio** *n.* advertisement
anterior *adj.* previous	**anus** *n.* anus
anteriormente *adj.* fore	**anverso** *n.* obverse
antes *adv.* before	**ao contrário** *prep.* unlike
anti *n.* anti	**ao lado de** *prep.* alongside
antiácido *adj.* antacid	**ao longo de** *prep.* along
antibiótico *n.* antibiotic	**ao redor** *adv.* around
anticlímax *n.* anticlimax	**apadrinhar** *v.* patronize
anticorpos *n.* antibody	**apagão** *n.* blackout
antídoto *n.* antidote	**apagar** *v.* erase
antigamente *adv.* formerly	**apaixonado** *adj.* impassioned
antigo *n.* & *adj.* antique & former	**apanhar** *v.* catch
antiguidade *n.* antiquity	**aparar** *v.* pare
antílope *n.* antelope	**aparato** *n.* apparatus
antinatural *adj.* unnatural	**aparecer** *v.* appear
antioxidante *n.* antioxidant	**aparência** *n.* appearance
antipatia *n.* antipathy	**aparente** *adj.* apparent
antipatizar *v.* dislike	**apartamento** *n.* apartment
antiquado *adj.* antiquated	**aparte** *adv.* aside
antiquado *n.* gentry	**apartheid** *n.* apartheid
antiquário *adj.* antiquarian	**apatia** *n.* apathy
anti-social *adj.* antisocial	**apático** *adj.* listless
antisséptico *adj.* antiseptic	**apátrida** *adj.* stateless
antítese *n.* antithesis	**apaziguar** *v.* appease

apelar v.t. appeal

apelativo adj. snazzy

apelido n. nickname

apelo n. plea

apenas adv. barely

apêndice n. appendage

apendicite n. appendicitis

aperfeiçoar v. meliorate

aperitivo n. appetizer

apertado adj. tight

apertar v. tighten

aperto n. stricture

aperto de mão n. handshake

apesar de conj. although

apesar de prep. despite

apetite n. appetite

ápice n apex

aplacar v. placate

aplaudir v. applaud

aplauso n. applause

aplausos n. plaudits

aplicação n. appliance

aplicar mal v. misapply

aplicável adj. applicable

apócalipse n. apocalypse

apodrecer v. rot

apogeu n. acme

apoiar v. support

apoio n. backing

apoio (moral) n. support

apontar v. pinpoint

apoplético adj. apoplectic

após prep. after

aposentadoria n. retirement

aposentar v. retire

aposta & apostar n. & v. wager

apostador n. gambler

apostar v. bet

apóstata n. apostate

apóstolo n. apostle

apóstrefe n. apostrophe

apreciação n. appreciation

apreciar v. appreciate

apreciável adj. appreciable

apreender v. apprehend

apreensão n. apprehension

apreensivo adj. apprehensive

aprender v. learn

aprendido adj. learned

aprendiz n. apprentice

aprendizagem n. learning

apresentação n. presentation

apresentar v. exhibit

apressado adj. hasty

apressar v. rush

aprisionar v. imprison

aprofundar v. delve

apropriação n. appropriation

apropriado adj. apposite

apropriado n. fitting

apropriar indevidam. v. misappropriate

aprovação n. approval

aprovar v. approve

aproveitar v. avail

aproveitável adj. serviceable

aprovisionamento n. stocking

aprovisionar v. purvey

aproximação n. rapprochement

aproximadamente *adv.* about
aproximado *adj.* approximate
aproximar *v.* approach
aprumo *n.* aplomb
aptidão *n.* capability
apto *adj.* apt
apurar *v.* canvass
apuro *n.* plight
aquário *n.* aquarium
aquático *adj.* aquatic
aquecedor *n.* heater
aquecer *v.* bask
aquecimento *n.* heating
aqui *adv.* here
aquietar *v.* quieten
aquisição *n.* acquisition
aquoso *adj.* aqueous
aquoso *adj.* watery
ar *n.* air
Árabe *n.* Arab
árabe *n.* Arabian
arábico *n.* Arabic
arado *n.* plough
arame *n.* wire
aranha *n.* spider
arável *adj.* arable
arbitragem *n.* arbitration
arbitrar *v.* arbitrate
arbitrário *adj.* arbitrary
árbitro *n.* arbiter
arborização *n.* afforestation
arborizado *adj.* wooded
arbusto *n.* bush
arbusto *n.* shrub

arca *n.* ark
arcada *n.* arcade
arcaico *adj.* archaic
arcanjo *n.* archangel
arcebispo *n.* archbishop
arco *n.* arc
arco-íris *n.* rainbow
ardente *adj.* ardent
ardil *n.* elusion
ardor *n.* ardour
ardósia *n.* slate
árduo *adj.* arduous
área *n.* area
areia *n.* sand
arejado *adj.* airy
arena *n.* arena
arenoso *adj.* sandy
arenque *n.* herring
arenque defumado *n.* bloater
arfar *v.* pant
argamassa *n.* grout
argila *n.* clay
argumentar *v.* argue
argumentativo *adj.* argumentative
argumento *n.* argument
árido *adj.* arid
aristocracia *n.* aristocracy
aristócrata *n.* aristocrat
aritmética *n.* arithmetic
aritmético *adj.* arithmetical
arlequim *n.* harlequin
arma *n.* gun
armação *n.* casement
armada *n.* armada

armadilha *n.* trap

armadura *n.* armour

Armagedão *n.* Armageddon

armamento *n.* armament

armário *n.* closet

armazém *n.* warehouse

armazenamento *n.* storage

armazenar *v.* stow

armazenista *n.* stockist

armistício *n.* armistice

aro *n.* hoop

aroma *n.* aroma

aromaterapia *n.* aromatherapy

arqueiro *n.* archer

arqueologia *n.* archaeology

arquiteto *n.* architect

arquitetura *n.* architecture

arquivo *n.* file

arquivos *n.* archives

arrancar *v.* pluck

arranha-céu *n.* skyscraper

arranhar *v.t.* scratch

arranjo *n.* arrangement

arranque *n.* starter

arrasar *v.* raze

arrastar *v.t* drag

arrastar-se *v.* trudge

arrebatado *adj.* rapt

arrebatamento *n.* rapture

arrebatar *v.* enrapture

arrecadar *v.* levy

arredondado *adj.* rounded

arreganhar *v.* grin

arreio *n.* harness

arreliar *v.* tease

arremessar *v.* hurl

arrendamento *n.* lease

arrendatário *n.* lessee

arrepender-se *v.* repent

arrependido *adj.* repentant

arrependimento *n.* repentance

arriscado *adj.* risky

arriscar *v.* endanger

arrivista *n.* upstart

arrogância *n.* arrogance

arrogante *adj.* arrogant

arrogar-se *v.* arrogate

arrojado *adj.* dashing

arrotar *v.* belch

arroz *n.* rice

arroz com casca *n.* paddy

arrumado *adj.* tidy

arsenal *n.* arsenal

arsénico *n.* arsenic

arstístico *adj.* artistic

arte *n.* art

artefato *n.* artefact

artéria *n.* artery

artesanato *n.* craft

artesanato *n.* handicraft

artesão *n.* craftsman

Ártico *adj.* Arctic

articulação *n.* joint

articulado *adj.* articulate

artificial *adj.* artificial

artifício *n.* artifice

artifício *n.* gimmick

artigo *n.* article

artigos higiene pessoal *n.* toiletries	**assegurar** *v.* assure
artigos de papelaria *n.* stationery	**asseio** *n.* tidiness
artilharia *n.* artillery	**assembléia** *n.* assembly
artimanha *n.* wile	**assemelhar** *v.* resemble
artista *n.* artist	**assento** *n.* seat
artrite *n.* arthritis	**asséptico** *adj.* aseptic
árvore *n.* tree	**assessor** *n.* aide
ás *n.* ace	**assexuado** *adj.* asexual
asa *n.* wing	**assíduo** *adj.* assiduous
ascenção *n.* ascent	**assim** *adv.* so
ascendente *adj.* ascendant	**assimétrico** *adj.* lopsided
ascender *v.* ascend	**assimilação** *n.* assimilation
ascético *adj.* ascetic	**assimilar** *v.* assimilate
asco *n.* revulsion	**assinatura** *n.* signature
asfixiar *v.* asphyxiate	**assistente** *n.* attendant
Asiático *adj.* Asian	**assobiar** *v.i* hiss
asilo *n.* asylum	**assobio** *n.* whistle
asinino *adj.* asinine	**associação** *n.* association
asma *n.* asthma	**associar** *v.* associate
asna *n.* truss	**assombrada** *adj.* haunted
aspereza *n.* asperity	**assombrar** *v.* haunt
áspero *adj.* harsh	**assombro** *n.* amazement
aspersão *n.* sprinkling	**assombroso** *adj.* wondrous
aspeto *n.* fettle	assonância *n.* assonance
aspiração *n.* aspiration	**assumir** *v.* assume
aspirante *n.* aspirant	**assunto** *n.* subject
aspirar *v.* aspire	**assustadiço** *adj.* skittish
assaltar *v.* assail	**assustador** *adj.* scary
assalto *n.* assault	**assustar** *v.* frighten
assar *v.* bake	**asterisco** *n.* asterisk
assar *v.* roast	**asteróide** *n.* asteroid
assassinar *v.* assassinate	**astigmatismo** *n.* astigmatism
assassinato *n.* murder	**astral** *adj.* astral
assassino *n.* assassin	**astraounata** *n.* astronaut

astrologia *n.* astrology
astrólogo *n.* astrologer
astronomia *n.* astronomy
astrónomo *n.* astronomer
astuto *adj.* astute
atacador *n.* shoestring
atacar *v.* attack
atalho *n.* shortcut
ataque *n.* bout
ataque repentino *n.* blitz
atarracado *adj.* stocky
atávico *adj.* atavistic
atazanar *v.* pester
até *prep.* until
até agora *adv.* hitherto
ateísmo *n.* atheism
atenção *n.* attention
atender *v.* attend
atentar *v.* attempt
atento *adj.* attentive
atento *adj.* mindful
aterragem *n.* landing
aterro *n.* embankment
aterrorizar *v.* terrify
atestar *v.* attest
ateu *n.* atheist
ateu *n.* heathen
atingir *v.* attain
atirar *v.* fling
atirar *v.* shoot
atitude *n.* attitude
ativar *v.* activate
atividade *n.* activity
ativista *n.* activist

ativo *adj. & n.* active & asset
atlas *n.* atlas
atleta *n.* athlete
atlético *adj.* athletic
atmosfera *n.* atmosphere
atoalhado *n.* towelling
atol *n.* atoll
atolar *n.* bog
atómico *adj.* atomic
átomo *n.* atom
ator *n.* actor
ator de pantominas *n.* mummer
atordoar *v.* daze
atordoar *v.* stun
atormentador *n.* tormentor
atormentar *v.* tantalize
atração *n.* attraction
atraente *adj.* catching
atraente *adj.* prepossessing
atrair *v.* attract
atrapalhar *v.* hinder
atrás *adv.* aback
atrás de *prep.* behind
atrasado *adj.* overdue
atrasar *v.* t delay
atraso *n.* lagging
atrativo *adj.* attractive
através *prep.* by
atravessar *n. & v.* cross & traverse
atrevido *adj.* cheeky
atribuição *n.* assignment
atribuir *v.* attribute
átrio *n.* atrium
atrito *n.* rub

atriz a. actress
atrocidade n. atrocity
atroz adj. atrocious
atuação n. acting
atual adj. current
atualizar v. update
atualmente adv. presently
atuário n. actuary
audaz adj. gutsy
audição n. audition
audiência n. audience
audio n. audio
audível adj. audible
aufitório n. auditorium
aula n. class
aumentar v. increase
aura n. aura
auscultadores n. headphone
ausente n.& adj. absence & absent
auspicioso adj. auspicious
austero adj. austere
Australiano n. Australian
autenticidade n. authenticity
autêntico adj. authentic
autismo n. autism
autobiografia n. autobiography
autocarro n. bus
autocracia n. autocracy
autocrata n. autocrat
autocrata adj. autocratic
autoestrada n. highway
autógrafo n. autograph
automático adj. automatic
automóvel n. automobile

autónomo adj. autonomous
autópsia n. autopsy
autor n. author
autoridade n. authority
autorizar v. authorize
auxiliar adj. & v. ancillary & assist
auxiliar adj. auxiliary
auxiliar de futuro v. will
auxílio n. assistance
avalanche n. avalanche
avaliação n. assessment
avaliar v. i evaluate
avançar v. advance
avanço n. advance
avante adv. onward
avarento adj.& n. miserly & scrooge
avareza n. avarice
avariar v. malfunction
ave limícola n. wader
aveia n. oat
aveludado adj. velvety
avenida n. avenue
avental n. apron
aventura n. adventure
aventureiro adj. adventurous
avermelhado adj. reddish
aversão n. aversion
aves domésticas n. poultry
avestruz n. ostrich
aviação n. aviation
aviador n. aviator
avião n. plane
aviário n. aviary
avidamente adv. avidly

ávido *adj.* avid

avisar *v.* advise

aviso *n.* warning

avistamento *n.* sighting

avivar *v.* smarten

avó *n.* grandmother

avuncular *adj.* avuncular

axilas *adj.* underarm

azedo *adj.* sour

azeitona *n.* olive

azevinho *n.* holly

azia *n.* heartburn

azul *adj.* blue

azulejo *n.* tile

B

babado *n.* frill

babar *v.* slobber

Babel *n.* Babel

babete *n.* bib

babuíno *n.* baboon

bacharel *n.* bachelor

bacia *n.* basin

baço *n.* spleen

bacon *n.* bacon

bactéria *n.* bacteria

badminton *n.* badminton

bafiento *adj.* frowsty

bafiento *n.* staleness

baga *n.* berry

bagagem *n.* baggage

baguete *n.* baguette

baía *n.* bay

bainha *n.* hem

baioneta *n.* bayonet

baixar *v.* subside

baixo *n.* bass

baixo *adj.* low

bajulação *n.* adulation

bajulador *n.* smoothie

bala *n.* bullet

balada *n.* ballad

balançar *v.* swing

balançar-se *v. i.* dangle

balancé *n.* see-saw

balanço *n.* swing

balão *n.* balloon

balbuciar *v.* babble

balde *n.* bucket

baleeiro *n.* whaler

baleia *n.* whale

balet *n.* ballet

balir *v. i* bleat

balsa *n.* ferry

bálsamo *n.* balsam

baluarte *n.* bulwark

baluarte *n.* rampart

bambolear *v.* shamble

bamboo *n.* bamboo

banal *adj.* commonplace

banana *n.* banana

bancada da frente *n.* frontbencher

banco *n.* bank

banda *n.* band

bandeira *n.* flag

bandeja *n.* tray

bandido *n.* bandit

bando *n.* bevy

banéfico *adj.* beneficial
banha de porco *n.* lard
banhar *v.* bathe
banho *n.* bath
banir *v.* banish
banjo *n.* banjo
banner *n.* banner
banqueiro *n.* banker
banquete *n.* banquet
banquinho *n.* stool
baque *n.* thud
bar *n.* bar
barafunda *n.* mayhem
barão *n.* baron
barata *n.* cockroach
barato *adj.* cheap
barato *adj.* inexpensive
barba *n.* beard
bárbaro *n.* barbarian
bárbaro *adj.* barbaric
barbatana *n.* flipper
barbeado *adj.* shaven
barbear *v.& n.* shave & shaving
barbeiro *n.* barber
barcaça *n.* barge
barco *n.* boat
bardo *n.* bard
barómetro *n.* barometer
barra *n.* stripe
barracão *n.* shed
barracuda *n.* barracuda
barragem *n.* dam
barreira *n.* barrier
barreira *n.* hurdle

barricada *n.* barricade
barriga *n.* belly
barril *n.* barrel
barulhento *adj.* noisy
barulho *n.* din
base *n.* base
base de dados *n.* database
básico *n.* basic
basílica *n.* basilica
bastante *adv.& adj.* fairly & pretty
bastão *n.* baton
bastar *v.* suffice
bastardo *n.* bastard
bastião *n.* bastion
bata *n.* smock
batalha *n.* battle
batalhão *n.* battalion
batata *n.* potato
batedeira *v.& n.* churn & mixer
batente *n.* mullion
bater *v.* flap
bateria *n.* battery
batido *n.* milkshake
batik *n.* batik
batina *n.* cassock
batismo *n.* baptism
Batista *n.* Baptist
batizar *v.* baptize
batota *n.* cheat
bazar *n.* bazaar
bazuca *n.* bazooka
beagle *n.* beagle
bêbado *adj.* drunkard
bébé *n.* baby

beber v. t drink

bebida n. beverage

beco n. alley

bege n. beige

beijar v.t. kiss

beijoca n. smack

beinal adj. biennial

beira n. brink

beira-mar n. seaside

bela n. belle

beleza n. beauty

beleza n. prettiness

beliche n. bunk

bélico adj. warlike

belicoso adj. bellicose

beliscar v. pinch

bem adv. well

bem sucedido adj. successful

bem-estar n. welfare

benção n. blessing

beneficiar v.t. advantage

beneficiário n. payee

beneficiente adj. beneficent

benefício n. benefice

benevolência n. benevolence

benevolente adj benevolent

benfeitor n. benefactor

benigno adj. benign

bens imóveis n. chattel

berçário n. nursery

berço n. cradle

bergamota n. bergamot

beringela n. brinjal

berma n. kerb

bermudas n. breeches

berrar v. bawl

besouro n. beetle

besta n. beast

bestial adj. beastly

betão n. concrete

beterraba n. beet

bétula n. birch

bexiga n. bladder

bezerro n. calf

bi comb. bi

Bíblia n. Bible

bibliófilo n. bibliophile

bibliografia n. bibliography

biblioteca n. library

bibliotecário n. librarian

bica n. spout

bicar v.i. peck

bicentenário n. bicentenary

bíceps n. biceps

bicha-de-rabear n. squib

bichano n. puss

bicharada n. vermin

bicho-da-seda n. silkworm

bicicleta n. bicycle

bico n. beak

bidão n. jerry can

bidé n. bidet

bife n. beef

bifocal adj. bifocal

bifurcar v. bisect

bigamia n. bigamy

bigode n. moustache

bigorna n. anvil

bilateral *adj.* bilateral
bilhão *n.* billion
bilhar *n.* billiards
bilhete *n.* ticket
bilingue *adj.* bilingual
bilionário *n.* billionaire
bílis *n.* bile
binário *adj.* binary
binocular *adj.* binocular
biodegradável *adj.* biodegradable
biodeversidade *n.* biodiversity
biografia *n.* biography
biologia *n.* biology
biologista *n.* biologist
biópsia *n.* biopsy
bioquímica *n.* biochemistry
bip *n.* beep
bipartidário *adj.* bipartisan
biquini *n.* bikini
birra *n.* tantrum
bis *n.* encore
bisão *n.* bison
bisbilhotar *v.* pry
biscoito *n.* biscuit
bisel *n.* bevel
bispo *n.* bishop
bissexual *adj.* bisexual
bizarro *adj.* bizarre
blazer *n.* blazer
bloco *n.* bloc
blog *n.* blog
bloquear *n.* block
bloqueio *n.* blockage
blusa *n.* blouse

blush *n.* blusher
boa vontade *n.* goodwill
boas-vindas *n.* welcome
bobina *n.* coil
bobinador *n.* winder
bobo *n. & adj.* jester & silly
boca *n.* mouth
bocadinho *n.* modicum
bocado *n.* bit
bocal *n.* nozzle
bocejar *v.* gape
bocejar *v.* yawn
bochecha *n.* cheek
bode expiatório *n.* scapegoat
boi *n.* ox
boi castrado *n.* bullock
bóia *n.* buoy
boicotar *v.* boycott
bola *n.* ball
bola de neve *n.* snowball
bolacha *n.* cookie
boletim *n.* bulletin
boleto *n.* billet
bolha *n.* bubble
bolinha *n.* pellet
bolo *n.* cake
bolor *n.* mould
bolorento *adj.* musty
bolota *n.* acorn
bolsa *n.* handbag
bolsa de estudo *n.* scholarship
bolso *n.* pocket
bom *adj.* good
bom atirador *n.* marksman

bomba *n.* bomb	**Braille** *n.* Braille
bombardeamento *n.* bombardment	**branco** *adj.* white
bombardear *v.* bombard	**brandir** *v.* brandish
bombista *n.* bomber	**brando** *adj.* lenient
bondade *n.* goodness	**brandy** *n.* brandy
boné *n.* cap	**branquear** *v.* blanch
boneca *n.* doll	**bravura** *n.* gallantry
bonito *adj.* beautiful	**bravura** *n.* valour
bónus *n.* bonus	**breve** *adj.* brief
boquiabertos *adj.* flabbergasted	**brevidade** *n.* brevity
borboleta *n.* butterfly	**brigada** *n.* brigade
borbulha *n.* pimple	**brigadeiro** *n.* brigadier
borda *n.* edge	**brigar** *v.* bicker
bordado *n.* embroidery	**brilhante** *adj.& n.* bright & sparkling
bordel *n.* brothel	**brilhar** *v.* shine
borla *n.* tassel	**brilho** *n.* brilliance
borracha *n.* rubber	**brincadeira** *n.* hoax
borrachão *n.* rummy	**brincalhão** *adj.* facetious
borrar *n.* blot	**brincar** *v.* gambol
borrasca *n.* squall	**brinde** *n.* toast
borrifador *n.* sprinkler	**brinquedo** *n.* toy
borrifar *v.i.* sprinkle	**brisa** *n.* breeze
bosque *n.* woodland	**Britânico** *adj.* British
bota *n.* boot	**broca** *n.* drill
botânica *n.* botany	**brocado** *n.* brocade
botão *n.* button	**brochura** *n.* brochure
boutique *n.* boutique	**bróculos** *n.* broccoli
boxe n boxing	**bronco** *n.* dullard
boxe *n.* infighting	**bronquial** *adj.* bronchial
braça *n.* fathom	**bronze** *n.* bronze
braçadeira *n.* brace	**bronzeado** *n.* tan
bracelete *n.* bangle	**brotar** *v.* sprout
braço *n.* arm	**bruscamente** *adv.* shortly
bradar *v.* roister	**brusco** *adj.* brusque

brutal *adj.* brutal
bruto *n.& adj.* brute & gross
bruxa *n.* witch
bruxaria *n.* witchcraft
buço *n.* fluff
bufalo *n.* buffalo
bufet *n.* buffet
bugiganga *n.* bauble
bulbo *n.* bulb
buldogue *n.* bulldog
bulimia *n.* bulimia
bungalow *n.* bungalow
buraco *n.* hole
buraco de fechadura *n.* keyhole
burlar *v.* rig
burlesco *n.* burlesque
burocracia *n.* bureaucracy
burocrata *n.* bureaucrat
burro *n.* donkey
busca *n.* pursuit
buscar *v.* fetch
bússola *n.* compass
busto *n.* bust
búzio *n.* whelk
byte *n.* byte

C

cá *adv.* hither
cabaça *n.* gourd
cabana *n.* wigwam
cabaré *n.* cabaret
cabeça *n.* head
cabelo *n.* hair
cabide *n.* hanger

cabine *n.* cabin
cabine do piloto *n.* cockpit
cablagem *n.* wiring
cabo *n.* cable
cabra *n.* goat
cabrestante *n.* capstan
cabresto *n.* halter
cabriolé *n.* chaise
cabrito-montês *n.* roe
caçador *n.* hunter
caçar *v.* hunt
cacarejar *v.* chuckle
caçarola *n.* casserole
cacau *n.* cacao
cacete *n.* bludgeon
cachecol *n.* scarf
cachorrinho *n.* whelp
cachorro *n.* puppy
cacifo *n.* locker
caco *n.* shard
cacrejo *n.* cackle
cato *n.* cactus
cada *adj.* each
cadáver *n.* cadaver
caddie *n.* caddy
cadeado *n.* padlock
cadeira *n.* chair
caderno *n.* notebook
cadete *n.* cadet
cádmio *n.* cadmium
caducar *v.* dote
café *n.* coffee
café com leite *n.* latte
café expresso *n.* espresso

Cafetãs n. kaftans
cafeteria n. cafeteria
cãibra n. cramp
cair v. drop
cair os dentes v. teethe
cais n. quay
caixa n. box
caixão n. coffin
caju n. cashew
cal n. whitewash
calabouço n. dungeon
calamidade n. calamity
calão n. slang
calçada n. pavement
calcanhar n. heel
calcar v. tamp
calças n. trousers
calcinhas n. panties
cálcio n. calcium
calço n. underlay
calculadora n. calculator
calcular v. calculate
calcular mal v. miscalculate
cálculo n. calculation
caldear v.t. slake
caldeira n. boiler
caldeirão n. cauldron
caldo n. broth
caleidoscópio n. kaleidoscope
calendário n. calendar
calibrar v. calibrate
calibre n. calibre
cálice n. chalice
caligrafia n. calligraphy

callha n. gutter
calmaria adj. becalmed
calmo adj. calm
calor n. heat
caloria n. calorie
caloroso adj. hearty
calúnia n. calumny
cama n. bed
camada n. layer
câmara n. chamber
camarada n. comrade
camaradagem n. camaraderie
camareiro n. chamberlain
cambaleante adj. staggering
cambalear v. stagger
cambalhota n. somersault
cambraia n. cambric
camelo n. camel
camião n. truck
caminhada n. hike
caminhar v. traipse
caminho n. path
caminho de ferro n. railway
camionista n. trucker
camisa n. shirt
camisa de noite n. nightie
camisola n. jersey
camisola interior (s/mangas) n. singlet
campainha n. bell
campanário n. steeple
campanha n. campaign
campeão n. champion
campo n. field
campo de gelo n. floe

camponês *n.* peasant

camponeses *n.* peasantry

campónio *n.* yokel

camurça *n.* suede

cana *n.* cane

canabis *n.* cannabis

canal *n.* canal

canalha *n.* scoundrel

canalizador *n.* plumber

canção *n.* song

cancela *n.* gateau

cancelamento *n.* cancellation

cancelar *v.* cancel

cancro *n.* cancer

candidato *n.* candidate

candura *n.* candour

caneca *n.* mug

canela *n.* cinnamon

canela (perna) *n.* shin

caneta *n.* pen

cânfora *n.* camphor

cangalheiro *n.* undertaker

canguru *n.* kangaroo

canhão *n.* cannon

canibal *n.* cannibal

canil *n.* kennel

canino *adj.* canine

canoa *n.* canoe

cansado *adj.* tired

cansar *v.* tire

cansativo *adj.* tiresome

cantado em coro *adj.* choral

cantão *n.* canton

cantar *v.* sing

cantar tirolês *v.* yodel

cântico *n.* carol

cântico *n.* chant

cantina *n.* canteen

cantor *a.* singer

cão *n.* dog

cão de caça *n.* hound

caos *n.* chaos

caótico *adj.* chaotic

capa *n.* cape

capa de chuva *n.* raincoat

capacete *n.* helmet

capacidade *n.* ability

capacitor *n.* capacitor

capar *v.* geld

capataz *n.* foreman

capaz *adj.* able

capela *n.* chapel

capelão *n.* chaplain

capitação *n.* capitation

capital *n.* capital

capitalismo *n.* capitalism

Capitalista *n.* &*adj.* capitalist

capitalizar *v.* capitalize

capitania *n.* captaincy

capitão *n.* captain

capitular *v.* capitulate

capítulo *n.* chapter

capota *n.* fairing

capricho *n.* caprice

caprichoso *adj.* capricious

cápsula *n.* capsule

captor *n.* captor

captura *v.* capture

capturar *v. t.* entrap

capuz *n.* hood

caracol *n.* snail

característica *n.* characteristic

caramanchão *n.* bower

caramelo *n.* caramel

caranguejo *n.* crab

caráter *n.* character

caravana *n.* caravan

carbohidrato *n.* carbohydrate

carbonato *adj.* carbonate

carbonizar *v.* char

carbono *n.* carbon

carcaça *n.* carcass

carcaça (navio velho) *n.* hulk

carcereiro *n.* jailer

cardamomo *n.* cardamom

cardíaco *adj.* cardiac

cardigã *n.* cardigan

cardinal *n.* cardinal

cardiógrafo *n.* cardiograph

cardiologia *n.* cardiology

cardo *n.* thistle

cardume *n.* shoal

careca *adj.* bald

careta *n.* frump

carga *n.* cargo

carga *n.* charge

caricatura *n* caricature

carícia *v.* caress

caridade *n.* charity

caridoso *adj.* charitable

caril *n.* curry

carimbar *v.* stamp

carimbo *n.* stamp

carinho *n.* endearment

carisma *n.* charisma

carismático *adj.* charismatic

carma *n.* karma

carmesin *n.* crimson

carmim *n.* carmine

carnal *adj.* carnal

carnaval *n.* carnival

carne *n.* flesh

carne *n.* meat

carne de porco *n.* pork

carneiro *n.* mutton

carnificina *n.* carnage

carnívoro *n.* carnivore

carnudo *adj.* beefy

caro *adj.* expensive

carpiano *adj.* carpal

carpintaria *n.* carpentry

carpinteiro *n.* carpenter

carrancudo *n.* scowl

carregado *n.* laden

carregador *n.* charger

carregar *n.* load

carreira *n.* career

carretel *n.* reel

carriça *n.* wren

carrilhão *n.* chime

carrinha *n.* van

carrinho *n.* cart

carrinho de bébé *n.* pram

carro *n.* car

carro fúnebre *n.* hearse

carroça *n.* wain

carrossel *n.* roundabout

carta *n.* letter

carta singular *n.* singleton

cartão *n.* card

carteira *n.* wallet

carteiro *n.* postman

cartel *n.* cartel

cartilagem *n.* cartilage

cartilha *n.* primer

cartucho *n.* cartridge

carvalho *n.* oak

carvão *n.* charcoal

casa *n.* house

casa de banho *n.* toilet

casaco *n.* coat

casal *n.* couple

casamenteiro *n.* matchmaker

casamento *n.* marriage

Casanova *n.* Casanova

casar *v.* marry

casca *n.* bark

cascalho *n.* gravel

cascata *n.* cascade

cascata *n.* waterfall

casco *n.* hoof

casimira *n.* cashmere

Casinha *n.* maisonette

casino *n.* casino

caso *n.* case

caspa *n.* dandruff

casquilho *n.* socket

cassetete *n.* truncheon

casta *n.* caste

castanha *n.* chestnut

castanha da índia *n.* conker

castanho *n.* brown

castanhola *n.* scallop

castelo *n.* castle

castidade *n.* chastity

castigar *v.* castigate

casting *n.* casting

casto *adj.* chaste

castor *n.* beaver

castrar *v.* castrate

casual *adj.* casual

casualidade *n.* casualty

casulo *n.* cocoon

cataclismo *n.* cataclysm

catalisador *n.* catalyst

catalisar *v.* catalyse

catálogo *n.* catalogue

catarata *n.* cataract

catarse *n.* catharsis

catástrofe *n.* catastrophe

cata-vento *n.* vane

catecismo *n.* catechism

catedral *n.* cathedral

categoria *n.* category

categórico *adj.* categorical

caterpillar *n.* caterpillar

cativante *adj.& n.* catchy & stunner

cativar *v.* captivate

cativeiro *n.* captivity

cativo *n.* captive

católico *adj.* catholic

catorze *adj.& n.* fourteen

Caucasiano *adj.* Caucasian

cauda *n.* tail

caule *n.* stem	**cegonha** *n.* stork
causa *n.* sake	**cegueira** *n.* blindness
causal *adj.* causal	**ceia** *n.* supper
causar *n.* cause	**ceifeiro** *n.* reaper
causar apreensões *v.* misgive	**celebração** *n.* celebration
cáustico *adj.* caustic	**celebrante** *n.* celebrant
causualidade *n.* causality	**celebrar** *v.* celebrate
cautela *n.* caution	**celebridade** *n.* celebrity
cautelosamente *adv.* gingerly	**celebridade** *n.* luminary
cauteloso *adj.* cautionary	**celeiro** *n.* barn
cavalaria *n.* cavalry	**célere** *adj.* speedy
cavaleiro *n.* knight	**celestial** *adj.* heavenly
cavalete *n.* trestle	**celibatário** *adj.* celibate
cavalgada *n.* cavalcade	**celibato** *n.* celibacy
cavalgar *v.* bestride	**celidónia** *n.* celandine
cavalheiresco *adj.* chivalrous	**Celsius** *n.* Celsius
cavalheirismo *n.* chivalry	**Céltico** *adj.* Celtic
cavalheiro *n.* gentleman	**célula** *n.* cell
cavalo *n.* horse	**celular** *adj.* cellular
cavalo de trote *n.* trotter	**celulite** *n.* cellulite
cavalo-vapor *n.* horsepower	**celulóide** *n.* celluloid
cavar *v.* dig	**celulose** *n.* cellulose
cave *n.* basement	**cem** *adj.& n.* hundred
caverna *n.* cavern	**cemitério** *n.* cemetery
cavernoso *adj.* cavernous	**cena** *n.* scene
cavidade *n.* cavity	**cenário** *n.* scenario
cavilha *n.* toggle	**cénico** *adj.* scenic
cebola *n.* onion	**cenoura** *n.* carrot
ceceio *n.* lisp	**censo** *n.* census
ceder *v.* cede	**censor** *n.* censor
cedo *adj.* early	**censura** *n.* censorship
cedro *n.* cedar	**censurar** *v.* censure
cédula *n.* ballot	**censurável** *adj.* objectionable
cego *adj.* blind	**centavo** *n.* penny

centeio n. rye
centenário n. centennial
centígrados adj. centigrade
centímetro n. centimetre
cêntimo n. cent
centopeia n. millipede
centralizar v. centralize
centro n. center
centro comercial n. mall
cepo n. stub
cera n. wax
cerâmica n. ceramic
cerca n. fence
cercado para cavalos n. paddock
cercar v. t encircle
cerco n. siege
cereal n. cereal
cerebral adj. cerebral
cérebro n. brain
cerimónia n. ceremony
cerimonial adj. ceremonial
cerimonioso adj. ceremonious
cerrar v. clench
certamente adv. certainly
certeza n. certitude
certidão n. certificate
certificado n. testimonial
certificar v. certify
certificável adj. certifiable
certo adj. certain
cerveja n. beer
cervejaria n. brewery
cervical adj. cervical
cerzir v. darn

cesariana n. caesarean
cessação n. cessation
cessão n. cession
cessar v. cease
cessar fogo n. ceasefire
cesto n. basket
cesto feito de tiras n. trug
cético n. sceptic
cetim n. satin
cetro n. sceptre
céu n. heaven
cevada n. barley
chá n. tea
chacal n. jackal
chafurdar v. wallow
chalé n. chalet
chaleira n. kettle
chama n. flame
chamada n. calling
chamar v. call
chamariz n. decoy
chaminé n. chimney
champanhe n. champagne
champô n. shampoo
chamuscar v. singe
Chancelaria n. Chancery
chanceler n. chancellor
chantagem n. blackmail
chão n. ground
chapa de ferro (culinária) n. griddle
chapéu n. hat
charco n. moor
charlatanismo n. quackery
charlatão n. charlatan

charneca *n.* heath

charuto *n.* cigar

chassis *n.* chassis

chatear *v.* upset

chauvinismo *n.* chauvinism

chauvinista *n.* &*adj.* chauvinist

chave *n.* key

chave de fenda *n.* screwdriver

chávena *n.* cup

chefe *n.* boss

chefe dos correios *n.* postmaster

chefia *n.* leadership

chegada *n.* arrival

chegar *v.* arrive

cheio *adj.* fraught

cheiro *n.* smell

cheque *n.* cheque

cheque-mate n checkmate

chiar *v.* sizzle

chicote *n.* whip

chicotear *v.* lash

chifre *n.* horn

chilrear *v.* tweet

chimpazé *n.* chimpanzee

China *n.* china

chinelo *n.* slipper

chita *n.* cheetah

chocalhar *v.* rattle

chocante *adj.* shocking

chocar *v.* shock

chocolate *n.* chocolate

choque *n.* shock

choradeira *n.* whine

choramingar *v.* whimper

chorar *n.* cry

chorar *v.* cry

choroso *adj.* tearful

choupana *n.* shanty

chumaço *n.* wad

chupa-chupa *n.* lollipop

chupar *v.* suck

churrasco *n.* barbecue

chutar *v.* kick

chuva n rain

chuveiro *n.* shower

chuvisco *n.* drizzle

chuvoso *adj.* rainy

cianeto *n.* cyanide

ciano *n.* cyan

ciática *n.* sciatica

ciberespaço *n.* cyberspace

cibernético comb. cyber

cicatriz *n.* scar

cíclico *adj.* cyclic

ciclista *n.* cyclist

ciclo *n.* cycle

ciclomotor *n.* moped

ciclone *n.* cyclone

cidadania *n.* citizenship

cidadão *n.* citizen

cidade *n.* city

cidra *n.* cider

ciência *n.* science

científico *adj.* scientific

cientista *n.* scientist

cigano *n.* gypsy

cigarra *n.* buzzer

cigarro *n.* cigarette

cilada *n.* snare

cilindro *n.* cylinder

cimento *n.* cement

cinco *adj. & n.* five

cinema n cinema

cinético *adj.* kinetic

cínico *n.* cynic

cinosura *n.* cynosure

cinquenta *adj. & n.* fifty

cintilante *adj.* scintillating

cintilar *v.* shimmer

cinto *n.* belt

cintura *n.* waist

cinturão *n.* girdle

cinza *n.* ash

cinzel *n.* chisel

cio *n.* rut

cipreste *n.* cypress

circo *n.* circus

circuito *n.* circuit

circuito *n.* speedway

circulação *n.* circulation

circular *adj. & v.* circular & circulate

círculo *n.* circle

circuncidar *v.* circumcise

circunferência *n.* circumference

circunscrever *v.* circumscribe

circunstância *n.* circumstance

circusnpecto *adj.* circumspect

cirurgia *n.* surgery

cirurgião *n.* surgeon

cisma *n.* schism

cisne *n.* swan

cista *n.* cist

cisterna *n.* cistern

cístico *adj.* cystic

cisto *n.* cyst

citação *n.* quotation

citadela *n.* citadel

citar *v.* cite

citar mal *v.* misquote

cítara *n.* zither

cítrico *n. & adj.* citrus & citric

ciúme *n.* jealousy

ciumento *adj.* jealous

cívico *adj.* civic

civil *adj. & n.* civil & civilian

civilização *n.* civilization

civilizar *v.* civilize

clã *n.* clan

clamor *n.* clamour

clandestinamente *adj.* underhand

clandestino *adj.* clandestine

clarabóia *n.* skylight

claramente *adv.* clearly

clarear *v.* brighten

clareira *n.* glade

clareza *n.* clarity

clarim *adj.* clarion

clássico *adj.* classic

classificação *n.* classification

classificar *v.* categorize

claustro *n.* cloister

claustrofobia *n.* claustrophobia

cláusula *n.* clause

clava *n.* cudgel

clemência *n.* clemency

clemente *adj.* clement

Clementina n. Clementine	**coche** n. chariot
clérigo n. cleric	**cocktail** n. cocktail
clero n. clergy	**côco** n. coconut
cliente n. client	**codificar** v. encode
clima n. climate	**código** n. code
clímax n. climax	**código postal** n. postcode
clínica n. clinic	**codorniz** n. quail
clip n. clip	**co-educação** n. co-education
clique n. click	**coeficiente** n. coefficient
clone n. clone	**coelheira** n. hutch
cloro n. chlorine	**coelho** n. rabbit
clorofórmio n. chloroform	**coentro** n. coriander
clube n. club	**coerente** adj. coherent
coabitar v. cohabit	**coesão** n. cohesion
coador n. percolator	**coesivo** adj. cohesive
coagir v. coerce	**coevo** adj. coeval
coágulo n. clot	**coexistência** n. coexistence
coalhada n. curd	**coexistir** v. coexist
coalho n. whey	**cofre** n. coffer
coar v. leach	**cogitar** v. cogitate
coaxar n. croak	**cognato** adj. cognate
cobalto n. cobalt	**cogumelo** n. mushroom
cobarde n. coward	**coincidência** n. coincidence
coberto adj. overgrown	**coincidir** v. coincide
cobertor n. blanket	**coisa** n. thing
cobertura n. roofing	**coisas** n. stuff
cobiçar v. covet	**cola** n. glue
cobra n. cobra	**colaboração** n. collaboration
cobrar v. charge	**colaborar** v. collaborate
cobre n. copper	**colagem** n. collage
cobrir n.& v. cover	**colapso** v. collapse
coca-cola n. coke	**colar** n. necklace
cocaína n. cocaine	**colarinho** n. collar
coçar v.i. itch	**colateral** n. collateral

colcha *n.* quilt		**com sarampo** *adj.* measly	
colchão *n.* mattress		**coma** *n.* coma	
coldre *n.* holster		**comandante** *n.* commandant	
coleção *n.* collection		**comandar** *v.* command	
colega *n.* colleague		**comando** *n.* commando	
coleira *n.* leash		**combate** *n.* combat	
cólera *n.* cholera		**combatente** n combatant	
coletar *v.* collect		**combinação** *n.* combination	
colete *n.* vest		**combinado** *adj.* concerted	
coletivo *adj.* collective		**combinar** *v.* combine	
coletor *n.* collector		**comboio** *n.* train	
colheita *n.* harvest		**combustão** *n.* combustion	
colher *v. & n.* reap & spoon		**combustível** *adj.* combustible	
colherada *n.* spoonful		**combustível** *n. &* fuel	
cólica *n.* colic		**começar** *v.* begin	
colidir *v.* clash		**começo** *n.* commencement	
colidir *v.* collide		**comédia** n comedy	
colina *n.* hill		**comédia leve** *n.* vaudeville	
colírio *n.* eyewash		**comediante** *n.* comedian	
colisão *n.* collision		**comemoração** *n.* commemoration	
colmeia *n.* apiary		**comemorar** *v.* commemorate	
colo *n.* lap		**comentador** *n.* commentator	
colocar *v.* lay		**comentário** *n.* comment	
colocar em prateleira *v.* shelve		**comer** *v.* eat	
cólon *n.* colon		**comer** (com os olhos) *v.* ogle	
colónia *n.* colony		**comercial** *adj.* commercial	
colonial *adj.* colonial		**comerciante** *n.* trader	
colono *n.* settler		**comerciante** *n.* tradesman	
coloquial *adj.& n.* colloquial & locum		**comestível** *adj.* eatable	
coloração *n.* colouring		**cometa** *n.* comet	
colossal *adj.* colossal		**cometer** *v.* commit	
colosso *n.& adj.* colossus & jumbo		**cómico** *adj.* comic	
coluna *n.* column		**comida** *n.* food	
com *prep.* with		**cominhos** *n.* cumin	

comissão n. commission
comissário n. commissioner
comissário de bordo n. purser
comissura n. commissure
comité n. committee
comitiva n. entourage
como adj. & adv. alike & as
como prep like
comoção n. commotion
cómoda n. commode
comodidade n. commodity
compacto adj. compact
compaixão n. compassion
companheiro n. companion
companhia n. company
comparação n. comparison
comparar v. compare
comparativo adj. comparative
comparecimento n. attendance
compartimento n. compartment
compatível adj. compatible
compatriota n. compatriot
compêndio n. compendium
compensação n. compensation
compensar v. compensate
competência n. competence
competente adj. adept
competição n. competition
competir v. cope
competitivo adj. competitive
compilar v. compile
complacente adj. complacent
compleição n. complexion
complementar n. complement

complementar adj. complementary
completamente adv. altogether
completar v. accomplish
completo adj. complete
complexidade n. complexity
complexo adj. complex
complicação n. complication
complicado adj. tricky
complicar v. complicate
componente n. component
compor v. compose
comporta n. sluice
comportamento n. behaviour
comportar-se v. behave
composição n. composition
compositor n. composer
composto adj composite
composto n. compound
compostura n. composure
comprador n. buyer
comprar v. buy
compras n. shop
compreender v. comprehend
compreender mal v. misapprehend
compreensão n. understanding
compreensível adj. comprehensible
compreensivo adj. comprehensive
compressão n. compression
compressor n. supercharger
comprimento n. length
comprimido n. tablet
comprimir v. compress
compromisso n. appointment
comprovação n. substantiation

compulsão n. compulsion

compulsivo adj. compulsive

compunção n. compunction

computação n. computation

computador n. computer

comum adj. communal

comuna n. commune

comunhão n. communion

comunicação n. communication

comunicante n. communicant

comunicar v. communicate

comunicável adj. communicable

comunidade n. commonwealth

comunismo n. communism

comutar v. commute

concatenação n. concatenation

côncavo adj. concave

conceber v. t conceive

concebível adj. conceivable

conceder v. accord

conceito n. concept

concentração n. concentration

concentrar v. concentrate

concepção n. conception

concernente prep. concerning

concerto n. concert

concessão n. concession

concha n. conch

conciliar v. conciliate

conciso adj. concise

concluído adj. accomplished

concluir n. conclude

conclusão n. conclusion

conclusão n. upshot

conclusivo adj. conclusive

concordância n. acquiescence

concordar v. agree

concordar com v. acquiesce

concórdia n. concord

concorrente n. competitor

concorrente adj. & concurrent

concorrer v. concur

concubina n. concubine

concurso n. concourse

concussão n. concussion

condado n. county

conde n. earl

condenação n. condemnation

condenado n. convict

condenar v. condemn

condenável adj. damnable

condensar v. condense

condescendente adj. compliant

condescender v. condescend

condição n. condition

condicionador n. conditioner

condicional adj. conditional

condimento n. condiment

condolências n. condolence

condomínio n. condominium

condutor n. conductor

conduzir n. conduct

cone n. cone

conectar v. connect

conexão n. connection

confecção n. confection

confederação n. confederation

confederado adj. confederate

confeitaria *n.* confectionery

confeiteiro *n.* confectioner

conferência *n.* conference

conferencista *n.* lecturer

conferir *v.* confer

confessar *v.* confess

congresso *n.* congress

confiança *n.* confidence

confiante *adj.* confident

confiar *v.* confide

confiável *adj.* reliable

confidencial *adj.* confidential

confidente *n.* confidant

configuração *n.* configuration

confinar *v.* abut

confirmação *n.* confirmation

confirmada *v.* confirm

confiscar *v.* confiscate

confisco *n.* confiscation

confissão *n.* confession

conflito *n.* conflict

conflituoso *adj.* quarrelsome

conforme *adv.* according

conformidade *n.* accordance

confortar *v.* comfort

confortável *adj.* comfortable

conforto *n.* comfort

confrontar *v.* collate

confronto *n.* confrontation

confundir *v.* baffle

confusão *n.* confusion

confuso *adj.* befuddled

congelador *n.* freezer

congelar *v.* freeze

congénito *adj.* congenital

congestão *n.* congestion

congestionado *adj.* congested

congestionamento *n.* jam

conglomeração *n.* conglomeration

conglomerado *n.* conglomerate

congregar *v.* congregate

congruente *adj.* congruent

conhecedor *adj.* knowing

conhecimento *n.* knowledge

conhecimento limitado *n.* smattering

cónico *adj.* conical

conjetura *n.* conjecture

conjeturar *v.* conjecture

conjugal *n.* conjugal

conjugar *v.* conjugate

cônjuge *n.* spouse

conjunção *n.* conjunction

conjunto *adj.&n.* conjunct & set

conjuntura *n.* conjuncture

conjurar *v.* conjure

conjutivite *n.* conjunctivitis

conotação *n.* overtone

conquanto *conj.* though

conquista *n.* conquest

conquistar *v.* conquer

consagrar *v.* consecrate

consaguíneo *adj.* akin

consciência *n.* conscience

consciente *adj.* aware

consecutivamente *adv.* consecutively

consecutivo *adj.* consecutive

conselheiro *n.* councillor

conselho *n.* advice

consenso n. consensus
consentimento n. assent
consentir v.t. consent
consequência n. consequence
consequente adj. consequent
consertar v. mend
consertar utensílios v. tinker
conserva n. pickle
conservação n. conservation
conservador adj. conservative
conservar v. t conserve
conservatório n. conservatory
consideração n. consideration
considerado adj. considerate
considerar v. consider
considerável adj. considerable
consignação n. consignment
consignar v. consign
consistência n. consistency
consistente adj. consistent
consistir em v. consist
consoante n. consonant
consolar v. t. console
consolidação n. consolidation
consolidar v. consolidate
consolo n. consolation
consorciar n. consort
consórcio n. consortium
conspícuo adj. conspicuous
conspiração n. collusion
conspirador n. conspirator
conspirar v. conspire
constante adj. constant
constelação n. constellation

consternação n. consternation
constitucional adj. constitutional
constituição n. constitution
constituinte adj. constituent
constituir v. constitute
constragimento n. constraint
constranger v. constrain
construção n. construction
construir v. construct
construtivo adj. constructive
cônsul n. consul
consulado n. consulate
consular n. consular
consultar v.& consult
consultar n. consultation
consultor n. consultant
consumar v. consummate
consumidor n. consumer
consumir v. consume
consumo n. consumption
conta n. account
contabilidade n. accountancy
contabilista n. accountant
contador n. teller
contágio n. contagion
contagioso adj. contagious
contaminar v. contaminate
contar v. count
contato n. contact
contemplação n. contemplation
contemplar v. contemplate
contemporâneo adj. contemporary
contenção n. containment
contentamento n. contentment

contente *adj.* content

contentor *n.* bin

conter *v.* restrain

contestante *n.* contestant

contexto *n.* context

contigência *n.* contingency

contíguo *adj.* contiguous

continental *adj.* continental

continente *n.* continent

continuação *n.* sequel

continuidade *n.* continuity

contínuo *adj.* continual

conto *n.* tale

contorcer *v.* contort

contorno *n.* outline

contra *prep.* against

contrabandear *v.* smuggle

contrabandista *n.* smuggler

contrabando *n.* contraband

contracepção *n.* contraception

contraceptivo *n.* contraceptive

contradição *n.* contradiction

contradizer *v.* contradict

contragolpe *n.* riposte

contrair *v.* constrict

contrapartida *n.* counterpart

contrariar *v.* counteract

contraste *n.* contrast

contratação *n.* contraction

contratante *n.* contractor

contratar *v.t* hire

contratempo *n.* misadventure

contrato *n.* contract

contratual *adj.* contractual

contravenção *n.* misdemeanour

contribuição *n.* contribution

contribuir *v.* contribute

controlador *n.* controller

controlar *n.* control

controvérsia *n.* controversy

controverso *adj.* controversial

contusão *n.* contusion

convenção *n.* convention

convencer *v.* convince

convencido *adj.* cocky

conveniência *n.* convenience

conveniente *adj.* convenient

convento *n.* convent

convento de freiras *n.* nunnery

convergir *v.* converge

conversa *n.* conversation

conversão *n.* conversion

conversar *v.* converse

converter *v.* convert

convertido *n.* convert

convés *n.* deck

convicente *adj.* cogent

convicente *adj.* forcible

convidado *n.* guest

convidar *v.* invite

convidativo *adj.* inviting

convir *v.* befit

convite *n.* invitation

convocação *n.* convocation

convocar *v.* convene

convulsão *n.* convulsion

convulsionar *n.* convulse

cooperação *n.* cooperation

cooperar v. cooperate

cooperativo adj. cooperative

coordenação n. coordination

coordenar v. t coordinate

cópia n. copy

cópia impressa n. printout

copiadora n. copier

copiar v. copy

copinho n. tot

copo n. tumbler

copular v. copulate

cor n. colour

coração n. heart

corado adj. blowsy

coragem n. courage

corajosamente adj. gamely

corajoso adj. brave

coral n. coral

corar v. blush

corça n. doe

corcel n. steed

corcunda n. hump

corda n. rope

cordame n. rigging

cordão n. cordon

cordeiro n. lamb

cordel n. cord

cordial adj. amicable

cordial adj. cordial

cornaca n. mahout

córnea n. cornea

corneta n. cornet

corno n. cuckold

coro n. chorus

coroa n. crown

coroação n. coronation

coroar v. crown

coronel n. colonel

corpete n. bodice

corpo n. body

corporação n. corporation

corporal n. corporal

corpulento adj. corpulent

correção n. correction

corredio adj. runny

corredor n. runner

correia n. strap

correio n. mail

correios n. post

correios n. post office

correlação n. correlation

correlacionar v. correlate

corrente n. chain

correr v. run

correr velozmente v. sprint

correspondência n. correspondence

correspondente n. correspondent

corresponder v. correspond

corretivo adj. corrective

correto adj. correct

corretor n. broker

corretor de bolsa n. stockbroker

corrida n. race

corrida obstáculos n. steeplechase

corrigir v. amend

corrimão n. railing

corriqueiro adj. unexceptional

corroborar v. corroborate

corroer v. corrode
corrosão n. corrosion
corrosivo adj. corrosive
corrupção n. corruption
corrupto adj.& n. corrupt
cortador n. cutter
cortante adj. biting
cortar v. cut
corte n. cutting
corte de cabelo n. haircut
cortejar v. woo
cortês adj. courteous
cortesã n. courtesan
cortesão n. courtier
cortesia n. courtesy
cortiça n. cork
cortina n. curtain
cortisona n. cortisone
coruja n. owl
corvo n. crow
cós n. waistband
cosmético adj.& n. cosmetic
cósmico adj. cosmic
cosmologia n. cosmology
cosmopólita adj. cosmopolitan
costa n. coast
costas n. back
costela n. rib
costoleta n. cutlet
costumeiro adj. wonted
costura n. seam
costurar v. sew
cotonete n. swab
cotovelo n. elbow

cotovia n. lark
couceira n. stile
coupe n. coupe
couro n. leather
couro cabeludo n. scalp
couve-flor n. cauliflower
cova n. pit
covarde adj. craven
covardia n. cowardice
covil n. lair
coxa n. thigh
coxo adj. lame
cozinha n. kitchen
cozinhar v. cook
cozinheiro n. cook
crânio n. skull
crasso adj. crass
creche n. creche
credenciais n. credentials
crédito n. credit
credível adj. credible
credo n. creed
credor n. creditor
credor hipotecário n. mortgagee
credulidade adv. credulity
crédulo adj. gullible
cremação n. cremation
cremar v. cremate
crematório n. crematorium
creme n. custard
crença n. belief
crepitação v. crackle
crepitar v. splutter
crepúsculo n. twilight

crescente *n.* crescent
crescer *v.i.* grow
crescimento *n.* growth
cria *n.* cub
criação *n.* creation
criado *n.* cad
criado *n.* outrider
criado *n.* servant
criador *n.* creator
criança *n.* kid
criar *v.* create
criativo *adj.* creative
criatura *n.* creature
crime *n.* crime
criminal *n.* criminal
criminologia *n.* criminology
criminoso *n.* felon
crina *n.* mane
cripta *n.* crypt
criptografar *v.* encrypt
críquete *n.* cricket
crise *n.* crisis
crista *n.* crest
cristal *n.* crystal
Cristandade *n.* Christianity
Cristão *adj.* Christian
Cristo *n.* Christ
critério *n.* criterion
crítica *n.* critique
criticar *v.* criticize
crítico *n.& adj.* critic & critical
crivado *adj.* riddled
crochet *n.* crochet
crocodilo *n.* crocodile

croissant *n.* croissant
cromo *n.* chrome
crónica *n.* chronicle
crónico *adj.* chronic
cronógrafo *n.* chronograph
cronologia *n.* chronology
crosta *n.* crust
cru *adj.* crude
cruciante *adj.* harrowing
cruel *adj.* cruel
crueldade *adv.* cruelty
cruzada *n.* crusade
cruzador *n.* cruiser
cruzeiro *v.* cruise
cú *n.* ass
cúbico *adj.* cubical
cúbiculo *n.* cubicle
cubo *n.* cube
cuco *n.* cuckoo
cuecas *n.* knickers
cuecas *n.* underpants
cuidador *n.* carer
cuidadoso *adj.* careful
cuidar *n.* care
cuidar de cavalo *v.* groom
cuidar-se *v.* fend
culatra *n.* breech
culinária *adj.* culinary
culminar *v.* culminate
culotes *n.* bloomers
culpa *n.* guilt
culpado *n.& adj.* culprit & guilty
culpar *v.* blame
culpável *adj.* culpable

cultivar v. cultivate
culto n. cult
cultura n. culture
cultural adj. cultural
cume n. ridge
cúmplice n. acoomplice
cúmplice adj. accomplice
cumplicidade n. complicity
cumprimentar n. greet
cumprimentar v. i compliment
cumprimento n. fulfilment
cumprir v. fulfil
cunha n. wedge
cunhagem n. coinage
cupão n. coupon
cúpula n. dome
curador n. curator
curar v. heal
curativo adj. curative
curável adj. curable
curcuma n. turmeric
curiosamente adv. quaintly
curiosidade n. curiosity
curioso adj. curious
currículo n. curriculum
cursivo adj. cursive
curso n. course
cursor n. cursor
curtidor n. tanner
curto adj. short
curtume n. tannery
curva n. curve
curvar v. bow
curvatura n. camber

curvo adj. hooked
cuspo n. spit
custar v. cost
custear v. defray
custódia n. custody
cutelo n. chopper

D

dado n.& adj. datum & given
dados n. dice
daí adv. thence
dama n. dame
dançar v. dance
dançarino n. dancer
dano n. damage
dar v. give
dar risadinhas v.t. giggle
dardo n. dart
das marés adj. tidal
data n. date
datilógrafo n. typist
de prep. from
de alguma maneira adv. somehow
de fato adv. indeed
de irmã adj. sisterly
de lã adj. woollen
de luxo adj. deluxe
de madeira adj. wooden
de noite adv. overnight
de onde adv. whence
de qualquer maneira adv. anyhow
de trigo adj. wheaten
deambular v. rove
debandada n. stampede

debate *n.* debate	**declaração** *n.* declaration
debater *v. t.* debate	**declarar** n declare
débil *adj.* feeble	**declive** *n.* declivity
debilidade *n.* debility	**decompor** *n.* decompose
debilitar *v.* debilitate	**decomposição** *v. t* decomposition
débito *n.* debit	**decoração** *n.* decor
débito (conta descoberto) *n.* overdraft	**decorar** *v.* decorate
debochar *v.* debauch	**decorativo** *adj.* decorative
debulhar *v.* thresh	**decoro** *n.* decorum
debutante *n.* debutante	**decoroso** *adj.* decorous
década *n.* decade	**decorrer** *v.* elapse
decadente *adj.* decadent	**decrépito** *adj.* decrepit
decair *v.* i decay	**decretar** *v.* enact
decalcar *v.* pounce	**decreto** *n.* decree
decano *n.* dean	**dedal** *n.* thimble
decantar *v.* decant	**dedicação** *n.* dedication
decanter *n.* decanter	**dedicar** *v.* dedicate
decapitar *v.* decapitate	**dedo** *n.* finger
deceção *n.* deception	**dedo** do pé *n.* toe
decência *n.* decency	**dedo** indicador *n.* forefinger
decente *adj.* decent	**dedução** *n.* deduction
decíbel *n.* decibel	**deduzir** *v.* deduce
decidido *adj.* decided	**defecar** *v.* defecate
decidir *v.* decide	**defeito** *n.* defect
decifrar *v.* decipher	**defeituoso** *adj.* defective
decimal *adj.* decimal	**defender** *v.* defend
décimo *adj. & n.* tenth	**defensiva** *adj.* defensive
décimo nono *adj. & n.* nineteenth	**defensor** *n.* advocate
décimo sétimo *adj. & n.* seventeenth	**deferência** *n.* deference
décimo sexto *adj. & n.* sixteenth	**defesa** *n.* defence
décimo terceiro *adj. & n.* thirteenth	**défice** *n.* deficit
decisão *n.* decision	**défice** *n.* shortfall
decisivo *adj.* decisive	**deficiência** *n.* deficiency
declamar *v.* declaim	**deficiente** *adj.* deficient

deficientes *n.* handicapped
definição *n.* definition
definido *adj.* definite
definir *v.* define
deflação *n.* deflation
deformação *n.* deformity
deformar *v.* warp
deformidade *n.* malformation
defraudar *v.* defraud
defunto *adj.* defunct
degenerar *v.* degenerate
degradar *v.* degrade
degrau *n.* rung
deitar *v.* lounge
deixa *n.* cue
deixar *v.* let
deja vu *n.* deja vu
dela *pron.* hers
delegação *n.* delegation
delegar *n.* delegate
deleitar *v.* pamper
deleite *n.* delectation
delgado *adj.* slender
deliberação *n.* deliberation
deliberado *adj.* deliberate
delicadeza *n.* delicacy
delicado *adj.* delicate
deliciar *v. t.* delight
delicioso *adj.* delectable
delicioso *adj.* delicious
delinear *v.* delineate
delinquente *adj.* delinquent
delirante *adj.* delirious
delirar *v.* rave

delírio *n.* delirium
delito *n.* misdeed
dell *n.* dell
delta *n.* delta
demarcação *n.* demarcation
demência *n.* dementia
demente *adj.* demented
demérito n demerit
demitir *v.* dismiss
democracia *n.* democracy
democrático *adj.* democratic
demografia *n.* demography
demolir *v.* demolish
demónio *n.* demon
demonstrar *v.* demonstrate
demorar *v.* linger
denegrir *v.* blacken
denegrir *v.* denigrate
denominação *n.* denomination
denominador *n.* denominator
denotar *v. t* denote
densidade *n.* density
denso *adj.* dense
dentado *adj.* serrated
dentadura *n.* denture
dental *adj.* dental
dente *n.* tooth
dente de alho *n.* clove
dente de leão *n.* dandelion
denteado *adj.* jagged
dentífrico *n.* toothpaste
dentista *n.* dentist
dentro *n.& prep.* inside & whithin
denúncia *n.* denunciation

denunciar *v.* denounce
departamento *n.* department
dependência *n.* dependency
dependente *n.* dependant
dependente *adj.* dependent
depender *v.* depend
depilatório *adj.* depilatory
deplorável *adj.* deplorable
depois *adv.* after
depois que *conj.* after
depor *v.* depose
deportar *v.* t deport
depositário *n.* depository
depósito *n.* deposit
depósito mercad. cais *n.* wharfage
depravado *adj.* deviant
depravar *v.* deprave
depreciação *n.* depreciation
depreciar *v.* depreciate
depreciativo *adj.* derogatory
depressão *n.* depression
deprimir *v.* depress
deputado *n.* deputy
derivado *adj.* derivative
derivar *v.* derive
derramamento *n.* overspill
derramamento sangue *n.* bloodshed
derramar *v.* spill
derrame *n.* spillage
derrapar *v.* skid
derreter *v.* melt
derrotar *v.* t. defeat
derrotista *n.* defeatist
derrubar *v.* tumble

desabrigado *adj.* bleak
desacampar *v.* decamp
desacelerar *v.* decelerate
desacompanhado *adj.* unattended
desacordo *n.* disagreement
desacreditar *v.* discredit
desafeto *adj.* disaffected
desafiar *v.* defy
desafio *n.* challenge
desafogar *v.* wreak
desagradável *adj.* disagreeable
desajustado *adj.* maladjusted
desalento *n.* dismay
desalojar *v.* dislodge
desamparado *adj.* helpless
desanimado *adj.* dispirited
desanimar *v.* dishearten
desânimo *n.* rally
desaparecer *v.* vanish
desaparecido *adj.* missing
desapoderar *v.* disempower
desapontado *adj.* disgruntled
desportivo *adj.* sporting
desaprovação *n.* disapproval
desaprovar *v.* disapprove
desarmado *adj.* unarmed
desarmamento *n.* disarmament
desarmar *v.* disarm
desastre *n.* disaster
desastroso *adj.* disastrous
desatento *adj.* inattentive
desatualizado *adj.* outdated
desavergonhado *adj.* shameless
desbotado *adj.* lacklustre

descafeínado adj. decaffeinated

descampado n. wold

descansar v. rest

descapotável antigo n. roadster

descarga v. discharge

descarnado adj. emaciated

descarregar v. unload

descarrilhar v. t. derail

descartar v. discard

descartável adj. disposable

descascar v.t. strip

descendência n. progeny

descendente n. descendant

descentralizar v. decentralize

descer v. descend

descida n. descent

desclassificar v. declassify

descoberta n. discovery

descobrir v. discover

descodificar v. decode

descolorante adj. bleach

descolorir v. discolour

descomprimir v. decompress

desconcertar v. disconcert

desconexo adj. scrappy

desconfiadamente adv. askance

desconfiança n. distrust

desconfiar v. mistrust

desconfortável adj. uncomfortable

desconforto n. discomfort

descongelar v. defrost

descongestionante n. decongestant

desconhecido n.& strange

desconhecido adj. unknown

desconsiderado adj. dismissive

desconsiderar v. t disregard

desconsolado adj. disconsolate

desconstruir v. deconstruct

descontaminar v. decontaminate

descontentamento n. displeasure

descontente n. malcontent

descontinuar v. discontinue

desconto n. discount

descortês adj. discourteous

descrédito n. disrepute

descrença n. disbelief

descrever v. describe

descrição n. description

descriminalizar v. decriminalize

descuidado adj. careless

desculpa n. apology

desculpar v. apologize

desde adv. & prep. ago & since

desdém n. disdain

desdenhoso adj. contemptuous

desdentado adj. toothless

desdobrar v. unfold

desejar v. wish

desejar saber v. wonder

desejável adj. desirable

desejo n. desire

desejoso adj. desirous

desembaraçar v. disentangle

desembarcar v. disembark

desembolsar v. disburse

desempacotar v. unpack

desempenhar v. officiate

desempregado adj. unemployed

desencaminhar v. misguide

desencantar v. disenchant

desencarnado adj. disembodied

desencorajar v. discourage

desenfreado adj. unbridled

desengatar v. disengage

desengonçado adj. gangling

desenhar v. draw

desenho n. drawing

desenho (padrão tecido) n. paisley

desenho animado n. cartoon

desenredar v. extricate

desenrolar v. unwind

desenterrar v. unearth

desentoxicar v. detoxify

desenvolto adj. jaunty

desenvolver v. develop

desenvolvimento n. development

desequilibrado adj. unbalanced

desequilibrar v. overbalance

desequilíbrio n. imbalance

deserção n. lurch

deserdar v. disinherit

deserto v. desert

desesperado adj. desperate

desespero n. despair

desestabilizar v. destabilize

desfalecer v. languish

desfavor n. disfavour

desfavorecido n. underdog

desfazer v. undo

desfeito adj. undone

desfigurado adj. haggard

desfigurar v. deform

desfiladeiro n. canyon

desfile n. parade

desflorestar v. deforest

desfraldar v. unfurl

desfrutar v. enjoy

desgastar v. fray

desgosto n. disgust

desgoverno n. maladministration

desgoverno n. misrule

desgraça n. disgrace

desgraçado n. wretch

desidratar v. dehydrate

designação n. assignation

designar v. designate

desigual adj. patchy

desigualdade n. inequality

desiludir v. disappoint

desilusão v. disillusion

desincentivo n. disincentive

desinfetar v. disinfect

desintegrar v. disintegrate

desistir v. quit

desleal adj. disloyal

desleixado adj. sloppy

desleixar v. slouch

desligar v. disconnect

deslizar v. slide

deslocado adj. disjointed

deslocar v. dislocate

deslumbrante adj. gorgeous

deslumbrar v.i glare

desmaiar v. swoon

desmamar v. wean

desmancha-prazeres n. spoiler

desmantelar v. dismantle
desmascarar v. unmask
desmedido adj. outsize
desmentir v. belie
desmiolado adj. witless
desmistificar v. demystify
desmobilizar v. demobilize
desmoralizar v. demoralize
desmoronar v. slump
desnacionalizar v. denationalize
desnecessário adj. needless
desnudar v. denude
desobedecer v. disobey
desobediente adj. disobedient
desocupar v. vacate
desodorizante n. deodorant
desolado adj. desolate
desolar v. bereaved
desonesto adj. dishonest
desonra n. dishonour
desordem n. disorder
desordenado adj. untidy
desordenar v. disarrange
desorganizado adj. disorganized
desorientar v. disorientate
desovar v. spawn
despedaçar v. rive
despedida interj. farewell
despedida n. parting
despeito n. spite
despejar v. evict
despejo n. eviction
despender v. expend
despensa n. larder

despenteado adj. unkempt
despentear v. tousle
desperdiçar v. waste
desperdício n. wastage
despertar v. awaken
desperto adj. wakeful
despesa n. expense
despesas n. outlay
despir v. undress
despistar v. outwit
despojar v. divest
desportista n. sportsman
desporto n. sport
desposar v. espouse
déspota n. despot
despreocupado adj. carefree
desprevenido adj. unprepared
desprezar v. despise
desprezível adj. despicable
desprezo n. scorn
desprivilegiado adj. underprivileged
desproporcionado adj. disproportionate
desprovido adj. devoid
desqualificação n. disqualification
desqualificar v. disqualify
desregado adj. licentious
desregramento n. profligacy
desregulamentar v. deregulate
desrespeito n. disrespect
destacamento n. detachment
destapar v. uncover
destemido adj. fearless
destemido adj. hardy
destilar v. distil

destilaria *n.* distillery
destinatário *n.* addressee
destino *n.* destiny
destituído *adj.* destitute
destituir *v.* unseat
destreza *n.* dexterity
destronar *v.* dethrone
destruição *n.* destruction
destruidor *n.* destroyer
destruir *v.* destroy
desumanizar *v.* dehumanize
desumano *adj.* inhuman
desvairar *v.* revel
desvalorizar *v.* devalue
desvanecer *v.*i fade
desvantagem *n.* disadvantage
desvelar *v.* unveil
desviar *v.* deviate
desviar-se *n.* veer
desvio *n.* detour
detenção *n.* detention
deter *v.* t detain
detergente *n.* detergent
deteriorar *v.* deteriorate
determinação *v.* t determination
determinante *n.* determinant
determinar *v.* t determine
detestar *v.* detest
detetive *n.* detective
detonar *v.* detonate
detrimento *n.* detriment
detrito *n.* detritus
detritos *n.* debris
deturpar *v.* misrepresent

Deus *n.* god
deusa *n.* goddess
devaneio *n.* reverie
devassidão *n.* debauchery
devastação *n.* havoc
devastar *v.* devastate
devedor *n.* debtor
dever *n.*& *v.* duty & must
dever (obrigatoriedade) *v.* should
devidamente *adv.* duly
devido *adj.* due
devoção *n.* devotion
devolução *n.* devolution
devolver *v.* devolve
devorar *v.* devour
devoto *n.*& *adj.* devotee & devout
dez *adj.* & *adv.* ten
dezanove *adj.* & *n.* nineteen
dezasseis *adj.* & *n.* sixteen
Dezembro *n.* December
dezessete *adj.* & *n.* seventeen
dezoito *adj.* & *n.* eighteen
dia *n.* day
dia da semana *n.* weekday
dia dos namorados *n.* valentine
dia seguinte *n.* morrow
diabetes *n.* diabetes
diabo *n.* devil
diabrete *n.* urchin
diadema *n.* coronet
diafragma *n.* midriff
diagnosticar *v.* diagnose
diagnóstico *n.* diagnosis
diagrama *n.* diagram

dialeto *n.* dialect

diálise *n.* dialysis

diálogo *n.* dialogue

diamante *n.* diamond

diâmetro *n.* diameter

diário *adj.& n.* daily & diary

diarréia *n.* diarrhoea

Diáspora *n.* Diaspora

dica *n.* hint

dicção *n.* diction

dicionário *n.* dictionary

didático *adj.* didactic

dieta *n.* diet

difamação *n.* defamation

difamações *n.* aspersions

difamar *v.* defame

difamatório *adj.* slanderous

diferença *n.* difference

diferente *adj.* different

diferir *v.* differ

difícil *adj.* hard

dificilmente *adv.* hardly

dificuldade *n.* difficulty

difundir *v.* diffuse

digerir *v.* digest

digestão *n.* digestion

digital *adj.* digital

digitalizador *n.* scanner

digitalizar *v.* scan

dígito *n.* digit

dignidade *n.* dignity

dignificar *v.* dignify

dignitário *n.* dignitary

digno *adj.* worth

dilacerar *v.* lacerate

dilapidado *adj.* dilapidated

dilatar *v.* dilate

dilema *n.* dilemma

diligência *n.* stagecoach

diligente *adj.* diligent

diluir *v.* dilute

dilúvio *n.* deluge

dimensão *n.* dimension

diminuição *n.* diminution

diminuir *v. t.* decline

diminuto *adj.* petite

dinâmica *n.* dynamics

dinâmico *adj.* dynamic

dinamite *n.* dynamite

dínamo *n.* dynamo

dinastia *n.* dynasty

dinheiro *n.* money

dinossauro *n.* dinosaur

diploma *n.* diploma

diplomacia *n.* diplomacy

diplomata *n.* diplomat

diplomático *adj.* diplomatic

dipsomania *n.* dipsomania

dique *n.* causeway

direção *n.* direction

directiva *n.* directive

direito *n* right

diretamente *adv.* directly

direto *adj.* direct

diretor *n.* director

diretório *n.* directory

dirigente *n.* ruling

dirigir *v.* steer

discar n. dial

discernir v. discern

disciplina n. discipline

discípulo n. disciple

disco n. disc

disco rígido n. hard drive

discordante adj. discordant

discordar v. disagree

discórdia n. discord

discoteca n. disco

discrepância n. discrepancy

discreto adj. discreet

discrição n. stealth

discriminar v. discriminate

discursivo adj. discursive

discurso n. speech

discussão n. discussion

discutir v. discuss

discutível adj. debatable

disenteria n. dysentery

disfarçar v. disguise

disforme adj. shapeless

disfuncional adj. dysfunctional

dislexia n. dyslexia

disparatado adj. senseless

disparate n. skittle

disparidade n. disparity

dispendioso adj. costly

dispensar v. dispense

dispensário n. dispensary

dispensável adj. dispensable

dispepsia n. dyspepsia

dispersar v. disband

disponível adj. available

dispor v. t dispose

disposição n. disposal

dispositivo n. device

disposto adj. willing

disputa n. quarrel

disputar v. i dispute

dissecar v. dissect

dissertação n. dissertation

dissidente n. dissident

dissimulado adj. disingenuous

dissimular v. dissimulate

dissipar v. dispel

dissipar v. dissipate

dissolver v. t dissolve

dissuadir v. dissuade

distância n. distance

distante adj. distant

distinção n. distinction

distinguir v. t distinguish

distintivo n. badge

distinto adj. distinct

distorcer v. distort

distração n. distraction

distrair v. distract

distribuição n. allotment

distribuidor n. distributor

distribuir v. distribute

distrito n. district

ditado n. dictation

ditador n. dictator

ditar adj. dictate

dito n. dictum

divã n. ottoman

divagar v. digress

divergir v. diverge
diversão n. entertainment
diversidade n. diversity
diverso adj. diverse
diversos adj. sundry
divertido adj. hilarious
divertimento n. amusement
divertir v. amuse
dívida n. debt
dividendo n. dividend
dividir v. split
divindade n. divinity
divinizar v. deify
divino adj. divine
divisa n. chevron
divisão n. division
divisória n. partition
divorciado n. divorcee
divórcio n. divorce
divulgar v. divulge
dizer v. tell
dizimar v. decimate
dízimo n. tithe
do norte adj. northern
do qual adj. whose
doador n. donor
doar v. donate
dobradiça n. hinge
dobrado adj. bent
dobrar v. bend
doca n. dock
doce n.& adj. candy & sweet
dócil adj. docile
documentário n. documentary

documentário viagem n. travelogue
documento n. document
doçura n. sweetness
doença n. illness
doente adj. ill
doentio adj. sickly
doer v. hurt
dogma n. dogma
dogmático adj. dogmatic
dois adj.&n. two
dólar n. dollar
dolorido adj. sore
doloroso adj. painful
doméstico adj. domestic
domicílio n. domicile
dominante adj. dominant
dominar v. dominate
dominar o conjuge adj. henpecked
Domingo n. Sunday
domínio n. domain
dona de casa n. housewife
doninha n. weasel
dono de restaurante n. restaurateur
donzela n. damsel
dor n. pain
dor de cabeça n. headache
dor de dente n. toothache
doravante adv. henceforth
dorminhoco n. sleeper
dormitar n. snooze
dormitório n. dormitory
dose n. dose
dossel n. canopy
dossier n. dossier

dotado *adj.* gifted

dotar *v.* endow

dote *n.* dowry

dourado *adj.* golden

dourar *v.* gild

doutorado *n.* doctorate

doutrina *n.* doctrine

dowload *v.* download

doze *adj.&n.* twelve

dragão *n.* dragon

drama *n.* drama

dramático *adj.* dramatic

dramatizar *v.* overreact

dramaturgo *n.* dramatist

drástico *adj.* drastic

drenar *v.* t drain

droga *n.* drug

duas vezes *adv.* twice

duelo *n.* duel

duende *n.* hobgoblin

dueto *n.* duet

duo *n.* duo

décimo segundo *adj.&n.* twelfth

duplicar *adj.* duplicate

duplicidade *n.* duplicity

duplo *adj. & n.* double & duplex

duração *n.* duration

duradouro *adj.* lasting

durante *prep.* during

durável *adj.* durable

dureza *n.* toughness

duro *adj.* stiff

duvido *n.* doubt

duvidoso *adj.* dubious

dúzia *n.* dozen

E

e *conj.* and

e comercial (&) *n.* ampersand

ébano *n.* ebony

eclesiástico *adj.* clerical

eclipse *n.* eclipse

eco *n.* echo

ecoar *v.* reverberate

ecografia *n.* ultrasound

ecologia *n.* ecology

economia *n.* economy

económico *adj.* economic

ecrã *n.* screen

edição *n.* edition

edifício *n.* edifice

editar *v.* edit

édito *n.* edict

editor *n.* editor

editorial *adj.* editorial

edredom *n.* duvet

educação *n.* education

educação cívica *n.* civics

educado *adj.* polite

educar *v.* educate

efeito *n.* effect

efeminado *adj.* effeminate

efeminar *v.* womanize

efervescente *adj.* ebullient

efetivamente *adv.* actually

eficácia *n.* efficacy

eficaz *adj.* effective

eficiência *n.* efficiency

eficiente *adj.* efficient

efígie *n.* effigy

égide *n.* aegis

ego *n.* ego

egoísmo *n.* egotism

egoísta *adj.* selfish

égua *n.* mare

eixo *n.* axle

ejacular *v.* ejaculate

ejetar *v.* t eject

ela *pron.* she

ela mesma *pron.* herself

elaborado *adj.* elaborate

elástico *adj.* elastic

ele *pron.* he

ele próprio *pron.* himself

eléctrico *n.* tram

elefante *n.* elephant

elegância *n.* elegance

elegante *adj.* chic

eleger *v.* elect

elegível *adj.* eligible

eleição *n.* election

eleitor *n.* voter

eleitorado *n.* electorate

elementar *adj.* elementary

elemento *n.* element

eles *pron.* they

eletivo *adj.* elective

eletricidade *n.* electricity

eletricista *n.* electrician

elétrico *adj.* electric

eletrificar *v.* electrify

eletrocutar *v.* electrocute

eletrónico *adj.* electronic

elevado *adj.* lofty

elevador *n.* elevator

elevar *v.* elevate

elfo *n.* elf

eliminação *n.* deletion

eliminar *v.* eliminate

elipse *n.* ellipse

elite *n.* elite

elocução *n.* elocution

elogiar *v.* laud

elogio *n.* compliment

eloquência *n.* eloquence

elucidar *v.* t elucidate

em *prep.* at

em alta *adj.* bullish

em chamas *adj.* aflame

em cima *adv.* overhead

em contradição *adv.* ajar

em exercício *adj.* acting

em movimento *adj.* moving

em nenhuma parte *adv.* nowhere

em pé *n.* standing

em perspectiva *adj.* prospective

em qualquer lugar *adv.* anywhere

em relação a *prep.* regarding

em segredo *adj.* subjudice

em terra firme *adv.* ashore

em vez *adv.* instead

e-mail *n.* email

emanar *v.* reek

emancipar *v.* t emancipate

emanecipar *v.* enfranchise

embaixada *n.* embassy

embaixador *n.* ambassador

embaixo *prep.* underneath

embalagem *n.* package

embalar *v.* dandle

embalsamar *v.* embalm

embaraçado *adj.* abashed

embaraçar *v.* embarrass

embarcar *v. t* embark

embargo *n.* embargo

embeber *v.* soak

embelezador *n.* trimmer

embelezar *v.* beautify

emblema *n.* emblem

embora *conj. & adv.* albeit & away

emborcar *v.* capsize

emboscada *n.* ambush

embriagado *adj.& n.* groggy & tipsy

embrião *n.* embryo

embuste *n.* trickery

embutir *v.* embed

emendar *v.* emend

emergência *n.* emergency

emergir *v.* emerge

emigrar *v.* emigrate

eminência *n.* eminence

eminente *adj.* eminent

emissário *n.* emissary

emitir *v.* emit

emoção *n.* emotion

emocional *adj.* emotional

emoliente *adj.* emollient

emolumento *n.* emolument

emotivo *adj.* emotive

empada *n.* patty

empalidecer *v.* blench

empanar *v.* tarnish

emparedar *v.* immure

empatia *n.* empathy

empenhar *v.* engage

empertigado *adj.* perky

empinar *v.* cram

emplastrar *v.* daub

empobrecer *v.* impoverish

empolado *adj.* overblown

empossar *v.* enthrone

empreender *v.* undertake

empregada *n.* maid

empregada de mesa *n.* waitress

empregado *n.* employee

empregado de mesa *n.* waiter

empregador *n.* employer

empregar *v.* employ

empresa *n.* enterprise

empresário *n.* businessman

emprestar *v.* borrow

empréstimo *n.* loan

empunhar *v.* wield

empurrar *v.* push

emular *v. t* emulate

enamorar *v. t* enamour

encadear *v.* interlink

encalhar *v.* strand

encantador *adj.* charming

encantar *v.* enchant

encanto *n.* charm

encapsular *v.* encapsulate

encarar *v.* envisage

encarcerar *v.* incarcerate

encarnação *n.* incarnation

encarnado *adj.* incarnate

encarquilhado *adj.* wizened

encerramento *n.* closure

encerrar *v.* encase

encharcado *adj.* sopping

enchedor *n.* filler

enchente *n.* spate

encher de pontos *v.* stipple

enchimento *n.* filling

enciclopédia *n.* encyclopaedia

enclave *n.* enclave

encoberto *adj.* covert

encolher *v.* shrink

encolher os ombros *v.* shrug

encolher-se *v.* cower

encolhimento *n.* shrinkage

encontrar *v.* find

encontro *n.* rendezvous

encorajar *v.* encourage

encurralar *v.* impound

encurtar *v.* shorten

endémico *adj.* endemic

endiabrar *v.* demonize

endireitar *v.* straighten

endividado *adj.* indebted

endoidecer *v.* rant

endossar *v.* endorse

endurecer *v.* harden

energia *n.* energy

enérgico *adj.* energetic

enervar *v.* unnerve

enfadonho *adj.* wearisome

enfaixar *v.* swaddle

ênfase *n.* emphasis

enfático *adj.* emphatic

enfatizar *v.* emphasize

enfatuar *v.* infatuate

enfeitado *adj.* swish

enfeitar *v.* garnish

enfeitiçar *v.* bewitch

enfermeira *n.* nurse

enfermidade *n.* infirmity

enfermo *adj.* infirm

enferrujado *adj.* rusty

enforcamento *n.* hanging

enfraquecer *v.* weaken

enfrentar *v.* confront

enfumaçado *adj.* smoky

enfurecer *v.* enrage

enfurecido *adj.* irate

enganador *adj.* specious

enganar *v.* cheat

engano *n.* deceit

enganoso *adj.* deceptive

engatar *v.* limber

engenheiro *n.* engineer

engenhoso *adj.* resourceful

engolir *v.* engulf

engolir *v.* swallow

engraçado *n.& adj.* crate & funny

engrenagem *n.* gear

engrenar *n.* mesh

engrossar *v.* thicken

enguiço *n.* jinx

enigma *n.* enigma

enjoado *adj.* queasy

enjoar *v.* nauseate

enjoativo *adj.* cloying

enlouquecer *v.* rampage

enlutado *n.* mourner

enorme *adj.* huge

enquanto *n. & conj.* while & whilst

enraizado *adj.* rooted

enredar *v.t.* tangle

enredo *n.* plot

enrijecer *v.* stiffen

enriquecer *v.* enrich

enrolar *v.* curl

ensaboado *adj.* soapy

ensaiar *v.* rehearse

ensaio *n.* essay

ensaio *n.* rehearsal

enseada *n.* cove

ensinar *v.* teach

ensino *n.* tuition

ensolarado *adj.* sunny

ensopado *n.* stew

ensurdecedor *adj.* deafening

entalhar *v.* gouge

entalhe *n.* notch

então *adv.* then

entender *v.t.* understand

enterrar *v.* bury

enterro *n.* burial

entidade *n.* entity

entoar *v.* intone

entomologia *n.* entomology

entorpecido *adj.* torpid

entortar (os olhos) *v.* squint

entrada *n.* entry

entranhas *n.* entrails

entrar *v.* enter

entre *prep.* among

entre *adv.* between

entrega *n.* delivery

entregar *v.* deliver

entrelaçar *v.* wreathe

entreligar *v.* interlock

entretanto *adv.* meanwhile

entreter *v.* entertain

entrevista *n.* interview

entrevistador *n.* pollster

entrincheirar *v.* entrench

entristecer *v.* sadden

entristecido *adj.* overcast

entusiasmante *adv.* ablaze

entusiasmo *n.* enthusiasm

entusiasta *n.* enthusiastic

enumerar *v. t* enumerate

enunciação *n.* utterance

enunciar *v.* enunciate

envelope *n.* envelope

envergonhado *adj.* ashamed

enviado *n.* envoy

enviar *v.* send

enviesar *v.* skew

envolver *v.* involve

enxaguar *v.* rinse

enxame *n.* swarm

enxaqueca *n.* migraine

enxerto *n.* graft

enxofre *n.* sulphur

enxoval de noiva *n.* trousseau

épico *n.* epic

epidemia *n.* epidemic

epiderme *n.* epidermis

epigrama *n.* epigram

epilepsia *n.* epilepsy

epílogo *n.* epilogue

episódio *n.* episode

epístola *n.* epistle

epitáfio *n.* epitaph

epítome *n.* epitome

época *n.* epoch

equação *n.* equation

equador *n.* equator

equestre *adj.* equestrian

equidade *n.* equity

equidistante *adj.* equidistant

equilátero *adj.* equilateral

equilíbrio *n.* equilibrium

equimose *n.* bruise

equipamento *n.* equipment

equipar *v.* equip

equiparar *v.* equate

equipe *n.* team

equitativo *adj.* equitable

equivalente *adj.* equivalent

equivocado *adj.* mistaken

equivocar *v.* misdirect

equívoco *adj* equivocal

equívoco *n.* misapprehension

equlibrar *n.* balance

era *n.* era

erário *n.* exchequer

eremita *n.* hermit

eremitério *n.* hermitage

erguer *adj.* erect

erógeno *adj.* erogenous

erosão *n.* erosion

erótico *adj.* erotic

erradamente *adv.* awry

erradicar *v.* eradicate

errado *adj.* wrong

errante *adj.* errant

errar *v.* err

errático *adj.* erratic

erro *n.* mistake

erro de cálculo *n.* miscalculation

erro de impressão *n.* misprint

erróneo *adj.* erroneous

erudito *adj.* erudite

erva *n.* herb

erva daninha *n.* weed

ervilha *n.* pea

esbanjar *v.* squander

esbelto *adj.* svelte

esboço *n.* sketch

esbofetear *v.t.* slap

escabeche *n.* marinade

escada *n.* stair

escada rolante *n.* escalator

escadaria *n.* staircase

escadote *n.* ladder

escala *n.* scale

escalar *v.* escalate

escaldar *v.* scald

escandalizar *v.* scandalize

escândalo *n.* scandal

escapada *n.* escapade

escapar *v.i* escape

escapulir *v.* slink

escaramuça *n.* skirmish

escarlate *n.* scarlet

escarnecer *v.* gibe

escárnio *n.* sneer

escarpa *n.* scarp

escarrador *n.* spittoon

escassez *n.* shortage

escasso *adj.* sparse

escavar *v.* excavate

esclarecer *v.* clarify

esclarecimento *n.* clarification

Escocês *n.* Scot

escola *n.* school

escolha *n.* choice

escolher *v.* t choose

escolta *n.* escort

esconder *v.*t hide

esconderijo *n.* cache

escora *n.* prop

escória *n.* slag

escoriar *v.* excoriate

escorpião *n.* scorpion

escorregadio *adj.* slippery

escorregar *v.* slip

escoteiro *n.* scout

escotilha *n.* hatch

escovar *n.* brush

escravidão *n.* slavery

escravizar *v.* enslave

escravo *n.* slave

escrever *v.* write

escriba *n.* scribe

escrita *n.* writing

escritor *n.* writer

escritório *n.* office

escritura *n.* scripture

escriturário *n.* clerk

escrivão *n.* registrar

escroque *n.* racketeer

escrúpulo *n.* qualm

escrúpulos *n.* scruple

escrupuloso *adj.* scrupulous

escrutinar *v.* scrutinize

escrutínio *n.* scrutiny

escudeiro *n.* varlet

escudo *n.* shield

esculpir *v.* sculpt

escultor *n.* sculptor

escultura *n.* sculpture

escultura *adj.* sculptural

escumalha *n.* scum

escurecer *v.* darken

escuridão *n.* darkness

escuro *adj.* dark

escutar *v.* hark

esfaquear *v.* stab

esfera *n.* sphere

esférico *n.* spherical

esforçar *v.* endeavour

esforçar (para vomitar) *v.* retch

esforço *n.* effort

esfregar *v.* rub

esfregona *n.* mop

esgotar *v.* deplete

esgoto *n.* sewer

esgrima *n.* fencing

esguichar *v.* spurt

esguio *adj.* lanky

eslinga *n.* sling

esmagador *adj.* smashing

esmagar *v.* crush

esmaltar *v.* glaze

esmalte *n.* enamel

esmeralda *n.* emerald

esmigalhar *v.* crumble

esmolas *n.* alms

esófago *n.* gullet

esotérico *adj.* esoteric

espacial *adj.* spatial

espaço *n.* space

espaçoso *adj.* spacious

espada *n.* sword

espadilha *n.* sprat

espalhafato *n.* fuss

espalhafatoso *adj.* fussy

espalhar *v.* spread

espamódico *adj.* spastic

espanador *n.* duster

espanar *v.* whisk

espancar *v.* spank

Espanhol *n.* Spanish

espantalho *n.* scarecrow

espantar *v.* astound

espanto *n.* astonishment

espargos *n.* asparagus

espasmo *n.* spasm

espasmódico *adj.* spasmodic

espasmos *n.* throes

espátula *n.* trowel

especial *adj.* especial

especialidade *n.* speciality

especialista *n.* expert

especialização *n.* specialization

especializar *v.* specialize

especialmente *adv.* especially

espécies *n.* species

especificação *n.* specification

especificar *v.* specify

específico *adj.* specific

espécime *n.* specimen

espectador *n.* onlooker

especulação *n.* speculation

especular *v.* speculate

espelhar *v.t.* glass

espelho *n.* mirror

espelunca *n.* rookery

esperança *n.* hope

esperançosamente *adv.* hopefully

esperar *v.* wait

esperma *n.* sperm

espernear *v.* flounce

espesso *adj.* bushy

espetacular *adj.* spectacular

espetáculo *n.* spectacle

espetador *n.* spectator

espetral *adj.* spectral

espetro *n.* spectre

espião *n.* spy

espigado *adj.* spindly

espinafre *n.* spinach

espinha dorsal *n.* backbone

espinhal *adj.* spinal

espinheiro-alvar *n.* hawthorn

espinhela *n.* stickleback

espinho *n.* thorn

espinhoso *adj.* thorny

espionagem *n.* espionage

espiral *adj.* spiral

espírito *n.* spirit

espiritual *adj.* spiritual

espiritualidade *n.* spirituality

espiritualismo *n.* spiritualism

espiritualista *n.* spiritualist

espirituoso *adj.* witty

espirrar *v.i.* sneeze

esplêndido *adj.* splendid

esplendor *n.* splendour

esplenético *adj.* splenetic

esponja *n.* sponge

espontaneidade *n.* spontaneity

espontâneo *adj.* spontaneous

espora *n.* spur

esporádico *adj.* sporadic

esporo *n.* spore

esposa *n.* wife

espreitar *v.* peek

espremer *v.* squeeze

espuma *n.* spume

espúrio *adj.* spurious

esquadra *n.* squad

esquadrão *n.* squadron

esquadrinhar *v.* rummage

esquálido *adj.* squalid

esquecer *v.* forget

esquecido *adj.* forgetful

esquecimento *n.* oblivion

esquelético *adj.* bony

esqueleto *n.* skeleton

esquema *n.* scheme

esquema (desonesto) *n.* scam

esquemático *adj.* schematic

esquerdista *n.* leftist

esquilo *n.* squirrel

esquina *n.* corner

esquisito *adj.* queer

esquivar *v.* shirk

esquivar-se *v.* sneak

esquizofrenia *n.* schizophrenia

esquerdo *n.* left

essência *n.* essence

essencial *adj.* essential

estabelecer *v.* establish

estabelecimento *n.* establishment

estabilidade *n.* stability

estabilização *n.* stabilization

estabilizar *v.* stabilize

estábulo *n.* stable

estábulos *n.* mews

estaca *n.* stake

estação *n.* station

estacionário *adj.* stationary

estadia *n.* sojourn

estádio *n.* stadium

estadista *n.* statesman

estado *n.* state

estado (posição social) *n.* status

estagiário *n.* trainee

estagnação *n.* stagnation

estagnado *adj.* stagnant

estagnar *v.* stagnate

estalar *v.* snap

estaleiro *n.* shipyard

estambre *n.* worsted

estame *n.* stamen

estanho *n.* tin

estar na marmelada v. smooch

estarola n. stooge

estatelar v. sprawl

estaticamente adv. statically

estático adj. static

estatística n. statistics

estatístico adj. statistical

estatístico n. statistician

estátua n. statue

estatuária n. statuary

estatueta n. statuette

estatura n. stature

estatutário adj. statutory

estatuto n. statute

estável adj. stable

esteio n. mainstay

estelar adj. stellar

estêncil n. stencil

estender v. extend

estenografia n. stenography

estenógrafo n. stenographer

estepe n. steppe

esterco n. dung

esterelizar v. spay

estéreo n. stereo

estereofónico adj. stereophonic

estereoscópico adj. stereoscopic

estereótipo n. stereotype

estéril adj. sterile

esterilidade n. sterility

esterilização n. sterilization

esterilizar v. sterilize

esterno n. sternum

esteróide n. steroid

estertorante adj. stertorous

estética n. aesthetics

esteticista n. beautician

estético adj. aesthetic

estetoscópio n. stethoscope

esticador n. stretcher

esticar v. stretch

estigma n. stigma

estigmas n. stigmata

estigmatizar v. stigmatize

estilete n. stylus

estilhaçar v.t. shatter

estilhaços n. shrapnel

estilista n. stylist

estilístico adj. stylistic

estilizado adj. stylized

estilo n. style

estiloso n. dandy

estima n. esteem

estimar v. t estimate

estimulante n. stimulant

estimular v. stimulate

estímulo n. stimulus

estipêndio n. stipend

estipulação n. stipulation

estipular v. stipulate

estofamento n. stuffing

estofamento n. upholstery

estofar v. upholster

estóico n. stoic

estola n. stole

estômago n. stomach

estorvo n. nuisance

estourar v. burst

estourar (entrar erupção) v. erupt

estouvado adj. madcap

estrada n. road

estrado n. dais

estragar v. spoil

estrangeiro adj. foreign

estrangulamento n. strangulation

estrangular v. strangle

estranho adj. weird

estratagema n. stratagem

estratégia n. strategy

estratégico adj. strategic

estrategista n. strategist

estratificar v. stratify

estrato n. stratum

estrebaria n. stall

estreia n. premiere

estreitar v. scrimp

estreito adj.& n. narrow & strait

estrela n. star

estrelado adj. starry

estrelinha n. starlet

estremecer v. shudder

estrias n. striation

estribo n. stirrup

estridente adj. strident

estritamente adv. strictly

estrito adj. strict

estroboscópio n. strobe

estrofe n. stanza

estrondo n. bang

estrume n. manure

estrutura n. structure

estrutural adj. structural

estudante n. student

estudante universit. n. undergraduate

estudar v. study

estúdio n. studio

estudioso adj. bookish

estudioso n. scholar

estudo n. study

estupendo adj. stupendous

estupidez n. stupidity

estúpido adj. stupid

estupor n. stupor

estuque n. stucco

esvaziar v. deflate

etapa n. stage

etc. adv. et cetera

eternidade n. eternity

eterno adj. eternal

ética n. ethos

éticamoral n. ethical

ético n ethic

etimologia n. etymology

etiqueta n. etiquette

étnico adj. ethnic

eu pron. & n. I & self

eu mesmo pron. myself

euforia n. euphoria

eunuco n. eunuch

euro n. euro

Europeu n. European

eutanásia n. euthanasia

evacuar v. evacuate

evadir v. t evade

evaporar v. evaporate

evasão n. evasion

evasivo *adj.* evasive

evento *n.* event

eventualmente *adv.* eventually

evidência *n.* evidence

evidenciar *v.* evince

evidente *adj.* evident

evitar *v.* avoid

evocar *v.* evoke

evolução *n.* evolution

exagerado *adj.* gaudy

exagerar *v.* exaggerate

exagero *n.* exaggeration

exalar *v.* exhale

exaltar *v.* exalt

exame *n.* exam

examinando *n.* examinee

examinar *v.* examine

exasperar *v.* exasperate

exato *adj.* exact

exaustivo *adj.* exhaustive

exceção *n.* exception

excedente *n.* surplus

exceder *v.* exceed

excelência *n.* excellence

Excelência *n.* Excellency

excelente *adj.* excellent

excentricidade *n.* oddity

excêntrico *adj.* eccentric

excerto *n.* excerpt

excessivamente *adv.* overly

excessivo *adj.* excessive

excesso *n.* excess

exceto *prep.* except

excitação *n.* excitement

excitar *v.i* excite

exclamação *n.* exclamation

exclamar *v.* exclaim

excluir *v.* exclude

exclusivo *adj.* exclusive

excretar *v.* excrete

excursão *n.* excursion

execução *n.* execution

executante *n.* performer

executar *v.* execute

executivo *n.* executive

executor *n.* executor

exemplo *n.* example

exequível *adj.* workable

exercer *v.* exert

exército *n.* army

exibir *v.* display

exigência *n.* exigency

exigente *adj.* demanding

exigir *v.* require

exílio *n.* exile

existência *n.* existence

existente *adj.* extant

existir *v.* exist

exonerar *v.* exonerate

exorbitante *adj.* exorbitant

exortar *v.* exhort

exótico *adj.* exotic

expandir *v.* expand

expatriado *n.* expatriate

expectante *adj.* expectant

expectativa *n.* suspense

expedição *n.* expedition

expediente *adj.* expedient

expedir v. expedite
expelir v. t expel
expelir jato v. squish
experiência n. experience
experimental adj. tentative
experimentar v. taste
expetoração n. sputum
expiar v. expiate
expirar v. expire
explicar v. explain
explícito adj. explicit
explodir v. explode
exploração n. exploration
explorar v. explore
explosão n. explosion
explosivo adj. explosive
expoente n. exponent
expor v. expose
expor v. jeopardize
exportar v. t. export
exposição n. exhibition
expositor n. showcase
expressão n. expression
expressivo adj. expressive
expresso v. express
exprimentar v. undergo
exprimir condolências v. condole
expropriar v. expropriate
expulsão n. banishment
expulsar v. extrude
êxtase n. ecstasy
extensão n. extension
extenuado adj. overwrought
exterior adj. exterior

exteriormente adv. outwardly
externo adj. external
extinguir v. extinguish
extinto adj. extinct
extirpar v. extirpate
extorquir v. extort
extra adj. extra
extração n. extraction
extrair v. t extract
extraordinário adj. extraordinary
extraterrestre adj. unworldly
extravagância n. extravagance
extravagante adj. extravagant
extravagante adj. garish
extraviado adv. astray
extraviar v. mislay
extremamente adv. sorely
extremista n. extremist
extremo adj. extreme
extremo adj. uttermost
extrovertido n. extrovert
extrovertido adj. outgoing
exuberante adj. exuberant

F

fábrica n. factory
fabricante n. manufacturer
fabricar v. manufacture
fábula n. fable
fabuloso adj. fabulous
faca n. knife
façanha n. feat
fação n. sect
facção n. faction

face *n.* face
faceta *n.* facet
fachada *n.* facade
facial *adj.* facial
fácil *adj.* easy
facilidade *n.* facility
facilitar *v.* facilitate
faculdade *n.* college
fadas *n.* fairy
fadiga *n.* fatigue
Fahrenheit *n.* Fahrenheit
faia *n.* beech
faísca *n.* spark
faixa *n.* bandage
faixa *n.* swathe
fala-barato *n.* windbag
falador *adj.* talkative
falante *n.* speaker
falar *v.* speak
falar fanhoso *v.* snuffle
falcão *n.* hawk
falecido *adj.* deceased
falecimento *n.* decease
falência *n.* bankruptcy
falha *n.* failure
falha *n.* glitch
falhar *v.* fail
falhar alvo *v.* misfire
falido *adj.* bankrupt
falível *adj.* fallible
falsidade *n.* falsehood
falsidade *adv.* insincerity
falsificação *adj.* fake
falsificar *v.* wangle

falso *adj.* false
falta *n.* failing
fama *n.* fame
família *n.* family
familiar *adj.* familiar
familiarizado *adj.* conversant
familiarizar *v.* acquaint
faminto *adj.* hungry
famoso *adj.* famous
famoso *adj.* renowned
fanático *n.& adj.* fanatic & rabid
fanfarra *n.* fanfare
fanfarrão *adj.* swashbuckling
fanfarronar *v.* swagger
fantasia *n.* fantasy
fantasiar *v.* fantasize
fantasma *n.* ghost
fantástico *adj.* fantastic
fantoche *n.* puppet
farda *n.* accoutrement
fardo *n.* bale
farejar *v.* sniff
farinha *n.* flour
farinhento *adj.* mealy
farmacêutico *adj.* pharmaceutical
farmacêutico *n.* pharmacist
farmácia *n.* pharmacy
faro *n.* flair
farol *n.* headlight
farpa *n.* barb
farpado *adj.* barbed
farra *n.* spree
farrapo *n.* shred
farsa *n.* farce

fascia *n.* fascia	**feder** *v.* stink
fascinação *n.* glamour	**federação** *n.* federation
fascinar *v.* fascinate	**federado** *v.* federate
fascismo *n.* fascism	**federal** *adj.* federal
fase *n.* phase	**fedor** *n.* stench
fatal *adj.* fatal	**feijão** *n.* bean
fatalidade *n.* fatality	**feio** *adj.* ugly
fatia *n.* slice	**feitiçaria** *n.* witchery
fatídico *adj.* fateful	**feiticeiro** *n.* wizard
fato *n.* fact	**feito sob medida** *adj.* bespoke
fato de treino *n.* tracksuit	**felicidade** *n.* happiness
fator *n.* factor	**felicitação** *n.* felicitation
fátuo *adj.* fatuous	**felicitar** *v.* felicitate
fatura *n.* invoice	**feliz** *adj.* happy
fauna *n.* fauna	**fêmea** *adj.* female
favela *n.* slum	**feminilidade** *n.* womanhood
favo de mel *n.* honeycomb	**feminino** *adj.* feminine
favor *n.* behalf	**feminismo** *n.* feminism
favorável *adj.* favourable	**fenda** *n.* cleft
favorecer *n.* favour	**fenda palatina** *n.* harelip
favorito *adj.* favourite	**fender** *v.* cleave
fax *n.* fax	**feng shui** *n.* feng shui
fazenda *n.* farm	**fénix** *n.* phoenix
fazer *v.* make	**feno** *n.* hay
fazer alarde *v.* brag	**fenomenal** *adj.* phenomenal
fazer cócegas *v.* tickle	**fenómeno** *n.* phenomenon
fazer mau uso *v.* misuse	**férias** *n.* holiday
fazer uma introspecção *v.* introspect	**ferida** *n.* wound
fé *n.* faith	**ferido** *adj.* stricken
fealdade *n.* ugliness	**ferimento** *n.* injury
febre *n.* fever	**ferir** *v.* injure
febril *adj.* febrile	**fermentação** *n.* fermentation
fechadura *n.* lock	**fermentar** *v.* ferment
fechar *v.* shut	**feroz** *adj.* ferocious

ferramenta *n.* tool
ferreiro *n.* blacksmith
ferro *n.* iron
ferrugem *n.* rust
fértil *adj.* fertile
fertilidade *n.* fertility
fertilizante *n.* fertilizer
fertilizar *v.* fertilize
fervente *adj.* fervent
ferver *v.i.* boil
festa *n.* party
festejar *n.* fete
festival *n.* festival
festividade *n.* festivity
festivo *adj.* festive
fetiche *n.* fetish
feto *n.* fern
feudalismo *n.* feudalism
feudo *n.* feud
Fevereiro *n.* February
fiador *n.* warrantor
fiança *n.* bail
fiandeira *n.* spinner
fiapos de neve *n.* sleet
fiasco *n.* fiasco
fibra *n.* fibre
fibra de coco *n.* coir
ficar *v.* stay
ficção *n.* fiction
ficha (elétrica) *n.* plug
fictício *adj.* fictitious
fidalguia *n.* knighthood
fidedigno *adj.* trustworthy
fidelidade *n.* allegiance

fidelidade *adj.* fidelity
fiel *adj.* trusty
fígado *n.* liver
figo *n.* fig
figura *n.* figure
figurativo *adj* figurative
fila *n.* tier
filamento *n.* filament
filantropia *n.* philanthropy
filantrópico *adj.* philanthropic
filantropo *n.* philanthropist
filatelia *n.* philately
filha *n.* daughter
filho *n.* son
filme *n.* film
filmes *n.* movies
filologia *n.* philology
filológico *adj.* philological
filólogo *n.* philologist
filosofia *n.* philosophy
filosófico *adj.* philosophical
filósofo *n.* philosopher
filtrado *n.* filtrate
filtro *n.* filter
final *n.* & *adj.* end & final
finalista *n.* finalist
finalmente *adv.* ultimately
finança *n.* finance
financeiro *adj.* financial
financeiro *n.* financier
fingir *v.* pretend
fino *adj.* fine
fio *n.* thread
fio dental *n.* floss

fiorde *n.* fjord

firewall *n.* firewall

firmamento *n.* firmament

firme *adj.* firm

fiscal *adj.* fiscal

fiscalização *n.* oversight

fiscalizar *adj.* invigilate

física *n.* physics

físico *adj.* physical

físico *n.* physique

fisionomia *n.* physiognomy

fisioterapia *n.* physiotherapy

fissura *n.* fissure

fita *n.* tape

fivela *n.* buckle

fixação *n.* fixation

fixar *v.* fix

flacidez *n.* flab

flácido *adj.* flaccid

flagelar *v.* flagellate

flagrante *adj.* flagrant

flâmula *n.* streamer

flanco *n.* flank

flanela *n.* flannel

flapjack *n.* flapjack

flash *v.* flash

flatulento *adj.* flatulent

flauta *n.* flute

flertar *v.* dally

fleumático *adj.* phlegmatic

flexitime *n.* flexitime

flexível *adj.* flexible

floco *n.* flake

flor *n.* flower

flora *n.* flora

floral *adj.* floral

florão *n.* finial

florescer *v.* bloom

floresta *n.* forest

florete *n.* rapier

florido *adj.* flowery

florir *n.* blossom

florista *n.* florist

fluente *adj.* fluent

fluído *n.* fluid

fluir *v.i* flow

fluorescente *adj.* fluorescent

fluoreto *n.* fluoride

flutuabilidade *n.* buoyancy

flutuação *n.* flotation

flutuante *adj.* afloat

flutuar *v.* fluctuate

fluvial *adj.* fluvial

fluxo *n.* flux

fobia *n.* phobia

focal *adj.* focal

focinho *n.* snout

foco *n.* focus

fofinho *adj.* cuddly

fogão *n.* stove

fogo *n.* fire

fogueira *n.* bonfire

fogueiro *n.* stoker

foguete *n.* rocket

foice *n.* sickle

fole *n.* bellows

folga *n.* clearance

folgado *adj.* baggy

folha *n.* sheet

folha de cálculo *n.* spreadsheet

folhagem *n.* foliage

folheado *n.* veneer

folheto *n.* booklet

fólio *n.* folio

fome *n.* hunger

fonético *adj.* phonetic

fonte *n.* font

fora *adv.&n.* out & outside

fora de moda *adj.* outmoded

forasteiro *n.* foreigner

forca *n.* gallows

força *n.* strength

força moral *n.* fortitude

forçar *v.* wrest

fórceps *n.* forceps

forense *adj.* forensic

forjar *v.t* forge

forma *n.* shape

formação *n.* formation

formal *adj.* formal

formalidade *n.* formality

formato *n.* format

formidável *adj.* formidable

formiga *n.* ant

fórmula *n.* formula

formular *v.* formulate

fornada *n.* batch

fornecedor *n.* supplier

fornecer *v.* supply

forno *n.* oven

forragem *n.* fodder

fortalecer *v.* strengthen

fortaleza *n.* fortress

forte *adj.& n.* forceful & fot«rt

fortificar *v.* fortify

fortuna *n.* fortune

fórum *n.* forum

fosfato *n.* phosphate

fósforo *n.* match

fossar *v.* nuzzle

fóssil *n.* fossil

fosso *n.* moat

foto *n.* photo

fotocópia *n.* photocopy

fotocopiadora *n.* photostat

fotografia *n.* photography

fotográfico *adj.* photographic

fotógrafo *n.* photographer

fração *n.* fraction

fracassar *v.* flop

fraco *adj.* weak

frágil *adj.* fragile

fragmentário *adv.* piecemeal

fragmento *n.* fragment

fragrância *n.* fragrance

fragrante *adj.* redolent

fralda *n.* diaper

framboesa *n.* raspberry

Francês *adj.* French

franco *adj.* frank

frango *n.* fowl

franja *n.* fringe

franquia *n.* postage

franzir *v.i* frown

fraqueza *n.* weakness

frasco *n.* flask

frase *n.* phrase
fraseologia *n.* phraseology
frasquinho *n.* vial
fraternal *adj.* fraternal
fraternidade *n.* fraternity
fraturar *v.t* fracture
fraude *n.* fraud
fraudulento *adj.* fraudulent
freio *n.* bridle
freira *n.* nun
frenesim *n.* frenzy
frenético *adj.* frenetic
frente *n.* front
frequência *n.* frequency
frequente *adj.* frequent
frequentemente *adv.* often
fresco *adj.* fresh
fretado *adj.* chartered
fretador *n.* freighter
fretar *n.* charter
frete *n.* freight
fricção *n.* friction
frígido *adj.* frigid
frigorífico *n.* fridge
frio *n* chill
frio *adj.* cold
frio e húmido *adj.* dank
friorento *adj.* chilly
frisado *n.* terry
fritar *v.* fry
frívolo *adj.* frivolous
fronteira *n.* frontier
frota *n.* fleet
frouxidão *n.* laxity

frouxo *adj.* floppy
frugal *adj.* frugal
frugalidade *n.* thrift
frustrar *v.* frustrate
fruta *n.* fruit
frutífero *adj.* fruitful
fuga *n.* leakage
fugir *v.* elope
fugitivo *n.* fugitive
fugitivo *adj.* runaway
fulcro *n.* fulcrum
fuligem *n.* soot
fumar *n.* smoke
fumigar *v.* fumigate
fumo *n.* fume
função *n.* function
funcho *n.* fennel
funcional *adj.* functional
funcionário *n.* functionary
fundação *n.* foundation
fundador *n.* founder
fundamentação lógica *n.* rationale
fundamental *adj.* fundamental
fundamentar *v.* substantiate
fundar *v.* found
fundição *n.* foundry
fundido *adj.* molten
fundir *v.* merge
fundo *n.* background
funeral *n.* funeral
fungar *v.* snuff
fungo *n.* fungus
funil *n.* funnel
furacão *n.* hurricane

fúria *n.* fury
furioso *adj.* furious
furor *n.* furore
furtar *v.* pilfer
furtivamente *adv.* stealthily
furtivo *adj.* stealthy
fusão *n.* merger
fusível *v.* fuse
fuso *n.* spindle
futebol *n.* football
fútil *adj.* futile
futilidade *n.* futility
futurista *adj.* futuristic
futuro *n.* future

G

gabinete *n.* cabinet
gadanha *n.* scythe
gado *n.* cattle
gafanhoto *n.* grasshopper
gafe *n.* gaffe
gaguejar *v.* stutter
gaio *n.* jay
gaivina *n.* tarn
gaivota *n.* seagull
gajo *n.* guy
gala *n.* gala
galão *n.* gallon
galáxia *n.* galaxy
galeria *n.* gallery
galgo *n.* greyhound
galho *n.* twig
galinha *n.* chicken
galo *n.* rooster

galochas *n.* wellington
galopar *v.* lope
galope *n.* gallop
galvanizar *v.i.* galvanize
gama *n.* gamut
gambito *n.* gambit
gamela *n.* trough
ganância *n.* greed
ganancioso *adj.* greedy
gancho *n.* hook
gancho (suspensão tecidos) *n.*tenterhook
ganhar *v.* win
ganido *n.* yelp
ganso *n.* goose
garagem *n.* garage
garanhão *n.* stallion
garantia *n.* warranty
garantir *v.t* guarantee
garfo *n.* fork
gargalhada *n.* guffaw
garganta *n.* throat
gargarejar *v.* gargle
garra *n.* claw
garrafa *n.* bottle
garrafão *n.* carboy
gás *n.* gas
gasóleo *n.* diesel
gasolina *n.* petrol
gáspea (de sapato) *n.* vamp
gastar *v.* spend
gasto *adj.* shabby
gástrico *adj.* gastric
gastronomia *n.* gastronomy
gastrónomo *n.* epicure

gatafunhar v. scrawl	**geólogo** n. geologist
gatilho n. trigger	**geometria** n. geometry
gatinhar v. creep	**geométrico** adj. geometric
gatinho n. kitten	**geração** n. generation
gato n. cat	**gerador** n. generator
gaveta n. drawer	**geral** adj. general
gaxeta n. gasket	**geralmente** adv. usually
gaze n. gauze	**gerar** v. generate
gazeta n. gazette	**gerente** n. manager
geada n. frost	**gerir** v. manage
gel n. gel	**germano** adj. germane
gelado adj.& n. frosty & icy	**germe** n. germ
gelados n. ice-cream	**germinação** n. germination
geléia n. jelly	**germinar** v. germinate
geleira n. glacier	**gerúndio** n. gerund
gelo n. ice	**gesso** n. plaster
gelosia n. lattice	**gestação** n. gestation
gema n. yolk	**gestão** n. management
gémeo n. twin	**gesto** n. gesture
gemer v. groan	**geyser** n. geyser
gemido n. moan	**gigabyte** n. gigabyte
generalizar v. generalize	**gigante** n. giant
género n. gender	**gigantesco** adj. gigantic
generosidade n. generosity	**ginásio** n. gymnasium
generoso adj. generous	**ginasta** n. gymnast
génese n. genesis	**ginástico** n. gymnastic
genético adj. genetic	**ginecologia** n. gynaecology
gengibre n. ginger	**girafa** n. giraffe
génio n. genius	**girar** v. spin
genuíno adj. genuine	**giratório** adj. pivotal
geografia n. geography	**giz** n. chalk
geográfico adj. geographical	**glacê** n. icing
geógrafo n. geographer	**glacial** adj. glacial
geologia n. geology	**glândula** n. gland

glicerina *n.* glycerine

glicínia *n.* wisteria

glicose *n.* glucose

global *adj.* global

globalização *n.* globalization

globo *n.* globe

globo ocular *n.* eyeball

glória *n.* glory

glorificação *n.* glorification

glorificar *v.* glorify

glorioso *adj.* glorious

glossário *n.* glossary

glutão *n.* glutton

godo *n.* cobble

goiaba *n.* guava

gola *n.* necklet

golfe *n.* golf

golfo *n.* gulf

golpe *n.* stroke

golpear *n.* batter

golpear *v.* strike

gôndola *n.* gondola

gongo *n.* gong

gordura *n.* fat

gorgolejar *v.* gurgle

gorgulho *n.* weevil

gorila *n.* gorilla

gorro *n.* bonnet

gosto *n.* taste

gostoso *adj.* tasty

gota *n.* gout

gotejar *v.* i drip

gourmet *n.* gourmet

governador *n.* governor

governamental *adj.* ministerial

governanta *n.* governess

governante *n.* ruler

governar *v.* rule

governo *n.* government

graça *n.* grace

graça *n.* witticism

gracioso *adj.* graceful

gradação *n.* gradation

grade *n.* grid

gradiente *n.* gradient

graduação *n.* rank

gradual *adj.* gradual

gráfico *n.*& *adj.* chart &graphic

grafite *n.* graphite

grafitti *n.* graffiti

gralha (pássaro) *n.* rook

grama *n.* gram

gramática *n.* grammar

gramofone *n.* gramophone

granada *n.* garnet

granada *a.* grenade

grande *adj.* grand

grandeza *n.* grandeur

grandioso *adj.* grandiose

granito *n.* granite

granizo *n.* hail

granja *n.* grange

grânulo *n.* granule

grão *n.* grain

grão de bico *n.* chickpea

grasnido do ganso *n.* honk

grasnir *v.* squawk

gratidão *n.* gratitude

gratificação *n.* gratification

gratificar *v.* gratify

grátis *adv.* &*adj.* gratis

grato *n.* & *adj.* grateful & thankful

gratuito *adj.* gratuitous

grau *n.* degree

gravador *n.* recorder

gravar *v.* engrave

gravata *n.* tie

grave *adj.* grievous

grávida *adj.* pregnant

gravidade *n.* severity

gravidez *n.* pregnancy

gravitação *n.* gravitation

gravitar *v.* gravitate

graxa *n.* grease

grelha *v.* grill

grevista *n.* striker

grinalda *n.* garland

gripe *n.* flu

gripe aviária *n.* bird flu

gritar *v.* scream

grito *n.* yell

grosa *n.* rasp

groselha *n.* gooseberry

grosseiro *adj.* coarse

grossista *n.* wholesaler

grosso *adj.* thick

grotesco *adj.* grotesque

grua *n.* crane

grupo *n.* group

gruta *n.* cave

guarda *n.* keeper

guarda-chuva *n.* umbrella

guarda-costas n bodyguard

guardado *adj.* guarded

guarda-florestal *n.* ranger

guardanapo *n.* napkin

guardar *v.* guard

guarda-redes *n.* goalkeeper

guarda-roupa *n.* wardrobe

guarda-sol *n.* parasol

guardião *n.* guardian

guedelha *n.* shag

guerra *n.* war

guerreiro *n.* warrior

guerrilha *n.* guerrilla

guia *n.* guide

guilhotina *n.* guillotine

guinar *v.* yaw

guinchar *v.* shriek

guincho *n.* screech

guitarra *n.* guitar

guligem *n.* grime

gulodice *n.* gluttony

guloseima *n.* sweetmeat

guloseimas *n.* delicatessen

guloso *n.* gourmand

gurdwara *n.* gurdwara

gutural *adj.* throaty

H

hábil *adj.* skilled

habilidade *n.* skill

habitação *n.* housing

habitante *n.* inhabitant

habitar v. inhabit

habitat n. habitat

habitável adj. habitable

hábito n. habit

habitual adj. customary

habituar v.t. habituate

habitué n. habitue

hadj n. hajj

halal adj. halal

hall de entrada n. hall

halogénio n. halogen

halterofilia n. weightlifting

hambúrguer n. burger

hamster n. hamster

hangar n. hangar

harém n. harem

harmonia n. harmony

harmónio n. harmonium

harmonioso adj. harmonious

harmonizar v. harmonize

harpa n. harp

haste n. haste

hectare n. hectare

hediondo adj. hideous

hedonismo n. hedonism

hegemonia n. hegemony

hélice n. propeller

helicóptero n. helicopter

heliporto n. heliport

hemisfério n. hemisphere

hemoglobina n. haemoglobin

hemorragia n. haemorrhage

hemostático adj. styptic

hena n. henna

hepatite adj. hepatitis

heptágono n. heptagon

hera n. ivy

herança n. heritage

hercúleo adj. herculean

herdar v. inherit

herdeiro n. heir

hereditariedade n. heredity

hereditário adj. hereditary

heresia n. misbelief

hermético adj. hermetic

hérnia n. hernia

herói n. hero

heróico adj. heroic

heroína n. heroine

herpes n. herpes

hesitante adj. hesitant

hesitar v. hesitate

heterodoxo adj. unorthodox

heterogéneo adj. heterogeneous

heterossexual adj. heterosexual

hexogeno n. hexogen

hibernar v. hibernate

híbrido n. hybrid

hidrante n. hydrant

hidratar v. moisturize

hidrato v. hydrate

hidráulico adj. hydraulic

hidrodinâmica n. hydrofoil

hidrogênio n. hydrogen

hidromel n. mead

hiena n. hyena

hierarquia n. hierarchy

hífen n. hyphen

higiene *n.* hygiene
higienizar *v.* sanitize
hilaridade *n.* hilarity
hino *n.* hymn
hiper *pref.* hyper
hiperativo *adj.* hyperactive
hipérbole *n.* hyperbole
hipermercado *n.* superstore
hipertensão *n.* hypertension
hipnose *n.* hypnosis
hipnotismo *n.* hypnotism
hipnotizar *v.* hypnotize
hipocrisia *n.* hypocrisy
hipócrita *n.* hypocrite
hipócrita *adj.* sanctimonious
hipoteca *n.* mortgage
hipotecário *n.* mortgagor
hipotensão *n.* hypotension
hipótese *n.* hypothesis
hipotético *adj.* hypothetical
hirsuto *adj.* hirsute
histeria *n.* hysteria
histérico *adj.* hysterical
histograma *n.* histogram
história *n.* history
historiador *n.* historian
histórico *adj.* historic
histórico *adj.* historical
hobby *n.* hobby
hoje *adv.* today
hoje à noite *adv.* tonight
holística *adj.* holistic
hólmio *n.* holmium
holocausto *n.* holocaust

holofote *n.* floodlight
holograma *n.* hologram
homem *n.* man
homenagem *n.* homage
homeopata *n.* homoeopath
homeopatia *n.* homeopathy
homicídio *n.* homicide
homofobia *n.* homophobia
homogéneo *adj.* & *n.* homogeneous
homologação *n.* probate
homónimo *n.* namesake
homossexual *n.* homosexual
honestidade *n.* honesty
honesto *adj.* honest
honorário *adj.* honorary
honra *n.* honour
honradez *n.* probity
honroso *adj.* honourable
Hoover *n.* Hoover
hóquei *n.* hockey
hora *n.* hour
horário *n.* schedule
horas extras *n* overtime
horda *n.* horde
horizontal *adj.* horizontal
horizonte *n.* horizon
hormona *n.* hormone
horóscopo *n.* horoscope
horrendo *adj.* horrendous
horrível *adj.* awful
horror *n.* horror
horrorizado *adj.* aghast
horrorizar *v.* horrify
horroroso *adj.* horrific

hortelã *n.* mint

hortelã-pimenta *n.* peppermint

horticultura *n.* horticulture

hospedeiro *n.* host

hospício *n.* hospice

hospital *n.* hospital

hospitaleiro *adj.* hospitable

hospitalidade *n.* hospitality

hostil *adj.* hostile

hostilidade *n.* hostility

hotel *n.* hotel

humanidade *n.* mankind

humanismo *n.* humanism

humanitário *adj.* humanitarian

humanizar *v.* humanize

humano *adj.* human

humedecer *v.* moisten

humedecer *v.* souse

humidade *n.* moisture

húmido *adj.* moist

humildade *n.* humility

humilde *adj.* humble

humilhar *v.* humiliate

humor *n.* humour

humorista *n.* humorist

I
---

iaque *n.* yak

iate *n.* yacht

içar *v.* hoist

icebergue *n.* iceberg

ícone *n.* icon

icterícia *n.* jaundice

ida *n.* going

idade *n.* age

ideal *n.& adj.* ideal & notional

idealismo *n.* idealism

idealista *n.* & *adj.* idealist & idealistic

idealizar *v.* idealize

idealmente *adv.* ideally

idéia *n.* idea

idem *n.* ditto

idêntico *adj.* identical

identidade *n.* identity

identificação *n.* identification

identificar *v.* identity

ideologia *n.* ideology

idílio *n.* idyll

idioma *n.* idiom

idiomático *adj.* idiomatic

idiossincrasia *n.* idiosyncrasy

idiota *n.& adj.* idiot & idiotic

idolatrar *v.* idolize

idolatria *n.* idolatry

ídolo *n.* idol

idoso *adj.* aged

iglu *n.* igloo

ígneo *adj.* igneous

ignição *n.* ignition

ignóbil *adj.* ignoble

ignorância *n.* ignorance

ignorante *n.& adj.* ignoramus & ignorant

ignorar *v.* ignore

igreja *n.* church

igual *adj.* equal

igualar *v. t* equalize

ilegal *adj.* illegal

ilegibilidade *n.* illegibility

ilegítimo *adj.* illegitimate
ilegível *adj.* illegible
ileso *adj.* unscathed
ilha *n.* island
ilhota *n.* islet
ilícito *adj.* illicit
ilimitado *adj.* unlimited
ilógico *adj.* illogical
iludir *v.* elude
iluminação *n.* lighting
iluminar *v.* lighten
ilusão *n.* illusion
ilusório *adj.* illusory
ilustração *n.* illustration
ilustrar *n.* illustrate
ilustre *adj.* illustrious
imaculado *adj.* immaculate
imagem *n.* image
imagens *n.* imagery
imaginação *n.* imagination
imaginar *v.t.* imagine
imaginário *adj.* imaginary
imaginativo *adj.* imaginative
íman *n.* magnet
imanente *adj.* immanent
imaterial *adj.* immaterial
imaturidade *n.* immaturity
imaturo *adj.* immature
imbecil *n.* oaf
imediatamente *adv.* straightway
imediato *adj.* immediate
imemorial *adj.* immemorial
imensidão *n.* immensity
imenso *adj.* immense

imensurável *adj.* immeasurable
imergir *v.* immerse
imersão *n.* immersion
imigração *n.* immigration
imigrante *n.* immigrant
imigrar *v.* immigrate
iminente *adj.* imminent
imitação *n.* imitation
imitador *n.* imitator
imitar *v.* imitate
imobilização *n.* standstill
imobilizadamente *adj.* aground
imoderado *adj.* immoderate
imodéstia *a.* immodesty
imodesto *n.* immodest
imolar *v.* immolate
imoral *adj.* immoral
imoralidade *n.* immorality
imortal *adj.* immortal
imortalidade *n.* immortality
imortalizar *v.* immortalize
imóvel *adj.* still
impaciente *adj.* impatient
impacto *n.* impact
impalpável *adj.* impalpable
imparcial *adj.* impartial
imparcialidade *n.* impartiality
impasse *n.* impasse
impassível *adj.* impassive
impecável *adj.* impeccable
impedido *adj.* offside
impedidor *n.* detainee
impedimento *n.* impediment
impedir *v.* impede

impelir v. impel
impenetrável adj. impenetrable
impensável adj. unthinkable
imperador n. emperor
imperativo adj. imperative
imperatriz n. empress
imperceptível adj. inconspicuous
imperfeição n. imperfection
imperfeito adj. imperfect
imperial adj. imperial
imperialismo n. imperialism
império n. empire
impermeável n. mackintosh
impermeável adj. waterproof
impertinência n impertinence
impertinente adj. impertinent
impessoal adj. impersonal
ímpeto n. impetus
impetuosidade n. mettle
impetuoso adj impetuous
impetuoso n. mettlesome
impiedoso adj. heartless
ímpio adj. impious
implacável adj. implacable
implantar v. implant
implementar n. implement
implicação n. implication
implicar v. implicate
implícito adj. implicit
implodir v. implode
implorar v. beg
imponente adj. imposing
impor v. impose
importador n. importer

importância n. importance
importante adj. important
importar v. import
importunar v. heckle
imposição n. imposition
impossibilidade n. impossibility
impossível adj. impossible
imposto n. tax
impostor n. imposter
impotência n. impotence
impotente adj. impotent
impraticável adj. impracticable
imprecisão n. vagueness
impregnado adj. ingrained
impregnar v. pervade
impressão n. impression
impressionante adj. impressive
impressionar v. impress
impressora n. printer
imprestável adj. unemployable
imprevisto adj. unforeseen
imprimir v. print
impróprio adj. improper
improvável adj. unlikely
improvisado adj. cavalier
improvisar v. improvise
imprudente adj. imprudent
impugnação n. impeachment
impulsionar v. propel
impulsivo adj. impulsive
impulso n. impulse
impune adv. scot-free
impunidade n. impunity
impureza n. impurity

impuro *adj.* impure

imputar *v.* impute

imundície *n.* filth

imundo *adj.* foul

imundo *adj.* unclean

imune *adj.* immune

imunidade *n.* immunity

imunizar *v.* immunize

imunologia *n.* immunology

imutável *adj.* immutable

inabalável *adj.* unshakeable

inábil *adj.* awkward

inabitado *adj.* uninhabited

inacreditável *adj.* unbelievable

inadaptado *n.* misfit

inadequado *adj.* inadequate

inadmissível *adj.* inadmissible

inadvertido *adj.* inadvertent

inalador *n.* inhaler

inalar *v.* inhale

inanimado *adj.* inanimate

inaplicável *adj.* inapplicable

inarticulado *adj.* inarticulate

inatacável *adj.* unassailable

inatividade *n.* inaction

inativo *adj.* inactive

inato *adj.* innate

inaudito *adj.* unprecedented

inaudível *adj.* inaudible

inaugural *adj.* inaugural

inaugurar *v.* inaugurate

incalculável *adj.* incalculable

incansável *adj.* tireless

incapacidade *n.* inability

incapacitar *v.* disable

incapaz *adj.* unable

incauto *adj.* improvident

incendiar *v.* ignite

incendiário *n. & adj.* arson & artless

incenso *n.* incense

incentivo *n.* incentive

incerto *adj.* uncertain

incessante *adj.* ceaseless

incesto *n.* incest

inchação *n.* swell

inchaço *n.* swelling

inchar *v.* swell

incidência *n.* incidence

incidente *n.* incident

incisivo *adj.* incisive

incitador *n.* prompter

incitamento *n.* inducement

incitar *v.* incite

inclinação *n.* inclination

inclinado *adj.* prone

inclinar *v.* incline

inclinar-se *v.* slope

incluir *v.* include

inclusão *n.* inclusion

inclusivo *adj.* inclusive

incoerente *adj.* incoherent

incolor *n.* colourless

incomodar *v.* bother

incómodo *adj.* worrisome

incomparável *adj.* incomparable

incompatibilidade *n.* mismatch

incompatível *adj.* incompatible

incompetente *adj.* incompetent

incompleto adj. incomplete

incomum adj. unusual

inconclusivo adj. inconclusive

incondicional adj. unconditional

inconformista n. nonconformist

inconsciente adj. unaware

inconsolável adj. inconsolable

inconstante adj. fickle

incontável adj. countless

incontrolável adj. ungovernable

inconveniência n. impropriety

inconveniente n. inconvenience

incorporação n. incorporation

incorporar v. incorporate

incorrer v. incur

incorreto adj. incorrect

incorrigível adj. incorrigible

incrédulo adj. sceptical

incrementar n. increment

incriminar v.i. incriminate

incrível adj. incredible

incubar v. incubate

inculcar v. inculcate

inculto adj. fallow

incumbência n. errand

incumbente adj. incumbent

incurável adj. incurable

incursão n. incursion

incutir v. imbue

indecência n. indecency

indecente adj. indecent

indecisão n. indecision

indeciso adj. undecided

indefinido adj. indefinite

indelicado adj. impolite

indemnização n. indemnity

independência n. independence

independente adj. independent

indescritível adj. indescribable

indesculpável adj. inexcusable

indesejável adj. undesirable

indevido adj. undue

Indiano n. Indian

indicação n. indication

indicador n. indicator

indicar v. indicate

indicativo adj. indicative

índice n. index

indiferença n. indifference

indiferente adj. indifferent

indígena adj. indigenous

indigente n. pauper

indigestão n. indigestion

indigesto adj. indigestible

indignação n. indignation

indignado adj. indignant

indignidade n. indignity

indigno adj. unworthy

índigo n. indigo

indireto adj. indirect

indisciplina n. indiscipline

indisciplinado adj. unruly

indiscreto adj. indiscreet

indiscrição n. indiscretion

indiscriminado adj. indiscriminate

indispensável adj. indispensable

indisposto adj. unwell

indisputável adj. indisputable

indistinto *adj.* indistinct

individual *adj.* individual

individualidade *n.* individuality

individualismo *n.* individualism

indivisível *adj.* indivisible

indolente *adj.* indolent

indomado *adj.* indomitable

indução *n.* induction

indulgência *n.* indulgence

indulgente *adj.* indulgent

indústria *n.* industry

industrial *adj.* industrial

induzir *v.* induce

inebriante *adj.* heady

ineficaz *adj.* nugatory

ineficiente *adj.* inefficient

inegável *adj.* undeniable

inelegível *adj.* ineligible

inequívoco *adj.* unmistakable

inércia *n.* inertia

inerente *adj.* inherent

inerte *adj.* inert

inesgotável *adj.* inexhaustible

inesperado *adj.* unexpected

inesquecível *adj.* unforgettable

inestimável *adj.* priceless

inevitável *adj.* unavoidable

inexato *adj.* inexact

inexorável *adj.* inexorable

inexperiência *n.* inexperience

inexperiente *adj.* callow

inexplicável *adj.* inexplicable

inexpressivo *adj.* blank

inexpriente *adj.* unskilled

inexprímivel *adj.* unutterable

inextricável *adj.* inextricable

infalível *adj.* infallible

infame *adj.* infamous

infâmia *n.* infamy

infância *n.* childhood

infância *n.* infancy

infantaria *n.* infantry

infanticídio *n.* infanticide

infantil *adj.& n.* childish & infant

infecção *n.* infection

infeccioso *adj.* infectious

infectar *v.* infect

infeliz *adj.* unhappy

infência *n* boyhood

inferior *adj.* inferior

inferioridade *n.* inferiority

infernal *adj.* infernal

inferno *n.* hell

infértil *adj.* infertile

infestado *n.* buggy

infestar *v.* infest

infidelidade *n.* infidelity

infiel *adj.* unfaithful

infiltrar *v.* infiltrate

infinidade *n.* infinity

infinito *adj.* infinite

inflação *n.* inflation

inflamação *n.* inflammation

inflamar *v.* inflame

inflamatório *adj.* inflammatory

inflamável *adj.* flammable

inflar *v.* inflate

inflexível *adj.* inflexible

infligir v. inflict

influenciar n. influence

influente adj. influential

informação n. information

informal n.& adj. hoopla & informal

informante n. informer

informar v. inform

informar mal v. misinform

informativo adj. informative

informatizar v. computerize

infortúnio n. misfortune

infra-estrutura n. infrastructure

infringir v. infringe

infundado adj. unfounded

infundir v. infuse

infusão n. infusion

ingenuidade n. naivety

Inglês n. English

ingratidão n. ingratitude

ingrato adj. ungrateful

ingrediente n. ingredient

íngreme adj. steep

inhame n. yam

inibição n. inhibition

inibir v. inhibit

inicial adj. initial

iniciar v. initiate

iniciativa n. initiative

início n. beginning

inigualável adj. unequalled

inimigo n. enemy

inimitável adj. inimitable

inimizade n. enmity

injeção n. injection

injetar v. inject

injunção n. injunction

injustiça n. injustice

injustificável adj. unwarranted

injusto adj. unfair

inocência n. innocence

inocente adj. innocent

inoculação n. inoculation

inocular v. inoculate

inofensivo adj. harmless

inoperante adj. inoperative

inoportuno adj. inopportune

inóspito adj. inhospitable

inovação n. innovation

inovador n. innovator

inovar v. innovate

inquérito n. enquiry

inquietação n. disquiet

inquieto adj. uneasy

inquilino n. lodger

inquirido n. respondent

inquirir v. enquire

inquisição n. inquisition

insaciável adj. insatiable

insalubre adj. unhealthy

insanidade n. insanity

insano adj. insane

inscrever v. inscribe

inscrição n. inscription

insegurança n. insecurity

inseguro adj. insecure

inseguro n. unreliable

insensível adj. insensible

insensório n. censer

inseparável *adj.* inseparable
inserção *n.* insertion
inserir *v.* insert
inseticida *n.* insecticide
inseto *n.* bug
insignificância *n.* insignificance
insignificante *adj.* insignificant
insinuação *n.* insinuation
insinuar *v.* insinuate
insípido *adj.* insipid
insistência *n.* insistence
insistente *adj.* insistent
insistir *v.* insist
insociável *adj.* unsocial
insolar *v.* sun
insolência *n.* insolence
insolente *adj.* insolent
insolúvel *adj.* insoluble
insolvência *n.* insolvency
insolvente *adj.* insolvent
inspeção *n.* inspection
inspecionar *v.* inspect
inspetor *n.* inspector
inspiração *n.* inspiration
inspirar *v.* inspire
instabilidade *n.* instability
instalação *n.* installation
instalar *v.* install
instância *n.* instance
instantâneo *adj.* instantaneous
instante *n.* tick
instar *v.* urge
instável *adj.* unstable
instigar *v.* instigate

instilar *v.* instil
instintivo *adj.* instinctive
instinto *n.* instinct
instituição *n.* institution
instituto *n.* institute
instrução *n.* instruction
instruções *n.* briefing
instruir *v.* instruct
instrumental *adj.* instrumental
instrumentalista *n.* instrumentalist
instrumento *n.* instrument
instrutor *n.* instructor
insubordinação *n.* insubordination
insubordinado *adj.* insubordinate
insubstituível *adj.* irreplaceable
insucesso *n.* miscarriage
insuficiente *adj.* insufficient
insular *adj.* insular
insulina *n.* insulin
insultar *v.t.* insult
insuportável *adj.* insupportable
insurgente *n.* insurgent
insurreição *n.* insurrection
insustentável *adj.* indefensible
intacto *adj.* intact
intangível *adj.* intangible
integral *adj.* integral
integridade *n.* integrity
íntegro *adj.* incorruptible
inteiro *adj.* whole
intelecto *n.* intellect
intelectual *adj.* intellectual
inteligência *n.* intelligence
inteligente *adj.* clever

inteligível *adj.* intelligible

intenção *n.* intent

intencional *adj.* intentional

intencionalmente *adv.* purposely

intensidade *n.* intensity

intensificador *n.* booster

intensificar *v.* intensify

intensivo *adj.* intensive

intenso *adj.* intense

interação *n.* interplay

interagir *v.* interact

interceder *v.* intercede

interceptação *n.* interception

intercetar *v.* intercept

intercomunicador *n.* intercom

interconectar *v.* interconnect

interdependente *adj.* interdependent

interessante *adj.* interesting

interessar *v.* concern

interesse *n.* interest

interestadual *n.* interstate

interface *n.* interface

interferência *n.* interference

interferir *v.* interfere

interino *n.* interim

interior *adj.* indoor

interlocutor *n.* interlocutor

interlúdio *n.* interlude

intermediário *n.* intermediary

intermédio *adj.* intermediate

interminável *adj.* interminable

intermitente *adj.* intermittent

internacional *adj.* international

internado *n.* inpatient

internar *v.* intern

Internet *n.* internet

interno *adj.* internal

interpor *v.* interject

interpretar *v.* interpret

interpretar mal *v.* misinterpret

intérprete *n.* interpreter

inter-relacionar *v.* interrelate

interrogar *v.* interrogate

interrogativo *adj.* interrogative

interromper *v.* interrupt

interrupção *n.* interruption

interruptor *n.* switch

intervalo *n.* recess

intervenção *n.* intervention

intervir *v.* intervene

intestino *n.* intestine

intimidação *n.* intimidation

intimidade *n.* intimacy

intimidar *v.* intimidate

íntimo *adj.* intimate

intitular *v.* entitle

intocável *adj.* untouchable

intolerância *n.* bigotry

intolerante *n.& adj.* bigot & intolerant

intolerável *adj.* intolerable

intoxicação *n.* intoxication

intoxicar *v.* intoxicate

intranet *n.* intranet

intransigente *adj.* uncompromising

intransitável *adj.* impassable

intransitivo *adj.* intransitive

intransponível *adj.* insurmountable

intratável *adj.* intractable

intrépido adj. intrepid
intricado adj. intricate
intriga v. intrigue
intrínseco adj. intrinsic
introdução n. introduction
introdutório adj. introductory
introduzir v. introduce
intrometer v. obtrude
intrometer-se v. meddle
intrometido adj. nosy
introspeção n. insight
introspeção n. introspection
introvertido n. introvert
intrusão n. intrusion
intrusivo adj. intrusive
intruso n. interloper
intuição n. intuition
intuitivo n. intuitive
inumerável adj. numberless
inundação n. flood
inundar v. inundate
inútil adj. useless
inutilmente adv. vainly
invadir v. encroach
invadir v. invade
invalidar v. invalidate
inválido adj.& n. disabled & invalid
invariável adj. invariable
invasão n. invasion
inveja n. envy
invejável adj. enviable
invejoso adj. envious
invenção n. invention
invencível adj. invincible

inventar v. invent
inventário n. inventory
inventor n. inventor
inverno n. winter
inverossímil adj. implausible
inverso adj. backward
inverter v. invert
investida n. onslaught
investigação n. investigation
investigar v. investigate
investimento n. investment
investir v.t. invest
invetiva n. invective
inviolável adj. inviolable
invisível adj. invisible
invocação n. invocation
invocar v. invoke
invólucro n. casing
involuntariamente adv. unwittingly
involuntário adj. involuntary
invulnerável adj. invulnerable
ioga n. yoga
iogue n. yogi
iogurte n. yogurt
ir v.t go
ira n. ire
irascível adj. waspish
íris n. iris
irmã n. sister
irmandade n. brotherhood
irmão n. brother
ironia n. irony
irónico adj. ironical
irracional adj. irrational

irradiar v. irradiate

irreconciliável adj. irreconcilable

irrefletido adj. thoughtless

irrefutável adj. irrefutable

irregular adj. irregular

irregularidade n. irregularity

irrelevante adj. irrelevant

irremediável adj. irredeemable

irrepreensível adj. unexceptionable

irresistível adj. irresistible

irresoluto adj. irresolute

irresponsável adj. irresponsible

irreverente adj. flippant

irreversível adj. irreversible

irrevogável adj. irrevocable

irrigação n. irrigation

irrigar v. irrigate

irritado adj. angry

irritante n. irritant

irritar v. irritate

irritável adj. irritable

irrupção n. irruption

isco n. bait

isento adj. exempt

Islão n. Islam

isóbaro n. isobar

isolado adj. secluded

isolador n. insulator

isolamento n. isolation

isolar v. insulate

isolar v. isolate

isqueiro n. lighter

isso & este pron.& adj. this

itálico adj. italic

item n. item

itinerário n itinerary

J

já adv. already

jacaré n. alligator

jactância n. huff

jacuzzi n. Jacuzzi

jade n. jade

Janeiro n. January

janela n. window

jangada n. raft

jantar n. dinner

jantar (ato de jantar) v. dine

jaqueta n. jacket

jardim n. garden

jardim de infância n. kindergarten

jardim zoológico n. zoo

jardineiro n. gardener

jargão n. jargon

jarra n. jar

jarro n. jug

jasmim n. jasmine

jato n. jet

jaula n. cage

javali n. boar

jazz n. jazz

jazzístico adj. jazzy

jeans n. jeans

jet lag n. jet lag

jipe n. jeep

joalheiro n. jeweller

joaninha n. ladybird

jocoso adj. jocose

joeirar v. winnow	**jurado** n. juror
joelho n. knee	**juramento** n. oath
jogador n. player	**jurar** v. swear
jogar v. gamble	**júri** n. jury
jogo n. game	**jurisdição** n. jurisdiction
jóia n. jewel	**jurisprudência** n. jurisprudence
jóias n. jewellery	**jurista** n. jurist
joker n. joker	**justiça** n. justice
jóquei n. jockey	**justificação** n. justification
jornada n. journey	**justificar** v. justify
jornalismo n. journalism	**justificável** adj. justifiable
jornalista n. journalist	**justilho** n. jerkin
jovem adj.& n. young & youngster	**justo** adj. fair
jovial adj. jovial	**justo** adj. just
jovialidade adv. joviality	**juta** n. jute
jubileu n. jubilee	**juvenil** adj. juvenile
júbilo n. jubilation	**juventude** n. youth
jubiloso adj. jubilant	
judicial adj. judicial	**K**
judiciário n. judiciary	**karaoke** n. karaoke
judicioso adj. judicious	**karaté** n. karate
judo n. judo	**kebab** n. kebab
jugo n. yoke	**ketchup** n. ketchup
juiz n. judge	**kilobyte** n. kilobyte
julgamento n. trial	**kilt** n. kilt
julgar v.t. adjudge	**kosher** adj. kosher
Julho n. July	**kung fu** n. kung fu
junção n. junction	
Junho n. June	**L**
júnior adj.& n. junior	**lá** adv. there
junta n. knuckle	**lã** n. wool
juntar v. join	**labareda** n. blaze
juntos adv. together	**labial** adj. labial
Júpiter n. Jupiter	**lábio** n. lip

labirinto n. maze
laborar v.i. toil
laboratório n. laboratory
labrego n. lout
laca n. lacquer
lacaio n. lackey
laço n. loop
laço (insígnia) n. cockade
lacónico adj. laconic
lacrimoso adj. lachrymose
lacrosse n. lacrosse
lactose n. lactose
lacuna n. lacuna
ladainha n. rigmarole
lado n. side
lado a lado adv. abreast
ladrão n. thief
ladrilho n. dale
lagarto n. lizard
lager (tipo de cerveja) n. lager
lago n. lake
lagoa n. lagoon
lagosta n. lobster
lágrima n. tear
laje n. slab
lama n. mud
lamaçal n. slough
lamacento adj. slushy
lamber v. lick
lambril n. wainscot
lamentar v. mourn
lamentável adj. lamentable
lamento n. lament
lâmina n. blade

laminar v. laminate
lâmpada n. lamp
lamurioso adj. plaintive
lança n. lance
lançar v. launch
lanceiro n. lancer
lanceta n. lancet
lanche n. snack
lânguido adj. languid
lanoso adj. woolly
lanterna n. flash light
lápis n. pencil
lapso n. lapse
lar n. home
laranja n. orange
lareira n. hearth
largura n. width
laringe n. larynx
larva n. larva
lasanha n. lasagne
lasca n. chip
lascivo adj. lascivious
laser n. laser
lastração n. weighting
lata n. can
latada n. trellis
latão n. brass
latente adj. latent
laticínio n. dairy
latido n. woof
latir v. yap
latitude n. latitude
latrina n. latrine
laureado n. laureate

lava *n.* lava

lavagem *n.* washing

lavanda *n.* lavender

lavandaria *n.* laundry

lavar *v.* wash

lavatório *n.* sink

lavável *adj.* washable

lavrador *n.* ploughman

lavrar (fogo) *v.* smoulder

laxante *n.* laxative

lazer *n.* leisure

leal *adj.* loyal

lealista *n.* loyalist

leão *n.* lion

lebre *n.* hare

legado *n.* bequest

legado *n.* legacy

legal *adj.* legal

legalidade *n.* legality

legalizar *v.* legalize

legar *v.* bequeath

legião *n.* legion

legislação *n.* legislation

legislador *n.* legislator

legislar *v.* legislate

legislativo *adj.* legislative

legislatura *n.* legislature

legitimidade *n.* legitimacy

legítimo *adj.* legitimate

legível *adj.* legible

lei *n.* law

leigo *n.* layman

leilão *n.* auction

leite *n.* milk

leitor *n.* reader

leitoso *adj.* milky

leitura *n.* reading

leitura (cuidadosa) *n.* perusal

lema *n.* watchword

lembrança *n.* souvenir

lembrar *v.* remind

lembrete *n.* reminder

leme *n.* helm

lenço *n.* handkerchief

lenda *n.* legend

lendário *adj.* legendary

lentamente *adv.* slowly

lente *n.* lens

lentidão *n.* slowness

lentilha *n.* lentil

lento *adj.* slow

Leo *n.* Leo

leopardo *n.* leopard

lepra *n.* leprosy

leproso *n.* leper

ler *v.* read

lésbica *n.* lesbian

lesma *n.* slug

leste *n.* east

letal *adj.* lethal

letargia *n.* lethargy

letárgico *adj.* lethargic

letreiro *n.* placard

levantado *adv.* up

levantar *v.* raise

leve *adj.* slight

levedura *n.* yeast

levemente *adv.* lightly

leviandade *n.* levity
lexical *adj.* lexical
léxico *n.* lexicon
liberal *adj.* liberal
liberdade *n.* freedom
libertação *n.* liberation
libertador *n.* liberator
libertar *v.* release
libertino *adj.* profligate
libidinoso *adj.* lustful
libido *n.* libido
libra *n.* pound
libra estrelina *n.* sterling
libré *n.* livery
lição *n.* lesson
licença *n.* licence
licenciado *n.* graduate
lichia *n.* lychee
licitante *n.* bidder
licitar *v.* bid
liço *n.* herald
licor *n.* liquor
líder *n.* leader
liderança *n.* lead
liga *n.* league
ligação *n.* link
ligação desigual *n.* misalliance
ligamento *n.* ligament
lilás *n.* lilac
lima *n.* lime
limalha *n.* filings
limão *n.* lemon
limbo *n.* limbo
limiar *n.* threshold

limitação *n.* limitation
limitado *adj.* limited
limitar *n.* limit
limite *n.* boundary
limonada *n.* lemonade
limpar *v.* cleanse
limpeza *n.* cleanliness
límpido *adj.* perspicuous
limpo *adj.* clean
limusine *n.* limousine
linchamento *n.* lynch
linfa *n.* lymph
lingerie *n.* lingerie
lingote *n.* bullion
língua *n.* tongue
linguagem *n.* language
lingual *n.* lingual
linguista *adj.* linguist
linguístico *adj.* linguistic
linha *n.* row
linha de assinatura *n.* by-line
linha lateral *n.* sideline
linhaça *n.* linseed
linhagem *n.* lineage
linhita *n.* lignite
linho *n.* linen
lintel *n.* lintel
lipoaspiração *n.* liposuction
liquidação *n.* liquidation
liquidar *v.* liquidate
liquidificador *n.* blender
liquidificar *v.* liquefy
líquido *n.* liquid
lira *n.* lyre

lírica *n.* lyric	**loção** *n.* lotion
lírico *n.* lyricist	**locomoção** *n.* locomotion
lírio *n.* lily	**locomotiva** *n.* locomotive
liso *adj.* smooth	**locução** *n.* locution
lisonja *n.* blarney	**lodo** *n.* slush
lisonjear *v.* flatter	**logaritmo** *n.* logarithm
lista *n.* list	**lógica** *n.* logic
lista de chamada *n.* roll-call	**lógico** *adj.* logical
lista negra *n.* blacklist	**logística** *n.* logistics
listra *n.* streak	**logotipo** *n.* logo
liteira *n.* litter	**loira** *adj.* blonde
literal *adj.* literal	**loja** *n.* store
literário *adj.* literary	**lombo** *n.* loin
literatura *n.* literature	**lona** *n.* canvas
litigante *n.* litigant	**longe** *adv.* far
litigar *v.* litigate	**longevidade** *n.* longevity
litigável *adj.* actionable	**longitude** *n.* longitude
litígio *n.* litigation	**longo** *adj.* long
litro *n.* litre	**lontra** *n.* otter
livrar *v.* dispossess	**lorpa** *n.* gull
livre *adj.* free	**losango** *n.* lozenge
livreiro *n.* bookseller	**lotaria** *n.* lottery
livro *n.* book	**lótus** *n.* lotus
livro de capa dura *n.* hardback	**louça de barro** *n.* crockery
lixa *n.* sandpaper	**louco** *adj.* mad
lixadeira *n.* sander	**loucura** *n.* lunacy
lixeira *n.* dump	**loureiro** *n.* laurel
lixo *n.* trash	**louvável** *adj.* laudable
lobo *n.* wolf	**Louvre** *n.* Louvre
lóbulo *n.* lobe	**lua** *n.* moon
local *adj.& n.* local & spot	**lua de mel** *n.* honeymoon
localidade *n.* locale	**luar** *n.* moonlight
localização *n.* location	**lubrificação** *n.* lubrication
localizar *v.* localize	**lubrificante** *n.* lubricant

lubrificar v. lubricate

lucidez adv. lucidity

lúcido adj. lucid

lucrativo adj. gainful

lucro n. profit

lufada n. whiff

lugar n. place

lugarejo n. hamlet

lugares sentados n. seating

lúgubre adj. lurid

lula n. squid

luminoso adj. luminous

lunar adj. lunar

lunático n. lunatic

lustre n. chandelier

lustro n. gloss

lustroso adj. sleek

luta n. tussle

lutador n. fighter

lutar v. struggle

luto n. mourning

luva n. glove

luva de lã n. mitten

luxo n. luxury

luxuoso adj. luxurious

luxúria n. lust

luxuriante adj. luxuriant

luz n. light

M

maçã n. apple

macabro adj. macabre

macaco n. monkey

maçador n. irksome

maçapão n. marzipan

macarronete n. noodles

macete n. mallet

machadinha n. hatchet

machado n. axe

macho adj. macho

maciço adj. massive

macular v. taint

madame n. madam

madeira n. wood

madeixa n. quiff

madrinha n. godmother

madrugada n. dawn

maduro adj. mature

mãe n. mother

máfia n. Mafia

magenta n. magenta

magia n. magic

mágico n. magician

magistrado n. magistrate

magistral adj. magisterial

magnânimo adj. magnanimous

magnata n. magnate

magnético adj. magnetic

magnetismo n. magnetism

magnífico adj. magnificent

magnitude n. magnitude

mágoa n. heartache

magoar v. rankle

magricela adj. scraggy

magricela adj. scrawny

magro adj. skinny

Maio n. May

maionese n. mayonnaise

maior *adj.* major

maioria *n.* majority

mais *adv.* further

mais *n.* more

mais *prep.* plus

mais uma vez *adv.* anew

mais velho *adj.* elder

majestade *n.* majesty

majestoso *adj.* majestic

mal *adj. & n.* evil & harm

mal vestido *adj.* scruffy

malabarista *n.* juggler

malandro *adj.* roguish

malária *n.* malaria

malbaratar *v.* potter

malcheiroso *adj.* smelly

maldição *n.* curse

maleável *adj.* malleable

maléfico *adj.* malign

mal-entendido *n.* misunderstanding

mal-estar *n.* malaise

malévolo *adj.* wicked

malfeitor *n.* malefactor

mal-humorado *adj.* moody

malícia *n.* malice

malicioso *adj.* malicious

maligno *adj.* malignant

malmequer *n.* marigold

malte *n.* malt

maltratar *v.* mistreat

maluco *adj.* crazy

malversação *v.* misappropriation

mamar *v.* suckle

mamário *adj.* mammary

mamífero *n.* mammal

mamilo *n.* nipple

mamona *n.* mammon

mamute *n.* mammoth

maná *n.* manna

mancar *v.* hobble

mancha *adj.* brindle

mancha pequena *n.* speck

manchar *v.* besmirch

manchar *v.t.* stain

manchete *n.* headline

mandão *adj.* bossy

mandato *n.* mandate

mandíbula *n.* jaw

mandrião *n.* shirker

mandriar *v.* dawdle

mandril *n.* arbour

maneira *n.* manner

maneirismo *n.* mannerism

manejável *adj.* manageable

manequim *n.* mannequin

manga *n.* mango

manganésio *n.* manganese

mangueira *n.* hose

mangusto *n.* mongoose

manhã *n.* morning

mania *n.* mania

maníaco *n.* maniac

manicure *n.* manicure

manifestação *n.* manifestation

manifesto *adj.* manifest

manifesto *n.* manifesto

manilha *n.* shackle

manipulação *n.* manipulation

manipular v. manipulate

manivela v. crank

manjedoura n. manger

manjericão n. basil

manobra n. manoeuvre

manopla n. gauntlet

mansamente adv. tamely

mansão n. mansion

manso adj. meek

manteiga n. butter

manter v. keep

mantimentos n. viands

manto n. mantle

mantra n. mantra

manual adj. manual

manual escolar n. textbook

manuscrito n. manuscript

manusear v.t handle

manutenção n. maintenance

mão n. hand

mão de obra n. manpower

mapa n. map

maquilhagem n. make-up

máquina n. machine

máquina de costurar n. shuttle

máquina de lavar n. washer

máquina fotográfica n. camera

maquinaria n. machinery

mar n. sea

maratona n. marathon

maravilhar-se v.i marvel

maravilhoso adj. marvellous

marca n. mark

marca d'água n. watermark

marca registrada n. trademark

marcador n. marker

marca comercial n. brand

marcador de livros n. bookmark

marcante adj. outstanding

marcas n. marking

marceneiro n. joiner

marcha n. march

marchar v. march

marcial adj. martial

marco miliário n. milestone

marechal n. marshal

marfim n. ivory

marga n. marl

margarida n. daisy

margarina n. margarine

margem n. margin

marginal adj. marginal

maria-rapaz n. tomboy

maricas n. sissy

marido n. husband

marina n. marina

marinar v. marinate

marinha adj.& n. marine & navy

marinheiro n. sailor

marioneta n. marionette

mariposa n. moth

marital adj. marital

marítimo adj. maritime

marketing n. marketing

marmelada n. marmalade

marmelo n. quince

mármore n. marble

maroto n. scamp

marquesinha *n.* marquee

marreta *n.* sledgehammer

marrom *n.* maroon

marshmallow *n.* marshmallow

marsupial *n.* marsupial

Marte *n.* Mars

martelo *n.* hammer

mártir *n.* martyr

martírio *n.* martyrdom

Marxismo *n.* Marxism

mas *conj.* but

máscara *n.* mask

mascarada *n.* masquerade

mascote *n.* mascot

masculinidade *n.* manhood

masculino *n.* male

masculino *adj.* masculine

masoquismo *n.* masochism

massa *n.* mass

massa (dinheiro) *n.* dough

massacre *n.* massacre

massagem *n.* massage

massagista *n.* masseur

mastigar *v.* chew

mastigar *v.* scrunch

mastro *n.* mast

masturbar *v.* masturbate

matador *n.* matador

matagal *n.* thicket

matança *n.* slaughter

matar *v.* kill

matemática *n.* mathematics

matemático *n.* mathematician

matemático *adj.* mathematical

material *n.* material

materialismo *n.* materialism

materializar *v.* materialize

maternal *adj.* maternal

maternidade *n.* maternity

matiné *n.* matinee

matiz *n.* hue

matreiro *adj.* shifty

matriarca *n.* matriarch

matricídio *n.* matricide

matrícula *n.* matriculation

matricular *v.* matriculate

matrimonial *adj.* matrimonial

matrimónio *n.* matrimony

matriz *n.* matrix

matrona *n.* matron

maturidade *n.* maturity

mau *adj.* bad

mau agouro *n.* portent

mau comportamento *n.* misbehaviour

mau hálito *n.* halitosis

mausoléu *n.* mausoleum

máxima *n.* maxim

maximizar *v.* maximize

máximo *n.& adj.* maximum & utmost

meada *n.* hank

mecânica *n.* mechanics

mecânico *n.* mechanic

mecânico *adj.* mechanical

mecanismo *n.* mechanism

mecha *n.* tinder

meda *n.* rick

medalha *n.* medal

medalhão *n.* medallion

medalhista *n.* medallist

media *n.* media

média *n.* average

mediação *n.* mediation

mediador *n.* trouble-shooter

mediana *adj.* median

mediar *v.* mediate

medicação *n.* medication

medição *n.* measurement

medicina *n.* medicine

medicinal *adj.* medicinal

médico *n.& adj.* doctor & medical

médico legista *n.* coroner

Medida comp.201 m *n.* furlong

medido *adj.* measured

medieval *adj.* medieval

médio *adj.* middle

medíocre *adj.* mediocre

mediocridade *n.* mediocrity

medir *v.* measure

meditar *v.* meditate

Mediterrâneo *adj.* Mediterranean

medium *n.* medium

medo *n.* fear

medroso *adj.* funky

medusa *n.* jellyfish

megabyte *n.* megabyte

megafone *n.* megaphone

megahertz *n.* megahertz

megalítico *adj.* megalithic

megálito *n.* megalith

megapixel *n.* megapixel

megera *n.* shrew

meia *n.* sock

meia-noite *n.* midnight

meias *n.* hosiery

meio *n.* centre

meio *adj.* midst

meio social *n.* milieu

meio-dia *n.* noon

meios *n.* means

meirinho *n.* bailiff

mel *n.* honey

melaço *n.* molasses

melamina *n.* melamine

melancia *n.* watermelon

melancolia *n.* melancholia

melão *n.* melon

melhor *adj.* better

melhoramento *n.pl.* amendment

melhorar *v.* upgrade

melhoria *n.* improvement

melodia *n.* melody

melódico *adj.* melodic

melodioso *adj.* melodious

melodrama *n.* melodrama

melodramático *adj.* melodramatic

membrana *n.* membrane

membro *n.* member

memorando *n.* memo

memorável *adj.* memorable

memória *n.* memory

memorial *n.* memorial

mencionar *v.* mention

mendicante *adj.* mendicant

mendigo *n.* beggar

menina *n.* girl

menina solteira *n.* miss

meningite *n.* meningitis
menopausa *n.* menopause
menor *adj.* lesser
menos *adj.& prep.* less & minus
menosprezar *v.* spurn
mensageiro *n.* messenger
mensagem *n.* message
mensal *adj.* monthly
menstruação *n.* menstruation
menstrual *adj.* menstrual
mental *adj.* mental
mentalidade *n.* mentality
mente *n.* mind
mentir *v.* lie
mentira *n.* canard
mentiroso *n.* liar
mentiroso *adj.* mendacious
mentor *n.* mentor
menu *n.* menu
mercado *n.* market
mercadoria *n.* merchandise
mercantil *adj.* mercantile
mercearia *n.* grocery
mercedor *adj.* worthy
merceeiro *n.* grocer
mercenário *adj.* mercenary
mercurial *adj.* mercurial
mercúrio *n.* mercury
merecer *v. t.* deserve
meretriz *adj.* meretricious
mergulhar *v. t* dip
mergulhar (verticalmente) *v.* plummet
mergulho *v.* dive
meridiano *n.* meridian

meridional *adj.* southerly
meritório *adj.* meritorious
mero *adj.* mere
mês *n.* month
mesa *n.* table
mesmérico *adj.* mesmeric
mesmo *adj.* even
mesquinhar *v.* niggle
mesquinho *n.* niggard
mesquinho *adj.* niggardly
mesquita *n.* mosque
messias *n.* messiah
mestiço *n.* mongrel
mestre *n.* master
mestria *n.* mastery
metabolismo *n.* metabolism
metafísica *n.* metaphysics
metafísico *adj.* metaphysical
metáfora *n.* metaphor
metal *n.* metal
metálico *adj.* metallic
metalurgia *n.* metallurgy
metamorfose *n.* metamorphosis
meteórico *adj.* meteoric
meteoro *n.* meteor
meteorologia *n.* meteorology
meticuloso *n.* martinet
meticuloso *adj.* meticulous
metódico *adj.* methodical
método *n.* method
metodologia *n.* methodology
metragem *n.* footage
métrico *adj.* metric
metro *n.& adj.* metro & metropolitan

metrópole *n.* metropolis

meu *pron.& adj.* mine & my

mexer *v.* wiggle

mexerico *n.* gossip

mexilhão *n.* mussel

mezanino *n.* mezzanine

mialgia *n.* myalgia

miasma *n.* miasma

mica *n.* mica

micose *n.* ringworm

microbiologia *n.* microbiology

microchip *n.* microchip

microcirurgia *n.* microsurgery

microfilme *n.* microfilm

microfone *n.* microphone

micrómetro *n.* micrometer

microondas *n.* microwave

microprocessador *n.* microprocessor

microscópico *adj.* microscopic

microscópio *n.* microscope

mictório *n.* urinal

migalha *n.* crumb

migração *n.* migration

migrante *n.* migrant

migrar *v.* migrate

mil *adj. & n.* thousand

milagre *n.* miracle

milagroso *adj.* miraculous

milénio *n.* millennium

milha *n.* mile

milhão *n.* million

milho *n.* corn

milícia *n.* militia

miligrama *n.* milligram

milímetro *n.* millimetre

milionário *n.* millionaire

militante *adj. & n.* militant

militar *adj.* military

militar *v.* militate

mim *pron.* me

mimado *adj.* finicky

mímico *n.* mimic

mimo *n.* mime

mina *n.* mine

mina de carvão *n.* colliery

minar *v.* undermine

minarete *n.* minaret

mineiro *n.* miner

mineral *n.* mineral

mineralogia *n.* mineralogy

minério *n.* ore

minestrone *n.* minestrone

Mini *adj.* mini

miniatura *adj.* miniature

miniautocarro *n.* minibus

minicarro *n.* minicab

mínima *n.* minim

minimizar *v.* minimize

mínimo *adj.& n.* minimal & minimum

minissaia *n.* miniskirt

ministério *n.* ministry

ministro *n.* minister

minoria *n.* minority

minuciosamente *adv.* minutely

minucioso *adj.* minute

minúscula *adj.* minuscule

minúsculo *adj.* tiny

minuto *n.* minute

míope *adj.* myopic
miopia *n.* myopia
miose *n.* myosis
miragem *n.* mirage
mirante *n.* gazebo
miríade *n.* myriad
mirra *n.* myrrh
miserável *adj.* miserable
miséria *n.* misery
misericórdia *n.* mercy
misericordioso *adj.* merciful
mísero *adj.* woeful
missão *n.* mission
míssil *n.* missile
missionário *n.* missionary
missiva *n.* missive
mistério *n.* mystery
misterioso *adj.* mysterious
mística *n.* mystique
misticismo *n.* mysticism
místico *n.* mystic
mistificar *v.* juggle
mistificar *v.* mystify
misto *adj.* interracial
mistura *n.* mixture
misturar *v.* mix
mítico *adj.* mythical
mitigação *n.* mitigation
mitigar *v.* mitigate
mito *n.* myth
mitologia *n.* mythology
mitra *n.* mitre
mobília *n.* furniture
mobiliário *n.* furnishing

mobilidade *n.* mobility
mobilizar *v.* mobilize
moca *n.* mocha
moça *n.* lass
mochila *n.* backpack
moda *n.* fashion
modalidade *n.* modality
modelagem *n.* moulding
modelo *n.* model
modem *n.* modem
moderação *n.* moderation
moderada *adj.* moderate
moderador *n.* moderator
modernidade *n.* modernity
modernismo *n.* modernism
modernizar *v.* modernize
moderno *adj.* modern
modéstia *n.* modesty
modesto *adj.* modest
modificação *n.* modification
modificar *v.t.* modify
modista *n.* milliner
modo *n.* mode
modular *v.* modulate
módulo *n.* module
moeda *n.* coin
moer *v.* grind
mogno *n.* mahogany
moinho *n.* mill
moinho de vento *n.* windmill
molar *n.* molar
molécula *n.* molecule
molecular *adj.* molecular
molestação *n.* molestation

molestar v. molest

molhado adj. wet

molho n. sauce

molho (de palha) n. sheaf

molho picante n. chutney

molinete n. windlass

molusco gastrópode n. winkle

momentâneo adj. momentary

momento n. moment

monaquismo n. monasticism

monarca n. monarch

monarquia n. monarchy

monástico adj. monastic

monção n. monsoon

monetário adj. monetary

monetarismo n. monetarism

monge n. monk

monitor n. monitor

monitorial adj. monitory

mono n. mono

monocarril n. monorail

monocromático n. monochrome

monocular adj. monocular

monóculo n. monocle

monofónico adj. monophonic

monogamia n. monogamy

monografia n. monograph

monograma n. monogram

monolatria n. monolatry

monolito n. monolith

monólogo n. monologue

monopólio n. monopoly

monopolista n. monopolist

monopolizar v. monopolize

monossílabo n. monosyllable

monoteísmo n. monotheism

monoteísta n. monotheist

monotonia n. monotony

monótono adj. monotonous

monstro n. monster

monstruoso adj.& n. monstrous

montado sobre prep. astride

montador n. fitter

montagem n. assemblage

montanha n. mountain

montanha-russa n. rollercoaster

montanhismo n. mountaineering

montanhista n. mountaineer

montanhoso adj. mountainous

montar v. assemble

monte n. pile

montículo n. mound

montículo de terra n. hummock

monumental adj. monumental

monumento n. monument

morada n. address

moral adj.& n. moral & morale

moralidade n. morality

moralista n. moralist

moralizar v. moralize

morango n. strawberry

morbidez adv. morbidity

mórbido adj. morbid

morcego n. bat

mordaça n. gag

mordacidade n. poignancy

mordaz adj. poignant

morder v. bite

mordidela v. nibble	**moto** n. motto
mordomo n. butler	**motocicleta** n. motorcycle
morena n. brunette	**motor** n. motor
moreno adj. swarthy	**motorista** n. motorist
morfina n. morphine	**mousse** n. mousse
morfologia n. morphology	**movedor** n. mover
morganático adj. morganatic	**móvel** adj. mobile
morgue n. morgue	**mover** v. move
moribundo adj. moribund	**movimentar** v. stir
mormacento adj. muggy	**movimentar avião na pista** v. taxi
morrer v. die	**movimento** n. movement
morrer de fome v. starve	**mozzarella** n. mozzarella
morsa n. walrus	**mucilagem** n. mucilage
mortal adj. mortal	**muco** n. mucus
mortalha n. pall	**mucoso** adj. mucous
mortalidade n. mortality	**Muçulmano** n. Muslim
morte n. death	**mudar** v. relocate
mortificar v. mortify	**mudar as penas** v. moult
morto adj. dead	**mudo** adj. speechless
mortuário n. mortuary	**muesli** n. muesli
mosaico n. mosaic	**mugir** v. moo
moscovita n. muscovite	**muito** adv. greatly
mosqueado n. mottle	**muito** pron. much
mosquete n. musket	**muito** adj. rare
mosqueteiro n. musketeer	**muito tempo** n. yonks
mosquito n. mosquito	**muitos** adj. many
mostarda n. mustard	**mula** n. mule
mosteiro n. monastery	**mulato** n. mulatto
mostrar v. show	**muleta** n. crutch
motel n. motel	**mulher** n. woman
motherboard n. motherboard	**mulher desmazelada** n. slattern
motivação n. motivation	**mullah** n. mullah
motivar v. motivate	**mulridão** n. mob
motivo n. motive	**multa** v. forfeit

multicolor *adj.* motley

multicultural *adj.* multicultural

multidão *n.* crowd

multiforme *adj.* multiform

multilateral *adj.* multilateral

multimédia *n.* multimedia

multíparo *adj.* multiparous

multiplex *n.* multiplex

multiplicação *n.* multiplication

multiplicar *v.* multiply

multiplicidade *n.* multiplicity

múltiplo *adj.* multiple

múmia *n.* mummy

mumificar *v.* mummify

mundano *adj.* mundane

mundo *n.* world

munição *n.* ammunition

municipal *adj.* municipal

municipalidade *n.* municipality

munições *n.* munitions

mural *n.* mural

murchar *v.* shrivel

murmurar *v.* murmur

murta *n.* myrtle

musa *n.* muse

muscular *adj.* muscular

músculo *n.* muscle

museu *n.* museum

musgo *n.* moss

música *n.* music

musical *adj.* musical

músico *n.* musician

musselina *n.* muslin

mustang *n.* mustang

mutação *n. & adj.* mutation & mutative

mutar *v.* mutate

mutável *adj.* mutable

mutilação *n.* mutilation

mutilar *v.* mutilate

mútuo *adj.* mutual

N

na frente *adv.* ahead

nababo *n.* nabob

nabo *n.* turnip

nação *n.* nation

nacho *n.* nacho

nacional *adj.* national

nacionalidade *n.* nationality

nacionalismo *n.* nationalism

nacionalista *n.* nationalist

nacionalização *n.* nationalization

nacionalizar *v.* nationalize

naco *n.* chunk

nada *pron. & n.* nothing & nil

nadador *n.* swimmer

nadante *adj.* natant

nadar *v.* swim

nádega *n.* buttock

nadir *n.* nadir

nado-morto *n.* stillborn

naftalina *n.* naphthalene

namorar *v.i* flirt

namorico *n.* dalliance

namoro *n.* courtship

não *adj.* no

não celebrado *adj.* unsung

não chamado *adj.* uncalled

não obstante adv. nevertheless &

não obstante prep notwithstanding

não tripulado adj. unmanned

não-alinhamento n. non-alignment

narcisismo n. narcissism

narciso n. narcissus

narcótico n. narcotic

narina n. nostril

nariz n. nose

narração n. narration

narrador n. narrator

narrar v. narrate

narrativa n. narrative

nasal adj. nasal

nascente adj. nascent

nascido adj. born

nascimento n. birth

Natal n. Christmas

natas n. cream

nativo n. native

natural adj. natural

naturalista n. naturalist

naturalização n. naturalization

naturalizar v. naturalize

naturalmente adv. naturally

natureza n. nature

naturismo n. naturism

naufrágio n. shipwreck

náufrago n. castaway

náusea n. nausea

nauseabundo adj. nauseous

náutico adj. nautical

naval adj. naval

navalha n. razor

nave n. nave

navegação n. navigation

navegador n. navigator

navegar v. navigate

navegável adj. navigable

navio n. ship

navio a vapor n. steamer

neblina n. haze

nébula n. nebula

nebuloso adj. nebulous

necessariamente adv. necessarily

necessário adj. necessary

necessidade v. need

necessitado adj. needy

necessitar v. necessitate

necromancia n. necromancy

necrópole n. necropolis

néctar n. nectar

nectarina n. nectarine

nefasto adj. nefarious

negação n. denial

negar v. i. deny

negatividade n. negativity

negativo adj. negative

negligência n. negligence

negligenciar v. neglect

negligente adj. negligent

negociação n. negotiation

negociador n. negotiator

negociante n. dealer

negociante de vinhos n. vintner

negociar v. negotiate

negociável adj. negotiable

negócio n. business

negrito *adj.* bold

negro *adj.& n.* black & negro

nem *adv.* not

nem *adj.* neither

nem *conj.* nor

nenhum *pron.* none

neoclássico *adj.* neoclassical

neófito *n.* neophyte

Neolítico *adj.* Neolithic

néon *n.* neon

nepotismo *n.* nepotism

Neptuno *n.* Neptune

nervo *n.* Nerve

nervosismo *n.* jitters

nervoso *adj.* nervous

neural *adj.* neural

neurologia *n.* neurology

neurologista *n.* neurologist

neurose *n.* neurosis

neurótico *adj.* neurotic

neutral *adj.* neutral

neutralizar *v.* neutralize

neutrão *n.* neutron

neutro *adj.* neuter

nevão *n.* blizzard

neve *n.* snow

névoa *n.* mist

nevoeiro *n.* fog

nevoso *adj.* snowy

nexo *n.* nexus

nicho *n.* niche

nicotina *n.* nicotine

niilismo *n.* nihilism

nimbo *n.* nimbus

ninfa nymph

ninguém *pron.* nobody

ninhada *n.* brood

ninharia *n.* trifle

ninho *n.* nest

ninho de pombo *n.* pigeonhole

níquel *n.* nickel

nirvana *n.* nirvana

nitrogénio *n.* nitrogen

nível *n.* level

nó *n.* knot

no entanto, a. nonetheless

no estrangeiro *adv.* abroad

no exterior *adv.* overseas

no fundo do palco *adv.* backstage

no verso *adv.* overleaf

nobre *adj..* noble

nobre *n.* nobleman

nobreza *n.* nobility

noção *n.* notion

nocivo *adj.* noxious

nodoso *adj.* knotty

nogado *n.* nougat

nogueira *n.* walnut

noite *n.* night

noiva *n.* bride

noivo *n.* bridegroom

nómado . nomad

nómado *adj.* nomadic

nome *n.* name

nome impróprio *n.* misnomer

nomeação *n.* nomination

nomeadamente *n.* namely

nomeado *n.* nominee

nomear v. nominate

nomenclatura n. nomenclature

nominal adj. nominal

nonagésimo adj. & n. ninetieth

nono adj. & n. ninth

nora n. daughter-in-law

Nórdico adj. Nordic

norma n. norm

normal adj. normal

normalidade n. normalcy

normalizar v. normalize

normalmente adv. ordinarily

normativo adj. normative

norte n.& adj. north & northerly

nós pron. we

nós mesmos pron. ourselves

nosso adj. our

nostalgia n. nostalgia

nota n. note

nota de publicidade n. blurb

notação n. notation

notar n. notice

notário n. notary

notável adj. notable

notícia n. news

notificação n. notification

notificar v. notify

notoriedade n. notoriety

notório prep. notorious

noturno adj. nocturnal

novamente adv. again

novato n. novice

nove adj. & n. nine

novela n. novel

Novembro n. November

noventa adj. & n. ninety

novidade n. novelty

novo adj. new

novo julgamento n. retrial

noz n. nut

noz-pecã n. pecan

nu adj. naked

nuance n. nuance

núbil adj. nubile

nublado adj. cloudy

nuca n. nape

nuclear adj. nuclear

núcleo n. core

nudez n. nudity

nudista n. nudist

nulidade n. nonentity

nulo adj. null

numerador n. numerator

numeral n. numeral

numerário n. cash

numérico adj. numerical

número n. number

numeroso adj. numerous

nunca adv. never

nupcial adj. nuptial

nutrição n. nutrition

nutricionista n. dietician

nutriente n. nutrient

nutrir v. nourish

nutritivo adj. nutritive

nuvem n. cloud

nylon n. nylon

o

o mais baixo *adj.* lower

o mais próximo *adj.* nearest

o melhor *adj.* best

o pior *adj.* worst

o que & qual *pron.* & *adj.* what

oásis *n.* oasis

obcecado *adj.* besotted

obcecar *v.* obsess

obedecer *v.* obey

obediência *n.* obedience

obediente *adj.* obedient

obesidade *n.* obesity

obeso *adj.* obese

obituário *n.* obituary

objeção *n.* objection

objetivamente *adv.* objectively

objetivo *n.* & *adj.* goal & objective

objeto *n.* object

oblação *n.* oblation

oblíquo *adj.* oblique

obliteração *n.* obliteration

obliterar *v.* obliterate

oblongo *adj.* oblong

obra *n.* handiwork

obra-prima *n.* masterpiece

obras na estrada *n.* roadwork

obrigação *n.* obligation

obrigacionista *n.* debenture

obrigado *adj.* obligated

obrigar *v.* oblige

obrigatório *adj.* obligatory

obscenidade *n.* obscenity

obsceno *adj.* obscene

obscuridade *n.* obscurity

obscuro *adj.* obscure

observação *n.* observation

observador *adj.* observant

observância *n.* observance

observar *v.* observe

observatório *n.* observatory

obsessão *n.* obsession

obsolescente *adj.* obsolescent

obsoleto *adj.* obsolete

obstáculo *n.* obstacle

obstinação *n.* obduracy

obstinação *n* obstinacy

obstinado *adj.* obstinate

obstipação *n.* constipation

obstrução *n.* obstruction

obstruir *v.* obstruct

obstrutivo *adj.* obstructive

obtenção *n.* procurement

obter *v.* obtain

obtuso *adj.* obtuse

óbvio *adj.* obvious

ocasião *n.* occasion

ocasional *adj.* occasional

ocasionalmente *adv.* occasionally

oceânico *adj.* oceanic

oceano *n.* ocean

ocidental *adj.* & *n.* western & westerner

ocidentalizar *v.* westernize

Ocidente *n.* occident

ociosidade *n.* idleness

ocioso *adj.* & *n.* otiose & idler

oco *adj.* hollow

ocorrência *n.* occurrence	**ofuscar** *v.* obfuscate
ocorrer *v.* occur	**oitava** *n.* octave
ocre *n.* umber	**oitenta** *adj.* & *n.* eighty
octavo *n.* octavo	**oito** *adj.* & *n.* eight
octogenário *n.* octogenarian	**Ok** *adj.* okay
octógono *n.* octagon	**óleo** *n.* oil
octroi *n.* octroi	**óleo** de rícino *a.* castor oil
ocular *adj.* ocular	**oleoso** *adj.* oily
oculista *n.* optician	**olhadela** n look
ocultar *v.* secrete	**olhar** *v.* look
oculto *n.* occult	**olho** *n.* eye
ocupação *n.* occupancy	**oligarquia** *n.* oligarchy
ocupado *adj.* busy	**olímpico** *adj.* Olympic
ocupante *n.* occupant	**ombro** *n.* shoulder
ocupar *v.* engross	**omelete** *n.* omelette
ode *n.* ode	**omissão** *n.* omission
odiar *v.t.* hate	**omitir** *v.* omit
ódio *n.* odium	**omnipotência** *n.* omnipotence
odioso *adj.* hateful	**omnipotente** *adj.* omnipotent
Odisseia *n.* odyssey	**omnipresença** *n.* omnipresence
odor *n.* odour	**omnipresente** *adj.* omnipresent
oeste *n.* west	**omnisciência** *n.* omniscience
ofegante *adj.* puffy	**omnisciente** *adj.* omniscient
ofegar *v.* wheeze	**omnomatopeia** *n.* onomatopoeia
ofender *v.* offend	**onça** *n.* ounce
ofensa *n.* offence	**onda** *n.* surge
ofensiva *adj.* offensive	**onde** *adv.* where
ofensor *n.* offender	**ondear** *v.* billow
oferecer *v.* offer	**ondulação** *n.* ripple
oferta *n.* offering	**ondulado** *adj.* wavy
oficial *adj.* authoritative	**ondular** *v.* wave
oficial *n.* officer	**oneroso** *adj.* onerous
oficialmente *adv.* officially	**ónix** *n.* onyx
oficioso *adj.* officious	**ontem** *adv.* yesterday

ontologia n. ontology
ónus n. onus
onze adj. & n. eleven
opacidade n. opacity
opaco adj. opaque
opala n. opal
opção n. option
opcional adj. optional
ópera n. opera
operação n. operation
operacional adj. operational
operador n. operator
operar v. operate
operativo adj. operative
opinar v. opine
opinião n. opinion
ópio n. opium
oponente n. opponent
opor v. oppose
oportunidade n. chance
oportunismo n. opportunism
oportuno adj. opportune
oposição n. opposition
oposto adj. opposite
opressão n. oppression
opressivo adj. oppressive
opressor n. oppressor
oprimir v. oppress
optar v. opt
opulência n. opulence
opulento adj. opulent
oração n. oration
oração n. prayer
oracular adj. oracular

oráculo n. oracle
orador n. orator
oral adj. oral
oralmente adv. orally
oratória n. oratory
orbe n. orb
órbita n. orbit
orbital adj. orbital
orçamento n. budget
ordem n. order
ordem de correio n. mail order
orfanato n. orphanage
órfão n. orphan
orgânico adj. organic
organismo n. organism
organização n. organization
organizar v. organize
órgão n. organ
orgasmo n. orgasm
orgia n. orgy
orgulho n. pride
orgulhoso adj. proud
orientação n. guidance
oriental adj. oriental
orientar v. orientate
oriente n. orient
origami n. origami
origem n. origin
originador n. originator
original adj. original
originalidade n. originality
originar v. originate
ornamentação n. ornamentation
ornamentado adj. ornate

ornamental *adj.* ornamental

ornamento *n.* ornament

orquestra *n.* orchestra

orquestral *adj.* orchestral

orquídea *n.* orchid

ortodoxia *n.* orthodoxy

ortodoxo *adj.* orthodox

ortopedia *n.* orthopaedics

orvalho *n.* dew

os, as, *pron.* them

oscilação *n.* oscillation

oscilar *v.* oscillate

ossificar *v.* ossify

osso *n.* bone

ostensivo *adj.* ostensible

ostentação *n.* ostentation

ostentado *adj.* vaunted

ostentar *v.* swank

osteopatia *n.* osteopathy

ostra *n.* oyster

ostracizar *v.* ostracize

ótico *adj.* optic

otimismo *n.* optimism

otimista *n.& adj.* optimist & optimistic

otimizar *v.* optimize

ótimo *adj.* optimum

ou *conj.* or

ou melhor *adv.* nay

ourela *n.* selvedge

ourives *n.* goldsmith

ouro *n.* gold

ouropel *n.* tinsel

ousadia *n.* boldness

ousado *adj.* daring

ousar *v.* dare

outeiro *n.* hillock

outono *n.* autumn

outorgar *v.* bestow

outra vez *adv.* afresh

outro *adj. & adv.* another & else

outro *adj. & pron.* other

outrora *adj.& n.* erstwhile & yore

Outubro *n.* October

ouvido *n.* ear

ouvinte *n.* listener

ouvir *v.* listen

ouvir por *v.* overhear

ovação *n.* ovation

ovadas *adj.* ovate

oval *adj.* oval

ovário *n.* ovary

ovelha *n.* sheep

overdose *n.* overdose

overdrive *n.* overdrive

ovo *n.* egg

ovular *v.* ovulate

óxido *n.* oxide

oxigénio *n.* oxygen

ozónio n ozone

pá *n.* shovel

pacemaker *n.* pacemaker

paciência *n.* patience

paciente *adj.& n.* patient

pacificar *v.* pacify

pacífico *n. & adj.* pacific & peaceful

pacifista *n.* pacifist

pacote *n.* pack

pacto *n.* pact

padaria *n.* bakery

padeiro *n.* baker

padrão *n.* pattern

padre *n.* priest

padrinho *n.* godfather

pagamento *n.* payment

pagão *n.* pagan

pagar *v.* pay

pagável *n.* payable

página *n.* page

pagode *n.* pagoda

pai *n.* father

painço *n.* millet

painel *n.* panel

painél instrumentos *n.* dashboard

paiol *n.* bunker

pairar *v.* hover

país *n.* country

paisagem *n.* landscape

paixão *n.* passion

palácio *n.* palace

paladar *n.* palate

palatal *adj.* palatal

palavra *n.* word

palavra de honra *n.* parole

palavreado *n.* verbiage

palavroso *adj.* wordy

palestra *n.* lecture

paleta *n.* palette

palete *n.* pallet

palha *n.* straw

palhaço *n.* clown

paliçada *n.* paling

pálido *adj.* pale

palito *n.* toothpick

palma *n.* palm

palmada *n.* spat

palmo *n.* span

palpável *adj.* palpable

palpitação *n.* palpitation

palpitar *v.* palpitate

palrar *v.t.* gabble

panaceia *n.* panacea

pança *n.* paunch

pâncreas *n.* pancreas

panda *n.* panda

pandeireta *n.* tambourine

pandemónio *n.* pandemonium

panegírico *n.* panegyric

panela *n.* pan

panela de barro *n.* crook

panfletista *n.* pamphleteer

panfleto *n.* pamphlet

pagaia *n.* paddle

pânico *n.* panic

pano *n.* cloth

pano de fundo *n.* backdrop

panorama *n.* panorama

panqueca *n.* pancake

pântano *n.* swamp

panteísmo *n.* pantheism

panteísta *adj.* pantheist

pantera *n.* panther

pantomima *n.* pantomime

pão *n.* bread

pão de forma *n.* bun

papa *n.* pope
papa de aveia *n.* gruel
papado *n.* papacy
papagaio *n.* parrot
papal *adj.* papal
papas *n.* mush
papeira *n.* mumps
papel *n.* paper
par *n.* pair
para *prep.* towards
para baixo *adv.* down
para cima *adv.* upward
para lá *adv.* thither
para o exterior *adj.* outboard
para oeste *adv.* westerly
para onde *adv.* whither
para que não *conj.* lest
para sempre *adv.* forever
parabéns *n.* congratulation
parábola *n.* parable
pára-choques *n.* bumper
paradoxal *adj.* paradoxical
paradoxo *n.* paradox
parafernália *n.* paraphernalia
parafina *n.* paraffin
parafrasear *v.* paraphrase
parafuso *n.* screw
parágrafo *n.* paragraph
paraíso *n.* paradise
paralelo *n.* parallel
paralelograma *n.* parallelogram
paralisar *v.* paralyse
paralisia *n.* paralysis
paralítico *adj.* paralytic

paramédico *n.* paramedic
parâmetro *n.* parameter
parapeito *n.* sill
paraquedas *n.* parachute
paraquedista *n.* parachutist
parar *v.* stop
parasita *n.* parasite
parceiro *n.* partner
parcela *n.* parcel
parceria *n.* partnership
parcial *adj.* partial
parcialidade *n.* partiality
parcialmente *adv.* partly
parcimónia *n.* parsimony
parco *adj.* skimp
pardal *n.* sparrow
parecer *v.* seem
paredão *n.* pier
parede *n.* wall
parental *adj.* parental
parente *n. & adj.* parent & relative
parentes *n.* kin
parentesco *n.* parentage
parênteses *n.* parenthesis
pargo (peixe) *n.* snapper
pária *n.* pariah
paridade *n.* par
paridade *n.* parity
parlamentar *n.* parley
parlamentar *adj.* parliamentary
parlamento *n.* parliament
paródia *n.* parody
paróquia *n.* parish
paroquial *adj.* parochial

parque *n.* park

parricídio *n.* parricide

parte *n.* part

parteira *n.* midwife

participação *n.* participation

participação obrigatória *adj.* notfiable

participante *n.* participant

participar *v.* participate

partícula *n.* particle

partida *n.* departure

partidário *n.* partisan

partir *v.* depart

parvo *n.* geek

Páscoa *n.* Easter

pasmar *v.* gaze

passa de uva *n.* raisin

passadeira *n.* zebra crossing

passadiço *n.* gangway

passado *adj.* past

passageiro *n.* passenger

passagem *n.* passage

passagem elevada *n.* overpass

passagem inferior *n.* underpass

passante *adj.* passing

passaporte *n.* passport

passar *v.* pass

pássaro *n.* bird

passatempo *n.* pastime

passável *adj.* passable

passear *v.* saunter

passeata *n.* jaunt

passeio *n.* outing

passeio público *n.* promenade

passiva *adj.* passive

passível *adj.* liable

passo *n.* step

pasta *n.* paste

pastel *n.* pastel

pastelaria *n.* pastry

pastel-dos-tintureiros (flor) *n.* woad

pasteurizado *adj.* pasteurized

pastilha *n.* gum

pasto *n.* pasture

pastor *n.* shepherd

pastoral *adj.* pastoral

pastoso *n.* pasty

pata *n.* paw

patente *n.* patent

paternal *adj.* paternal

paternidade *n.* paternity

pateta *n.* slob

patético *adj.& n.* pathetic & pathos

paticídio *n.* patricide

patife *n.* rascal

patim *n.* skate

patinhar *v.* wade

pátio *n.* patio

pato *n.* duck

patologia *n.* pathology

patrão *n.* compere

patriarca *n.* patriarch

património *n.* patrimony

patriota *n.* patriot

patriótico *adj.* patriotic

patriotismo *n.* patriotism

patrocinador *n.* sponsor

patrocínio *n.* patronage

patrocínio *n.* sponsorship

patrulha *v.* patrol	**pedregoso** *adj.* stony
pau *n.* stick	**pedregulho** *n.* boulder
pausa *n.* pause	**pedreira** *n.* quarry
pauzinho *n.* chopstick	**pedreiro** *n.* mason
pavão *n.* peacock	**pega** *n.* magpie
pavilhão *n.* pavilion	**pegajoso** *adj.* sticky
pavimentar *v.* pave	**peito** *n.* breast
pavimento *n.* storey	**peixe** *n.* fish
pavio *n.* wick	**pejorativo** *adj.* pejorative
pavoa *n.* peahen	**pela borda fora** *adv.* overboard
pavor *v.t* dread	**pele** *n.* skin
pavoroso *adj.* awesome	**pelicano** *n.* pelican
paz *n.* peace	**pêlos** *n.* bristle
pé *n.* foot	**pelotão** *n.* platoon
peão *n.* pawn	**pelúcia** *n.* plush
peça *n.* piece	**peludo** *adj.* hairy
pecado *n.* sin	**pélvis** *n.* pelvis
pecador *adj.& n.* sinful & sinner	**pena** *n.* feather
pechincha *n.* bargain	**penacho** *n.* panache
pechinchar *v. t.* cheapen	**penal** *adj.* penal
peculiar *adj.* peculiar	**penalizar** *v.* penalize
pedaço *n.* lump	**pensando bem** *prep.* considering
pedagogia *n.* pedagogy	**pendente** *adj.* pending
pedagogo *n.* pedagogue	**pêndulo** *n.* pendulum
pedal *n.* pedal	**pendurar** *v.i.* hang
pedante *n. & adj.* pedant & pedantic	**peneira** *n.* sieve
pedestal *n.* pedestal	**peneirar** *v.* sift
pedestre *n.* pedestrian	**penetração** *n.* penetration
pediatra *n.* paediatrician	**penetrar** *v.* penetrate
pedicure *n.* pedicure	**penhasco** *n.* cliff
pedido *n.* request	**penhor** *n.* lien
pedófilo *n.* paedophile	**penhorista** *n.* pawnbroker
pedómetro *n.* pedometer	**península** *n.* peninsula
pedra *n.* stone	**pénis** *n.* penis

penitência *n.* penance

penitente *adj.* penitent

penoso *adj.* laborious

pensador *n.* thinker

pensão *n.* pension

pensar *v.* think

pensativo *adj.* thoughtful

pensionista *n.* pensioner

pentágono *n.* pentagon

pente *n.* comb

penteado *n.* hairstyle

penthouse *n.* penthouse

penúltimo *adj.* penultimate

pepino *n.* cucumber

pepita *n.* nugget

péptico *adj.* peptic

pequena mala viagem *n.* valise

pequeno *adj.* small

pequeno proprietário *n.* yeoman

pequeno-almoço *n.* breakfast

peq-almoço reforçado *n.* brunch

pera *n.* pear

perambular *v.t.* perambulate

perceber *v.* realize

percentagem *n.* percentage

percepção *n.* perception

perceptível *adj.* perceptible

perceptivo *adj.* perceptive

perda *n.* loss

perdão *n.* pardon

perder *v.* miss

perdição *n.* perdition

perdoar *v.* forgive

perdoável *adj.* pardonable

perdulário *n.* spendthrift

perecer *v.* perish

perecível *adj.* perishable

peregrinação *n.* pilgrimage

peregrino *n.* pilgrim

perene *adj.* perennial

perfeição *n.* perfection

perfeito *adj.* perfect

pérfida *adj.* perfidious

perfil *n.* profile

perfumado *adj.* fragrant

perfume *n.&* adv perfume

perfurar *v.* perforate

pergunta *n.* query

perguntar *v.* ask

perícia *n.* expertise

periferia *n.* periphery

perigar *v.* imperil

perigo *n.* danger

perigoso *adj.* dangerous

perímetro *n.* girth

periódico *adj.* periodic

período *n.* period

perjúrio *n.* perjury

permanecer *v.* remain

permanência *n.* permanence

permanente *adj.* permanent

permeável *adj.* permeable

permissão *n.* permission

permissível *adj.* permissible

permissivo *adj.* permissive

permitir *v.* allow

permutação *n.* permutation

permutar *v.* interchange

perna *n.* leg

perna dianteira *n.* foreleg

perneiras *n.* leggings

pernicioso *adj.* pernicious

pernil *n.* haunch

pernilongo *n.* stilt

pérola *n.* pearl

perpendicular *adj.* perpendicular

perpetrar *v.* perpetrate

perpetuar *v.t.* perpetuate

perpétuo *adj.* perpetual

perplexidade *n.* perplexity

perplexo *adj.* nonplussed

Perry *n.* Perry

perscrutar *v.* peer

perseguição *n.* persecution

perseguidor *n.* stalker

perseguir *v.* pursue

perseverança *n.* perseverance

perseverar *v.i.* persevere

persiana *n.* shutter

persistência *n.* persistence

persistente *adj.* persistent

persistir *v.* persist

personagem *n.* personage

personalidade *n.* personality

personalizado *n.* custom

personalizar *v.* customize

personificação *n.* personification

personificar *v.* personify

perspetiva *n.* perspective

perspicácia *n.* keenness

perspicaz *adj.* acute

persuadir *v.* persuade

persuasão *n.* persuasion

pertencer *v.* belong

pertences *n.* belongings

pertinente *adj.* pertinent

perto *adv.* near

perto daqui *adv.* hereabouts

perturbação *n.* upheaval

perturbador *adj.* troublesome

perturbar *v.* disturb

peru *n.* turkey

peruca *n.* wig

perversão *n.* perversion

perversidade *n.* perversity

perverso *adj.* perverse

perverter *v.* pervert

pesadelo *n.* nightmare

pesado *adj.* weighty

pesar *v.* weigh

pesaroso *adj.* sorry

pesca *n.* fishery

pesca à baleia *n.* whaling

pesca à rede *n.* netting

pescador *n.* fisherman

pescoço *n.* neck

peso *n.* weight

peso troy *n.* troy

pesquisa *n.* research

pêssego *n.* peach

pessimismo *n.* pessimism

pessimista *n.* pessimist

pessimista *adj.* pessimistic

pessoa *n.* person

pessoa ausente *n.* absentee

pessoa fraca *n.* weakling

pessoal *adj.& n.* personal & personnel
pessoal *n.* personnel
pessoas *n.* people
pestanejar *v.* blink
peste *n.* pestilence
pesticida *n.* pesticide
pétala *n.* petal
petição *n.* petition
peticionário *n.* petitioner
petrificar *v.* petrify
petroleiro *n.* tanker
petróleo *n.* petroleum
petulância *n.* petulance
petulante *adj.* petulant
peúga *n.* anklet
peva *n.* zilch
piada *n.* joke
pianista *n.* pianist
piano *n.* piano
piar *v.* peep
picada *n.* sting
picadeiro *n.* lunge
picante *adj.* spicy
picar *v.* prick
pico *n.* peak
pico rochoso *n.* tor
pictograma *n.* pictograph
pictórico *adj.* pictorial
picuinhas *n.* stickler
piedade *n.* piety
piedoso *adj.* pious
pigmento *n.* pigment
pigmeu *n.* pigmy
pijama *n.* pyjamas

pilar *n.* pillar
pilha *n.* stack
pilhagem *n.* loot
pilhar *v.* ransack
piloto *n.* pilot
pílula *n.* pill
pimenta *n.* pepper
pimenta-caiena *n.* chilli
pimento *n.* capsicum
pináculo *n.* spire
pinça *n.* pincer
pinça *n.* tweezers
pingente *n.* pendant
pinguim *n.* penguin
pinho *v.* pine
pinote *n.* buck
pinotear *v.* cavort
pintar *n.* paint
pintor *n.* painter
pintura *n.* painting
pio *n.* cheep
piolhento *adj.* lousy
piolho *n.* louse
pioneiro *n.* pioneer
pior *adj.* worse
piorar *v.* worsen
piorreia *n.* pyorrhoea
pipa *n.* kite
pipeta *n.* pipette
pique *n.* pike
piquenique *n.* picnic
piquete *n.* picket
pira funerária *n.* pyre
pirâmide *n.* pyramid

pirata *n.* pirate	**platónico** *adj.* platonic
pirataria *n.* piracy	**plausível** *adj.* plausible
piratear *v.* hack	**plebeu** *n.* commoner
pires *n.* saucer	**plebeu** *adj.* plebeian
piromania *n.* pyromania	**plebiscito** *n.* plebiscite
pisar *v.* trample	**pletora** *n.* plethora
piscar *v.* twinkle	**plinto** *n.* plinth
piscar os olhos *v.* wink	**pluma** *n.* plume
piscina *n.* pool	**plumagem** *n.* plumage
piso *n.* floor	**plúmbeo** *adj.* leaden
pista *n.* clue	**plural** *adj.* plural
pista de gelo *n.* rink	**pluralidade** *n.* plurality
pistão *n.* piston	**pneu** *n.* tyre
pistola *n.* pistol	**pneumático** *adj.* pneumatic
pitada *n.* smidgen	**pneumonia** *n.* pneumonia
píton python	**pó** *n.* dust
pitoresco *adj.* picturesque	**pobre** *adj.* poor
pivete *n.* chit	**pobremente** *adv.* poorly
pixel *n.* pixel	**pobreza** *n.* poverty
pizza *n.* pizza	**pocilga** *n.* piggery
placa *n.* plaque	**poço** *n.* well
plácido *adj.* placid	**podar** *v.* lop
planador *n.* glider	**podcast** *n.* podcast
planalto *n.* plateau	**poder** *v.* may
planar *v.i.* soar	**poder** *n.* power
planeta *n.* planet	**poderoso** *adj.* mighty
planetário *adj.* planetary	**pódio** *n.* podium
plano *adj.& n.* flat & plan	**podre** *adj.* rotten
planta *n.* plant	**poema** *n.* poem
plantação *n.* plantation	**poesia** *n.* poetry
plaqueta *n.* platelet	**poeta** *n.* poet
plástico *n.* plastic	**poker** *n.* poker
plataforma *n.* platform	**polar** *adj.* polar
platina *n.* platinum	**polegada** *n.* inch

polegar *n.* thumb

poleiro *n.* roost

polémica *n.* polemic

pólen *n.* pollen

polia *n.* pulley

poliandria *n.* polyandry

polícia *n.* police

policial *n.* constable

polidez *n.* politeness

polido *adj.* courtly

poligamia *n.* polygamy

polígamo *adj.* polygamous

poliglota *adj.* polyglot

polígrafo *n.* polygraph

polimento *n.* polish

politécnico *n.* polytechnic

politeísmo *n.* polytheism

politeísta *adj.* polytheistic

política *n.* politics

político *adj.& n.* politic & politician

pólo *n.* pole

polpa *n.* pulp

poluição *n.* pollution

poluir *v.* pollute

polvo *n.* octopus

pomada *n.* ointment

pomar *n.* orchard

pombo *n.* pigeon

pompa *n.* pomp

pompom *n.* bobble

pomposidade *n.* pomposity

pomposo *adj.* pompous

ponderar *v.* ponder

pónei *n.* pony

ponta *n.* tip

ponta de lança *n.* spearhead

pontada *n.* twinge

ponte *n.* bridge

pontiagudo *adj.* spiky

pontífice *n.* pontiff

ponto *n.* point

ponto crucial *n.* crux

ponto de vista *n.* standpoint

ponto e vírgula (;) *n.* semicolon

pontuação *n.* punctuation

pontual *adj.* punctual

pontualidade *n.* punctuality

pontuar *v.* score

pop *v.* pop

popelina *n.* poplin

população *n.* population

popular *adj.* popular

popularidade *n.* popularity

popularizar *v.* popularize

populoso *adj.* populous

por *prep.* per

pôr *v.* set

por algum tempo *adv.* awhile

por este meio *adv.* hereby

por favor *v.* please

por intermédio *n.* by-election

por isso *adv.* hence

por onde *adv.* whereabouts

por que *adv.* why

por si mesmo *adj.* self-made

por todo *prep.* throughout

porca *n.* sow

porcelana *n.* porcelain

porco n. pig

porco-espinho n. porcupine

porém adv. however

pormenor n. detail

pornografia n. pornography

poro n. pore

porque conj. because

porta n. door

portador n. carrier

portagem n. toll

portal n. portal

portão n. gate

portaria n. ordinance

portar-se mal v. misbehave

portátil adj. portable

porta-voz n. spokesman

porteiro n. porter

pórtico n. portico

porto n. port

pose v. pose

posfácio n. postscript

pós-graduado n. postgraduate

posição n. position

positivo adj. positive

possante adj. stentorian

posse n. possession

possessivo adj. possessive

possesso de fúria adv. amok

possibilidade n. possibility

possível adj. possible

possuir v. possess

postal adj.& n. postal & postcard

poster n. poster

posteridade n. posterity

posterior adj. posterior

postigo n. wicket

posto avançado (militar) n. outpost

póstumo adj. posthumous

postura n. posture

pote n. pot

potência n. potency

potencial adj. potential

potencialidade n. potentiality

potente adj. potent

pouco adj. little

pouco auspicioso adj. inauspicious

poucos adj. few

poupado adj. sparing

poupança n. savings

poupar v. indulge

pousada n. inn

pousar v.t. alight

povo n. folk

povoar v. populate

praça n. plaza

prado n. meadow

praga n. plague

pragmático adj. pragmatic

pragmatismo n. pragmatism

praia n. beach

pralina n. praline

prancha n. plank

pranto n. wail

prata n. silver

prateleira n. shelf

prateleira do fogão n. mantel

prática n. practice

praticabilidade n. practicability

praticar v. practise

praticável adj. practicable

prático adj. practical

prato n. dish

prazer n. pleasure

prazo n. term

prazo de entrega n. deadline

preâmbulo n. preamble

precário adj. precarious

precaução n. precaution

precaucionário adj. precautionary

precedência n. precedence

precedente n. precedent

preceder v. precede

preceito n. precept

precioso adj. precious

precipitado adj. rash

precipitar v. precipitate

precisão n. precision

preciso adj. precise

preço n. price

precursor n. precursor

predador n. predator

pré-datar v. backdate

predestinação n. predestination

predeterminar v. predetermine

predicado n. predicate

predicamento n. predicament

predição n. prediction

predizer v. foretell

predizer v. predict

predominante adj. predominant

predominar v. predominate

predomínio n. predominance

preeminência n. pre-eminence

preeminente adj. pre-eminent

preencher v. fill

pré-fabricadas adj. prefabricated

prefácio n. preface

prefeito n. prefect

preferência n. preference

preferencial adj. preferential

preferir v. prefer

prefixo n. prefix

prega n. pleat

pregar v. sermonize

prego n. spike

preguiça n. sloth

preguiçar v. laze

preguiçoso adj. lazy

preguiçoso n. sluggard

pré-histórico adj. prehistoric

prejudicar v. impair

prejudicial adj. prejudicial

prejuízo n. prejudice

pré-julgar v. prejudge

prelado n. prelate

preliminar adj. preliminary

preliminares n. foreplay

prelúdio n. prelude

prematuro adj. premature

premeditação n. premeditation

premeditar v. premeditate

premiar v. award

prémio n. prize

premissa n. premise

premissa n. premises

prender v. arrest

prenome *n.* forename
pré-nupcial *adj.* premarital
preocupação *n.* preoccupation
preocupado *adj.* worried
preocupar *v.* worry
preparação *n.* preparation
preparado p/ combate *adj.* embattled
preparar *v.* prepare
preparatória *adj.* preparatory
preponderância *n.* preponderance
preponderar *v.* preponderate
preposição *n.* preposition
pré-requisito *n.* prerequisite
prerrogativa *n.* prerogative
presa *n.* prey
presa (dente) *n.* tusk
presciência *n.* prescience
prescindir *v.* waive
prescrever *v.* prescribe
prescrição *n.* prescription
presença *n.* presence
presente *adj.& n.* present
preservação *n.* preservation
preservar *v.* preserve
preservativo *n.* condom
presidencial *adj.* presidential
presidente *n.* president
Presidente da Câmara *n.* mayor
presidir *v.* preside
presságio *n.* omen
presságio *v.* presage
pressão *n.* pressure
pressentimento *n.* premonition
pressionar *v.t.* stress

pressupor *v.* presuppose
pressuposto *n.* presupposition
pressurizar *v.* pressurize
prestação *n.* instalment
prestar atenção *v.* heed
prestidigitação *n.* sleight
prestígio *n.* prestige
prestigioso *adj.* prestigious
presumir *v.* presume
presunção *n.* presumption
presunçoso *adj.* smug
presunto *n.* ham
preta *n.* negress
pretencioso *v.* swanky
pretender *v.* intend
pretensão *n.* pretension
pretensioso *adj.* pretentious
pretexto *n.* pretext
preto *n.* nigger
prevalecer *v.* prevail
prevenção *n.* prevention
prevenir *v.* forestall
preventivo *adj.* preventive
prever *v.* foresee
previdência *n.* foresight
prévio *adj.* prior
previsão *n.* foreknowledge
primário *adj.* primary
primata *n.* primate
primazia *n.* primacy
primeiro *adj.* prime
primeiros socorros *n.* first aid
primitivo *adj.* primitive
primo *n.* cousin

princesa n. princess

principal adj.& n. principal

primeiro adj. & n. first

principalmente adv. primarily

príncipe n. prince

princípesco adj. princely

princípio n. principle

priorado n. priory

prioridade n. priority

prisão n. jail

prisioneiro n. prisoner

prisma n. prism

privação n. privation

privacidade n. privacy

privado adj. private

privar v. deprive

privar-se v.t. refrain

privatizar v. privatize

privilégio n. privilege

pró n. pro

proativa adj. proactive

probabilidade n. likelihood

problema n. problem

problemático adj. problematic

procedimento n. procedure

processar v.t. sue

processo n. process

procissão n. procession

proclamação n. proclamation

proclamar v. proclaim

procriar v. procreate

procura n. demand

procuração n. proxy

procurar v. search

prodígio n. prodigy

prodigioso adj. prodigious

pródigo adj. prodigal

produção n. production

produtividade n. productivity

produtivo adj. productive

produto n. product

produtor n. producer

produzir v. produce

proeminência n. prominence

proeminente adj. prominent

proeza n. prowess

profano adj. profane

profecia n. prophecy

professar v. profess

professor n. teacher

profeta n. prophet

profético adj. prophetic

profetizar v. prophesy

proficiência n. proficiency

proficiente adj. proficient

profissão n. profession

profissional n. practitioner

profissional adj. profissional

profundidade n. depth

profundo adj. deep

profusão n. profusion

profuso adj. profuse

prognosticar v. prognosticate

prognóstico n. prognosis

programa n. programme

programa de estudos n. syllabus

progressivo adj. progressive

progressivo n progress

proibição n. prohibition
proibir v. forbid
proibitivo adj. prohibitive
projeção n. projection
projétil n. projectile
projeto n. project
projetor n. projector
prolapso n. prolapse
prole n. offspring
proliferação n. proliferation
proliferar v. proliferate
prolífico adj. prolific
prólogo n. prologue
prolongado adj. protracted
prolongamento n. prolongation
prolongar v. prolong
promessa n. promise
promíscuo adj. promiscuous
promissor adj. promising
promoção n. promotion
promotor n. prosecutor
promover v. promote
promulgar v. promulgate
pronome n. pronoun
prontamente adv. readily
pronto adj. ready
pronúncia n. pronunciation
pronunciar v. pronounce
propagação n. propagation
propaganda n. propaganda
propagar v. propagate
propensão n. proclivity
propiciar v. propitiate
propor v. propose

proporção n. proportion
proporcionado adj. proportionate
proporcional adj. proportional
proporcionar v.t. afford
proposição n. proposition
propósito n. purpose
proposta n. proposal
propriedade n. propriety
proprietário n. owner
proprietário adj. propritary
proprietário adj. proprietary
proprietário papelaria n. stationer
próprio adj. own
próprio para venda adj. saleable
prorrogar v. prorogue
prosa n. prose
prosaico adj. prosaic
prospecto n. prospectus
prosperar v. prosper
prosperidade n. prosperity
próspero adj. prosperous
prosseguir v. continue
próstata n. prostate
prostituição n. prostitution
prostituta n. whore
prostração n. prostration
prostrado adj. prostrate
protagonista n. protagonist
proteburância n. bulge
proteção n. protection
proteção militar n. muniment
proteger v. protect
protegido adj. secure
proteína n. protein

protestar v. remonstrate

protesto n. protest

protetor adj.& n. protective & patron

protetorado n. protectorate

protocolo n. protocol

protótipo n. prototype

prova n. proof

provação n. probation

provar v. prove

provável adj. likely

provavelmente adv. probably

provedor n. trustee

proveniência n. provenance

proverbial adj. proverbial

provérbio n. proverb

proveta n. beaker

providência n. providence

providencial adj. providential

providente adj. provident

província n. province

provincial adj. provincial

provisão n. provision

provisório adj. provisional

provocação n. provocation

provocador naufrágios n. wrecker

provocante adj. provocative

provocar v. provoke

proximidade n. proximity

próximo adj. close

prudência n. prudence

prudencial adj. prudential

prudente adj. cautious

prurido n. tingle

pseudo adj. pseudo

pseudónimo n. pseudonym

psicologia n. psychology

psicológico adj. psychological

psicólogo n. psychologist

psicopata n. psychopath

psicose n. psychosis

psicoterapia n. psychotherapy

psique n. psyche

psiquiatra n. psychiatrist

psiquiatria n. psychiatry

psíquico adj. psychic

pua n. wimble

pub n. pub

puberdade n. puberty

púbico adj. pubic

publicação n. publication

publicar v. publish

publicidade n. publicity

público adj. public

pudim n. pudding

pueril adj. puerile

puff n. hassock

pugilista n. boxer

puído adj. seedy

pular v. skip

pulga n. flea

pulmão n. lung

pulôver n. pullover

púlpito n. pulpit

pulsação n. pulsation

pulsar v. pulsate

pulseira n. bracelet

pulso n. wrist

punção n. puncture

pungência *n.* pungency

pungente *adj.* pungent

punhado *n.* bunch

punhal *n.* stiletto

punho *n.* fist

punição *n.* punishment

punir *v.* punish

punitivo *adj.* punitive

pureza *n.* purity

purga *v.* purge

purgação *n.* purgation

purgante *adj.* purgative

purgatório *n.* purgatory

purificação *n.* purification

purificar *v.* purify

purista *n.* purist

puritana *n.* prude

puritana *adj.* puritanical

puritano *n.* puritan

puro *adj.* pure

pus *n.* pus

pústula *n.* blain

putativo *adj.* putative

puto *n.* lad

pútrido *adj.* putrid

puxar *v.* pull

puzzle *n.* jigsaw

Quacre *n.* Quaker

quádruplo *adj.* quadruple

quadrado *n.* square

quadrangular *n.* quadrangular

quadrângulo *n.* quad

quadrante *n.* quadrant

quadrilátero *a.* quadrangle

quadrilha *n.* gang

quadro *n.* tableau

quadro (de lousa) *n.* blackboard

quadro de notícias *n.* noticeboard

quadrúpede *n.* quadruped

quádrupla *n.* quadruplet

qualidade *n.* quality

qualificação *n.* qualification

qualificar *v.* qualify

qualitativo *adj.* qualitative

qualquer *adj.* any

qualquer um *pron.* anyone

quando *adv.* when

quango *n.* quango

quantia *n.* amount

quantidade *n.* quantity

quantificar *v.* quantify

quantitativo *adj.* quantitative

quanto *adv.* the

quarenta *adj.& n.* forty

quarentena *n.* quarantine

quark *n.* quark

Quarta-feira *n.* Wednesday

quartel *n.* barrack

quarteto *n.* quartet

quartilho *n.* pint

quarto *adj.& n.* fourth

quartzo *n.* quartz

quase *adv.* almost

quatro *adj.& n.* four

que *pron.* who

que deixou *adj.* testate

que ressurge *adj.* resurgent

que vale a pena *adj.* worthwhile

quebradiço *adj.* crisp

quebrado *adj.* broke

quebrar *v.* break

queda *n.* downfall

queijo *n.* cheese

queimador *n.* burner

queimar *v.* burn

queixa *n.* complaint

queixar *v.* whinge

queixinhas *adj.* telltale

queixo *n.* chin

queixoso *n.* plaintiff

quem *pron.* whom

quem colhe *n.* harvester

quem quer que *pron.* whoever

quente *adj.* hot

queque *n.* muffin

querer *v.* want

querida *n.* darling

querido *adj.& n.* dear & sweet

querosene *n.* kerosene

questão *n.* issue

questionário *n.* questionnaire

questionável *adj.* questionable

quiescente *adj.* quiescent

quietetude *n.* quietetude

quilate *n.* carat

quilha *n.* keel

quilo *n.* kilo

quilometragem *n.* mileage

quilómetro *n.* kilometre

química *n.* chemistry

químico *adj.& n.* chemical & chemist

quimioterapia *n.* chemotherapy

quimono *n.* kimono

quinina *n.* quinine

Quinn *n.* Quinn

quinta-essência *n.* quintessence

quinta-feira *n.* Thursday

quintal *n.* yard

quintilha humorística *n.* limerick

quinze *adj.& n.* fifteen

quinzena *n.* fortnight

quiromante *n.* palmist

quiromantia *n.* palmistry

quisto sebáceo *n.* wen

quite *adj.* quits

quixotesco *adj.* quixotic

quociente *n.* quotient

quorum *n.* quorum

quota *n.* quota

R

rabanete *n.* radish

rabeca *n.* fiddle

rabiscar *v.* scrabble

rabugento *adj.* pettish

ração *n.* ration

rachar *n.* crack

racial *adj.* racial

racional *adj.* rational

racionalismo *n.* rationalism

racionalizar *v.* rationalize

racismo *n.* racialism

radar *n.* radar

radiação *n.* radiation

radial *adj.* radial

radiante *adj.* radiant

radical *adj.* radical

rádio *n.* radio

radioativo *adj.* radioactive

radiografia *n.* x-ray

radiologia *n.* radiology

raiado *adj.* streaky

rainha *n.* queen

raio *n.* radius

raiva *n.* rage

raiz *n.* root

raiz de beterraba *n.* beetroot

rajada *n.* gust

ralador *n.* grater

ralar *v.t* grate

ramificação *n.* ramification

ramificar *v.* ramify

raminho *n.* sprig

ramo (de negócios) *n.* branch

ramo (flores) *n.* bouquet

rampa *n.* ramp

rancho *n.* ranch

rancor *n.* rancour

rancoroso *adj.* spiteful

rançoso *adj.* rancid

ranger *v.* creak

rangido *n.* creak

ranhura *n.* slot

ranzinza *adj.* surly

rapaz *n.* boy

rapaziada *n.* jig

rapidamente *adv.* quickly

rapidez *n.* rapidity

rápido *adj.* fast

raposa *n.* fox

rapsódia *n.* rhapsody

raptar *v.* kidnap

rapto *n.* abduction

raquete *n.* racket

raquitismo *n.* rickets

raramente *adv.* seldom

raro *adj.* scarce

rascunho *n.* draft

rasgar *v.* rip

raso *adj.* shallow

raspar *v.* scrape

rastejar *v.* crawl

rasto *n.* track

rastreável *adj.* traceable

ratificar *v.* ratify

rato *n.* mouse

ravina *n.* ravine

razão *n.* reason

razoável *adj.* reasonable

reabastecer *v.* refill

reabilitação *n.* rehabilitation

reabilitar *v.* rehabilitate

reação *n.* reaction

reacionário *adj.* reactionary

reafirmar *v.* reaffirm

reagir *v.* react

reajustar *v.* readjust

real *adj.& n.* real & royal

realçar *v.* highlight

realce *n.* underling

realeza *n.* royalty

realidade *n.* reality

realismo *n.* realism

realista *adj.& n.* realistic & royalist

realização *n.* realization

realizar *v.* perform

realmente *adv.* really

reaparação *n.* atonement

reaparecer *v.* reappear

rearranjar *v.* rearrange

reassegurar *v.* reassure

reator *n.* reactor

reavaliação *n.* reappraisal

reavaliar *v.* reassess

reaver *v.* recover

rebaixar *v.* debase

rebanho *n.* flock

rebelar *v.* rebel

rebelde *adj.* rebellious

rebelião *n.* rebellion

rebitar *v.* clinch

rebite *n.* rivet

rebobinar *v.* rewind

rebocar *v.* tug

recanto *n.* nook

recapitular *v.* recap

recapturar *v.* recapture

recarregar *v.* recharge

recatado *adj.* coy

recauchutar *v.* retread

recebedor *n.* receiver

receber *v.* receive

recebimento *n.* receipt

receção *n.* reception

rececionista *n.* receptionist

receita *n.* recipe

receitas (dinheiro) *n.* proceeds

recente *adj.* recent

recentemente *adv.* recently

receoso *adj.* afraid

recessão *n.* recession

recetáculo *n.* receptacle

recetivo *adj.* receptive

reciclar *v.* recycle

recife *n.* reef

recinto *n.* precinct

recíproco *adj.* reciprocal

recital *n.* recital

recitar *v.* recite

reclamante *n.* claimant

reclinado *adj.* recumbent

reclinar *v.* recline

reclusão *n.* confinement

recluso *n.* recluse

recomeço *n.* resumption

recomendação *n.* recommendation

recomendar *v.* recommend

recompensa *n.* reward

recompensar *v.* recompense

reconciliação *n.* reconciliation

reconciliar *v.* reconcile

recondicionar *v.* recondition

reconhecer *v.i.* recognize

reconhecido *adj.* beholden

reconhecimento *n.* recognition

reconsiderar *v.* reconsider

reconstruir *v.* reconstruct

recordação *n.* recollection

recordar *v.* recall

recordativo *adj.* reminiscent

recorrente *adj.* recurrent
recorrer *v.* betake
recortar *v.* indent
recorte *n.* indenture
recreação *n.* recreation
recrear *v.* recreate
recreio *n.* playground
recriminação *n.* recrimination
recrutar *v.* recruit
recuar *v.* recede
recuperação *n.* recovery
recuperar *v.* recuperate
recurso *n.* recourse
recusa *n.* refusal
recusar *v.* refuse
redação *n.* wording
rede *n.* net
rede de esgotos *n.* sewerage
rédea *n.* rein
redenção *n.* redemption
redimir *v.* redeem
redobrar *v.* redouble
redondamente *adv.* roundly
redondo *adj.* round
redução *n.* reduction
redundância *n.* redundancy
redundante *adj.* redundant
reduzir *v.* reduce
reembolsar *v.* refund
reembolso *n.* repayment
reencarnar *v.* reincarnate
refeição *n.* meal
refém *n.* hostage
referência *n.* reference

referendo *n.* referendum
referir *v.* refer
refinação *n.* refinement
refinar *v.* refine
refinaria *n.* refinery
refletir *v.* reflect
reflexão *n.* reflection
reflexivo *adj.* reflexive
reflexo *adj.& n.* reflective & reflex
reflexologia *n.* reflexology
reforçar *v.* reinforce
reforço *n.* reinforcement
reforma *n.* reformation
reformador *n.* reformer
reformar *v.* reform
refração *n.* refraction
refrear *v. t* curb
refrescar *v.* refresh
refresco *n.* refreshment
refrigeração *n.* refrigeration
refrigerador *n.* cooler
refrigerante *n.* coolant
refrigerar *v.* refrigerate
refugiado *n.* refugee
refúgio *n.* haven
refúgio *n.* refuge
refulgente *adj.* refulgent
refutação *n.* refutation
refutar *v.* refute
regabofe *v.* guzzle
regalia *n.* perquisite
regato *n.* rivulet
regeneração *n.* regeneration
regenerar *v.* regenerate

regente *n.* regent

reggae *n.* reggae

região *n.* region

regicídio *n.* regicide

regime *n.* regime

regimento *n.* regiment

regional *adj.* regional

registo *n.* record

registro *n.* ledger

regozijar *v.* rejoice

regra *n.* rule

regressivo *adj.* recessive

regulação *n.* regulation

regulador *n.* regulator

regular *v.* regulate

regularidade *n.* regularity

regularizar *v.* regularize

rei *n.* king

reimprimir *v.* reprint

reinar *v.* reign

reincidir *v.* relapse

reino *n.* kingdom

reintegração *n.* reinstatement

reinvidicar *v.* claim

reiteração *n.* reiteration

reiterar *v.* reiterate

rejeição *n.* rejection

rejeitar *v.* reject

rejuvenescer *v.* rejuvenate

rejuvenescimento *n.* rejuvenation

relação *n.* relation

relaçar *v.t.* underline

relacionamento *n.* relationship

relacionar (-se) *v.* relate

relações *n.* intercourse

relâmpago *n.* lightening

relatividade *n.* relativity

relativo a alfaiate *adj.* sartorial

relaxamento *n.* relaxation

relaxar *v.* relax

relaxar-se *v.* loll

relé *n.* relay

relegar *v.* relegate

relembrar *v.* remember

relevância *n.* relevance

relevante *adj.* relevant

religião *n.* religion

religioso *adj.* religious

relincho *n.* whinny

relinga *v.* baulk

relíquia *n.* relic

relógio *n.* clock

relutância *n.* reluctance

relutante *adj.* reluctant

relva *n.* grass

relvado *n.* lawn

remédio *n.* remedy

remendo *n.* patch

remessa *n.* remittance

reminiscência *n.* reminiscence

remissão *n.* remission

remisso *adj.* remiss

remo *n.* oar

remoção *n.* removal

remodelar *v.* reshuffle

remontar *v.t.* retrace

remorso *n.* remorse

remoto *adj.* remote

remover v. remove
removível adj. removable
remuneração n. remuneration
remunerar v. remunerate
remunerativo adj. remunerative
renascimento n. renaissance
renda n. rent
rendado adj. lacy
render-se v. surrender
rendição n. surrender
rendimento n. output
renegado n. renegade
renegar v. forswear
renome n. renown
renovação adj.. renewal
renovação n. renovation
renovar v. renew
rentável adj. profitable
renúncia n. renunciation
renunciar v. disclaim
renunciar a v.t. renounce
reorganizar v. reorganize
reparar v. repair
repartir v.t. apportion
repatriação n. repatriation
repatriar v. repatriate
repelente adj. repellent
repelir v. repel
repensar v. rethink
repentino adj. sudden
repercussão n. repercussion
repetição n. repetition
repetir v. repeat
repique n. peal

repleto adj. replete
réplica n. replica
replicar v. retort
repolho n. cabbage
reportagem n. reportage
repórter n. reporter
repositório n. repository
repousante adj. restful
repousar v. slumber
repouso n. repose
repreender v. reproach
repreensível adj. reprehensible
represália n. reprisal
representação n. representation
representar v. represent
representativo adj. representative
repressão n. repression
reprimenda v. reprimand
reprimir v. repress
réprobo n. reprobate
reprodução n. reproduction
reprodutivo adj. reproductive
reproduzir v. reproduce
reprovar v. reprove
réptil n. reptile
república n. republic
republicano adj. republican
repudiar v. repudiate
repúdio n. repudiation
repugante adj. abhorrent
repugnância n. repugnance
repugnante adj. repulsive
repulsão n. repulsion
reputação n. reputation

réquiem n. requiem
requisição n. requisition
requisito n. requisite
rescindir v. rescind
reserva n. reservation
reservar v. reserve
reservatório n. reservoir
resfôlego n. snort
resgatar v. rescue
resgate n. ransom
residência n. residence
residencial adj. residential
residente n. resident
residir v. reside
residual adj. residual
resíduo n. residue
resíduos n. refuse
resistência n. resistance
resistente adj. resistant
resistir v. withstand
resma n. ream
resmungar v. grumble
resolução n. resolution
resoluto adj. resolute
resolver v. solve
respeitado adj. revered
respeitar v. regard
respeitável adj. respectable
respeito n. respect
respeitoso adj. respectful
respetivo adj. respective
respigar v. glean
respingar v. squirt
respiração n. breath

respirador n. respirator
respiradouro n. vent
respirar v. breathe
resplandecente adj. resplendent
resplendor adj. refulgence
responder v. reply
responsabilidade n. liability
responsável adj. responsible
responsivo adj. responsive
resposta n. answer
ressaca n. hangover
ressaltar v. rebound
ressalto n. tappet
ressentimento n. resentment
ressentir v. resent
ressequido adj. parched
ressoar v. resound
ressonância n. resonance
ressonante adj. resonant
ressurgimento a. resurgence
ressuscitar v. resurrect
restabelecer v. reinstate
restante n. remainder
restauração adj. restoration
restaurante n. restaurant
restaurar v. restore
restituição n. restitution
resto n. remnant
restolho n. stubble
restos n. remains
restrição n. restriction
restringir n. & v. restrict & retrench
restritivo adj. restrictive
resultado n. outcome

resultante *adj.* resultant
resumido *adj.* compendious
resumir *v.* summarize
resumo *adj.* rundown
resumo *n.* summary
retalhar *v.* slash
retalhista *n.* retailer
retalho *n.* retail
retaliação *n.* retaliation
retaliar *v.* retaliate
retangular *adj.* rectangular
retângulo *n.* rectangle
retardado *adj.* retarded
retardar *v.* retard
retardo *n.* retardation
retenção *n.* retention
retentivo *adj.* retentive
retentor *n.* retainer
reter *v.i.* retain
retesar *v.* flex
reticente *adj.* reticent
reticulado *adj.* webby
retidão *n.* rectitude
retificação *n.* rectification
retificar *v.* rectify
retina *n.* retina
retirada *n.* withdrawal
retirar *v.* withdraw
reto *n.& adj.* rectum & straight
retocar *v.* retouch
retomar *v.* resume
retórica *n.* rhetoric
retórico *adj.* rhetorical
retornar *v.* recur

retorno *n.* return
retraído *adj.* retiring
retrair *v.* retract
retratar *v.* portray
retrato *n.* portrait
retribuição *n.* retribution
retribuir *v.* reciprocate
retriever *n.* retriever
rétro *adj.* retro
retroativo *adj.* retroactive
retroceder *v.* regress
retrógrado *adj.* retrograde
retrós *n.* twine
retrospecto *n..* retrospect
retrospetiva *n.* hindsight
retrospetivo *adj.* retrospective
retumbar *v.* rumble
réu *n.* defendant
reumático *adj.* rheumatic
reumatismo *n.* rheumatism
reunião *n.* meeting
reunir *v.* meet
reutilizar *v.* reuse
revelação *n.* revelation
revelar *v.* reveal
rever *v.* revise
reverência *n.* reverence
reverencial *adj.* reverential
reversão *n.* reversal
reversível *adj.* reversible
reverter *v.* revert
revés *n.* backhand
revestido *adj.* clad
revestimento *n.* coating

revigorar v. perk
revisão n. revision
revista n. magazine
revivalismo n. revivalism
reviver v. revive
revogação n. revocation
revogar v. revoke
revogável adj. revocable
revolta n. mutiny
revoltar v. revolt
revolução n. revolution
revolucionar v. revolutionize
revolucionário adj. revolutionary
revolver v. revolve
revólver n. revolver
rezar v. pray
riacho n. streamlet
ribalta n. limelight
ribeiro n. brook
ricamente adv. richly
rico adj. wealthy
ridicularizar v. belabour
ridículo adj. ridiculous
rígido adj. rigid
rigor n. rigour
rigoroso adj. rigorous
rim n. kidney
rima n. rhyme
rímel n. mascara
rinoceronte n. rhinoceros
rio n. river
ripa n. lath
riquexó n. rickshaw
riqueza n. wealth

rir v. laugh
rir à socapa n. snigger
risco n. risk
riso n. laughter
rítmico adj. rhythmic
ritmo n. rhythm
rito n. rite
ritual n. ritual
rival n. rival
rivalidade n. rivalry
rixa n. scuffle
robe n. robe
robô n. robot
robusto adj. robust
roçar v. skim
rocha n. rock
rochoso adj. rocky
roda n. wheel
roda dentada n. cog
rodapé n. skirting
rodar v. rotate
rodeio n. rodeo
ródio n. rhodium
rodízio n. carvery
rodopiar v. twirl
roedor n. rodent
roer v. gnaw
rolamento n. bearing
rolar v. trundle
roleta n. roulette
rolete n. roller
roliço adj. plump
rolo n. roll
rolo de pergaminho n. scroll

romã *n.* pomegranate	**rubi** *n.* ruby
romance *n.* romance	**rubrica** *n.* rubric
romancista *n.* novelist	**rude** *adj.* rude
romântico *adj.* romantic	**rudimentar** *adj.* rudimentary
rombo *n.* rhombus	**rudimento** *n.* rudiment
romper *v.* disrupt	**rufião** *n.* ruffian
roncar *v.i.* grunt	**ruga** *n.* wrinkle
ronco *n.* snore	**rugby** *n.* rugby
ronronar *v.* purr	**rugido** *n.* roar
roquete *n.* ratchet	**rugir** *v.* roar
rosa *adj.& n.* pink & rose	**ruído** *n.* noise
rosado *adj.* rosy	**ruidoso** *adj.* blatant
rosário *n.* rosary	**ruína** *n.* ruin
roseta *n.* rosette	**ruínas** *n.* shambles
rosnar *v.* growl	**ruinoso** *adj.* ruinous
rosquilha *n.* pretzel	**rum** *n.* rum
rosto *n.* visage	**ruminação** *n.* rumination
rota *n.* rota	**ruminante** *n.* ruminant
rotação *n.* rotation	**ruminar** *v.* ruminate
rotar *v.* swivel	**rumor** *n.* rumour
rotativo *adj.* rotary	**rural** *adj.* rural
roteiro *n.* guidebook	**Rusk** *n.* Rusk
rotina *n.* routine	**rusticidade** *n.* rusticity
rotor *n.* rotor	**rústico** *n.& adj.* bumpkin & rustic
rótulo *n.* docket	**rutura** *n.* breakage
roubar *v.* steal	
roubo *n.* robbery	
roubo em lojas *n.* shoplifting	**S**
rouco *adj.* raucous	
roupa *n.* clothes	**Sábado** *n.* Saturday
roupa interior *n.* underwear	**sabão** *n.* soap
rouxinol *n.* nightingale	**Sabbat** *n.* Sabbath
roxo *n.* purple	**sabedoria** *n.* wisdom
rua *n.* street	**saber** *v.* know
	sábio *adj.* wise

sabor *n.* flavour

saborear *v.t.* savour

saboroso *adj.* tasteful

sabotar *v.* sabotage

sabre *n.* sabre

sabujo *n.* sleuth

sacarina *n.* saccharin

sacarina *adj.* saccharine

sacerdócio *n.* priesthood

saché *n.* sachet

saciado *adj.* sated

saciar *v.* satiate

saciável *adj.* satiable

saciedade *n.* satiety

saco *n.* bag

saco de viagem *n.* holdall

sacola *n.* satchel

sacramento *n.* sacrament

sacrário *n.* sanctum

sacrificar *v.* sacrifice

sacrificial *adj.* sacrificial

sacrifício *n.* sacrifice

sacrilégio *n.* sacrilege

sacrílego *adj.* sacrilegious

sacristão *n.* sexton

sacristia *n.* vestry

sacrossanto *adj.* sacrosanct

sacudir *v.* jiggle

sádico *n.* sadist

sadismo *n.* sadism

safari *n.* safari

safira *n.* sapphire

saga *n.* saga

sagacidade *n.* sagacity

sagaz *adj.* sagacious

sagrado *adj.* sacred

saia *n.* skirt

saída *n.* outlet

saiote *n.* petticoat

sair *n.* exit

sal *n.* salt

salada *n.* salad

salão *n.* saloon

salário *n.* salary

salgado *adj.* salty

salgueiro *n.* willow

saliência *n.* ledge

saliente *adj.* salient

salinidade *n.* salinity

salino *adj.* saline

saliva *n.* spit

salmão *n.* salmon

salmo *n.* psalm

salmoura *n.* brine

salpicar *v.* splash

salsa *n.* salsa

salsicha *n.* sausage

salsichão *n.* frankfurter

saltador *n.* jumper

saltar *v.i* jump

salteador *n.* dacoit

salto *v.* hop

salutar *adj.* salutary

salva *n.* sage

salvação *n.* salvation

salvador *n.* saviour

salvaguarda *n.* safeguard

salvar *v.* save

Samaritano *n.* Samaritan	**sarcófago** *n.* sarcophagus
sanatório *n.* sanatorium	**sardas** *n.* freckle
sancionar *v.* sanction	**sardónico** *adj.* sardonic
sandália *n.* sandal	**sargaço** *n.* wrack
sândalo *n.* sandalwood	**sargento** *n.* sergeant
sanduíche *n.* sandwich	**sari** *n.* sari
saneamento *n.* sanitation	**sarja** *n.* serge
sanefa *n.* valance	**sarna** *n.* scabies
sangrar *v.* bleed	**sarnenta** *n.* scab
sangrento *adj.* bloody	**sarnento** *adj.* itchy
sangue *n.* blood	**sarrafo** *n.* batten
sangue derramado *n.* gore	**Satanás** *n.* Satan
sangue-frio *n.* sangfroid	**satânico** *adj.* satanic
sanguessuga *n.* leech	**Satanismo** *n.* Satanism
sanguinário *adj.* sanguinary	**satélite** *n.* satellite
sanguíneo *adj.* sanguine	**sátira** *n.* satire
sanidade *n.* sanity	**satírico** *adj.* satirical
sanita *n.* loo	**satirista** *n.* satirist
sanitário *adj.* sanitary	**satirizar** *v.* satirize
santidade *n.* sanctity	**satisfação** *n.* satisfaction
santificação *n.* sanctification	**satisfatório** *adj.* satisfactory
santificar *v.* sanctify	**satisfazer** *v.* satisfy
santo *adj. & n.* holy & saint	**saturação** *n.* saturation
santuário *n.* sanctuary	**saturar** *v.* saturate
são *adj.* sane	**saturnino** *adj.* saturnine
sapateado *n.* stomp	**saudação** *n.* greeting
sapato *n.* shoe	**saudável** *adj.* healthy
sapo *n.* frog	**saúde** *n.* health
saque *n.* booty	**saudoso** *adj.* wistful
saqueador *n.* marauder	**sauna** *n.* sauna
saquear *v.* maraud	**saxofone** *n.* saxophone
sarampo *n.* measles	**sazonal** *adj.* seasonal
sarcasmo *n.* sarcasm	**scooter** *n.* scooter
sarcástico *adj.* sarcastic	**se** *conj.& pron.* if & itself

sebe *n.* hedge

seca *n.* drought

secador *n.* dryer

seção *n.* section

secessão *n.* secession

seco *adj.* dry

secreção *n.* secretion

secretária *n.* desk

secretariado *n.* secretariat

secretário *n.* secretary

secreto *adj.* secret

sectário *adj.* sectarian

secular *n.* centenary

secular *n.* secular

século *n.* century

secundário *adj.* secondary

seda *n.* silk

sedação *n.* sedation

sedan *n.* sedan

sedativo *n.* sedative

sede *n.* headquarters

sedentário *adj.* sedentary

sedento *adj.* thirsty

sedição *n.* sedition

sedicioso *adj.* seditious

sedimento *n.* sediment

sedoso *adj.* silken

sedução *n.* seduction

sedutor *adj.* seductive

seduzir *v.* seduce

segmento *n.* segment

seguidor *n.* follower

seguir *v.* follow

Segunda-feira *n.* Monday

segundo *adj.* second

segurança *n.* safety

seguro *n.* insurance

seguro *adj.* safe

seio *n.* sinus

seis *adj.& n.* six

seiva *n.* sap

seixo *n.* pebble

seja qual for *pron.* whichever

sela *n.* seal

selante *n.* sealant

seleção *n.* selection

selecionar *v.* select

seleiro *n.* saddler

seletivo *adj.* selective

selo (referente qualidade) *n.* cachet

selva *n.* jungle

selvagem *adj.* savage

selvageria *n.* savagery

sem *prep.* without

sem costura *adj.* seamless

sem escrúpulos *adj.* unscrupulous

sem esperança *adj.* hopeless

sem fio *adj.* wireless

sem lei *adj.* lawless

sem nervos *adj.* nerveless

sem objetivo *adj.* aimless

sem princípios *adj.* unprincipled

sem proteção *adj.* unguarded

sem rumo *adj.* adrift

sem topo *adj.* topless

semana *n.* week

semanal *adj.* weekly

semântico *adj.* semantic

semblante *n.* countenance

semelhança *n.* resemblance

sémen *n.* semen

semente *n.* seed

semestral *adj.* biannual

semestre *n.* semester

semicírculo *n.* semicircle

seminal *adj.* seminal

seminário *n.* seminar

Semítico *adj.* Semitic

sempre *adv.* always

sempre que *conj.* whenever

senado *n.* senate

senador *n.* senator

senão *adv.* otherwise

senão *conj.* unless

senatorial *adj.* senatorial

senciente *adj.* sentient

senhor *n.* lord

senhora *n.* lady

senhoria *n.* landlady

senhorio *n.* landlord

senil *adj.* senile

senilidade *n.* senility

sénior *adj.* senior

sensação *n.* sensation

sensacional *adj.* sensational

sensato *adj.* sensible

sensibilidade *n.* sensibility

sensibilizar *v.* sensitize

sensível *adj.* sensitive

sensor *n.* sensor

sensorial *adj.* sensory

sensual *adj.* sensual

sensualidade *n.* sensuality

sensualista *n.* sensualist

sentar *v.* sit

sentença *n.* sentence

sentencioso *adj.* sententious

sentido *n.* sense

sentimental *adj.* sentimental

sentimento *n.* feeling

sentinela *n.* sentinel

sentir *v.* feel

separação *n.* separation

separadamente *adv.* asunder

separar *v.* separate

separatista *n.* separatist

separável *adj.* separable

sepentear *v.* meander

sepsia *n.* sepsis

septuagésimo *adj. & n.* seventieth

sepulcral *adj.* sepulchral

sepulcro *n.* sepulchre

sepultura *n.* grave

sequência *n.* sequence

sequente *adj.* sequential

sequestrar *v.* sequester

séquito *n.* retinue

ser humano *n.* being

ser *v.* be

sereia *n.* mermaid

sereidade *n.* gravitas

serenidade *n.* serenity

sereno *adj.* serene

seria *v.* would

serial *adj.* serial

seriar *v.* serialize

série n. series
seringa n. syringe
sério adj. serious
sermão n. sermon
serpente n. snake
serpentear v. swirl
serra n. saw
serradura n. sawdust
serrar v. saw
serviço n. service
servidão n. bondage
servidor n. server
servil adj. servile
servilismo n. servility
servir v. serve
servo n. serf
sésamo n. sesame
sessão n. session
sessenta adj. & n. sixty
sesta n. siesta
seta n. arrow
sete adj. & n. seven
Setembro n. September
setenta adj. & n. seventy
sético adj. septic
sétimo adj. & n. seventh
setor n. sector
seu pron. & adj. her & their
severo adj. censorious
severo adj. stern
sexagésimo adj. & n. sixtieth
sexismo n. sexism
sexo n. sex
Sexta-feira n. Friday

sexto adj. & n. sixth
sêxtuplo n. sextuplet
sexual adj. sexual
sexualidade n. sexuality
sibarita n. sybarite
sibilante adj. sibilant
sicofanta n. sycophant
sicofantismo n. sycophancy
sicómoro n. sycamore
sida n. aids
sifão n. siphon
sigilo n. secrecy
signatário n. signatory
significado n. meaning
significar v. mean
significativo n. significant
signo n. sign
sílaba n. syllable
silábico adj. syllabic
silenciador n. silencer
silêncio n. silence
silencioso adj. silent
silfo n. sylph
silhueta n. silhouette
silício n. silicon
silogismo n. syllogism
silvestre adj. sylvan
silvicultura n. forestry
silvo n. zing
sim excl. yes
simbiose n. symbiosis
simbólico adj. symbolic
simbolismo n. symbolism
simbolizar v. symbolize

símbolo *n.* symbol
simetria *n.* symmetry
simétrico *adj.* symmetrical
similar *adj.* similar
similaridade *n.* similarity
símile *n.* simile
simpatia *n.* sympathy
simpático *adj.* likeable
simpatizar *v.* sympathize
simples *adj.* simple
simplicidade *n.* simplicity
simplificação *n.* simplification
simplificar *v.* simplify
simplista *adj.* reductive
simplório *n.* simpleton
simpósio *n.* symposium
simular *v.* simulate
simultâneo *adj.* simultaneous
sinal *n.* signal
sincelo *n.* icicle
sinceridade *n.* sincerity
sincero *adj.* sincere
sincronizar *v.* synchronize
síncrono *adj.* synchronous
sindicalista *n.* unionist
sindicato *n.* syndicate
síndrome *n.* syndrome
sinecura *n.* sinecure
sinergia *n.* synergy
sinfonia *n.* symphony
singular *adj.* quaint
singularidade *n.* singularity
singularmente *adv.* singularly
sinistro *adj.* sinister

sinónimo *adj.* synonymous
sinónimo *n.* synonym
sinopse *n.* synopsis
sintaxe *n.* syntax
síntese *n.* synthesis
sintético *adj.* synthetic
sintetizar *v.* synthesize
sintoma *n.* symptom
sintomático *adj.* symptomatic
sintonia *n.* tune
sintonizador *n.* tuner
sinuoso *adj.* sinuous
sirigaita *n.* minx
sísmico *adj.* seismic
sistema *n.* system
sistemático *adj.* systematic
sistematizar *v.* systematize
sistémico *adj.* systemic
site *n.* website
sitiada *adj.* beleaguered
sitiar *v.* besiege
situação *n.,* a situation
situar *v.* situate
skate *n.* skateboard
ski *n.* ski
slogan *n.* slogan
smoking *n.* tuxedo
snobe *n.& adj.* snob & snobbish
snobismo *n.* snobbery
snooker *n.* snooker
só *adj.* lonesome
soberania *n.* sovereignty
soberano *n.* sovereign
soberbo *adj.* superb

sobrancelha *n.* brow	**sodomia** *n.* sodomy
sobras *n.* pickings	**sofá** *n.* couch
sobre *prep.* over	**sofisma** *n.* sophism
sobrecarregar *v.* overload	**sofismar** *n.* sophisticate
sobrecasaca *n.* frock	**sofista** *n.* sophist
sobre-humano *adj.* superhuman	**sofisticação** *n.* sophistication
sobremesa *n.* dessert	**sofisticado** *adj.* sophisticated
sobrenatural *adj.* supernatural	**sofrer** *v.i.* suffer
sobrenome *n.* surname	**sofrimento** *n.* sufferance
sobrepor *v.* overlap	**sogra** *n.* mother-in-law
sobrescrito *adj.* superscript	**sol** *n.* sun
sobressair *v.* protrude	**solar** *adj.* solar
sobressalente *adj.* spare	**solda** *n.* solder
sobrestimar *v.* overrate	**soldado** *n.* soldier
sobretaxa *n.* surtax	**soldado de cavalaria** *n.* trooper
sobretudo *n.* overcoat	**soldar** *v.* weld
sobrevir *v.* supervene	**solene** *adj.* solemn
sobrevivência *n.* survival	**solenidade** *n.* solemnity
sobreviver *v.* survive	**solenizar** *v.* solemnize
sobriedade *n.* sobriety	**soletração** *n.* spelling
sobrinha *n.* niece	**soletrar** *v.t.* spell
sobrinho *n.* nephew	**soletrar mal** *v.* misspell
sóbrio *adj.* sober	**solicitação** *n.* solicitation
sociabilidade *n.* sociability	**solicitador** *n.* solicitor
social *adj.* social	**solicitar** *v.* solicit
socialismo *n.* socialism	**solícito** *adj.* solicitous
socialista *n. & adj.* socialist	**solicitude** *n.* solicitude
socializar *v.* socialize	**solidão** *n.* loneliness
sociável *adj.* sociable	**solidariedade** *n.* solidarity
sociedade *n.* society	**solidez** *n.* fastness
sociologia *n.* sociology	**sólido** *adj.* solid
soco *v.* punch	**solilóquio** *n.* soliloquy
socorro *n.* succour	**solista** *n.* soloist
soda *n.* soda	**solstício do verão** *adj.* midsummer

solitário *adj.& n.* lone & loner
solo *n.* soil
soltar *v.* unleash
solteirona *n.* spinster
solto *adj.* loose
solubilidade *n.* solubility
solução *n.* solution
soluçar *v.* sob
soluço *n.* hiccup
solúvel *adj.* soluble
solvência *n.* solvency
solvente *n.* solvent
som *n.* sound
som intermitente *n.* blip
soma *n.* sum
sombra *a.* shadow
sombrio *adj.* shadowy
sonambulismo *n.* somnambulism
sonâmbulo *n.* somnambulist
sonda *n.* probe
sondagem *n.* poll
sondar *v.* plumb
soneca *n.* nap
sonegar *v.* withhold
soneto *n.* sonnet
sonho *n.* dream
sónico *adj.* sonic
sono *n.* sleep
sonolência *n.* somnolence
sonolento *adj.* sleepy
sonoridade *n.* sonority
sopa *n.* soup
soporífero *adj.* soporific
soprar *v.* blow

sopro *n.* puff
sórdido *adj.* sordid
sorrir *v.* smile
sorrir afetadamente *v.* simper
sorte *n.* luck
sortudo *adj.* lucky
sorver *v.* sip
sorver (ruidosamente) *v.* slurp
sorvete *n.* sorbet
sósia *n.* lookalike
sótão *n.* attic
sotaque *n.* accent
soterrar *v.* whelm
sovar *v.* thrash
sozinho *adv.* alone
spa *n.* spa
spam *n.* spam
spaniel *n.* spaniel
spray *n.* spray
sprinter *n.* sprinter
stock *n.* stock
stress *n.* stress
Stripper *n.* stripper
strudel *n.* strudel
Stuart *n.* Stuart
suave *adj.* gentle
suavidade *n.* leniency
subalterno *n.* subaltern
subalugar *v.t.* sublet
subconsciente *adj.* subconscious
subcontratar *v.* subcontract
subestimar *v.* underestimate
subestimar *v.* underrate
subida *n.* rising

subir *v.* rise

subitamente *adv.* suddenly

subjetivo *adj.* subjective

subjugação *n.* subjugation

subjugar *v.* subjugate

subjuntivo *adj.* subjunctive

sublimar *v.* sublimate

sublime *adj.* sublime

subliminar *adj.* subliminal

sublinhar *v.* underscore

submarino *n.* submarine

submergir *v.* submerge

submersível *adj.* submersible

submerso *adj.* sunken

submeter *v.* submit

submissão *n.* submission

submisso *adj.* submissive

submundo *n.* underworld

subnutrição *n.* malnutrition

subordinação *n.* subordination

subordinado *adj.* subordinate

subornar *v.* suborn

sub-reptício *adj.* surreptitious

subscrever *v.* subscribe

subscrito *adj.* subscript

subsequente *adj.* subsequent

subserviência *n.* subservience

subserviente *adj.* subservient

subsidiar *v.* subsidize

subsidiário *adj.* subsidiary

subsídio *n.* subsidy

subsistência *n.* subsistence

subsistir *v.* subsist

subsónico *adj.* subsonic

substância *n.* substance

substancial *adj.* substantial

substancialmente *adv.* substantially

substantivo *n.& adj.* substantive

substituição *n.* substitution

substituir *v.* replace

substituto *n.* substitute

subsumir *v.* subsume

subterfúgio *n.* subterfuge

subterrâneo *adj.* underground

subtil *adj.* subtle

subtileza *n.* subtlety

subtítulo *n.* subtitle

subtotal *n.* subtotal

subtração *n.* subtraction

subtrair *v.* subtract

subtropical *adj.* subtropical

suburbano *adj.* suburban

subúrbio *n.* suburb

subúrbios *n.* suburbia

subversão *n.* subversion

subversivo *adj.* subversive

subverter *v.i.* subvert

sucata *n.* scrap

sucção *n.* suction

suceder *v.* succeed

sucessão *n.* succession

sucessivo *adj.* successive

sucesso *n.* success

sucessor *n.* successor

sucinto *adj.* succinct

suculento *adj.* juicy

sucumbir *v.* succumb

Sudoku *n.* Sudoku

suéter *n.* sweater
suficiência *n.* sufficiency
suficiente *adj.* sufficient
sufixo *n.* suffix
sufocar *v.* choke
sufoco *n.* suffocation
sufrágio *n.* suffrage
sugerir *v.* suggest
sugestão *n.* suggestion
sugestionável *adj.* suggestible
sugestivo *adj.* suggestive
suíças *n.* whisker
suicida *adj.* suicidal
suicídio *n.* suicide
suíno *n.* swine
suite *n.* suite
sujar *v.* smudge
sujeição *n.* subjection
sujeito *n.* bloke
sujo *n.& adj.* dirt & dirty
sul *n.* south
sulco *n.* furrow
sulista *adj.* southern
sultana *n.* sultana
sumariamente *adv.* summarily
sumo *n.* juice
sumptuoso *adj.* sumptuous
sundae *n.* sundae
suor *n.* sweat
superabundância *adj.* superabundance
superabundância *n.* surfeit
superabundante *adj.* superabundant
superar *v.* overcome
superficial *adj.* superficial

superficialidade *n.* superficiality
superfície *n.* surface
superfino *adj.* superfine
superfluidade *n.* superfluity
supérfluo *adj.* superfluous
superintendência *n.* superintendence
superintendente *n.* superintendent
superintender *v.* superintend
superior *adj.* superior
superioridade *n.* superiority
superlativo *adj.* superlative
supermercado *n.* supermarket
superpotência *n.* superpower
supersónico *adj.* supersonic
superstição *n.* superstition
supersticioso *adj.* superstitious
supervisão *n.* supervision
supervisionar *v.* supervise
supervisionar a redação *v.* subedit
supervisor *n.* supervisor
suplantar *v.* supplant
suplementar *adj.* supplementary
suplemento *n.* supplement
súplica *v.* t entreaty
suplicante *n.* suppliant
suplicar *v.* supplicate
supor *v.* suppose
suportar *v.t* bear
suporte *n.* bracket
suposição *n.* assumption
supositório *n.* suppository
supremacia *n.* supremacy
supremo *adj.* supreme
supressão *n.* suppression

suprimir v. suppress

supurar v. suppurate

surdo adj. deaf

surf n. surf

surgir v. arise

surpreendente n. startling

surpreender v. amaze

surpresa n. surprise

surreal adj. surreal

surrealismo n. surrealism

surtida n. sortie

surto n. outbreak

suscetível adj. touchy

suserano n. liege

suspeita n. suspicion

suspeitar v. suspect

suspeito adj. suspicious

suspeito n. suspect

suspender v. suspend

suspensão n. suspension

suspirar v.i. sigh

suspiro v.i gasp

sussurrar v. whisper

sussurro v. rustle

sustentar v. sustain

sustentável adj. sustainable

sustento n. sustenance

sutiã n. bra

subtileza n. finesse

sutura n. suture

T

tabaco n. tobacco

tablóide n. tabloid

tabu n. taboo

tabulador v. tabulator

tabular adj. tabular

taça n. goblet

tacha n. tack

tácito adj. tacit

taciturno adj. taciturn

tacómetro n. tachometer

tagalerice v. chatter

tagarela adj. garrulous

tagarelar v. blab

tagarelar (modo·infantil) v. prattle

tagarelice n. tattle

takeaway n. takeaway

tal adj. such

tala n. splint

talão de cheques n. counterfoil

talco n. talc

talento n. talent

talentoso adj. talented

talhar v. hew

talismã n. talisman

talvez adv. maybe

tamanho n. size

tamarindo n. tamarind

também adv. also

tambor n. drum

tampa n. lid

tampão n. tampon

tanchagem n. plantain

tandem n. tandem

tangente n. tangent

tangerina n. tangerine

tangível adj. tangible

tanoeiro *n.* cooper
tanque *n.* tank
tapar *v.* occlude
tapas *n.* tapas
tapeçaria *n.* tapestry
tapete *n.* carpet
tardar *v.* loiter
tarde *adj.* late
tardio *adj.* tardy
tarefa *n.* task
tarifa *n.* tariff
tarot *n.* tarot
tartaruga *n.* turtle
tarte *n.* pie
tarte de frutas *n.* cobbler
tástaro *n.* tartar
tatear *v.* fumble
tática *n.* tactic
tático *n. & adj.* tactician & tactical
tátil *adj.* tactile
tato *n.* tact
tatuagem *n.* tattoo
taverna *n.* tavern
taxa *n.* fee
táxi *n.* taxi
taxonomia *n.* taxonomy
tear *n.* loom
teatral *adj.* theatrical
teatro *n.* theatre
teca *n.* teak
tecelão *n.* weaver
tecer *v.* weave
tecido *n.* tissue
teclado *n.* keyboard

técnica *n.* technique
tecnicismo *n.* technicality
técnico *adj.* technical
técnico *n.* technician
tecnologia *n.* technology
tecnológica *adj.* technological
tecnólogo *n.* technologist
tédio *n.* tedium
tedioso *adj.* tedious
teia *n.* web
teia de aranha *n.* cobweb
teimoso *adj.* stubborn
teísmo *n.* theism
teixo *n.* yew
telecomunicações *n.* telecommunicat.
telefone *n.* phone
telegrafia *n.* telegraphy
telegráfico *adj.* telegraphic
telégrafo *n.* telegraph
telegrama *n.* telegram
teleimpressor *n.* teleprinter
telemóvel *n.* cell phone
telepata *n.* telepathist
telepatia *n.* telepathy
telepática *adj.* telepathic
telescópio *n.* telescope
teletexto *n.* teletext
televisão *n.* television
televisionar *v.t.* telecast
telha *n.* shingle
telhado *n.* roof
telheiro *n.* outhouse
tema *n.* theme
temático *adj.* thematic

temeridade *n.* temerity

temível *adj.* redoubtable

temor *n.* awe

temperado *adj.* temperate

temperamental *adj.* temperamental

temperamento *n.* temper

temperança *n.* temperance

temperatura *n.* temperature

tempero *n.* spice

tempestade *n.* storm

tempestuoso *adj.* stormy

templo *n.* temple

tempo *n.* time

tempo (música) *n.* tempo

temporada *n.* season

temporal *adj.* temporal

temporário *adj.* temporary

temporizar *v.* temporize

tenacidade *n.* tenacity

tenaz *adj.* tenacious

tenda *n.* tent

tendão *n.* tendon

tendência *n.* trend

tendencioso *adj.* tendentious

tenente *n.* lieutenant

ténis *n.* sneaker

tenor *n.* tenor

tenro *adj.* tender

tensão *n.* strain

tênsil *adj.* tensile

tenso *adj.* tense

tentação *n.* temptation

tentáculo *n.* tentacle

tentador *n.* tempter

tentar *v.* try

ténue *adj.* tenuous

teocracia *n.* theocracy

teodolito *n.* theodolite

teologia *n.* theology

teólogo *n.* theologian

teor *n.* content

teorema *n.* theorem

teoria *n.* theory

teórico *adj.& n.* theoretical & teorist

teorizar *v.* theorize

teosofia *n.* theosophy

tépido *adj.* tepid

ter *v.* have

ter cuidado *v.* beware

terapeuta *n.* therapist

terapêutico *adj.* therapeutic

terapia *n.* therapy

Terça-feira *n.* Tuesday

terceirizar *v.* outsource

terceiro *adj.* third

terciário *adj.* tertiary

terebintina *n.* turpentine

térmico *adj.* thermal

terminação *n.* termination

terminal *adj.* terminal

terminar *v.* finish

término *n.* terminus

terminologia *n.* terminology

terminológico *adj.* terminological

térmite (formiga) *n.* termite

termo *n.* thermos

termodinâmica *n.* thermodynamics

termoendurecíveis *adj.* thermosetting

termómetro *n.* thermometer	**têxtil** n textile
termóstato *n.* thermostat	**texto** *n.* text
terra *n.* earth	**textual** *adj.* textual
terraço *n.* terrace	**textura** *n.* texture
terracota *n.* terracotta	**tia** *n.* aunt
terremoto *n.* earthquake	**tiara** *n.* tiara
terreno *n.* terrain	**tidally** *n.* tidally
terrenos universidade *n.* campus	**tifo** *n.* typhus
térreo *adj.* earthen	**tifóide** *n.* typhoid
terrestre *adj.* earthly	**tigela** *n.* bowl
terrier *n.* terrier	**tigre** *n.* tiger
territorial *adj.* territorial	**tijolo** *n.* brick
território *n.* territory	**tilintar** *n.* jingle
terrível *adj.* terrible	**tilintar** *v.* tinkle
terrivelmente *adj.* ghastly	**timidez** *n.* timidity
terror *n.* terror	**tímido** *adj.* shy
terrorismo *n.* terrorism	**timorato** *adj.* timorous
terrorista *n.* terrorist	**tina** *n.* tub
tese *n.* thesis	**tingir** *n.* dye
tesoura *n.* scissors	**tinido** *n.* clink
tesouraria *n.* treasury	**tinta** *n.* ink
tesoureiro *n.* treasurer	**tintura** *n.* tincture
tesouro *n.* treasure	**tio** *n.* uncle
tesouro escondido *n.* hoard	**típico** *adj.* typical
testa *n.* forehead	**tipificar** *v.* typify
testamento *n.* testament	**tipo** *n.* type
teste *n.* test	**tiquetaque** *n.* ticking
testemunha *n.* witness	**tira de couro** *n.* strop
testemunha ocular *n.* eyewitness	**tirada** *n.* tirade
testemunhar *v.* testify	**tirania** *n.* tyranny
testemunho *n.* testimony	**tiranizar** *v.* tyrannize
testículo *n.* testicle	**tirano** *n.* tyrant
testosterona *n.* testosterone	**tiritar** *v.* shiver
teto *n.* ceiling	**tiro pela culatra** *v.* backfire

tiróide n. thyroid		**tonto** adj. spellbound	
tiroteio n. shooting		**topázio** n. topaz	
titânico adj. titanic		**topiária** n. topiary	
titular adj. titled		**tópico** n.& adj. topic & topical	
título n. title		**topo** n. top	
toalha n. towel		**topografia** n. topography	
toca n. burrow		**topográfico** adj. topographical	
tocante adj. touching		**topógrafo** n. topographer	
tocar v. touch		**toque de recolher** n. curfew	
tocar (sino) v. ring		**torção** n. torsion	
tocha n. torch		**torcer** v. wrick	
toco n. stump		**tordo** n. thrush	
todo adj. all		**tormento** n. torment	
toga n. gown		**tornado** n. tornado	
toga n. toga		**torneio** n. tournament	
tolerância n. tolerance		**torneira** n. tap	
tolerante adj. tolerant		**torneiro** n. turner	
tolerar v. tolerate		**torno mecânico** n. lathe	
tolerável adj. tolerable		**tornozelo** n. ankle	
tolice n. tomfoolery		**toro** n. log	
tolo adj. foolish		**torpedo** n. torpedo	
tom n. tone		**torradeira** n. toaster	
tomada n. jack		**torre** n. tower	
tomar v. take		**torrencial** adj. torrential	
tomate n. tomato		**torrente** n. torrent	
tombar v. topple		**tórrido** adj. torrid	
tômbola n. raffle		**torso** n. torso	
tomo n. tome		**torto** adj. wry	
tonel n. tun		**tortuoso** adj. tortuous	
tonelada n. tonne		**tortura** n. torture	
tonelagem n. tonnage		**tosquiar** v. shear	
toner n. toner		**tossir** v. cough	
tónico n. tonic		**tostar** v. sear	
tonsura n. tonsure		**total** adj.& n. total	

totalidade *n.* entirety	**traineira** *n.* trawler
totalitário *adj.* totalitarian	**trair** *v.* betray
totalmente *adv.* wholly	**traje** *n.* costume
totó *n.* nerd	**trajetória** *n.* trajectory
toupeira *n.* mole	**tralha** *n.* junk
toureiro *n.* toreador	**trampolim** *n.* trampoline
touro *n.* bull	**trança** *n.* tress
tóxico *adj.* toxic	**tranquilidade** *n.* tranquillity
toxicologia *n.* toxicology	**tranquilizar** *v.* tranquillize
toxina *n.* toxin	**tranquilo** *adj.* tranquil
trabalhador *adj.* industrious	**transação** *n.* transaction
trabalhador *n.* worker	**transacionar** *v.* transact
trabalhar duro *v.* moil	**transatlântico** *adj.* transatlantic
trabalho *n.* job	**transbordar** *v.* overflow
traçado *n.* tracing	**transcendental** *adj.* transcendental
tração *n.* traction	**transcendente** *adj.* transcendent
traçar *v.t.* trace	**transcender** *v.* transcend
traço *n.* trait	**transceptor** *n.* transceiver
tradição *n.* tradition	**transcontinental** *adj.* transcontinental
tradicional *adj.* traditional	**transcrever** *v.* transcribe
tradicionalista *n.* traditionalist	**transcrição** *n.* transcription
tradução *n.* translation	**transe** *n.* trance
traduzir *v.* translate	**transferidor** *n.* protractor
tráfego *n.* traffic	**transferir** *v.* transfer
traficante *n.* trafficker	**transferível** *adj.* transferable
traficar *v.* peddle	**transferir** *v.* redeploy
tráfico *n.* trafficking	**transfiguração** *n.* transfiguration
tragar *v.* gulp	**transfigurar** *v.* transfigure
tragédia *n.* tragedy	**transformação** *n.* transformation
trageódico *n.* tragedian	**transformador** *n.* transformer
trágico *adj.* tragic	**transformar** *v.* transform
traição *n.* treason	**transfusão** *n.* transfusion
traiçoeiro *adj.* treacherous	**transgredir** *v.* transgress
traidor *n.* traitor	**transgressão** *n.* transgression

transição *n.* transition	**tratável** *adj.* tractable
transístor *n.* transistor	**trato** *n.* tract
transitivo *adj.* transitive	**trator** *n.* tractor
trânsito *n.* transit	**trauma** *n.* trauma
transitório *adj.* transitory	**travão** *n.* brake
transliterar *v.* transliterate	**travessa** *n.* platter
translúcido *adj.* translucent	**travesseiro** *n.* pillow
transmigração *n.* transmigration	**travessia** *n.* crossing
transmissão *n.* transmission	**travessura** *n.* mischief
transmissor *n.* transmitter	**travesti** *n.* transvestite
transmitir *v.* transmit	**travo** *n.* tang
transmutar *v.* transmute	**trazer** *v.* bring
transparência *n.* transparency	**trégua** *n.* truce
transparente *adj.* transparent	**treinador** *n.* coach
transpiração *n.* perspiration	**treino** *n.* training
transpirar *v.* transpire	**tremendo** *adj.* tremendous
transplantar *v.* transplant	**tremer** *v.* shake
transpor *v.* transpose	**tremor** *n.* tremor
transportador *n.* transporter	**trémulo** *adj.* tremulous
transportar *v.* carry	**trenó** *n.* sledge
transporte *n.* transportation	**trepadeira** *n.* creeper
transsexual *n.* transsexual	**trepidação** *n.* trepidation
transversalmente *adv.* across	**três** *adj. & n.* three
transverso *adj.* transverse	**treze** *adj. & n.* thirteen
trapaceiro *n.* trickster	**triangular** *adj.* triangular
trapalhão *adj.* clumsy	**triângulo** *n.* triangle
trapézio *n.* trapeze	**triatlo** *n.* triathlon
trapo *n.* rag	**tribal** *adj.* tribal
traquinar *v.* romp	**tribo** *n.* tribe
traseiro *n.* backside	**tribulação** *n.* tribulation
traste *n.* boor	**tribuna** *n.* rostrum
tratado *n.* treaty	**tribunal** *n.* tribunal
tratamento *n.* treatment	**tributação** *n.* taxation
tratar *v.* treat	**tributário** *n.* tributary

tributável *adj.* taxable
tributo *n.* tribute
triciclo *n.* tricycle
tricípite *n.* triceps
tricolor *n.* tricolour
tricotar *v.* knit
tridente *n.* trident
Trier *n.* Trier
trigésimo *adj. & n.* thirtieth
trigo *n.* wheat
trigonometria *n.* trigonometry
triler *n.* thriller
trilha *n.* trail
trilho *n.* rail
trilião *adj & n.* trillion
trilogia *n.* trilogy
trimestral *adj.* quarterly
trimestre *n.* quarter
trinado *n.* trill
trinar *v.* quaver
trincheira *n.* trench
trinco *n.* latch
trindade *n.* trinity
trinta *adj. & n.* thirty
trio *n.* trio
tripartido *adj.* tripartite
tripé *n.* tripod
triplamente *adv.* thrice
triplicado *adj.* triplicate
triplo *adj.& n.* treble & triple
tríptico *n.* triptych
tripulação *n.* crew
triste *adj.* sad
tristeza *n.* sorrow

triturar *v.* crunch
triunfal *adj.* triumphal
triunfante *adj.* triumphant
triunfo *n.* triumph
trivial *adj.* trivial
trivialidades *n.* trivia
troça *n.* ridicule
trocadilho *n.* pun
trocar *v. t* exchange
troféu *n.* trophy
troll *n.* troll
trombeta *n.* trumpet
tronco *n.* trunk
trono *n.* throne
tropa *n.* troop
tropeçar *v.* stumble
tropical *adj.* tropical
trópico *n.* tropic
trotar *v.* trot
trote *n.* canter
trovão *n.* thunder
trovejante *adj.* thunderous
trufa *n.* truffle
truísmo *n.* truism
truncar *v.* truncate
trunfo *n.* trump
truque *n.* trick
truta *n.* trout
tsunami *n.* tsunami
tubarão *n.* shark
tubérculo *n.* tubercle
tuberculose *n.* tuberculosis
tubo *n.* pipe
tubular *adj.* tubular

tudo *pron.* lot

tudo o que *pron.* whatever

tufão *n.* typhoon

tulipa *n.* tulip

tumescente *adj.* tumescent

tumor *n.* tumour

túmulo *n.* tomb

tumulto *n.* tumult

tumultuoso *adj.* tumultuous

túnel *n.* tunnel

túnica *n.* tunic

turbante *n.* turban

turbilhão *n.* whirlpool

turbina *n.* turbine

turbocompressor *n.* turbocharger

turbulência *n.* turbulence

turbulento *adj.* turbulent

túrgido *adj.* turgid

turismo *n.* tourism

turista *n.* tourist

turno *n.* innings

turquesa *n.* turquoise

turvo *adj.* turbid

tutela *n.* tutelage

tutor *n.* tutor

tutorial *n.* tutorial

tweed *n.* tweed

U

uádi *n.* wadi

úbere *n.* udder

ubíquo *adj.* ubiquitous

uísque *n.* whisky

uivo *n.* yowl

úlcera *n.* ulcer

ulterior *adj.* ulterior

ultimato *n.* ultimatum

último *adj.* last

ultrajante *adj.* outrageous

ultraje *n.* outrage

ultramarino *n.* ultramarine

ultrapassar *v.* overtake

ultrapassar (em peso) *v.* outweigh

ultrassónico *adj.* ultrasonic

um *a.* a

um *n.* & *adj.* one

um pouco *adv.* somewhat

uma *adj.* an

uma vez *adv.* once

umbilical *adj.* umbilical

unânime *adj.* unanimous

unanimidade *a.* unanimity

ungir *v.* anoint

unha *n.* nail

união *n.* union

unicamente *adv.* solely

unicidade *n.* oneness

único *adj.* & *n.* single & sole

unidade *n.* unit

unificação *n.* unification

unificar *v.* unify

uniforme *adj.* uniform

uniformização *n.* standardization

uniformizar *v.* standardize

unilateral *adj.* unilateral

unir *v.* unite

unissexo *adj.* unisex

unissonância *n.* unison

universal *adj.* universal	**utópico** *adj.* utopian
universalidade *adv.* universality	**uva** *n.* grape
universidade *n.* university	
universo *n.* universe	
untar *v.* smear	**V**
untuoso *adj.* unctuous	**vaca** *n.* cow
upload *v.* upload	**vacaria** *n.* byre
urbanidade *n.* urbanity	**vacilação** *n.* vacillation
urbano *adj.* urban	**vacilante** *adj.* wonky
urgente *adj.* urgent	**vacilar** *v.* vacillate
urina *n.* urine	**vacina** *n.* vaccine
urinar *v.* urinate	**vacinação** *n.* vaccination
urinário *adj.* urinary	**vacinar** *v.* vaccinate
urna *n.* urn	**vácuo** *n.* vacuum
urso *n.* bear	**vaga** *n.* vacancy
urtiga *n.* nettle	**vagabundear** *v.* tramp
urubu *n.* buzzard	**vagabundo** *n.* bum
urze *n.* heather	**vagão** *n.* wagon
usar *v.t.* use	**vagaroso** *adj.* leisurely
uso *n.* usage	**vagem** *n.* pod
usual *adj.* usual	**vagina** *n.* vagina
usuário *n.* user	**vago** *adj.* vague
usura *n.* usury	**vaguear** *v.* maunder
usurpação *n.* usurpation	**vaidade** *n.* vanity
usurpar *v.* usurp	**vaidoso** *adj.* vain
utensílio *n.* utensil	**vala** *n.* manhole
útero *n.* womb	**vale** *n.* valley
útil *adj.* useful	**vale postal** *n.* giro
utilidade *n.* utility	**valência** *n.* valency
utilitário *adj.* utilitarian	**valentão** *n.* bully
utilização *n.* utilization	**valente** *adj.* valiant
utilizar *v.* utilize	**valete** *n.* knave
utilizável *adj.* usable	**valetudinário** *n.* valetudinarian
utopia *n.* utopia	**validade** *n.* validity

validar *v.* validate

válido *adj.* valid

valioso *adj.* valuable

valor *n.* value

valsa *n.* waltz

válvula *n.* valve

vampiro *n.* vampire

vandalizar *v.* vandalize

vândalo *n.* vandal

vanglorioso *adj.* vainglorious

vanguarda *n.* vanguard

vantagem *n.* advantage

vantajoso *adj.* advantageous

vapor *n.* steam

vaporizar *v.* vaporize

varanda *n.* balcony

variação *n.* variation

variado *adj.* assorted

variante *n.* variant

variar *v.* vary

variável *adj.* variable

varicoso *adj.* varicose

variedade *n.* variety

varinha *n.* wand

vário *adj.* various

varíola *n.* smallpox

vários *adj.* several

varredor *n.* sweeper

varrer *v.* sweep

vascular *adj.* vascular

vasectomia *n.* vasectomy

vasilha *n.* canister

vaso *n.* vase

vassalo *n.* vassal

vassoura *n.* broom

vazante *n.* ebb

vazar *v.* leak

vazio *adj.* empty

veado *n.* deer

veemente *adj.* vehement

vegan *n.* vegan

vegetação *n.* vegetation

vegetal *n.* vegetable

vegetar *v.* vegetate

vegetariano *n.* vegetarian

vegetativo *adj.* vegetative

veia *n.* vein

veicular *adj.* vehicular

veículo *n.* vehicle

veículo bom estado *adj.* roadworthy

veio *n.* cameo

vela *n.* candle

velejador *n.* yachtsman

velejar *v.* sail

velhacaria *n.* roguery

velho *adj.* old

velo *n.* fleece

velocidade *n.* speed

veludo *n.* velvet

venal *adj.* venal

venalidade *n.* venality

vencedor *n.& adj.* winner & winning

vencer *v.* vanquish

venda *n.* sale

venda por grosso *n.* wholesale

vendar os olhos *v.* blindfold

vendedor *n.* seller

vendedor ambulante *n.* pedlar

vender v. sell
vendeta n. vendetta
veneno n. poison
venenoso adj. poisonous
veneração n. worship
venerar v. venerate
venerável adj. venerable
veneziano adj. venetian
venial adj. venial
venoso adj. venous
ventania n. gale
ventilação n. ventilation
ventilador n. ventilator
ventilar v. ventilate
vento n. wind
ventoinha n. fan
ventoso adj. windy
ver v. see
veracidade n. veracity
verão n. summer
verbal adj. verbal
verbalizar v. verbalize
verbalmente adv. verbally
verbo n. verb
verbosidade n. verbosity
verboso adj. verbose
verdade n. truth
verdade n. verity
verdadeiramente adv. verily
verdadeiro adj. true
verde adj. & n. green
verdejante adj. verdant
verdinho (peixe) n. whiting
verdura v.t. greenery

veredito n. verdict
verga n. withe
vergonha n. shame
vergonhoso adj. disreputable
vergonhoso adj. shameful
verídico adj. veracious
verificação n. verification
verificar v. verify
verme n. worm
vermelhão n. rouge
vermelho adj. red
vernáculo n. vernacular
vernal adj. vernal
verniz n. varnish
verossimilhança n. verisimilitude
verruga n. wart
versado adj. versed
versão n. version
versátil adj. versatile
versatilidade n. versatility
versificação n. versification
versificar v. versify
verso n. verse
vértebra n. vertebra
vertebrado n. vertebrate
vertical adj. vertical
vértice n. vertex
vertigem n. vertigo
vertiginoso adj. giddy
vertiginoso adj. vertiginous
verve n. verve
vesícula n. vesicle
vespa n. wasp
vespão n. hornet

véspera *n.* eve

vestíbulo *n.* vestibule

vestígio *n.* vestige

vestir *v.* dress

vestuário *n.* vestment

veterano *n.* veteran

veterinário *adj.* veterinary

veto *n.* veto

vetor *n.* vector

véu *n.* veil

via *prep.* via

via pública *n.* thoroughfare

viaduto *n.* viaduct

viagem *n.* voyage

viajante *n.* traveller

viajante incansável *n.* globetrotter

viajar *v.* travel

vibração *n.* vibe

vibrador *n.* vibrator

vibrafone *n.* vibraphone

vibrante *adj.* vibrant

vibrar *v.* vibrate

vicário *adj.* vicarious

vice-rei *n.* viceroy

vice-versa *adv.* vice-versa

viciado *n.* & *adj.* addict & addicted

viciar *v.* vitiate

vício *n.* addiction

vício *adj.* vicious

vicissitude *n.* vicissitude

vida *n.* life

vida rural *n.* rustication

videira *n.* vine

vidente *n.* seer

vídeo *n.* video

vídeo câmara *n.* camcorder

vidraça *n.* pane

vidraceiro *n.* glazier

viés *n.* bias

viga *n.* beam

vigário *n.* vicar

vigarista *n.* swindler

vigésimo *adj.&n.* twentieth

vigia *n.* sentry

vigiar *v.* oversee

vigilância *n.* surveillance

vigilante *n.* invigilator

vigilante *n..* vigilant

vigília *n.* vigil

vigor *n.* vigour

vigoroso *adj.* vigorous

Viking *n.* Viking

vil *adj.* vile

vila *n.* villa

vilão *n.* villain

vilipendiar *v.* vilify

vime *n.* wicker

vinagre *n.* vinegar

vincular *v.* bind

vínculo *n.* bond

vindouro *adj.* unborn

vingança *n.* revenge

vingativo *adj.* vengeful

vinheta *n.* vignette

vinho *n.* wine

vinícola *n.* winery

vinil *n.* vinyl

vintage *n.* vintage

violação *n.* violation	**visibilidade** *n.* visibility
violador *n.* rapist	**visionário** *adj.* visionary
violar *v.* violate	**visita oficial** *n.* visitation
violência *n.* violence	**visitante** *n.* visitor
violento *adj.* violent	**visitar** *v.* visit
violeta *n.* violet	**visível** *adj.* visible
violinista *n.* violinist	**vislumbrar** *v.* glimmer
violino *n.* violin	**vislumbre** *n.* glimpse
vir a ser *v.* become	**vison** *n.* mink
vira (de calçado) *n.* welt	**vista** *n.* sight
virago *n.* virago	**visto** *n.* visa
viral *adj.* viral	**visto que** *n.* whereas
vira-lata *n.* waif	**vistoso** *adj.* showy
virgem *n.* virgin	**visual** *adj.* visual
virgindade *n.* virginity	**visualização** *n.* preview
vírgula *n.* comma	**visualizar** *v.* visualize
viril *adj.* virile	**vital** *adj.* vital
virilha *n.* groin	**vitalício** *adj.* lifelong
virilidade *n.* virility	**vitalidade** *n.* vitality
virtual *adj.* virtual	**vitalizar** *v.* vitalize
virtude *n.* virtue	**vitamina** *n.* vitamin
virtuoso *adj.* virtuous	**vitela** *n.* veal
virulência *n.* virulence	**viticultura** *n.* viticulture
virulento *adj.* virulent	**vítima** *n.* victim
vírus *n.* virus	**vitimar** *n.* victimize
visão *n.* vision	**vitória** *n.* victory
visão global *n.* overview	**vitorioso** *adj.* victorious
visar *v.i.* aim	**vítreo** *adj.* vitreous
visco-branco *n.* mistletoe	**vitrificar** *v.* vitrify
visconde *n.* viscount	**vitríolo** *n.* vitriol
viscondessa *n.* viscountess	**vitupério** *n.* vituperation
viscose *n.* viscose	**viúva** *n.* widow
viscoso *adj.* viscous	**viúvo** *n.* widower
viseira *n.* visor	**vivacidade** *n.* vivacity

vivaz *adj.* vivacious

viveiro *n.* vivarium

viver *v.* live

viver no campo *v.* rusticate

vívido *adj.* vivid

vivificar *v.* vivify

vivo *adj.* alive

vizinhança *n.* neighbourhood

vizinho *n.* neighbour

voar *v.i* fly

vocabulário *n.* vocabulary

vocação *n.* vocation

vocal *adj.* vocal

vocalista *n.* vocalist

vocalizar *v.* vocalize

você *pron.* you

você mesmo *pron.* yourself

vociferador *adj.* vociferous

vociferar *v.* bluster

vodu *n.* voodoo

voga *n.* vogue

vogal *n.* vowel

voicemail *n.* voicemail

voile *n.* voile

volante (badminton) *n.* shuttlecock

volátil *adj.* volatile

vólei *n.* volley

volição *n.* volition

volt *n.* volt

volta *n.* turning

voltar *v.* return

volume *n.* volume

volume de negócios *n.* turnover

volumoso *adj.* voluminous

voluntariamente *adv.* voluntarily

voluntário *adj.* voluntary

voluntário *n.* volunteer

voluptuário *n.* voluptuary

voluptuoso *adj.* voluptuous

vomitar *v.* vomit

vôo *n.* flight

voraz *adj.* voracious

vórtice *n.* vortex

votivo *adj.* votive

voto *n.* vow

voz *n.* voice

vulcânico *adj.* volcanic

vulcanizar *v.* vulcanize

vulcão *n.* volcano

vulgar *adj.&n.* vulgar & vulgarian

vulgaridade *n.* vulgarity

vulnerável *adj.* vulnerable

vulpino *adj.* vulpine

W

waffle *v.* waffle

Wally *n.* Wally

watt *n.* watt

webpage *n.* webpage

whisky *n.* whist

Wight (ilha) *n.* Wight

wok *n.* wok

woofer *n.* woofer

workshop *n.* workshop

X

xadrez *n.* chess

xaile *n.* shawl

xarope *n.* syrup
xenofobia *n.* xenophobia
xenon *n.* xenon
Xerox *n.* Xerox
xilófagos *adj.* xylophages
xilófilo *adj.* xylophilous
xilofone *n.* xylophone

yashmak (véu) *n.* yashmak
Yen *n.* Yen
yeti *n.* yeti

zaragata *n.* ruckus
zebra *n.* zebra
zéfiro *n.* zephyr
zelador *n.* caretaker
zelo *n.* zeal
zeloso *adj.* zealous
zénite *n.* zenith
zero *adj.* zero
ziguezague *n.* zigzag
ziguezaguear *v.* wriggle
zinco *n.* zinc
zircão *n.* zircon
zodíaco *n.* zodiac
zombar *v.* mock
zombaria *n.* mockery
zombie *n.* zombie
zona *n.* zone
zonal *adj.* zonal
zoologia *n.* zoology
zoológico *adj.* zoological

zoólogo *n.* zoologist
zumbido *n.* buzz
zumbir *v.* whirr
zunido *n.* whir
zunir *v.* zoom